Burgess
CAMPING SERIES

Consulting Editors
BARBARA ELLEN JOY and MARJORIE CAMP

CREATIVE NATURE CRAFTS....................Bale
STEPPING STONES TO NATURE................Bale
OUTDOOR LIVING ....Bale
INSPIRATIONAL POETRY FOR CAMP
   AND YOUTH GROUPS....................Berger
PROGRAM ACTIVITIES FOR CAMPS............Berger
PHILOSOPHY OF OUTDOOR
   EDUCATION ....Freeberg, Taylor
DANCE A WHILE.............Harris, Pittman, Waller
CHILDREN ARE HUMAN..............Hartwig, Myers
   Even at Camp—
   So the Counselors Are Puzzled—
   If the Counselors Really Know Them—
   Are the Counselors Prepared?
WORKBOOK FOR CAMP COUNSELOR
   TRAINING ....Hartwig
TEACHING OF TENNIS..............Jaeger, Leighton
CAMP CRAFT ....Joy
CAMPING ....Joy
THE NATURE PROGRAM AT CAMP........Nickelsburg
A MANUAL OF RIDING........................Orr
GAMES for the ELEM. SCHOOL GRADES.....Richardson
GAMES for JR. and SR. HIGH SCHOOLS.....Richardson
BEGINNING SYNCHRONIZED SWIMMING......Spears
A SAILING MANUAL.........................Storm
TALKS FOR TEENAGERS....................Welch
MANUAL OF RIFLE MARKSMANSHIP...........Wilson

PHILOSOPHY OF

OUTDOOR EDUCATION

by

WILLIAM H. FREEBERG

Chairman, Recreation and Outdoor
Education Department

and

LOREN E. TAYLOR

Outdoor Education Specialist
Southern Illinois University
Carbondale, Illinois

BURGESS PUBLISHING COMPANY

426 South Sixth Street, Minneapolis 15, Minn.

INTRODUCTION

Because of automobiles, television, radio, movies, and a thousand and one distractions in contemporary life, especially urban life, teen-agers in the 1960's tend to get further and further away from a sense of compatibility with the earth. They no longer have opportunity to observe the processes of life and to appreciate man's place in the order of nature.

Outdoor education awakens them to a whole world of new ideas. It tends to give them a reverence for life. City dwellers too often see human life as the only thing worth preserving. Children who grow up close to nature know that human life could not exist on the planet without a multitude of other forms of life. Little by little, as they know more about animals and plants and the evolution of living forms all about them they are less inclined to be cruel in their relationships with one another.

Outdoor education can serve a great many ends, but central to all of it is this awakening in youth of a sense of proportion, a feeling of orientation in the all embracing scheme of life on the earth. It has been a source of great satisfaction to me to see the rapid development of outdoor education in this country. Nothing could be more useful at this time than a good textbook for the use of people of all ages but particularly for the use of children and youth who are being taught in every part of the country that all outdoors is a classroom. The authors of this book have, for a number of years, been recognized as leaders in recreation and outdoor education. The book deserves wide use.

John E. Grinnell
Vice-President for Operations
Carbondale Campus
Southern Illinois University

- i -

PREFACE

This book is intended to clarify for school adminstrators, teachers, parents and other citizens the real meaning and significance of outdoor education in the school curriculum. There appears to be a great deal of conflict in thought and interpretations throughout the country concerning outdoor education in terms of; its definition; its need; its concepts; its place in the curriculum; and its scope.

A deliberate attempt has been made to keep the text in accord with recognized professional standards of writing; but at the same time to eliminate educational and sociological terminology that might prohibit understanding by parents and other citizens.

It was felt that in order to properly present the outdoor education program in its true perspective, it would be necessary to present several influential social and educational factors as an orientation to detailed discussion concerning outdoor education. This discussion is presented in the first few chapters.

The text has been influenced by fundamental beliefs held by the authors which have been substantiated and reinforced through more than two decades of teaching in elementary school, high school, and universities; both in the classroom and outside the classroom. Some of these beliefs are:

1. Learning takes place faster and is more meaningful when it is associated with experience.
2. The emphasis in education today is on drill, memorization, and textbook knowledge. Little opportunity exists for critical thinking or creativity.
3. The school curriculum is not designed to provide students with many opportunities for direct experiences

with nature and real life situations. As a result, there are not enough opportunities for students to discover, explore, observe, investigate and learn things first hand.

4. It is difficult to interpret or to associate factual knowledge learned in the classroom with things real in nature, life, and the community; particularly when students have not been given opportunities to apply their knowledge to a real experience.

5. Outdoor education provides the best teaching opportunities in the curriculum for developing attitudes, appreciations, knowledge and skills in democratic group living; conservation education; healthful living; and leisure time education.

Throughout the text it is necessary to repeat these principles often since they apply to many of the different concepts of outdoor education.

These beliefs are fundamental to successful education at any level of the school curriculum whether it be elementary school, high school or college.

The authors may have been overly critical of the public schools in several areas of the text. The criticism is meant to be constructive and is made with the full realization that in many instances there are realistic factors which limit full acceptance of outdoor education programs.

William H. Freeberg
Loren E. Taylor

ACKNOWLEDGMENTS

The authors are very much aware of their dependence upon others for background materials and interpretive material used to focus attention to the importance of outdoor education in the school curriculum.

There is a vast amount of literature in the educational and sociological fields that directly relates to outdoor education. The authors are greatly indebted to those who have made this literature available to help interpret in our own way the many ramifications involved in outdoor education programs. The authors assume responsibility for any shortcomings involved in the use of this literature for interpretive purposes.

The authors owe a great deal to D. W. Morris, President of Southern Illinois University for his vision and his courage in providing the university with an extensive outdoor education laboratory; to John E. Grinnell, former Dean of the College of Education, Southern Illinois University for his encouragement, guidance and council in the development of the outdoor education program at this university; to the 30 or more staff members of Southern Illinois University representing various departments who have planned and worked to develop the outdoor education program in terms of instruction and research; and also to the many university students and campers who have participated in the program over the past eleven years.

Recognition must also be given to the many consultants who have aided in developing the outdoor education program at Southern Illinois University. Among those most helpful have been L. B. Sharp, executive director of Outdoor Education Association, Julian Smith, Michigan State University, Reynold E. Carlson, Indiana University, Kenneth R. Miller, Southern Illinois University, and Robert E. McBride, San Francisco State College, California.

TABLE OF CONTENTS

CHAPTER I   OUR CHANGING SOCIETY   1
Technology, Automation, and In-
creased Productivity   5
Transportation and Communication   9
The Population Problem   14
Social Disorganization and Re-
Orientation   18
The Equalization of Social Status . .   21
Depletion of Natural Resources. . .   25
The New Leisure   29
One World   34
Summary   37

CHAPTER II   EDUCATION FOR A CHANGING
SOCIETY   41
Society and Education   43
The Philosophies of Education . . .   48
Modern Day Concern For Education   55
The Need For A Realistic Approach
to Education   62
The Educational Needs of Modern
Society   73
Implication For Teacher Education   81
Summary   85

CHAPTER III   OUTDOOR EDUCATION
A METHOD OF EDUCATION . . .   89
Observation   95
Investigation.   103
Cooperation   106
Integration and Correlation   109
Meditation   112
Informality   115

CHAPTER III   (continued)
Participation   120
Creativity   121
Total Fitness   125
Summary   129

CHAPTER IV   PHILOSOPHICAL AND HISTORICAL
FOUNDATIONS OF OUTDOOR
EDUCATION   134
Education In The Ancient World . .   136
The Medieval World   154
The Renaissance and Reformation   159
Modern Times . . ₒ   167
Summary   175

CHAPTER V   THE DEVELOPMENT OF CAMP-
ING IN THE UNITED STATES . .   180
The Private Camp   186
Church Camps   191
School Camps   193
Agency Camps . ₒ   199
Summary   202

CHAPTER VI   MODERN CONCEPTS OF OUT-
DOOR EDUCATION   205
Atlanta (Georgia) Outdoor Educa-
tion Program   208
Battle Creeek (Michigan) Outdoor
Education Program   211
Western New York State Outdoor
Education Program   213
Los Angeles (California) Outdoor
Education Program   223
Frederick County (Maryland)
Outdoor Education Program . . .   226
Criteria For A Good School Camp .   228
General Considerations   230
Concepts Regarding Outdoor
Education   233
Curricula   244

CHAPTER VII   DEMOCRATIC GROUP LIVING . .   250
               American Democracy   259
               Democracy in The Modern Camp .   298
               Summary   301

CHAPTER VIII   CONSERVATION EDUCATION . .   305
               Conservation and Democracy . . .   306
               The Schools' Responsibility For
               Conservation Education   308
               Outdoor Education and Conserva-
               tion   319
               Summary   323

CHAPTER IX   HEALTHFUL OUTDOOR LIVING .   327
               New Threats To Man's Health . . .   328
               Health Education   330
               Outdoor Education and Health . . .   335
               Summary   352

CHAPTER X   LEISURE TIME EDUCATION . . .   356
               New Leisure   356
               Leisure Time and Youth   365
               Leisure Time Education and the
               Schools   368
               Outdoor Education and Leisure
               Time   375
               Summary   381

CHAPTER XI   SCOPE OF OUTDOOR EDUCA-
               TION IN THE UNITED STATES .   384
               Outdoor Education in the Schools .   385
               Outdoor Education in Colleges and
               Universities   397
               Organized Camping in the United
               States   400
               National Outdoor Education Or-
               ganizations   409
               Summary   428

CHAPTER XII   A LOOK TO THE FUTURE   432
              Why Has Mankind Failed?   433
              The Schools New Functions   435
              New Youth Program   438

Chapter 1

OUR CHANGING SOCIETY

A creative portrait of our contemporary society . . . An honest and intelligible description of the modern social order . . . This is an indispensable first step, both in social reconstruction and in the launching of a sound program of educational reconstruction.
—Harold Rugg[1]

How to live in a modern world has been the problem of every generation of mankind. The aims of primitive education and the aims of modern education are identical but in the artificial society of today the nature of the individual, the needs of society and the aims of education are hard to visualize. Since school and society go hand in hand, complexities in society bring complexities in education. The modern school library, the classrooms, the gymnasia and the swimming pools are replacements for the forests, the fields and the streams of an earlier age. The modern libraries have become the source of information which was formerly gathered through direct experience from nature and the out of doors. The textbook has largely displaced the teacher and parent and at the same time robbed the children of opportunities to make new discoveries of their own.

Prospective teachers and leaders in the American public schools and youth agencies should keep abreast of their contemporary social order. Since education is responsible for helping children adjust to their society it is imperative that educators consider the social forces operating within the American social structure. This is not always an easy task especially in the turmoil of modern changing times created by the advances in nuclear science. No sooner does society adjust to the modern ways of doing things than new ways have been developed.

[1]Harold Rugg, Culture and Education in America. New York: Harcourt, Brace and Company, 1931. p. 259.

2

In May, 1945, Archibald MacLeish speaking on the radio, during the San Francisco Conference of the United Nations, pointed out the difficulty in examining and defining culture:

"Culture is one of the things you don't define. It is too close to life itself to be defined. You describe it. You begin by clearing your head of the notion which Webster's dictionary gives you that culture has something to do with taste and aesthetics. Maybe it did in the nineteenth century in the ladies' Browning societies. Actually what you mean by the culture of a people is the way of life of that people, its civilization--its contribution to common civilization-- the things its people value and the things they don't value-- the way they make music--the way they express themselves --their habits of life--their works of art--their novels-- their history--the things they have learned in their effort to penetrate the common mystery and experience of mankind by the instruments of poetry and science--briefly, what they are, what they do, what they are like."

Every society in every age has been, and is, a changing society. One age serves as a transition period for the next. Until the middle of the nineteenth century, however, change was almost imperceptible. It was continuous, of course, but rather gradual and even-flowing with one society slowly building upon the society of the past. The wheels of the stagecoach in George Washington's time turned no faster than those of the chariots in the days of Julius Caesar. It took just as long to cultivate and harvest a wheat field at the turn of the nineteenth century as it did in Egypt in 5,000 B.C.

Then suddenly man's achievements seemed, with the advent of steam and electricity, to crystallize into the most cataclysmic period in all history. More changes were made in technology in two generations than in all the thousands of years of previous history combined. Sometime around the middle of the nineteenth century, with the beginning of the Industrial Revolution, man began his move from hand to machine production, from home to factory, and from farm to city. This touched off a chain reaction of one revolution after another in every field of human endeavor--all closely related and interrelated so that improvement in one field spread to another, resulting in the fastest changing society in the history of mankind.

Sociologists, anthropologists, and other educators are asking themselves and each other the reason for this sudden colossal and cumulative apex of man's achievements. Why should civilization move so slowly for century upon century then suddenly enter an age of gigantic and stupendous change? In studying this question, scholars and educators are turning to a closer examination of a universally acceptable answer-- science, research, and education.

Science, the father of man's fantastic achievements, did not develop overnight. Nor was it the doing of any one man or any one country. The advent of modern scientific thought and research techniques is built on the scholarly efforts of scores of scientists from many ages and from many lands.

Science was born when man devised new ways of think- ing and new ways of gathering and recording facts. Many, many centuries were required for this important step in man's struggle for enlightenment. For history shows that the greater part of man's existence was guided by dogma, authority, and divine rights. Man's struggle for a better life has been a history of unceasing conflict between change and stability, new ideas and dogma, insight and habit, science and authority. Man, on the one hand, clings to tradition and custom which he has firmly established by repetition. Man becomes emotionally attached and bound to the *status quo* because it is familiar, safe, dependable, and offers security. On the other hand, man in his quest for wisdom has used his imagination, his intelligence, and his insight to create new technological and social devices to improve his living conditions and add to his culture and leisure hours.

The history of man's long fight to free himself from authority and tradition is interspersed by the stimulating thinking and achievements of great scientists and scholars such as Socrates, Comenius, Descartes, Plutarch, Roger Bacon, Isaac Newton, John Dewey, Albert Einstein and many others. These men pleaded with their contemporaries to search for evidence--to look at the world and see things as they are rather than to accept a heritage of dogmatic and authoritative rule from previous generations.

It is to these men and their cumulative inventions, discoveries, and experimentation; their accumulation of accurate measured data and scientific knowledge; their new mathematical ways of treating the data; their steady improvement in organization and support of scientific research; and the rapidity with which scientific discoveries have been applied to technology and industry that modern civilization owes its tremendous cultural and technological achievements.

Science has drastically changed man's way of living. It has changed his spiritual and moral life. It has changed the focus of moral issues and changed the emphasis on what is right and what is wrong. For example, slavery in the golden age of Greece was acceptable and the success of the Greek civilization depended upon slavery. Today, technology, born of science, has forced man to deal with slavery as a moral issue.

The most manifest changes brought about in man's life are materialistic. This chapter deals with the most obvious changes in man's way of living. The discussion of these transformations or revolutions is not simple. The areas of man's life cannot be isolated, catalogued, or classified in a neat and orderly manner. Man's social life is affected by his spiritual life, his political life, his economic life, and his mental and physical health. A revolution in one field causes changes in other fields. Only for the sake of emphasis and ease of communication are the most obvious revolutions in the affairs of men isolated to show how science and research have brought about such drastic and universal change.

Science has made possible machines for power and increased productivity. It has made the world, in its physical dimension, a smaller place to live through revolutions in transportation and communication. Science has brought about a change in family and community life--a social reorientation. It has increased the life span, improved the standard of living, improved medicine, decreased the mortality rate--which, combined with the population explosion, has created a challenging problem to modern society. Science has given leisure time to an ever-widening segment of society and has tended to break down social structure and equalize the status of man. It has confronted mankind with problems of urbanization, suburbanization, and corollary problems such as crime, juvenile delinquency, housing, sanitation, and many other social ills inherent in the massing of humanity in large population centers. Science has brought to man the sudden realization that many of the natural resources are rapidly approaching depletion. Lastly, science is indirectly responsible for the world battle of political ideologies--the struggle of minority groups for equality of rights, the struggle between free countries and totalitarianism, and the trend toward a world government or "one-world."

TECHNOLOGY, AUTOMATION, AND INCREASED PRODUCTIVITY

Automation is not new. It is another step in man's continuous technological advancement. However, it is a giant step and probably the most advanced in man's many stages of accelerating change. Although man's march toward improved methods of work, a higher standard of living, increased leisure time, and a higher cultural attainment has been slow and continuous, it has been marked by three rather significant steps, each building on and accelerating the newest stages of advancement.

Many centuries were required for the first stage: the use of simple tools. The Stone Age lasted from about 200,000 years ago to about 6,000 years ago.

Man existed little better than an animal 200,000 years ago. Yet during the Stone Age, he brought about great changes and important inventions. Over the millennia he discovered how to shape stones into useful objects that enabled him to better cope with his environment. In fashioning crude and simple hand tools such as the axe, the saw, the hammer, and the knife man magnified and extended the use of his own body.

Many centuries more were required for the second step--harnessing the ox, the horse, and the waterwheel which more or less freed man's body through the use of simple power machines.

The essential feature of man's newest step in technological progress--automation--is the application of electronics to the control of mechanical and chemical processes. The substitution of mechanical control (the mechanical brain) for manual control at many points in the physical process of production not only makes it possible to relieve man at these points, but also to do things that man could not do--the production of atomic power being the most notable example. Another example is the electronic calculator which can make a computation in one week that would have taken forty-five years with an earlier machine. Automation, like the age of tools, or the era of simple power machines, cannot be said to have begun on any certain date, nor can it be predicted that it will end at a definite time.

It has been said that automation was used in one form or another even before the Industrial Revolution. The Industrial Revolution itself cannot be limited to the 1750-1850 era often ascribed to it. To do so does not take into account the progressive application of discoveries and inventions in industrial production preceding this period. Small tools worked by muscle through the centuries grew into complex machines run by steam, by electricity, and now by electronics. Although James Watt's steam engine ushered in the great "Industrial Revolution," many inventions and conditions led to this great achievement, including the utilization of water power. Soule points out this interaction very clearly.

> A revolution in technology was the core of the process which transformed the middle ages into the modern world. That whole process, to be sure, included other indispensable elements, such as new ideas, social mores, economic and political institutions. But how could the ideas have been broadcast so rapidly without the invention of printing and movable type? How could community life and government have changed as they did without trade and communication among provinces, nations, and continents?

And how could trade have expanded without the improvement of roads, the construction of canals' and railways,
the invention of the mariner's compass? How could large
urban populations, the base of modern civilization, have
been fed without the birth of scientific agriculture,
and how, without the surplus farm population--a surplus
to which a renovated agriculture gave rise--could mills
and factories have recruited their workers? And how
could factory chimneys have cast their long shadows over
civilization without the successive advances in the use
of energy-transforming engines or the machinery which
only great sources of mechanical power could activate?[2]

Many of the earlier inventions used the principle of
automation in that they controlled themselves. Ancient
clocks as early as the fourteenth century were self running.
James Watt perfected the governor on the steam engine
which regulated the speed of the engine. The "spinning
jenny" could very well be considered as another fore-runner
of automation. Likewise, Thomas Edison made possible a
multitude of inventions leading to automation with his experimentation in electricity. Thus, automation, like the
Industrial Revolution, is in truth another phase in man's
technological advancement, another improvement in the
tools man has been using, and another progression in man's
work methods.

While it took century upon countless century for man
to shape stones and develop the simple hand tool, yet only
200 years have elapsed since man ushered in the age of
steam. Yet, since the turn of the century, steam power
has all but disappeared, giving way to electric power. The
internal combustion engine is a product of the last fifty
years and electronics and synthetic chemistry have been
developed today. Sociologists claim that man advanced
more culturally in the leap from electric power to electronics than he did from steam power to electric power. There
is no doubt that electronics has, and will, greatly alter the
economic and cultural life of man.

Economically man stands to profit from increased
production. Automatic machines are making it possible

[2] George Soule, Time For Living. New York: The Viking Press, 1956. pp. 4-5.

to increase production at an incredible rate with less human labor. In 1909, Henry Ford produced 10,609 automobiles which sold at $950. In 1914, he increased his production through his assembly line technique to 24,800 and the price per automobile dropped to $490. Mass production methods reduces the cost of production by distributing costs over a larger number of automobiles.

Today electric light bulbs are made by an automatic machine that produces 150,000 bulbs in a twenty-four hour period. The machine replaced about one-thousand men and, at the same time, dropped the cost of producing the bulbs from $50 a thousand to less than $13 a thousand.

Many fear that automation will bring about severe unemployment. They point to the many hand-spinners and weavers that were quickly replaced by the "spinning jennies" and power looms. They point to the decline of small farms replaced by large farms and machine-cultivated crops. The truth is that although some skills will be made obsolete, a greater demand will be created for upgraded skills. Man will become an overseer of a machine that now does the menial tasks he once performed. His work will be more challenging, less strenuous, consume fewer hours per day, and possibly fewer days per week.

Furthermore, scientists claim that new jobs are being created by automation before the old ones are destroyed. They point out that the dial system has replaced human operators, but telephone companies are employing more people than ever. Installation of dial equipment, far from throwing thousands of telephone operators out of work, has actually meant a seventy-five percent increase in the number of telephone operators in the past ten years. The automobile replaced the stableman and the village blacksmith, but their modern counterparts have multiplied many-fold in the gasoline stations, highway construction, and the tire industries. Edison put the lamplighter out of work, but the light bulb industry employs thousands of modern lamplighters.

Throughout history employment has increased. The water wheel brought the miller, the wheel itself brought the wheelwright, the steam engine brought the engineer and fireman and opened up many new jobs on railroads and in factories. Electricity again increased employment.

Will not countless numbers of men be required to make and repair the automatic machines themselves? Therefore, why should not automation increase employment or leisure time, or both? Scientists forecast new and more complex machines. The sociologists predict greater consumer needs as population increases and the standard of living increases throughout the world. Increased production, greater distribution, and more employment as well as an expansion of new areas and services seem assured, providing man can manage the social and political problems of the immediate future. As atomic power becomes available, it may be used in remote areas and in new lands heretofore unfit because of a lack of water power, creating new opportunities for increased investment and trade expansion.

TRANSPORTATION AND COMMUNICATION

The rapid evolution in industrial production is paralleled in every phase of human affairs. Every segment of modern society is closely related and interrelated. Transportation and communication has developed and improved side by side in the movement of men, goods, and ideas.

Advances in transportation speeds the improvement of communication. The network of highways, railways and airways is supplemented by a network of wires, cables, and air channels. The revolution in transportation and communication is a history of inventions, each new one an improvement over its predecessor. Transportation has grown from the stagecoach and riverboat through the railroad era to the modern day automobiles and airplanes. Communication has made the long climb from the pony express, to the telegraph, the telephone, the modern press, the radio, and television.

Railroads were the first to challenge man's basic means of transportation--boats and horse drawn vehicles. But less than one-hundred years ago, wooden railroad tracks were still in existence in some parts of the United

States. The railroads did not reach maturity until World War I, and they have had to fight hard since that time to meet the competition of new forms of transportation, including the automobile, the airplane, and the pipe line.

Whether railroads continue as an important means of transportation is a moot question. Through mergers, new types of engines and other gains in efficiency, the railroads are still carrying a great percentage of the nation's freight and passengers. Scientists are now working on a wingless, air-supported vehicle that hovers above a rail and is propelled by forced air. Ford Motor Company already has such a vehicle developed that can obtain a safe speed up to 500 miles per hour. The car rides suspended a few thousandths of an inch above the roadbed. Thus, by combining the principle of railroad travel with the airplane, the railroads may soon compete again with the automobile for passenger traffic.

Waterway transportation, too, has made great strides and has grown steadily in volume of freight moved. Soon the St. Lawrence Seaway will open the Great Lakes to sea traffic. Improvements in loading an unloading cargo, greater comfort aboard ships, and greater speed of travel has made the waterways important movers of freight in the United States and movers of materials and passengers to other countries of the world. The January, 1961, issue of *Changing Times* reports the coming of atomic-powered ships that will skim over the water at 100 knots and haul over 300 passengers at $30 each.

Pipe lines have made steady growth in the number of miles of lines in operation and the number of gallons pumped from the oil fields to practically every major city in the United States. Pipe lines today carry almost as much of the nation's traffic in freight as do trucks, and more and more pipe lines are being installed to perform more and more service. The statistical abstract of the United States for 1960 shows an increase from 88,727 miles of line in 1930 to 144,354 miles of line today.

The automobile, developed after the invention and improvement of the internal combustion engine, has brought about the greatest and most phenomenal revolution in the history of transportation. In 1920, the automobile registration for the United States was 9,239,000. Today there are more than 75,000,000 automobiles on the road, and this road now weaves a network more than 3,500,000 miles long throughout the United States. Some scientists are predicting transportation by fast-moving conveyors or continuous rubber belts which slow down at intervals for the discharge and loading of passengers.

Almost as phenomenal as the development of the automobile is the rapid rise of the airplane. In 1926, less than 6,000 passengers were carried by airplanes. Today, commercial airlines serve every major city in the United States and travel over 66 billion passenger-miles a year. Improvement in airplane transportation is so rapid that a very comfortable and safe airplane one year may become practically obsolete the next. The jet plane is quickly supplementing the piston engine plane. Improvements in radar, blind landing devices, weather forecasting, speed of travel, and passenger comfort are making air travel safer, faster, and more universally popular. The new United States Air Force's B-70, which is expected to be in operation by 1962, will travel about 2,000 miles per hour--three times the speed of sound. This, of course, means that soon afterward commercial airlines will have planes to match this speed. Vertical take-off and vertical landing may open the doors for family flying cars operated from the roof top or the back yard.

Communications, too, compared to the slow evolution of previous decades has made stupendous progress in the last fifty years. Since tribesmen first learned to speed messages from drummer to drummer across the jungle, man has constantly striven to improve his communication. The Romans passed information across the country by relays of trained runners; Napoleon experimented with semaphores; in pioneer America the Pony Express riders linked the East with the West.

A citizen of the United States today enjoys a functioning network of communication through the post office, the telephone, the telegraph, the press, and through the broad-

cast media. National events of great importance may be
seen instantaneously by the entire nation. In the presidential election of 1960, the candidates of the two major parties
explained their stands on current issues before an audience
of over 75,000,000 people for each of their telecast debates.

Professor Howes in a report to the Senate of McGill
University on the use of television for instruction made this
statement.

Television is to the public lecture much as the printed
page was to the manuscript. Stimulating teachers in a
single effort may reach innumerable homes. The leading
authority in any field may in one television lecture
accomplish more than in thousands of separate appear-
ances before small groups. If a hundred persons show
up for a civic meeting, it is considered a success. If
a thousand attend a lecture, that is a large number;
but educational television can deliver tens of thousands
of persons to the meeting, the lecture hall, or the campus.

Scarcely more than one hundred years ago, the United
States government refused to buy Morse's invention because
it would not pay. Today, the Western Union Company operates over 2,000,000 miles of line with an annual income of
over $275,000,000.

An equally remarkable growth has taken place with the
invention and improvement of the telephone. The industry
has grown from less than 80,000,000 miles of wire and
17,000,000 telephones in 1930 to over 260,000,000 miles
of cable, 7,000,000 miles of aerial wire and 60,000,000
telephones today. The telephone is being made more and
more automatic as first local and then long distance dialing
has been perfected. Direct distance dialing is one of the
greatest advances in the speed and convenience of telephone
service. Already more than 8,000,000 telephone customers
in more than 700 localities can dial direct to as many as
46,000,000 telephones throughout the United States. Western Electric Company has designed a new machine which
automatically assembles 360 switches an hour at a very
small cost. Calls as far as 3,000 miles away go through
in seconds.

The newest innovation in telephones is a telephone-
television arrangement. It will be possible to see as well
as talk to the person at the other end of the line. In a few
years telephones in cars will be common, and it is highly
probable that the shopping mother may pull a miniature
telephone from her purse to check on the babysitter.

The radio as late as 1921 was regarded as a luxury,
with only 58,000 sets in operation. In January, 1960, the
National Association of Manufacturers reported over
50,000,000 homes owning radios. Radios have improved
over the years with automatic tuning, better reception, and
models of all sizes and for many purposes. The latest
development is the replacement of the vacuum tube with
the transister tube.

The advances in printing over the years have been
paralleled by better means of assimilation and dissemination of news. Special edition newspapers are on the streets
sometimes in a matter of minutes after an important news
break. The latest experimentation in newspapers is a re-
ceiver in the home which can pick up a radio edition of a
newspaper through a process of transmitting the paper
through the wave lengths.

Television, the latest entry in the field of communication, has developed in the last quarter of a century. With
television considered still in its infancy, there are over
45,000,000 homes in the United States with at least one
television set.

Billions of dollars will be spent on the nation's already
intricate transportation and communication system in the
next few years. Turnpikes and four-lane highways will
criss-cross the nation so that drivers may span the nation
east and west or north and south without stopping for a traffic light. Similar gains are expected in communication.
Progress in both fields will speed further revolution in
other directions.

THE POPULATION PROBLEM

The most striking an unexpected development of modern times is the large increase in the number of marriages and the phenomenal rise in the birth rate. The population problem has a three-fold impact upon society--the explosion or increase in the number of people, urbanization or concentration of humanity in limited areas, and mobility or the movement of families from one community to another.

From the time of the first man and woman on earth, it took thousands upon thousands of years for the human race to reach the one billion mark which it did in 1830. It took only one-hundred years (1930) for the population to double. The world population is expected to reach the third billion in only thirty-five years--sometime in the mid-sixties. The United Nations estimates that the fourth billion will be added in only fifteen years (1980), and the fifth billion in another ten years, around 1990. Researchers in population trends are pretty well agreed that by the end of this century, if the present rate of growth should continue the population of the earth will be over six billion people.

The population growth of the United States has been extraordinarily rapid throughout history. This has been due to a high birth rate, together with a heavy volume of immigration. During the second half of the nineteenth century, the increase of foreign-born, from a little over two million to over ten million, far exceeded the birth rate of the native born.

The United States has been a melting pot for many races and nationalities throughout its history. As the labor force grew, labor leaders began to fight mass immigration and, as a result, the rate of immigration was eventually restricted to a very small percentage. During World War II immigration was practically nil, but the end of the war brought a sharp increase due to the Displaced Persons Act of 1948. The act increased by several times the normal annual quota assigned to the various countries, with the understanding that the quotas for future years would be cut back by 50 per cent.

In the 1920's and 1930's, the population of the United States was less than 130,000,000 and was rather static. Today the population is over 175,000,000 and is growing at a very rapid rate. Every eleven seconds a new citizen is born. This is 327 per hour, almost 3,000,000 every year.

Increase in the birth rate and immigration are only two reasons for the population explosion. The mortality rate has been greatly reduced. In George Washington's day, reliable estimates have placed the infant death rate at seventy out of every one-hundred births. Today, thanks to the modern use of incubation, oxygen, sterilization, and immunization, the infant death rate has been reduced to fewer than three deaths out of every one-hundred babies born.

Furthermore, the life span of man has been lengthened due to the modern miracles of science and medical research which have opened the way to a fuller understanding of the human body. The x-ray machine, and other improvements in the detection of disease, along with the development of the modern "wonder" drugs, have increased man's life expectancy from forty-one years of age in 1850 to over seventy years today.

Paralleling the problem of feeding, housing, and educating an ever-increasing population are the problems caused by urbanization and more recently suburbanization. Urbanization is the flow of population to the cities and suburbanization is the counter-movement of people from the center of cities to the outlying areas. Within a little more than a century, the United States has changed from an agricultural economy to the most highly industrialized country in the world. Only 5 per cent of the nation's 41,000,000 inhabitants lived in urban communities in 1790. At the turn of the century the proportion was 39 per cent of a total of 76,000,000, and today over 69 per cent of the total population live in cities. Furthermore, metropolitan areas have grown so fast that some 35 to 40 per cent of the total population now live in areas of one million people or more.

Dr. Jerome P. Pickard of the Urban Land Institute

forecasts that by the year 2,000 A.D. cities will dominate
the United States with eighty-five per cent of the population
living in urban areas. Dr. Pickard predicts, according to
a *U.S. News and World Report* article in the November 9,
1959, issue, that by the turn of the century, one-third of
all Americans will live in ten grand "super-cities." These
cities will be formed by the merger of small cities and
suburbs with existing metropolises. The super-cities will
be: A New England city centering on Boston with a population of 6,500,000; New York City with a population of
23,000,000; Delaware Valley City centering on Philadelphia
with a population of 8,500,000; Chesapeake and Potomac
centering on Washington, D.C. and Baltimore with a population of 8,500,000; Southeast Florida City centering on
Miami and Palm Beach with a population of 6,500,000;
Cayahoga Valley City centering on Cleveland with a population of 5,000,000; Detroit City with a population of 9,500,-
000; Chicago City with a population of 11,000,000; San Francisco Bay City with a population of 7,500,000; and Los
Angeles City with a population of 20,000,000 people.

The rapidity with which the concentration and over-
crowding of people into large cities occurred has created
serious problems. They may be briefly summarized as:

1. Drastic inequalities of income and wealth.
2. Lack of articulation (coordination and balance)
   among various industries within the urban community.
3. Rapid obsolescense of the plysical plan and plant.
4. Disrupting imprint made by competing forms of transportation.
5. Uncontrolled subdivisions, speculative practices,
   and fantastic real estate booms.
6. Urban housing is one of the most burdensome problems
   the country now has to face.
7. Urban public health is endangered, particularly in
   blighted areas and among low income groups.
8. That very heterogeneity and specialization so pecu-
   liar to urban life leaves the community socially
   disconnected, lacking in a position civic program
   and in cooperation.
9. Opportunities for free higher education are limited.
10. Juvenile delinquency, organized crime, and commer-
    cial rackets are persistent urban problems.
11. Urban finance is an emerging problem of vast propor-
    tions.

12. There is lack of adjustment between urban powers as dictated by state legislative bodies.
13. Overlapping independent governments exist in great profusion, and these are unsuited to metropolitan areas.
14. Cities continue to be faced with evasions of civil service laws, irresponsible political leadership, and discriminatory or questionable administrative practices.[3]

As the cities became more and more crowded and uncomfortable, and as one problem after another weakened their political, economic and social life, people who could afford to do so began moving to the suburbs. The rapidity of urban growth with little time for planning, created a hodge-podge of factories, tenement houses, warehouses, a vast network of streets and many objectionable barriers to comfortable living. The automobile and transit lines accelerated the move from the decaying centers of cities to the nearby countryside. Shopping centers and suburban towns skirted and spread cities into large metropolitan centers. Suburban growth has in recent years increased at a rate six times greater than the growth of cities themselves.

Downtown shopping centers, becoming alarmed, are now trying to recapture their trade volume by a belated urban planning program which includes improvements in transportation and other comforts and conveniences to the shopper.

The third phase of the population problem is the mobility of the American people, or population shifts.

The United States, born because of an immigrant population, has always been characterized by the mobility of its people as witness the steady movement to the west during more than half the nation's history. Today, a large segment of the population is not identified with any given community. People are moving from the farms and rural communities to the cities, from the center of cities to the urban fringes and suburbs, from the Eastern Plains to the Pacific

[3]United States National Resources Committee, Our Cities--Their Role in the National Economy. Washington, D.C.: U.S. Government Printing Office, 1937. pp. VIII-X.

Coast, from one section of the country to another, and from one harvest to another. California, Florida, and Arizona are among the nation's fastest growing states. The once remote Pacific Coast is today a burgeoning empire and is due for continuous growth in the years ahead. The Old South is beginning to industrialize and is increasing in population. The spread of industrial civilization with the vast network of super highways across the nation has tended to obliterate the boundary lines of local communities and provides opportunities for people to move swiftly and easily from one section of the country to another in endless streams.

The constant shift in population poses major problems of readjustment and re-orientation for the migrant and serious problems of providing schooling, housing, and recreation for the community.

SOCIAL DISORGANIZATION AND RE-ORIENTATION

Social organization as well as economic and political structures were drastically changed with the coming of the industrial civilization. During the frontier days and throughout the agrarian period in United States history, social life was influenced by the family, the church, the farm, the rural neighborhood, and small villages and cities. During this period the family with its self-contained household provided not only education and moral discipline, but also occupational training. Families were large and self-sufficient with every member of the group sharing the chores of the home. Members of the family were closely and intimately associated, and ties were strengthened due to the interdependence of family members and their relative isolation from other groups.

About the only contact with other families or groups came on Sunday at church meetings or an occasional neighborhood gathering. These small and informal community get-togethers were simple in political structure, but there were apparently no problems of mutual concern that could not be solved by a meeting of family heads or appointed trustees.

Although the family is still the primary social unit, many factors in modern society have served to make inroads into the unified family life of one-hundred years ago. Stanley states that:

> Modern life is everywhere complicated, but especially so in the United States, where immigration from many lands, rapid mobility within the country itself, the lack of established classes or castes to act as a brake on social changes, the tendency to seize upon new types of machines, rich natural resources and vast driving power, have hurried us dizzily away from the days of the frontier into a whirl of modernisms which almost passes belief.[4]

Industrial civilization has seriously disrupted the traditional way of rearing the young, but at the same time has immeasurably increased the resources for education and enlightenment of its citizenry. It has brought new ways of education and new ways of living with the factory and the mechanized farm, new forms of communication and new ways to travel. These innovations have, in turn, brought new patterns or group life with clubs, unions, cooperatives, religious associations, and new agencies of recreation, including the community theater, orchestras, dance studios, parks, swimming pools, playgrounds, summer camps, gymnasiums, arenas, and organized sports.

At the same time industrialization has brought many forces that have tended to undermine the process of social control and weaken the family unit.

One basic change has been the gradual decrease in family size. Although the number of marriages and births has increased, the number of children in each household has decreased. As the United States was settled, as industrialization developed, as education spread and the standard of living rose, American parents had fewer and fewer children. The United States Bureau of the Census shows a decrease from about six children per family in 1850 to less than three in 1900, and to less than two children today. This steady decrease in family size is due to many factors,

[4] William O. Stanley, B. Othaniel Smith, Kenneth D. Benne, and Archibald W. Anderson, Social Foundations of Education. New York: Holt, Rinehart and Winston, 1956. p. 429.

including the wish to keep the family standard of living
higher, the increase in cost of rearing and educating children, growing uncertainty of work and income with a fear of
not being able to support children, child labor laws, the
fact that children are no longer needed for home chores,
and because more and more women are entering business
and industry. Accepting employment as an emergency war-
time measure, women have stayed on in industry and have
become a permanent segment of the laboring force.

In 1880, some 2,359,000 or 14 per cent of all workers
in the United Sates were women. Today, 10,546,000 or
nearly 22 per cent of the labor force are women, and 60
per cent of these women are married. Women have greater
economic responsibility in the home today, with more political rights and a higher status in community life.

This trend toward working mothers has raised many
problems. Children are often locked out of homes or forced
to prepare their own meals. An increasing number of di-
vorces and broken-homes have left children without security.

Another change in family life has to do with housing.
The traditional American family lived in a single family
dwelling on a farm, village, or small city. Today, with
the growth of an urban civilization, there is a perennial
increase of large duplexes, four-plexes, and apartment
houses. Almost 50 per cent of the American population
lives in multiple dwellings.

The family has changed, too, in its function. Much
of the work which was done in the homes of 1800 is now done
in factories and shops or has been radically reduced with
push-button appliances and modern household conveniences.
Many work responsibilities of earlier days are not now
necessary. Children grow up today without sharing work
experiences as the community takes over more and more
of the responsibilities of the family. Families that once
worked and played together are now working and playing
in the community--and more often than not as individuals
rather than a family unit. A fairly typical night might find
father at a club meeting, mother at a bridge party, daughter
at a movie, and son at a basketball game.

Education of the family, formerly undertaken in the home, today is accomplished in large modern schools and other community agencies. Children who once played around the home during their few leisure hours now find more and more time to attend community playgrounds and recreation centers. Spiritual values and morals are increasingly being conditioned by influences, both positive and negative, outside the family--from the church, the community center, dance halls, youth organizations and gangs. Where once the family assumed practically all the responsibility of rearing and educating the young, today the entire community shares this obligation.

THE EQUALIZATION OF SOCIAL STATUS

The emphasis on the equality of man as a dominant feature of American values and behavior has persisted throughout the history of the United States. This is not to say that class distinctions do not exist; the axiom "all men are created equal" has been contradicted on every side. But the masses of the population of the United States believe that a democratic way of life forbids the formation of class lines or social stratification. The American value system has never denied existing differences in rank or status, but these are regarded as accidental, not essential, to the American way of life.

Foreign travelers as early as 1830 were impressed with the apparent lack of class lines. Some were alarmed at this situation. They complained, as did Frances Trollope, about the "coarse familiarity, untempered by any shadows of respect, which is assumed by the grossest and the lowest in their intercourse with the highest and most refined."[5]

These visitors noted, too, that employees were completely independent of their employers in their private lives. Then, as now, they often dressed as well as their employers, enjoyed as many of the finer things of life, and bought their broadcloth or other apparel from the same haberdashery.

[5]Lyman Bryson (Ed.), An Outline of Man's Knowledge of the Modern World. Garden City, N.Y.: Nelson Doubleday, Inc., 1960. p. 392.

Nevertheless, class discrimination existed then and it exists today, particularly among the very poor and the very rich, and in the larger cities. In the 1830's, Harriet Martineau noted the status discrimination in Philadelphia which stemmed from the fact that the "fathers of the Arch Street ladies having made their fortunes, while the Chestnut Street ladies owed theirs to their grandfathers."[6]

Upper class families paid great sums of money to get their names published in an early New York social register in the 1840's. Such stratagems along with the forming and joining exclusive clubs, and parading family coats of arms are not uncommon today. Most unbecoming to the true aristocrat, they could be reactions to a feeling of uncertainty in a society whose basic values deny anyone the right to claim higher status than his neighbor. The would-be status seekers in the United States are so ingrained with democracy that they are sensitive to the ridicule and judgment of others, and concerned with public opinion.

At the other end of the diminishing social ladder are the groups whose income is so low as to create one of America's most perplexing social problems. These are the unskilled laborers, the farm laborers and sharecroppers, the Puerto Ricans of New York, the Mexicans of the Southwest and the French Canadians of New England, who make up a large proportion of the plighted who are "in the society but not of it."

Three forces, however, have tended to equalize or eliminate social stratification in the United States: (1) The frontier, (2) free public education, and (3) automation.

The frontier in America was a vital factor in breaking down the caste system of the old world. The rifle and axe tended to make all men equal. Brawn was worth as much as brains, and either was more important than family history. Men came to America to break away from despotism and the caste system of the old world; they came to carve a new world of freedom and were willing to make personal sacrifices to assure liberty and justice for each individual.

[6]Lyman Bryson (Ed.), An Outline of Man's Knowledge of the Modern World. Garden City, N.Y.: Nelson Doubleday, Inc., 1960. p. 394.

As despotism and religious bigots fell back into old world habits, rebels pushed out into the frontiers of America to start over again. Migration divorced the pioneers from their past. Class lines or social caste could be left behind, freeing the migrant to build a new status on the frontier. Even today, thanks to the automobile, a family may leave the past, move several states away, and start a new life unfettered by traditions and social status.

Free public schools and tax-supported colleges serve to weaken social strata and abolish class lines still more. Education does it by liberating the mind and establishing a more objective and sensible set of values. Young people are rated for their academic achievement without regard to family background. As early as fifty years ago, a wealthy scion was almost sure to be dropped from the social register for marrying below his class. Today, chiefly due to the influence of education, love and marriage are no respecters of social status.

Shaw's *Pygmalion* shows how education tends to abolish class lines. The world famous speech instructor, on a bet, chooses the lowest of the lowliest, a common flower girl from the streets of London, and through the process of education, he converts her into a charming and beautiful lady sought after by the males of all classes.

Technological advances such as modern developments in automation are eliminating menial tasks as well as heavy back-breaking unskilled labor. Along with better physical working conditions, automation increases the need for more intellectual and technical ability. Man becomes the master of machinery which now does his work.

Paralleling advances in technology is the tremendous increase and steady upgrading of both income and position of the ordinary individual in the United States. This increase has been shared by groups of all regions and occupations. In 1930, seven states had a per capita income of less than $250, while in 1950 only one state had an income of less than $400 and only seven states had a per capita income of less than $550. In 1930, no state had a per capita income as high as $850 while in 1950 sixteen states had per capita incomes equal to or higher than this amount, and fifteen additional states had per capita incomes in excess of $700. A survey of consumer finances sponsored by the Federal Reserve Board shows that since 1950 the number of families with less than $5,000 of annual income has decreased by nearly seven million. The number of families with an income of $5,000 or more has increased by more than eleven million. The number of families with incomes of $7,500 or more has increased by over seven million.

America is fast becoming a nation of middle class capitalists. Today there are very few rich and few who are very poor. The average wage-earner enjoys a very comfortable life, owning his own home, owning one or more cars, putting money in savings account, and often investing in the stock market. The wealthy man of today has few enjoyments denied to the wage earner or salaried man except for larger savings account and more investments.

One of the reasons for the revolution in equalization of income is the modern income tax laws that supplement low income through exemptions and skim off and redistribute sizable incomes. Pressures from labor unions are another cause. Pension systems for workers in practically all fields help protect workers against unemployment and old age. Government subsidies to farmers, widows, orphans, and other groups in society also tend to equalize or spread the income.

Thus, industrialization has brought about a new occupational structure, marked by a shift of workers from production to distribution and service occupations, the emergence of women into the working force, and the spread of income, all of which tends to account for the upward trend in the social-economic compositions of society.

America has made great progress since the depression of the 1930's when President Franklin D. Roosevelt commented that one-third of the American people were "ill-housed, ill-clad, and ill-nourished."

DEPLETION OF NATURAL RESOURCES

More natural resources have been consumed since 1900 than in all of human history before that time. The great industrial economy of the modern age, twice geared to war-time needs, plus the rapid and ever-increasing requirement of a growing population, are constantly multiplying the demands for natural resources.

During the frontier days when the young nation had acres and acres of untouched wilderness, natural resources were regarded as inexhaustible. As the pioneers depleted the resources or wore out the farms, they moved to new farms or new frontiers. But when the West was settled, the farmers plowed the farms over and over again and windstorms began to blow the Western prairie dust down the streets of Eastern cities. At the same time, huge industrial machines were gutting the forests and turning the earth over in search for minerals and fuel. The needs for natural resources were increasing while their source of supply was rapidly decreasing.

In the several generations it took to settle the United States from coast to coast the land was mis-used, forests were depleted, wildlife was expended, and the rivers ran rampant and uncontrolled. It soon became clear that the supply of natural resources was not limitless and that appropriate conservation measures must be taken if the United States was to continue her economic and industrial progress. Many citizens were suddenly awakened and alarmed by the realization that the nation had been recklessly and wantonly plundered and stripped of its forests, grasslands, top soil, and wildlife. Public opinion began to swing to the conservation movements and conservationists previously unheeded began to find an audience.

Today, the United States with only 6 per cent of the world's population and 7 per cent of the land area is producing an incredible share of the world's manufactured goods--over 40 per cent of the total output. In order to expand--indeed, in order to keep this pace--the supply of abundant raw materials must continue to be available. Wise management and use of the natural resources are

imperative for continuous productivity and prosperity but
poor management and misuse will lead to depression and
poverty. Dale and Carter sound the grim warnings:

> All across the continent of Asia and into Europe and
> north Africa, you find the seats of former leading
> civilizations that are now among the backward areas of
> the world. You need not search to find such areas.
> Just call the roll of the ancients and then look at the
> lands they live on, as they are today. You will soon
> see what the man meant when he said that civilized man
> has left a desert in his footprints as he moved from
> place to place across the face of the earth.[7]

Flagrant waste of natural resources must be sharply
reduced, new mineral and fuel deposits must be found and
developed, processes for using low grade ores must be improved, plentiful resources must be substituted for limited
resources, and wise use and reuse of materials must be
practiced. It is more than a matter of maintaining prosper-
ous production. *It is the price of survival.*

Shortly after the Revolutionary War, Patrick Henry
said, "Since the achievement of our independence, he is the
greatest patriot who stops the most gullies." Thomas Jefferson, too, was concerned with soil erosion. But they and
the few other conservation-minded patriots went unheeded.
For the most part, early American leaders had no understanding of conservation. Moreover, the scope and meaning of the term as applied to natural resources has changed
through the years.

Earliest efforts to save the resources tended to focus
on those that were being badly exploited. The dwindling
forests were the first concern of leaders in conservation.
Then, in turn, they became alarmed at the thoughtless
treatment of the soil, the stripping away of the grasslands,
the gradual extinction of wildlife, the muddy and rampant
rivers, and finally the deplorable condition of human resources.

In 1871, a committee was appointed by the Commis-

---

[7] Tom Dale and Vernon Gill Carter, Topsoil and Civilization. Norman, Oklahoma:
University of Oklahoma Press, 1955. p. 14.

sioner of Agriculture to study and report on the status of
the natural resources. They found that in less than two-
hundred years nearly one-half of the original forest land
had been cleared. As a result of this report, a Division of
Forestry was created within the Department of Agriculture
to work toward the wise use of the remaining forests and to
start a program of reforestation. In 1878, Gifford Pinchot
was named head of the Forestry Division. It was through
his energy and dynamic leadership and the support of his
friend, President Theodore Roosevelt, that conservation
took on its modern significance.

"The word conservation in its present meaning was
unknown until the early part of 1907," said Pinchot. "It
occurred to me one day that forestry, irrigation, soil protection, flood control, waterpower, and a lot of other matters were all part of a problem. That problem was and is
the use of the whole earth and all its resources for the en-
during good of men."

Pinchot was a prophet. It soon became clear that the
conservation of natural resources will not be effective unless the planning takes into account the essential unity of
all resources, including man. An old Chinese proverb
says: "To rule the mountain is to rule the river." The destruction of the forests threatened other resources, including the soil, the rivers, the wildlife, and the welfare
of the people--the greatest resource of the United States.

In spite of the great work and progress in conservation
education today, in spite of legislation which has set up Soil
Conservation Service districts in every state and territory,
and in spite of the belated admission of conservation courses
into the public school curricula, America has no cause to be
complacent. Few Americans realize that:

1. Timber resources which have been relatively plentiful in the United States are now being used 50 per cent
faster than it is currently being grown. Ninety per cent
of the virgin timber has been cut away. Today the United
States has less than 25 per cent of its original timber land
and has had to import timber to meet national need.

2. Every year the United States is losing nearly 800

square miles of crop land, or the equivalent of 3000 farms of 160 acres each due to erosion. Almost one-fourth of the potential good crop land--115,000,000 acres are being damaged so rapidly that they will be a total loss if protective measures are not taken soon.

3. Nearly two-thirds of America's drinking water comes from rivers, lakes, and reservoirs. Of the 11,800 sources of municipal pollution, only 50 per cent of those responsible treat their sewage. Of the 10,400 factory waste outlets, only 25 per cent are treating what they dump into the rivers and lakes. It would cost $10 billion and take ten years to clean our rivers of polluted waters.

In 1955, over 1,000 American cities had to ration their normal water supply. Several cities have to import water via pipe lines for many miles. New York City has to reach out 125 miles for her water. Los Angeles gets her supply from Parker Dam on the Colorado River, more than 400 miles away. Industrial demands, a growing population, poor practices in sewage disposal, poor conservation practices resulting in clogged streams and a lag in water development projects increase the water problem.

4. When the United States became a nation, there were over 600 acres of land to every man, woman, and child. Today there is less than thirteen acres and this will decrease in the years to come.

5. In 1944, the United States Geological Survey and Bureau of Mines reported that on the basis of current domestic consumption, of the forty-one basic minerals--

15 would last less than 50 years,
3 would last less than 39 years,
14 would last less than 25 years, and
9 would last less than 10 years.

6. Human resources are being wasted too. In spite of free public education and in spite of modern medical science, many people are illiterate and uneducated and many are ill or in poor health. Over 50 per cent of the first 3,000,000 men examined for World War II were turned down because of physical defects. On any given day, over

7,000,000 people in the United States, or one in every twenty, are ill.

THE NEW LEISURE

Mass leisure could well be the most profound and revolutionary force affecting modern society. Changes in the social and economic structure of the United States-- the transformation from a predominantly agrarian to a highly industrial society--have been accompanied by an increasing amount of leisure time, a new and larger leisure time, a new and larger leisure class, new attitudes toward leisure, and the most perplexing problem of how to use the sudden and ever-expanding leisure hours.

One of the most significant and persistent trends in the American economy has been the steady and continuous decline in the work-week. The trend of working hours both in industry and agriculture has been steadily downward with rapid acceleration in the last twenty-five years. As the work week declines, man's capacity to increase production increases. Statistics released by the Twentieth Century Fund show that while the work week had decreased on an average of three hours every decade for the past century, the average rate of increase in productivity has increased about 18 per cent every ten years. This increase in productivity is by no means limited to industry. The rapid scientific and technological advances of the last twenty-five years now make it possible for few farmers operating larger farms to meet the demands for farm products. It is quite evident that man is able to produce more goods with greater ease in less time, and this trend is likely to continue.

The Machine Age has almost reversed the proportion of time man spent at work and the time he spends in leisure. In 1800, the work week averaged eighty-four hours; in 1850, seventy hours; in 1900, sixty-four hours; in 1950, forty hours. It is predicted that by 1975 the average work week will be thirty-two hours or less. Even now many of the rubber produce factories of Akron, Ohio, are working a six-hour day and a five-day week. The United Rubber

Workers have written into their union constitution the intent "to establish the six-hour day and the thirty-hour week with wage increases to compensate for the shorter time so that there will be no reduction in weekly earnings from such action."

There is every likelihood of a three-day weekend and many predict a twenty-hour work week by the year 2,000.

In addition to a shorter working week, the masses are getting more and more leisure hours through paid vacations, holidays, and early retirement. By 1975, some 42,000,000 workers will be eligible for paid vacations ranging from one to four weeks in length, and over 20,000,000 will be in retirement at the age of sixty rather than sixty-five. The working class is fast becoming the new leisure class.

Less than fifty years ago the term "leisure class" was very descriptive and referred to a select group who enjoyed an exclusive way of life. Work was the primary objective of an industrial society and very few could afford to leave their work for leisure pursuits. Those who did were regarded as aristocrats, the elite, the industrial barons, the very rich, or the leisure class.

In those days men and women were working ten to fourteen hours a day and children were working without the protection of the child labor laws.

Within the past twenty-five years this picture has completely changed. For the first time in history, the dream of leisure time for all mankind is becoming a reality. The term "leisure class" has lost its meaning and no longer is identified with any one segment of society. Increased productivity, labor unions, legislation, and the development of the democratic ideals have given Americans free time and money to enjoy it. For the first time in history, it is possible for men to spend more time on the problem of how to live than on the problem of earning a living.

The following statistics and reports released by the various recreational and governmental agencies serve to show the growth and ever-expanding recreational habits of the masses of American people.

The number of visitors to National and State Parks and National Forests increased from just over 200,000 in 1910 to over 225,000,000 in 1960.

In 1910, the nickelodeon had so captivated the audience that over 10,000 theaters were playing to an audience of over 10,000,000 weekly. Movie attendance steadily increased over the years until it reached a peak audience of 81,000,000 weekly in 1946. Since that time there has been a gradual decrease due in part to the advent of television.

Today there are over 40,000,000 non-professional camera owners who spend $400,000,000 on supplies and equipment. Over 200,000 owners belong to 6 to 8,000 camera clubs.

Water sports have become increasingly popular in recent years. A Gallup poll survey in 1950 indicated that over 50 per cent of the adults in America can swim, and it is safe to assume that the percentage of swimmers is even greater today. Boating with around 30,000,000 Americans afloat in 7,500,000 boats last summer shows an increase of over 400 per cent over the 1947 statistics.

Other recent estimates in leisure time participation show a yearly total as follows:

Over 50 million people play coin-operated machines.
20 to 25 million people bought fishing licenses.
18 to 20 million people buy bicycles.
18 to 20 million people play softball.
18 to 20 million people roller skate.
18 to 20 million people bowl.
18 to 20 million people buy hunting licenses.
10 to 16 million people play table-tennis.
10 to 12 million people play billiards.
2 to 5 million people play tennis.
5 to 7 million people play volleyball.
3 to 5 million people participate in skiing.
6 to 8 million people pitch horseshoes.
6 to 8 million people play shuffleboard, and
6 to 8 million people play golf.

Estimates of the numbers who annually attend various sports as spectators are as follows:

125 to 130 million people watch softball.
125 to 130 million people watch basketball.
75 to 80 million people watch football.
50 to 60 million people attend horse races.
60 to 80 million people attend major and minor league baseball games.
40 to 45 million people attend auto speed races.
20 to 25 million people attend boxing matches.
20 to 25 million people attend roller-skating contests.
10 to 15 million people attend ice skating contests and carnivals.
5 to 6 million people attend wrestling matches, and
6 to 7 million people attend rodeos.

The above estimates are cited to show the great numbers of people who engage in recreation today. This does not include other untold millions who engage in such hobbies and activities as gardening, do-it-yourself projects, amateur radio, model airplanes, service organizations, theater organizations, recreational reading, television viewing, birdwatching, camping, nature clubs, and the many, many other recreational pursuits.

The attitude toward leisure and recreation has changed considerably from that of one hundred years ago. Idleness was regarded as sinful and the crocheted wall mottoes found in many colonial homes warned that "Idleness is the devil's workshop."

The Puritans quoted their Bible to prove that idleness was wrong; "Six days shalt thou labor," and "Man shall earn his bread by the sweat of his brow." The Discipline of the Methodist Episcopal Church in 1792 stated that "the student shall be indulged with nothing which the world calls play. Let this rule be observed with the strictest nicety for those who play when they are young will play when they are old." But the Bible was written before machines did man's work and some men as early as Henry David Thoreau wrote "It is not necessary that a man should earn his living by the sweat of his brow, unless he sweats easier than I do."

"Men, " he complained, "have become tools' of their tools. "

Man has bettered his state immeasurably from the time it took all his waking hours to provide food, clothing, and shelter. In colonial days, about the only recreation he could afford was what little fun he could inject into his work. Social interplay, conversation, feasting, and joking were tied to communal activities such as quiltings, corn huskings, house raisings, and log rollings.

Man has progressed in a short span of just over a century from the stage of "keeping alive" to that of "living fully. "

Science and technology have mastered the art of saving time but not the art of spending it. How people spend their abundance of leisure is of considerable concern to social scientist and scientist alike. Educators see a great opportunity for a cultural renaissance with more time for reading, painting, composing, sculpting, discussion, participation in government, personal fulfillment and adult education. But will the use of leisure reach such sought-for heights?

For many people leisure time is already proving to be a curse rather than a blessing. The present use of leisure has not advanced much beyond the loafing bench and the backyard hammock. Some children today spend more time in front of the television screen than they do in school. Many people have not been able to acquire new interests, and they are living a leisure-time life of boredom, manifested by more drinking, more sleep, and indulgence in cheap and time-wasting activities.

Because of a lack of education for leisure and their previous background, many will value work above leisure and money above recreational and cultural activities. They will seek the second job or baby sit while the wife works, and some will undertake both.

It is already quite evident that modern society needs a different set of values than those that guided society in the nineteenth and early twentieth centuries. Educators as early as 1918 realized the growing problem of leisure time and were beginning to become concerned with what children did with their leisure hours. The seven cardinal principles of education, evolved as the result of many meetings and the best thinking of outstanding educators throughout the country, included "The worthy use of leisure time" as one of the primary concerns of the schools. Evidently the educators included this worthy objective in order to placate the critics or to protect themselves from the pointed finger of posterity. At any rate, the principle was practically ignored except for lip service and was seldom discussed by the curriculum planners.

But why should educators be expected to support this "leisure-time" principle? Even when they do begin to make progress, they are under constant criticism from those that like the way "children were educated one-hundred years ago." Did not they grow up in a society which believed that education was salvation and recreation was sin? Was not one of the chief aims of education to increase one's earning power?

The December, 1960, issue of the National Education Research Quarterly has statistics to show that the more education a person has the more money he will earn. Surely there must be other more worthy aims for education!

If the educators have not waited too late to prepare the citizenry for the coming age of leisure, they have most certainly seriously handicapped many millions of young men and women today in their quest for adventure and escape from a life of boredom.

ONE WORLD

The earth is a much smaller planet than it was one-hundred years ago. This seeming shrinkage has been due to the tremendous revolutions brought about in transportation and communication. Today, no city or country is more than hours away. Many millions of people from all parts of the world visit Europe and the United States annually. The Far East, until recently, was practically left out of the geography and world history courses in America. Now Asiatic countries are of prime importance in world affairs.

The new developments in transportation have put world neighbors across the street and will soon put them on the doorstep.

Developments in communication have been equally amazing. Happenings in central Africa can be common knowledge--to citizens of all parts of the world--within minutes. It is possible for the entire world to view an event in practically any part of the globe the instant it happens.

Accompanying this shrinkage of the earth, although a cursory look does not reveal it, is the irresistible trend toward world unity. No nation, today can live apart and to itself. Each is affected by the demands and accomplishments of the others.

The forces which are bringing about greater interdependence and world unity in spite of two world wars are the scientific revolution, international economic interdependence, the imperative need for world organization, and widespread education and understanding among the peoples of the earth.

The relatively recent development and use of scientific knowledge has been a strong force for international understanding and unity. Science knows no national boundary. Scientists, in all fields of human endeavor, talk more or less the same language the world over. Fundamental scientific principles are not affected by race, religion, politics, or nationalities. Medicine, mathematics, physics, astronomy, biology, and other sciences are idealogically the same in all countries. Too, the application of scientific principles often requires the cooperation of many nations. For example, science is beginning to unite all nations in stamping out disease and virus. Action from all nations working in atomic development is especially important to prevent nuclear fall-out, for radioactive fall-out is no respecter of friend or foe, attacker or attacked.

The world today stands on the threshold of its greatest economic opportunity. Technological and scientific know-how has made it possible through international cooperation to raise the standard of living and abolish starvation and famine in all parts of the universe. The underlying crisis in economic life is primarily moral. With a new set of values which must come for the new age, the stashing away of money will be secondary to the golden rule. Industrial countries through a cooperative world organization may be able to find a much needed market for their much needed produce.

A nation cannot develop economically in the twentieth century without depending to a more or less degree on the resources of other countries. Highly developed industrial countries must draw from and exchange products with nations throughout the world. The day when countries could subsist by using resources within their own border is gone.

Recently a cartoon carried in the St. Louis *Post Dispatch* was titled "In the Laboratory of Human Affairs." The cartoon showed two large question marks. One was covered by a large atomic bomb. The other was entirely visible. Two scientists were contemplating the large questions. One said to the other, "We have solved the first question with an exclamation point! Can we solve the other question in time?" The first problem was, "How to kill everybody." The second one, still unanswered, was "How to live with everybody."

The danger of world destruction makes it imperative for nations to work together through some type of world organization. People from all over the world need to come together to build common world policies. It is either a matter of cooperation and survival or a matter of isolation and destruction. America cannot run the world alone. No nation can. The bright glare produced by the atomic bomb has blurred out man-made barriers and national boundary lines. Man has been transformed from a national to a world citizen. Tribal loyalties and instinct are not appropriate in the twentieth century. Security can no longer be found in armies and navies. Wealth and disproportionate abundance of resources by any nation can no longer be used for coercion or bargaining purposes. Any nation, however small, is potentially as strong as the largest nation. Two hundred powerful atomic bombs well placed are just as deadly and just as effective as 2000 bombs. It will take vision, skill, and ingenuity of leaders from all nations planning and working together through a world organization to insure peace and prosperity for all the people of the earth.

Science and technology has brought nations closer to world unity than ever before through its advancement in transportation, communication, control of natural forces, increased productivity and the solution of many mysteries of the modern world. The paradox is that these very advancements will divide rather than unite the world until men learn to solve the most perplexing problem of how to live together.

Today, the whole world is entering upon a new renaissance of learning as the mobility of people and ideas is breaking down traditional beliefs and customary designs for living in each community of the world. Every group of people is being exposed to new knowledge, new understanding and techniques, and new modes of living.

Realizing the importance of education and the exchange of ideas among nations, many statesmen are making it possible to send their scholars to other nations for study. The Fulbright Act passed by the seventy-ninth congress set up an educational exchange program "to further good will and understanding between the United States and other countries through the exchange of students, teachers, research scholars, and specialists." The purpose of the Fulbright Act is to strengthen the intellectual ties between the United States and the rest of the free world. Perhaps its one weakness is that no communist countries are participating in the exchange. It will be hard to get together on ideologies if there is not intercourse between the two major political factions in the world--democracy and communism.

Other agencies and institutions in the United States and other nations as well are promoting inter-visitations and scholarships to other nations. In 1949, about 16,000 American students studied in foreign countries and 26,000 foreign students came to America. The number of exchanges is steadily rising.

The United Nations Educational Scientific and Cultural

Organization (UNESCO), working within the framework of the United Nations, is designed to forward education and educational standards on a world-wide scale.

SUMMARY

Modern living is more and more complicated with each new day. The pattern of world economic, social, and political life is changing as a result of the tremendous impact of science and technology. Change is so fast that a widely acclaimed invention may become obsolete or improved upon so much that it is hardly recognizable within a year. Society is being reshaped in a new age of unlimited power.

The world had not yet adjusted to the vast changes brought about by the age of electricity when it found itself suddenly thrust into a new age of atomic energy resulting in unlimited power and unbelievable advances in human affairs.

Automation and electronics have brought new goods, new materials, and new processes. A new economic structure and a new pattern of living is emerging. The need for unskilled labor is diminishing as men master machines which do their work easier, faster, and more efficiently. The productivity of labor has been increased as working hours have decreased. Technological advances have assured an ever-increasing leisure for all mankind. Indications are that man will have more and more leisure time to develop his interests, talents, and abilities.

Transportation and communication have surmounted the barriers of oceans, mountains, and deserts. Planes now fly faster than the speed of sound and the most remote city in the world is only hours away. Press, radio, and television pour out information from all parts of the world.

Paralleling the mobility of ideas and information is the unprecedented mobility of people. Men are no longer rooted to the soil. Today men live in one community and work in another, creating new problems in home and community life. Migrant workers move from one area to another, their children victims of inadequate care and education.

A large segment of the population is moving from the farm to the city, from the city to the suburbs, and from one section of the country to another.

Urbanization and suburbanization have brought untold problems in crime, sanitation, merchandising, traffic and parking, juvenile delinquency, health, education, political graft, and many others. The trend in all parts of the nation is toward larger and larger shopping centers with acres of parking space and bigger and bigger stores. Mass production and mass distribution is gradually eliminating the small businessman.

International affairs are becoming vitally important to each individual. The age of isolation is past. Science has shaken individual and group composure with the development of nuclear weapons. Unless individuals and institutions from every nation can come to understand and accept the sacrifices necessary for world brotherhood and the concept of "one world", civilization may be wiped from the face of the earth.

Questions and Projects

1. A person's social position is usually measured by his occupation, income, and level of education. Do you know of an exception--a person whose social status is high regardless of his shortcomings in the above criteria? Describe him and tell how he obtained this status.

2. Write a brief paragraph on what you consider the most significant cultural characteristics of the United States.

3. Why did the League of Nations fail? Did the organizers of the United Nations profit from the mistakes of the League of Nations?

4. Why is the advance of science in the realm of human relationships so often opposed?

5. Make a study of the leisure time activities of the community.

6. Make a list of the things you do in your leisure time. Which of these meet the test of good recreation?

7. What are the causes of population shifts and the increased mobility of the population?

8. What are some of the factors which break down social strata and class distinction in the United States?

9. What are the determining factors in city planning. How would you plan to improve your own city?

10. How have new developments in transportation and communications affected your own community economically? Socially? Recreationally?

11. Read recent magazines and periodicals to prepare a paper on the new things to come in the continuing revolution in human affairs.

12. What evidence is there for the statement that the social sciences have not kept pace with the advances brought about by science?

13. Is there evidence in American society that there is confusion and uncertainty regarding both the means and ends of social progress.

14. What are some of the major problems of the "one-world" concept advanced by Wendell Wilkie?

15. Interview an old resident of your community in order to compare life in your community with that of 58 or 60 years ago.

Selected References

Chase, Stuart, *Men and Machines*. New York: The Macmillan Company, 1937.
Barnes, Harry Elmer, *Society In Transition*. New York: Prentice-Hall, Inc., 1952.

Cleator, P. E., *The Robot Era*. New York: Thomas Y. Crowell, 1955.

Dale, Tom and Carter, Vernon Gill, *Topsoil and Civilization*. Norman, Oklahoma: University of Oklahoma Press, 1955.

Dreher, Carl, *Automation; What It Is, How It Works, Who Can Use It*. New York: W. W. Norton and Company, 1957

Gillette, John M. and Reinhardt, James M., *Problems of A Changing Social Order*. New York: American Book Company, 1942.

Jacobson, Howard Boone and Roucek, Joseph S., *Automation and Society*. New York: Philosophical Library, 1959.

Landis, Paul H., *Introductory Sociology*. New York: The Ronald Press Company, 1958.

Larrabee, Eric and Meyersohn, Rolf (Eds.), *Mass Leisure*. Glencoe, Ill.: The Free Press, 1958.

Neumeyer, Martin H. and Neumeyer, Ester S., *Leisure and Recreation*. New York: The Ronald Press Company, 1958.

Reisman, David, *The Lonely Crowd*. New Haven: Yale University Press, 1956.

Rosen, S. McKee and Rosen, Laura, *Technology and Society*. New York: The Macmillan Company, 1941.

Rugg, Harold, *The Great Technology*. New York: The John Day Company, 1933.

Soule, George, *Time For Living*. New York: The Viking Press, 1956.

Steiner, Jessee Frederick, *Americans at Play*. New York: McGraw-Hill Book Company, 1933.

Willkie, Wendell L., *One World*. New York: Simon and Schuster, 1943.

Wish, Harvey, *Socieity and Thought In Modern America*. New York: Longmans, Green and Company, 1952.

Chapter 2

EDUCATION FOR
A CHANGING SOCIETY

Greeting his pupils, the master asked:
What would you learn of me?
And the reply came:
How shall we care for our bodies?
How shall we rear our children?
How shall we work together?
How shall we live with our fellowmen?
How shall we play?
For what ends shall we live?
And the teacher pondered these words,
and sorrow was in his heart, for his own
learning touched not these things.[1]

The profound prophecy of H. G. Wells that "civilization is a race between education and catastrophe" is now accepted as a universal truism. Only through education can men learn to live together in peace and prosperity in a family of nations.

Living in a modern world has been the problem of each generation since the beginning of man's life on earth. It has been the function of education to bring man in harmony with his surroundings. Education involves not only molding the individual to fit his environment but also changing the environment to further man's comforts and goals of life.

Education is an essential part of the fabric of life and it must be interwoven with the society which it fosters. The history of education reveals that education and culture are closely interrelated. Education and culture shape and reshape each other.

Education is the key to permanent social reconstruction. It is the only way man can solve the modern social, economic, and political problems which have been thrust upon him by the revolutions in science and industry. Only through education can man master the machine and create

[1] From the flyleaf of J. Crosby Chapman and George S. Counts, Principles of Education. Boston: Houghton Mifflin, 1924.

new leisure hours beyond the expectations of the most optimistic philosphers. Only through education can man be taught to use this leisure wisely and purposefully. Only through education can he find himself by acquiring the habit of meditation and reflection. Democracy can be made safe and the democratic ideal of government by the consent of the governed can be made to work only through the enlightenment and education of minority groups.

Mankind is in the first epoch of history in which he can devote more time to his culture and education than to the business of earning a living.

For the first time in history man has become the master and not the slave of nature. He has through his ingenuity and intelligence finally broken the barrier to a more abundant culture. He has in his power to build a civilization in which he may eliminate the age-old problems which have molested him for century upon century. A civilization of beauty, of unheralded cultural achievements, of tolerance and brotherhood and plenty of free time to enjoy life is now his.

Man can now live on a cultural plane which has never been equaled in the history of the world--a truly great epoch in man's march toward achieving or fulfilling his goals of self realization and enrichment of community living.

Mankind is at the crossroads of this new epoch. The road to the future is dependent on his kind and quality of education. If a functional and realistic philosophy can be adopted the road will lead to peace, productivity beyond all imagination, and prosperity beyond man's wildest dreams. If an unrealistic and traditional philosphy is to guide the future of society the road will lead to war, social chaos, and the possible destruction of civilization.

Education in a democracy can no longer be left to the educators. It must become the concern of every thinking citizen of society. For today, more than in any other era in history, man's very survival depends upon his education. Education has more than ever before become the first line of defense.

SOCIETY AND EDUCATION

No society, whether primitive or modern, simple or complex, has ever existed without some provision for education. As the youth learn the customs, traditions and ideas of their culture, society is entrenched and perpetuated. The many centuries of sub-standard existence by man in prehistoric times was the result of a lack of education of the youth in the ways and beliefs of their elders. Each generation had to begin anew to work out ways to satisfy their basic needs. Cultures developed and civilizations flourished when mankind began passing on the cultural accumulation from one generation to the next. Each new generation then, instead of beginning over again, built on to an already rich cultural tradition and advanced to a higher level of social existence than its predecessor. The task of education is to cling to the good, weed out the useless, and add the new cultural elements which have the greatest promise of contributing to the advancement of society.

An examination of the objectives of education and a parallel study of society reveals that through the ages the educational objectives of a given era gave expression to the goals of society. These objectives and goals have passed through various stages of development. For example, informal education of primitive societies was designed to maintain the *status quo*, to teach the learner to acquire food, clothing, and shelter.

As societies became more involved in their organization, education undertook to instruct youth the means of preserving the social order. As the cultures became more permanent, they acquired a system of values and morals and it became the purpose of education to inculcate these values in the youth of the society. It soon became apparent that purposes could not be automatically achieved through mastery of school subjects. This realization ushered in the mental discipline theory of education. Subject matter was classified and formalized and every student was given the same course of study in order to train his mind. Although each of these theories have been discarded for the most part, their influence is still felt in varying degrees in our modern school curriculum.

The expression of the purposes and objectives of education is as old as formal education. At the beginning of the fifteenth century Vergerius wrote:

> We call those studies liberal which are worthy of a free man, those studies by which we attain and practice virtue and wisdom; that education which calls forth, trains, and develops those highest gifts of body and mind which ennoble men and which are rightly judged to rank next in dignity to virtue only, for to a vulgar temper gain and pleasure are the one aim of existence, to a lofty nature, moral worth and fame.[2]

Nearly three hundred years later John Locke wrote that the purposes of education are virtue, wisdom, breeding, and learning. A hundred years or so later Herbart was still discussing the purposes of education in much the same terms. "The term 'virtue', says Herbart, expresses the whole purpose of education."

Education, to writers and scholars of the early modern age, was seen as a great force to make men good. Their education seems relatively simple in comparison to the complex and more inclusive statements of modern educators.

It is generally agreed among educators that the primary purpose of education today is to meet the needs of the individual and preserve and extend democracy as a way of life. The seven cardinal objectives of education formulated in 1918 by the National Education Association's Commission on the Reorganization of Secondary Schools were the most complete, functional, and influential set of objectives in the history of education. These objectives, which gave a new direction to education are as follows: (1) health, (2) command of fundamental processes, (3) worthy home membership, (4) vocation, (5) citizenship, (6) worthy use of leisure time, and (7) ethical character.

In an ever-changing and complex society, educators, in order to meet the present day needs of the students in the schools, should examine and re-evaluate the objectives of education. This presents extensive and perplexing problems

[2]Harry G. Good. A History of Western Education. New York: The Macmillan Company, 1947, p. 126.

to those concerned with keeping the schools abreast of the changing society. Educators must constantly evaluate their methods of teaching and the instructional material used to influence the development of the individual and the reinforcement of the cultural system. Culture changes day by day and year by year bringing new demands upon the schools, for it is the purpose of the schools to assist its citizenry in meeting the demands of a changing society. Such changes and such demands may mean new subjects, new methods of teaching, and new administrative structure in order to better meet the responsibilities of cultural changes and reforms. This requires a constant appraisal, interpretation and restating of the goals of society and the objectives of education.

Since 1918, most attempts to clarify and interpret the objectives of education have been a more re-wording or re-stating of the seven cardinal principles. The most significant and worthwhile contribution to educational objectives was made in 1938 by the National Education Association's Educational Policies Commission. They clarified vague statements, defined purposes, and gave further direction to the accomplishment of educational objectives by placing the responsibility of education on parents, the church, and social agencies as well as the school. The objectives of education which they broke down into four categories thus became a joint responsibility of a number of community educative forces. The four objectives of the Educational Policies Commission are:

1. The Objectives of Self-Realization

    The Inquiring Mind. The educated person has an
       appetite for learning.
    Speech. The educated person can speak the mother
       tongue clearly.
    Reading. The educated person can read the mother
       tongue efficiently.
    Writing. The educated person writes the mother
       tongue effectively.
    Number. The educated person solves his problems
       of counting and calculating.

Sight and Hearing. The educated person is skilled
in listening and observing.

Health Knowledge. The educated person understands
the basic facts concerning health and disease.

Health Habits. The educated person protects his
own health and that of his dependents.

Public Health. The educated person works to improve the health of the community.

Recreation. The educated person is participant and
spectator in many sports and other pastimes.

Intellectual Interests. The educated person appreciates beauty.

Character. The educated person gives responsible
direction to his own life.

2. The Objectives of Human Relationship

Respect for Humanity. The educated person puts
human relationships first.

Friendships. The educated person enjoys a rich,
sincere, and varied social life.

Cooperation. The educated person can work and
play with others.

Courtesy. The educated person observes the
amenities of social behavior.

Appreciation of the Home. The educated person
appreciates the family as a social institution.

Conservation of the Home. The educated person
conserves family ideals.

Homemaking. The educated person is skilled in
homemaking.

Democracy in the Home. The educated person
maintains democratic family relationships.

3. The Objectives of Economic Efficiency

Work. The educated producer knows the satisfaction
of good workmanship.

Occupational Information. The educated producer
understands the requirements and opportunities
for various jobs.

Occupational Choice. The educated producer has
selected his occupation.

Occupational Efficiency. The educated producer succeeds in his chosen vocation.

Occupational Adjustment. The educated producer maintains and improves his efficiency.

Occupational Appreciation. The educated producer appreciates the social value of his work.

Personal Economics. The educated consumer plans the economics of his own life.

Consumer Judgment. The educated consumer develops standards for guiding his expenditures.

Efficiency in Buying. The educated consumer is an informed and skillful buyer.

Consumer Protection. The educated consumer takes appropriate measures to safeguard his interests.

4. The Objectives of Civic Responsibility

Social Justice. The educated citizen is sensitive to the disparities of human circumstance.

Social Activity. The educated citizen acts to correct unsatisfactory conditions.

Social Understanding. The educated citizen seeks to understand social structures and social processes.

Critical Judgment. The educated citizen has defense against propaganda.

Tolerance. The educated citizen respects honest differences of opinion.

Conservation. The educated citizen has a regard for the nation's resources.

Social Applications of Science. The educated citizen measures scientific advance by its contribution to the general welfare.

World Citizenship. The educated citizen is a cooperating member of the world community.

Law Observance. The educated citizen respects the law.

Economic Literacy. The educated citizen is economically literate.

Political Citizenship. The educated citizen accepts his civic duties.

Devotion to Democracy. The educated citizen acts upon an unswerving loyalty to democratic ideals.[4]

[3]Educational Policies Commission, The Purposes of Education in American Democracy. Washington, D.C.: National Education Association, 1938.

Objectives of education reflect the goals and characteristics of the society in which they serve. The objectives of education clearly reflected the purpose of the Nazi party in Germany. Communist Russia uses her schools to shape the minds of her young citizens to Party loyalty. Neither educational system mentioned such objectives as "worthy use of leisure time" or "worthy home membership" which so vividly reflects the democratic way of life in America.

The detailed enumeration and description of the functions of education of the Educational Policies Commission is more concrete and useful than the ideal of teaching virtue and truth. Furthermore, these objectives and hundreds of other statements worked out by teachers on curriculum committees through the nation spell out more clearly the functions of education. The statement and restatement of educational objectives and accompanying revision of the school curriculum has served good administrators well in awakening the teachers to the purpose of education through inservice workshops and curriculum study groups.

THE PHILOSOPHIES OF EDUCATION

It is difficult except for the most astute scholar to make sense out of the many and varied philosophies of education. Philosophy has been divided, sub-divided, specialized, and confined until it has become almost as compartmentalized as the disciplines of human endeavor, almost as confusing as the confusion it is supposed to clear up.

In the days of Socrates, philosophy was closely related to life; it was discussed in ordinary language and it was debated by ordinary citizens in the market place. As the modern world has become more and more complex and technical, philosophy has become more and more to be regarded as a separate "ivory towerish" profession with a trade vocabulary to be understood and discussed only by learned and scholarly specialists. Indeed, so divorced is philosophy from culture today that it contributes to, rather than clarifies, the superficiality and confusion of the modern world.

Among the many philosophies listed in current literature are progressivism, perennialism, traditionalism, essentialism, reconstructionism, pragmatism, idealism, naturalism, realism, humanism, supernaturalism, absolutism, positivism, empiricism, existentialism, liberalism, eclecticism, pluralism, rationalism, instrumentalism, and utilitarianism.

Fortunately most of the above mentioned viewpoints have common elements of similarity and have somewhat crystallized into four main schools of philosophy--essentialism, perennialism, progressivism and reconstructionism.

ESSENTIALISM

Essentialism, as the name implies, holds that education must be based upon the "essentials"--the tried and tested heritage of facts, knowledge, principles and skills that have been proven over the centuries. The essentialist, sometimes called traditionalist, believes that the present culture has errored in straying too far from the road laid out for it by the past. The function of the schools, as they see it, is to strengthen and refine rather than to alter the time-tested and inherited principles, attitudes, and beliefs of the culture inherited from past generations.

Essentialism like most other philosophies of education draws its ideas and viewpoints from several philosophies and especially from the idealist and realist. Although the ideas of essentialism may be found in the works of Plato, Aristotle, and many early philosophers, its heritage started with the Renaissance. Modern essentialists do not hold with the ancient and medieval dogmatism and absolutism symbolized by the church. Instead their aim is to provide a systematized and unified philosophy of man and the universe that will meet the needs of both man and the church.

Among modern philosophers contributing to the essentialist belief are Immanuel Kant, G. W. F. Hegel, John Locke, Thomas Hobbes, David Hume, Ralph Waldo Emerson, Bertrand Russell, Alfred North Whitehead, and George Santayana.

The educational theory of essentialism had its beginning with such educators as Erasmus and Comenius in their revolt against medieval dogma and other-worldliness. Pestalozzi, Froebel and Herbart, although influencing other educational philosophies, gave authority to essentialism in their transcendalism. They believed that children learn through their senses and through nature the true meaning of Divine Unity, the oneness of the world, and their true God, the creator of all.

The most recent essentialist, William C. Bagley, spearheaded the Essentialist Committee for the Advancement of Education in the 1930's until his death in 1946. Bagley and his followers renewed the warning that progressive education was failing to teach the youth the truths and values of society and the realities of scientific fact. Students, they warned, must not only acquire this information but must learn to adjust themselves to it.

PERENNIALISM

Perennialism holds that the only hope for a sound educational system--and thus a sound culture--is through restoration of the eternal and absolute principles of truth, goodness, and beauty. Perennialists would return to the common principles which governed education of ancient and medieval culture. They believe that in all ages individuals come and go but the forms common to all things and common to all men are eternal and everlasting, and therefore perennial.

Like essentialism, perennialism draws from many philosophers and many philosophies--realism, humanism, and supernaturalism--for its sustenance. Although it gets support from many outstanding philosophers through the ages, perennialism draws most heavily upon Plato, Aristotle, and Aquinas.

The best known perennialists in contemporary America are Robert M. Hutchins and his associate, Mortimer J. Adler. Hutchins concurs that exercising and disciplining the mind is the primary obligation of education, and knowledge is valuable for knowledge's sake. He regards the schools as an agency for the improvement of man as man not as an agency of social reform. Hutchins believes that higher education is a privilege and not a right. The college student should be one of demonstrated ability and, in order to gain admittance to a university, he would have to meet standards prescribed for the best scholars. Hutchins and his contemporaries agree that the major cause of the confusion and bewilderment of the twentieth century world is the intellectual and spiritual bankruptcy of modern man.

PROGRESSIVISM

Progressivism, the most influential, exciting, and controversial philosophy of education today, carried the initiative in the reconstruction of modern education. Progressivism holds that the primary purpose of education is to teach people to think effectively and not to absorb knowledge as an end in itself. It places explicit faith in man and his ability to face the world with his own skills and solve his problems with his own intelligence. The primary purpose for acquiring knowledge is to use it in the solution of problems. "Applied research and the application of knowledge to the problems of government, industry, agriculture, labor, and society in general are the true goals of knowledge. "[4]

Although progressivism is largely a product of the twentieth century, it had its beginnings in the minds of such men as Socrates, Rousseau, Pestalozzi and later William James, Horace Mann, and Francis Parker.

John Dewey, with assistance from such able contemporaries as William Kilpatrick and Boyd Bode, was the main force behind progressivism. He carved from the priceless contributions of a large number of thinkers and theorists of other philosophies, the most influential and widely accepted philosophy of education in the history of the world. Dewey maintained that a philosophy of education is also a philosophy of life. He succeeded, at least for the time being, in developing a philosophy closely related to the changing culture of the day. His basic tenets

[4]R. Freeman Butts and Lawrence A. Cremins. A History of Education in American Culture. New York: Holt, Rinehart and Winston, 1953, p. 509.

that education is life, one learns by doing, and his concepts
of educating the "whole child" makes the community as well
as the school responsible for the education of youth.

With the development of industry came the achievements of science. Inextricably woven into the fabric of
modern culture are three strands or influences--industry,
science, and democracy. Industry and science accelerated
the growth of democracy. In order for industry to expand
and science to flourish, the social and political climate had
to be freed from the restrictions of the medieval church and
state. These joint influences--science, industry, and de-
mocracy--coupled with the encouragement of progressivism
resulted in men's freedom and right to rule themselves. The
schools, through practices in democratic procedures and
freedom for self-expression, promoted the unique worth
of the individual and the principles of democracy.

RECONSTRUCTIONISM

The reconstructionist, whose philosophy is an outgrowth of progressivism, regards the latter as a transition
philosophy standing between an obsolete cultural pattern and
a new cultural pattern which is now being formulated from
the ruins of the old.

Reconstructionism, realizing that civilization is beset
with frustrations and bewilderment and that there is need
for clarity and certainty in modern civilization, would combine with the constructive achievements of other philosophies their own knowledge and research for a reconstruction
of civilization for the advancement of the common man.
Brameld, the forerunner of reconstructionism, lists the
basic characteristics of this philosophy:

The world of the future should be a world which the common man rules not merely in theory, but in fact. It
should be a world in which the technological potentialities already clearly discernible are released for the
creation of health, abundance, security for the great
masses of every color, every creed, every nationality.
It should be a world in which national sovereignty is
utterly subordinated in international authority. In
short, it should be a world in which the dream of both
ancient Christianity and modern democracy are fused with

> modern technology and art into a society under the con-
> trol of the great majority of the people who are rightly
> the determiners of their destiny. Reconstructionism is
> thus a philosophy of magnetic foresight--a philosophy of
> ends attainable through the development of powerful
> means possessed latently by the people. To learn how
> to exercise that power for these ends is the first
> priority of education.[5]

Brameld and his followers are convinced that the world is undergoing a revolution for which no existing philosophy will provide the needed direction and goals.

Just as the four modern philosophies of education--essentialism, perennialism, progressivism, and reconstructionism--drew from many philosophies over the ages, they also qualify their outlook by elements contained in each other's philosophy.

Philosophy of education as a subject for study too often emphasizes the differences or disagreements among theories of education. While disagreements are necessary to creative thinking, there must be common ground or an orderly basis of agreement from which to start. Perhaps by concentrating on the similarities or commonness in all philosophies and seeking common denominators for the differences of each viewpoint, more agreement could be reached and greater professional cooperation attained.

Surprising as it may seem, all four philosophies accept the Seven Cardinal Principles of Education--command of the fundamental processes, worthy use of leisure time, health, worthy home membership, vocation, citizenship, and ethical character. Educators may differ on how these aims should be accomplished, but even in curriculum they agree that there are certain experiences which should become the common heritage of all.

Likewise, educators are in agreement on general educational tenets, such as the need for motivation of instruction, recognition of individual interests and capacities, and

[5]Theodore Brameld, Ends and Means In Education. New York: Harper and Brothers, 1950. pp. 16-17.

that the school should conserve the social heritage of man's experience.

Although progressivism and closely allied philosophies have dominated educational thinking the past quarter of a century, a careful analysis of the present educational system in America reveals strong traces of essentialism and perennialism. There are many desirable qualities in the educational viewpoints presented by these philosophies but their weakness is in providing opportunity for greater variety in the educational program. There is still emphasis on memorization of the classics, a concentration on mastery of foreign languages, and, in general, a concept that mastery of books and documents is the distinguishing mark of culture. Among these educators and their followers is heard in varied language the criticism of various methods of education, including outdoor education.

People voice protest when they see a teacher with her class in the city getting first hand experience and knowledge about some governmental service. To some people and some educators there can be no knowledge gained unless it is secured in the classroom from the many volumes of books. Among the group of people holding this educational viewpoint, there still exists the concepts that informal approaches to teaching cannot be as effective as formal disciplined teaching; teachings other than "book learning" are a waste of time and money; play and recreation are synonymous with sin; man is born in sin and materialistic teachings in the schools are evil; and to deviate from teaching the three R's in school is an educational blunder.

Another educational viewpoint allows for a more realistic approach to education and tolerates some experimental work and diverted experiences in the classroom. This viewpoint is considered less conservative than the above name groups but nevertheless advocates strong formal discipline in presenting instructional materials. This particular group sees value in a varied and changing curriculum but still clings to many of the idealist and humanistic concepts of education.

A third educational viewpoint which has considerable national support advocates a more progressive approach to education. Knowledge and experience for practical purposes are the basis of their educational theories and some of these educational practices have not met with the most highly acceptable results.

Combinations of all three educational viewpoints can be easily detected in most school systems throughout the United States.

The outdoor education program coincides most successfully with the latter two viewpoints but adds a tremendous amount of real meaning to things memorized and learned in the first viewpoint. By and large, the majority of public schools in the United States today are patterned with some modification after the progressive educational viewpoint.

Systematic and sequential learning has no substitute and the selection and organization of subject matter for study and learning is fundamental to all education. Outdoor education serves a very useful supplementary function in the total education picture.

Outdoor education makes many of the aims and objectives of general education more easily obtainable. This is primarily due to the fact that knowledge gained in the classroom is supplemented by "learning by doing" in the many educational opportunities offered in school camping and outdoor education experiences. Some of the more acceptable experiences in outdoor education which help to achieve the aims and objectives of general education are found in four general areas: democratic group living, healthful outdoor living, conservation education, and leisure-time education.

MODERN DAY CONCERN FOR EDUCATION

In time of peace and tranquility, in times of "normalcy, " and when "all's right with the world, " the problem of educating the youth of a nation is left to the educators. Conflicts and disagreements on the theories of education are found only in teachers colleges and professional education periodicals. Schools are taken for granted by the public. Nor is there concern shown over the caliber of the educators. The person who has a college degree, or who meets the state certification requirements, and who will work for the least possible salary is usually considered good enough to mold the lives of the future citizens of the country.

In times of political strife, in times of social and economic upheavals and revolutions, in times of war, crisis, and threat, education suddenly becomes the business and concern of everyone. Doctors, lawyers, military experts, politicians, ministers, and practically any man on the street not only knows what is wrong with education but becomes highly indignant if their ideas are not given immediate attention by the community educators. Many of the country's leading authorities, often in fields other than education, take advantage of their position to tell the nation in highly emotional tones and with little actual knowledge or research in education what is wrong with the public schools. These self-styled educators have access to the popular magazines--magazines, incidentally, that would not publish articles dealing with education in normal times--to speak from their own experience regardless of their profession as to why education is failing. Professional educators, themselves, take advantage of the climate to argue their cause and to state their case against the *status quo* in education. Indeed there are so many theories, ideas, and a babel of voices on how to educate the young that it is difficult for many professional educators, not to speak of the parents and lay citizens, to know the aims and purposes of education.

The history of civilization reveals that such periods of confusion and uncertainty were not unusual. Over twenty-five hundred years ago, Aristotle wrote:

> As things are . . . mankind are by no means agreed about the things to be taught, whether we look to virtue or the best life. Neither is it clear whether education is more concerned with intellectual or moral virtue. The existing practice is perplexing; no one knowing on what principle we should proceed--should the useful in life, or should virtue, or should the higher knowledge be the aim of our training; all three opinions have been entertained. Again about the means there is no agreement;

> for different persons, starting with different ideas
> about the nature of virtue, naturally disagree about
> the practice of it.[6]

Twenty-five hundred years ago the Empire of Greece
was in the midst of political and social unrest, threats of
war, and economic change due to flourishing trade and commerce on the Mediterranean. Aristotle and his contemporaries could not agree on the ends and means of education.
Some felt that the traditional educational system which had
served the nation so well would do equally as well for the
new time; others demanded a revision of the educational
program.

Twentieth century United States may be compared to
Greece, only the situation now is more acute. Never before
has a nation, or the world, gone through a social, political,
scientific, and economic revolution of such magnitude.
Twice in the first half of the twentieth century men have
engaged in war to test their political and economic idealo-
gies. The fear of a third world war brings anxiety and uncertainty. More than half the world is enslaved in the bonds
of communism and the rest of the world is threatened by
such enslavement. America is fighting unemployment,
surplus farm commodities, inflation, and socialism. The
American colony which started with 98 per cent of her
population living in rural communities and 2 per cent in
the cities has almost the exact reverse ratio today. Urbanization brought slums, traffic problems, juvenile delinquency, and new problems in health, housing, recreation,
education, and government. Rapid changes in communication, transportation, technology, control of natural forces,
achievements in space, and the solution of many mysteries
of the universe have presented as many problems as they
have contributed answers. Scientists seem to be more interested in perfecting instruments of destruction than in
instruments of social and economic betterment.

In spite of the dynamic and revolutionary upheavals in
contemporary culture and society, the schools are for the
most part shut within the narrow and protecting walls of the

[6]Aristotle, _Politics_ Book VIII, Chapter 2.

classroom. Yet many educators are confused by the rapid
changes in the world outside. They have lost the security
of the textbook, for what is taught as important and basic
facts today become out-dated and unrealistic tomorrow.
Still they cling to the old methods to teach in a new era.

In almost every field of human endeavor, although much
more slowly in education, new patterns and new conceptions
are being developed to challenge the old and, with sometimes
extraordinary rapidity, to supersede the long accustomed
ways of living, thinking, and believing. Teachers are
troubled and perplexed as they experience the loss of security and the passing of the old order. They are compelled
to modify, to discard or improve, and to learn new methods
in order to carry on activities in modern society. Too
many teachers are conducting classes without much aware-
ness or understanding of what should be taught and how it
should be taught.

Meanwhile, individuals and groups in society are advocating nationalism and internationalism, more academic
courses, more vocational courses, a more traditional school
system and a more progressive system of education.
Strong and vehement arguments are made in behalf of change
and equally strong and vehement opposition pleads for the
status quo and a return to old books.

Constructive criticism by capable and thinking citizens
is the wellspring of democracy. But many critics have been
yelling "fire" and causing unnecessary panic. This is no
time for hysteria, crash programs, rash and unfounded
statements and intuitive criticism with little thought and
no research. Many modern day critics have leveled their
blasts at the public schools without once visiting the target
of their vehemence. Clever paradoxical questions in popular magazines attract the eye of the American public and
create unrest and suspicion in the minds of those not close
to the schools. Fortunately, the public that is closest to
the school through citizens groups and parent-teacher organizations knows what is going on and they are amazed at
the lack of understanding on the part of the critics.

Commentators who are sincerely interested in the

welfare of the public education usually at least make a cursory investigation of the schools before sitting down to write against them.

For example, articles by George Leonard for *Look* Magazine and Robert Shayon's "Frontiers of Learning" in the September 13, 1958 issue of the *Saturday Review* of Literature were preceded by months of research in classrooms in all parts of the nation. It is no surprise that these articles had many valid criticisms and food-for-thought by American school administrators, teachers, and parents.

Probably the most intensive and thorough piece of research done on the status of American education is the continuing study of James B. Conant in the high schools, junior high schools, and elementary schools of the nation. Conant, an astute scholar and former president of Harvard University, has become probably the foremost authority on both American and European school systems through visitations to scores and scores of schools and talks to the men who run them.

In his close first-hand analysis of American high schools, Conant has developed a great deal of respect for school men and has not proposed a revolutionary change in the goals of American secondary education. He has wisely suggested changes in emphasis and organization for learning to more effectively meet the basic goals of democracy. As he points out, he was concerned with the problem of the American high school long before the "Russian success with rockets started the landslide of words about the alleged shortcomings of our public schools. "[7]

Conant's report on the American high school was published in a paperback book and was widely ready by educators and the lay public. The book could conceivably be as influential on American education as the publication of the cardinal principles of secondary education in 1918.

Among the conclusions drawn after his extensive

---

[7]James B. Conant, "Some Problems of the American High School", Phi Delta Kappan, November 1958. p. 50.

research, some of the most interesting are:

1. There are some 23, 000 high schools; how would it be possible to hazard an opinion as to the success or failure of the American high school, even if there was a typical American high school?

2. The high school principal should be asked to provide the superintendent with an academic inventory of the graduating class. This inventory could show the board of education to what extent high school students were studying those subjects they ought to study.

3. Since we are living in a free country, the decision regarding what subjects high school children study is, in the last analysis, a decision of the child and parent. But good guidance and good counselors can influence this decision. In the satisfactory schools, there is almost invariably a good guidance program.

4. For the welfare of citizens, for the preservation of freedom, for the maintenance of a highly industrialized society, many men and women with highly specialized skills are required. Today such skills may require twenty or more years of formal schooling and only those with certain kinds of ability can hope to complete such arduous academic labors. These are the academically talented and compose about 15 per cent of the high school population.

5. The academically talented should be identified as soon as possible, (as early as in the higher elementary grades) and ought to study the following in high school:

    4 years of English
    3-4 years of history and other social studies
    3 years of mathematics
    3 years of foreign languages and
    1 extra year of mathematics and science or
    3 years of a foreign language.

This program demands five subjects each year, with fifteen or more hours of homework each week. This is not an impossible task; many schools are offering this program now.

6. Some schools have an eight-period day (with forty-five minute periods) and an additional summer session so the academically talented may get a few elective subjects.

7. While academically talented boys are studying mathematics and science, there is a waste of the girl's academic talents. They, probably because of parental influence and social mores, are not choosing courses in mathematics and science. Good guidance programs could persuade a high percentage of both boys and girls to elect more academic subjects.

8. It is difficult to measure how well the subjects are being taught in the high schools. The success or failure of the academically talented youth in college entrance examinations and other external examinations provides some information.

9. There should be more ability grouping on a subject-by-subject basis. There should be sections for the more able pupils in English, the social studies, and courses in mathematics, science and foreign language. Exceptions should be made in courses dealing with the problems of American democracy.

10. In all the schools visited, instruction in most instances appeared to range from satisfactory to excellent.

11. In English courses half the time should be devoted to composition and half to literature. The school board should see to it that good English teachers are employed and that each teacher has responsibility for not more than 100 pupils.

12. Students not academically talented should occupy themselves, one-half to two-thirds of their time, to general education and the rest of the time to specialized talent or vocation. The majority should be electing a set of courses that fit into a vocational pattern. For the girls this might be typing and stenography, office practice, or distributive education with work experience. For the boys it might be one of a number of shop courses, or mechanical drawing, or both. There is no need for the establishment of separate schools for vocational education.

13. The introduction of special arrangements for gifted pupils is one of the changes that mark the transformation of a satisfactory high school into a generally good one.

14. To provide adequately for its range of students, a high school must be of sufficient size. The minimum should be 100 in the graduating class. In some states more than half the boys and girls are in high schools too small to provide a satisfactory education. These states should follow the lead of New Jersey, New York, California and others in re-organizing the school districts to eliminate so far as possible the small high school.

While the authors do not agree with every criticism and recommendation made by Dr. Conant, they feel that his study is based on scientific evidence and research. He has a good foundation in the problem of the American high school and has scientific data, not intuitive guesses, to present logical argument for his very fine and very thorough appraisal of American secondary education.

Education, as never before, is at the crossroads and the crossroads are crowded with traffic directors pointing in practically every direction their personal recommendation to the road of success. Unfortunately, many school advisors have not studied the problem as well as Dr. Conant. Uncertain and confusing times bring confusing answers. There is a need for educators to examine the philosophies of education in search for a clarifying solution to their problem. The nature of knowledge, of man, of value, of society, and of the world must each be considered before a satisfactory system of education can be hewn to fit modern society.

THE NEED FOR A REALISTIC APPROACH TO EDUCATION

Education must be geared to the society which it serves. If the society is static as it was during the Middle Ages, the educational system will remain static. In order for society to change, the educational system must change for it is the agent of society and the objectives of education are designed to further the goals of society.

Because of the rapidly changing society of modern times, education is receiving more attention than ever before. Instructional materials which were valid only five or ten years ago are obsolete today. The magnitude of the problem is discussed by Whitehead:

> Our sociological theories, our political philosophy, our practical maxims of business, our political economy, and our doctrines of education are derived from an unbroken tradition and practical examples from the age of Plato . . . to the end of last century. The whole of this tradition is warped by the vicious assumption that each generation will substantially live amid the conditions governing the lives of their fathers and will transmit those conditions to mould with equal force the lives of its children. We are living in the first period of human history for which this assumption is false.[8]

Imagine the implication for education, the seriousness of the problem, and the need for realistic and constructive thinking. With our democratic society threatened on all sides and communism encroaching on free people of the world, education must not fail. The twentieth century is characterized by the struggle for the survival of democracy against other ideologies. In order for it to do so there must be a realistic approach to the education of the youth and adults for living in the world today.

There must be an awakening, a new renaissance, a realistic and functional preparation of students for modern living. No longer can the problem be delayed. The United States has arrived at a time of decision. More money, more thinking, and more interest must be given to the leadership and quality of the educational system designed to promote democracy and equip its youth to live within the democratic society. The people of the United States must face reality and fight for democracy, or run and cease to be a democratic people.

Never in all history has an experiment in education

[8]Alfred North Whitehead, Adventures of Ideas, New York: The Macmillan Company, 1933. p. 117.

been conceived on so grand a scale as in the United States. Universal education has become a reality as the ideals and promises of democracy have unfolded in America's changing society. But quantity is not enough. It is now imperative that the quality of education is sufficient to serve the needs of both the individual and society. History has shown that if education loses sight of the true purpose of education the society becomes weak. Should poor education continue the society loses strength, disintegrates, and soon declines.

Too often in the past the goals to be achieved in education and the degree to which these goals have been reached have been determined by hunches, intuition, and inherited attitudes. Educators assumed that the success of pupils could be measured by academic marks and especially of these marks were in the so-called hard-core subjects. Lydgate points a vivid picture of an American school, a school incidentally, which is supposed to preserve democracy:

> There is something radically wrong with education in America. Our schools have been turning out too many people who have shockingly little knowledge about the world around and--worse still--<u>whose</u> <u>interest</u> <u>in</u> <u>learning</u> <u>has</u> <u>been</u> <u>killed</u> . . . . Our schools . . . have <u>squeezed</u> <u>all</u> <u>subjects</u> <u>dry</u> <u>of</u> <u>interest</u>. When these students get through dry-as-dust courses in history, government, economics, literature, they're so profoundly sunk in ennui that they never want to hear about these topics again. Schools have failed to make what they teach seem significant, compelling, worth remembering. No wonder such a large proportion of young people in the classrooms register nothing but colossal boredom. They squirm and fret under the irritating burden of dull lectures, dull teachers, dull textbooks. They can hardly wait until the whole boring process of school is over . . . . What countless thousands of perfectly normal people have gotten out of school is (1) a lack of interest in government, (2) a lack of interest in history and foreign affairs, (3) a lack of interest in worthwhile literature, (4) a lack of interest in geography, economics, and social sciences, (5) a total lack of interest in economics--in short, they've become allergic to learning.[9]

[9]William A. Lydgate, "What's Wrong With Our Schools?" Redbook Magazine February 1948.

Because of the quick rate of change in the modern world, education has become an increasingly difficult and engaging task. The youth of today has a need for a different kind of education than that which was adequate for their parents. Although many skills needed for living in a former day are still valuable and essential, new demands are constantly made on educators and educational institutions. The world of electronics, the new atomic age, and the dynamic vortex of world society which has brought man closer together through the use of technology, has failed to bring man closer together in understanding and brotherhood. It is in this lack of skill in communication and understanding that the schools have failed society. There is rather general agreement that the schools must make changes to meet the new demands imposed upon them. What changes, and how the changes are to be made, is a subject of great controversy.

Blind acceptance of advice from every admiral, beautician, or mortician who would return to the educational system of one-hundred years ago, or to adapt the Russian system of education, is not only unrealistic but ridiculous. The educational objectives of the horse and buggy era would hardly suffice to advance the highly technical society of the atomic age. The little one-room school provided ample housing for the purposes of education in the agrarian age but would not even house the facilities and equipment necessary for education today. Those who would return to the good old days should read the charming book, *The Age of Indiscretion*. In this book Davis describes the school of just sixty years ago:

> The town (Chillicothe) was proud of its educational system . . . . The Eugene Field School, which I entered in 1900, consisted of a three-room brick building set in a small cindery yeard. Each room was heated by a round bellied soft-coal stove. Each room owned a red composition water bucket and tin dipper which was shared by about 60 pupils--a democratic gesture designed for equitable distribution of all communicable maladies.[10]

[10] Clyde Brion Davis, The Age of Indiscretion. Philadelphia: J. B. Lippincott Company, 1950. p. 26.

Likewise, the educational system designed to promote communism is hardly the answer to solving the problems of a free and democratic society. A teacher concerned with equipping children for participation in a democratic society will not employ the same techniques used by the Russians who train their children to become subservient to the Communist Party.

Extending educational opportunities to include new kinds of experiences which will foster wholesome living in the modern world involves two major problems: (1) to devise a functional philosophy and (2) to involve a larger segment of society in the business of running the school. It is not enough for educators to devise a workable philosophy of education. In a democracy, education is much too great a problem to leave to the educators. This perhaps is one of the reasons why education has failed democracy to the extent that it has.

There must be a clear understanding and reasonable agreement by all concerned as to the goals of education, and how they can best be achieved. Citizens cannot possibly understand education in a democracy unless they are involved in its operation. The founding fathers of the United States, in their great dream, wrote and preached that a democratic form of government would succeed only if the masses of the people are educated, trained, and involved in, and for, that purpose. Democracy derives its form and system from the people themselves. Each generation must come to grips anew with its own problems and deal with them in a manner they judge best to serve their society. Reliance on the solution of past generations will no longer suffice and reliance on a few chosen educators is not in keeping with the democratic system of government.

Furthermore, those who foot the bill for education have a right to protect their investment. Schools throughout the United States which have strong parent-teacher organizations and citizen study groups have been immune to the wild attacks on education. Too few educators are involving the citizenry of their community. Too many educators either feel that they cannot take the time or feel that they have all the answers. Administrators who rule by authority are seldom bothered by the problem of participation.

Sometimes school administrators complain that there is a lack of interest in education on the part of the parents and citizens of their community. The difficulty does not stem from a lack of interest so much as a lack of opportunity for communication. The fact that the school is the agency of the democratic society is not clearly understood by parents and lay people, and educators do not usually have time for public relations. They are so busy managing the finances and the physical plant that the very important task of concentrating on the educational program has been neglected. Furthermore, to add to the difficulty, so many people from all walks of life have already assumed a position and are not willing to listen to others. Many, including school men themselves, have set themselves up as prophets and have declared themselves authorities. This does not make for good democratic procedure. Educators must become more public minded and public conscious than ever before.

A practical and functional philosophy must be designed by the entire community--for what profits can a society derive from a philosophy not of its own making and therefore not within its comprehension. A blueprint is no good to a carpenter unless he can read it. A good carpenter not only knows how to read a blueprint, but he also knows how to use it as a guide to construction. A good citizen will know the purpose of education and will be able to help in carrying out the objectives which he helped formulate.

Philosophy is not a private subject designed for philosophers only. It is for administrators, teachers, parents, and students. Administrators often are lacking a central purpose or their practice is not consistent with their pretension. Too often education becomes a matter of saving money at the expense of teachers and pleasing the public with fine athletic teams and beautiful stadiums.

Too often the teacher, either through a lack of interest or because she is saddled with too many unimportant details, does not keep up with current research. She becomes intel-

lectually sterile as year after year she parrots the contents
of the textbook to her children. She is usually so exhausted
at the end of the day that no time is left for improving her
cultural background or entering the social stream of the
community. The teacher needs time and encouragement to
explore the possibilities of teaching through nature, to examine her methods, and to seek inspiration from great
teachers both living (through visitations) and dead (through
books).

Parents should not be excluded from the realistic
philosophy for the modern day school. With an understanding of what the schools are trying to do they will be able to
give aid and support. It is hard to support that which is
not understood. In addition parents may use more democratic methods of conducting their home life if they are
given a chance to think along with leaders of their community on the problems of rearing their young. Neither au-
thoritarianism nor *laissez-faire* methods are ideal in a
democratic society. Cooperation and understanding between
parents and children in accepting responsibilities around the
home makes for a truly democratic education which can be
enlarged upon in the schools.

Students, too, need to be concerned with working out
a philosophy of life. Students choosing snap courses, going
to high school or college just to partake in athletics, avoiding the eight o'clock class, and attending college for social
prestige are examples of those who are in need of a constructive philosophy of education. Other students follow
their special interests too closely. Students of science
avoid the liberal arts courses and liberal arts students will
shy away from science. Students with a realistic approach
to education will try to build their education on a broad general education foundation.

The democratic way of life rests on the assumption
that individuals and groups within society will remain alert,
will offer constructive criticism, and will engage in study
and work to improve their schools. The schools will likewise teach the children through the democratic procedures
in the art of self-study, free inquiry, open-mindedness and
willingness to work and improve both their school and society.

Citizen study groups, parent-teacher committees and the students themselves should all be involved in a continuous process of setting objectives and evaluating results of their educational program. Schools cannot keep up with, much less propagate, a changing society unless pupils, teachers, supervisors, administrators, and parents continually appraise what they are trying to do and have the courage to change the school curriculum to reach the objectives which they set for themselves.

No longer can modern society afford to heed panic-stricken leaders who council retreat, back to old books, back to authority and obedience. The rigid class structures, entrenched institutions, deep-seated customs and traditions of the Middle Ages will hardly be the answer to the dynamic needs of the atomic age. The educational system of America has from the beginning lagged behind a healthy and growing society, although the gap, usually referred to as the social lag between life and education or society and the school, has been considerably narrowed in the past decade. It still has not taken the lead. Rugg and Withers comment on the failure of education to build understanding:

> Unfortunately, the reasons for World War II are much clearer in the 1950's than they were in 1939. The allied nations, especially the United States, had no accurate view of the world situation before the war. The failure of Americans to sense world realities caused millions to be amazed when Japan attacked Pearl Harbor. We were not prepared, either mentally or physically, for the attack. It is a reflection upon American public opinion that it was so ill-informed, and not a little of the blame for this ignorance rests with our public schools and colleges. Our school curricual included history and foreign affairs, but the treatment given these subjects were not sufficiently realistic.[11]

All of the resources of all the best teachers and schools will be required to teach young America to live intelligently and to comprehend and solve the basic problems of our complex society.

---

[11]Harold Rugg and William Withers, Social Foundations of Education. New York: Prentice-Hall, Inc., 1955. pp. 187-188.

This does not mean that the traditional philosophies will be overthrown. It does mean that they will be critically examined for the functional and practical guides that have more or less been unchanging truisms. These will be used along with new values to guide the direction of education.

The philosophy of the modern age must be a functional system of values which are derived from experience in the society which it proposes to serve. It must be based on inquiries, investigations, scientific research and observation. Thinking and reconstruction of abstract and often meaningless terms is not enough. Philosophy must not return to the past, to the glorification of old books and traditions for its strength. It must look to the present to implement and give direction to a progressive and forward moving program of education.

Emerson condemned the practice of depending on the old for guidance of the new:

> To be as good a scholar as Englishmen are; to have as much learning as our contemporaries; to have written a book that is read; satisfies us. We assume, that all thoughts are already long ago adequately set down in books,--all the imagination in poems; and what we say, we only throw in as confirmatory of this supposed body of literature. A very shallow assumption. Say rather all literature is yet to be written. Poetry has scarce chanted its first song. The perpetual admonition of nature to us, is "The world is new, untried. Do not believe the past. I give you the universe a virgin today.[12]

Mankind is constantly searching for possible signs that will guide his way to the good life. This eternal quest for knowledge of the good is the concern of philosophers and the system of values and beliefs as to what is the good of philosophy. As each generation faces a new life it must begin at its own stage in history with problems unique to the times. It is for this reason that philosophy, too, must change. Educators must turn to philosophy in order to determine what is the good, what is to be taught to children,

---

[12]The Works of Ralph Waldo Emerson. New York: Bigelow, Brown and Company, Vol. II. p. 115.

and what is to be allowed to disappear through neglect. It is for this reason that philosophy, education, and society must be closely related.

John Dewey was the most eloquent spokesman for education in a democracy. He stressed co-operation. He held that philosophy should come down from the clouds and be put to use in clarifying problems on earth. John Dewey conceived education in much broader terms than the school. Although the school was regarded by Dewey as a special agency of education, many important functions of education are performed by the home, the church, recreation department, church, agencies, and other neighborhood and other community organizations. The gist of John Dewey's philosophy may be briefly explained under the headings of "education is life," "education is growth," "education is a social process," and "education is reconstruction of experience."

EDUCATION IS LIFE

Many educators believe that the purpose of education is to prepare a child for society. Although this is true, education is more than a preparation. It is life. It does not stop at graduation. Education is a continuous process from birth to death and takes place both in and out of school. This philosophy makes education more acceptable to the student who sometimes feels that he has to spend most of his life in school learning to live.

EDUCATION IS GROWTH

A child builds on his experience. As long as growth is continuous the child is being educated. Growth that begins at birth, continues in school and progresses throughout life is the goal of education in a democratic society. For example, it is no longer considered enough for a child to learn skills; he must be given ample opportunity to use those skills. Knowing how to read is of little value unless a child learns what to read. Skills learned in school thus help him enjoy good music, appreciate beautiful pictures, engage in worthwhile leisure activities, practice good health habits, and, in short, adapt all the salutary habits, ideals, and attitudes that were acquired in school. Such growths in habits, attitudes, skills, and appreciations is education.

Education is an unfolding process. The school must provide a vital and stimulating environment in order to encourage growth and education.

EDUCATION IS A SOCIAL PROCESS

Education, being life and growth, has its setting within a social group. In the past many scholars believed that education could best be accomplished in a quiet secluded place. They confused education with knowledge. A man may be a walking encyclopedia and yet not be educated, for education means living. The schools must provide miniature democratic societies and communities where children may live naturally and practice good citizenship as a part of their experience. There is a difference in being a good citizen and knowing how to be a good citizen. The first is learned through practice and experience while the second is learned through knowledge and memorization of rules for good citizenship.

EDUCATION IS THE CONTINUOUS RECONSTRUCTION OF EXPERIENCE

Activities of the day are based on experiences of yesterday. Every activity is conditioned by what went before. The continuous reconstruction and reorganization of past experience to add to the meaning of present experience requires reflection and thought; that is education.

John Dewey believed that democracy is the very essence of education. Democracy is a way of life and not a set of theoretical rules. Before Dewey, dictatorial methods of teaching were employed to teach the rules and demands of democracy. Teachers had little freedom and students had less. Through a reconstruction of philosophy and education, John Dewey became the champion of the democratic faith.

The world has changed since John Dewey's day, recent though it has been. How long will his philosophy serve the new society of the atomic age? The "one world" of today? Just as educators, parents and students examine the philosophies of old, they need to continually evaluate and reconstruct the modern day philosophies.

Brameld, in advancing the reconstruction philosophy, repudiates nothing of the constructive achievements of Dewey's philosophy, but is critical that it focuses too much upon means at the expense of ends. He contends that Dewey rightfully expresses the spirit of open-mindedness, tolerance, and experimentation but fails to answer the question of what are the goals. Brameld would combine the good from Dewey's philosophy with the good of other philosophies and add values and guides deduced from modern society to derive a philosophy that would reconstruct world culture. His philosophy advanced in his very worthwhile book *Ends and Means In Education* should be read by all concerned with the problems of education.

THE EDUCATIONAL NEEDS OF MODERN SOCIETY

The function of education is fundamentally to equip youth for useful lives in their society and to assist men and women in making adjustments to a changing society by learning new ways of being useful. To serve this end, education must (1) provide for the basic needs of all human beings, and (2) pass the cultural heritage on to the next generation.

History shows that to fail in either of the above two functions of education society remains static and unchanging. The fulfullment of both individual needs and society's needs are imperative for a realistic and constructive, democratic way of life. No past society has succeeded in perfecting an educational system which has fully accomplished its dual responsibility. Education for the propagation of traditional values soon grows static unless the individual is prepared to live in the society and is encouraged to express himself in reshaping the society in which he lives.

Since education is given the responsibility for equipping youth to live in modern society, it has little business stressing the culture of the Middle Ages. In order to survive, every society expects its citizens to learn the ways of that society and to acquire the desire and ability to help that society meet the challenges of the changing world. The expressed needs cannot be met unless the individual has the knowledge to live effectively, with himself and in association with other individuals and groups. The needs of the individual, then, are closely allied with the society in which he lives. In a democracy, education can only meet the needs of its youth and the needs of society in one integrated process.

The basic and closely related needs of the individual and the parallel demands of society may be grouped in the following twelve categories:

1. *All members of society need to develop and maintain good habits, attitudes and appreciation in health, safety, and physical fitness.*

The Greeks probably more than any civilization appreciated the importance of a beautiful and healthy body. This was reflected in their art, their philosophy, and their daily lives.

Strong bodies are needed to develop keen minds. Poor physical condition is not only expensive and detrimental to the individual but it weakens the moral and physical vigor of a society. It goes without saying that a healthy person is an asset to society while an unhealthy person is a burden to himself, his family, and to society.

A child needs to learn the attitudes, habits, and appreciations in health and safety necessary to carry on life's activities without undue fatigue or strain. He should be coordinated sufficiently to enjoy sports and play and to be able to perform his work safely and efficiently in all areas of activity associated with effective living.

Good health and physical fitness involve freedom from disease and physical defects, muscular activity and good muscular tone, mental health, adequate nutrition, proper clothing, proper medical and dental care, proper environmental factors (good lighting, sanitation, fresh air, furniture, etc.), and a balanced schedule of work, recreation and sleep.

2. All members of society need the tools of learning --the skills and knowledges, and the wisdom and understanding to use them to advantage in becoming a more effective citizen of the democratic society.

For many centuries, imparting knowledge was considered the major purpose of education. Education was almost entirely a method of instruction. Culture in the Middle Ages remained static for century upon century, not because of a lack of knowledge but because of the acceptance of knowledge, and knowledge alone, as the proper function of education. Today, educators realize that there are better ways to knowledge than through formal instruction, and education must be concerned with other aspects as important, or more so, than knowledge for its own sake. Knowledge, although the first step in real education, is not enough. Individuals must have the know-how and the desire to use knowledge to further their personal well-being and that of their society.

It is to these ends--to gain more knowledge and to make knowledge more meaningful--that outdoor education is dedicated. Through firsthand, direct experience, knowledge becomes practical and therefore more valuable, as it is seen in context. It is not regarded as something to be stored or memorized for future use, but it is something to be sought from past experience and from books and then utilized to solve real and worthwhile problems here and now.

The ability to use the tools of learning--reading, writing, speaking, arithmetic, spelling, and so on--for effective, constructive, and creative thinking and living is the essence of a democratic society's expectation of its citizenry.

Knowledge whether stored in encyclopedias and great books or in the minds of men can be of very little value unless it can find expression in everyday living.

3. All members of society need to know and accept the responsibilities of citizenship.

As a child grows into an adult, he should learn his responsibilities as a member of his family, school, community, nation and as a world citizen. He should not only understand but practice desirable social attitudes toward other individuals, toward groups, and as a member of the many and varied groups. He must know the obligations of being a good neighbor and, especially, a good citizen of his country and the world.

People cannot be good citizens in a democratic society unless they know what they want of their government, know the problems which their government faces, and accept the responsibilities which democracy requires of well-informed citizens.

4. All members of society need to develop skills in human relations.

The ability and the desire to work with others is essential in a democratic society. If the majority of the citizens in America had the know-how and the real desire to work together, many perplexing problems such as crime, juvenile delinquency, highway slaughter, and other domestic evils could be solved as quickly and easily as technological problems. The apathy of the citizens toward issues that do not directly concern them, the lethargy of voters in the all-important decision of choosing leaders to represent them, and the universal practice of putting selfish and personal desires and gains ahead of the neighbor or community are all detrimental to good human relations and good democratic government.

Competition has been the controlling factor of America's business and economic life and this has tended to dominate every phase of man's activity. He competes with his neighbors to have the biggest and best house or car; he competes with his church members for status and leadership positions; his children compete with the neighbors' children to make the highest grades in school or to win athletic contests.

Competition, although necessary and desirable, need not permeate all of man's existence. Cooperation also is essential and may gradually supersede the highly competitive urge which now guides his destiny; the atomic bomb has brought the world to the point where man must practice the Golden Rule or perish.

Perhaps greater understanding and world peace would be realized if more people today could pray as Benjamin Franklin did in 1780, "That moral science were in as fair a way of improvement, that men would cease to be wolves to one another and that human beings would at length learn what they now improperly call humanity. "

5. *All members of society need to develop skills in consumer education.*

With the increased pressure of competition, products are constantly kept before the public by advertising through the media of television, radio, newspapers and magazines, and through unsightly billboards along the highways. It is a known fact that many products could sell for half the asking price if it were not necessary for consumers to bear the cost of advertising. Proper advertising is essential and helpful.

In addition to advertising, practically every company has highly skilled salesmen to move its product. Many a purchaser signs a dotted line or pays for a product that is practically useless to him because he "fell for a line" from a clever and fast-talking salesman.

All members of society need to know how to purchase and use both goods and services intelligently and wisely.

6. *All members of society need to use their leisure time wisely.*

The community has a responsibility not only to provide areas, facilities, and equipment for recreation but also an education that includes the skills, knowledge, and background to make wise and constructive use of leisure time.

Leisure education should give youth experience in a variety of the best recreational and cultural experiences. The schools have finally begun to offer courses, sponsor clubs, and support activities in music, art, drama, crafts, informal games, carry-over sports and many other areas of interest which will help each individual discover the type of recreation that will bring the richest and most rewarding satisfaction.

Instead of regarding recreation as a lesser component

to education, the community must put it on equal footing; for the day has finally arrived when it is just as important to educate a man for leisure time as it is to educate him for a profession or vocation.

The awakening of numerous interests and hobbies is an important phase of education. Childhood is the best time to learn to appreciate and enjoy the world of nature, to learn to swim, to learn the many enjoyable games, to develop an interest in picnicking, hosteling, skating, camping, and outdoor life, to learn to care for plants and animals, to learn to do things with the hands, and to learn to read and enjoy good sports. The public schools have it within their power to make the lives of every individual a rich and rewarding experience by opening doors to new and creative leisure time pursuits.

7. *All members of society need to develop sound moral and spiritual values.*

Standing in the dawn of the scientific age--an age that is soon to give man more time to himself--humanity is on the threshold of a new spiritual awakening. More people go to church today than ever before. The teachings of Darwin are being refuted in all nations; science has uncovered phenomena today that were unknown to Darwin, such as the wonders of ultramicroscopic genes. All mankind, including the great scientists, is more than ever before aware that the heavens declare the glory of God and the firmament showeth His handiwork.

Public schools do not spend enough time developing good moral and spiritual values in children. This important phase of life is left to the parents, to the church and often times to chance. A good teacher can instill morality and Christian education in a child both by example and by incidental instruction. This is not in violation of the principle of democracy which states that religion should not be taught in the schools; it is not a plea for indoctrination of children in religious dogma. It does mean that the teacher should stress those spiritual and moral tenets which transcend all religions or are held in common by all denominations-- the Golden Rule, respect for others, and faith in a Supreme Being.

8. All members of society need to develop aesthetic appreciation.

Too many citizens of the modern age never have the opportunity to develop an appreciation for the finer things of life. Yet life can be made more complete and more meaningful if one learns to become aware of beauty and aesthetic expression through music, art, poetry, literature, and nature.

Too many schools today are so intent on the mastery of subject matter they do not give enough attention to the development of the children's capacities to appreciate beauty in their everyday life.

9. All members of society need to develop a sense of wholeness.

Children need to achieve a feeling of belonging and a sense of wholeness with their fellow men, with nature, and with the universe. Alexander Pope wrote, "All are but parts of one stupendous whole."

As children grow up, they become socialized by learning to satisfy their personal needs within the framework of their culture. Their ego is formed somewhere between their natural desires and drives and the pressures of society. When the personality is successfully balanced between those two forces--personal and social--the child feels an increased sense of his wholeness and of unity with his fellow man. Beginning as a respected and rightful member of a family, he becomes, in turn, a member of various groups in school, church, community, nation and finally world affairs. In this way, realizing that cooperation is an expedient for his own well-being, he adjusts even if unwillingly to living cooperatively with others.

Man needs to find himself in relation to his environment. All his life the school has placed him on the outside of life. He has been looking in and fails many times to relate his knowledge to himself and his environment.

The ultimate goal of education is to help people find themselves. The goal of education should be closely identified with that of living--the achievement of dignity and integrity, the development of a unified personality and the integration into a feeling of wholeness with fellow men, with nature, and with local, national, and world culture. In the out-of-doors man can more realistically see that he is a part of nature and fits into a beautiful and well-organized pattern.

10. All members of society need to develop an understanding of science and the laws of nature.

People who understand are no longer afraid. To know the laws of nature, to understand scientific principles concerning the world of nature and man, and to know the influence of science on human affairs, is to allay fear and increase reverence and humility.

Every high school graduate should have a good background in biological, physical and earth sciences, if for no other reason than to give him a better understanding of his environment. Natural science, in its true perspective, is not to be feared as impious and anti-Christian, but is a good thing which brings benefits and comfort to human life.

It is not science but a few of the lesser gifted scientists who sometimes become destructive critics of religion and cynical about ancient and respected philosophy. Science seen in its totality tends to make its followers more creative, more humble, more reverent, and more religious.

11. All members of society need opportunites for reflection and meditation.

God made man in his own image. He didn't mean for man to become insignificant and subservient to a machine-dominated culture. Man needs time to think and to meditate--"to hold communion with nature"--and to be able to speak to himself in quiet and in solitude. Man does not use his time to take inventory, to search his soul, and to achieve spiritual and aesthetic fulfillment.

In modern civilization man is so far removed from his heritage that it is difficult for him to see his relationship with his fellow man, with his society, and with his God. Crowded together in large cities, living in the shadows of large factories, stacked one on top of another in apartment houses, and caught in the traffic of modern innovations, man has no longer an opportunity to walk the quiet streams or the still pastures. More and more public parks, forests, sanctuaries and gardens need to be set aside for the spiritual and mental relief which man requires in the age of machines.

12. *All members of society need opportunities for creative self-expression.*

Man must have opportunities to try new ways of doing things, new ways of living, and new forms of behavior, without fear. Children should be allowed to work in a permissive climate, unafraid of trial and error, or criticism. The failure of individuals today to accept constructive criticism rather than to take it as a personal affront does not speak well of the efforts of the public schools in a democracy. Creativity is much needed to put a spark of life into every subject matter field in the school curriculum. Knowledge, facts, and skills used to construct or reconstruct experience in a creative and constructive way is the very principle of education at its highest level of attainment.

IMPLICATION FOR TEACHER EDUCATION

There is a strange inconsistency in the innovations and imagination of the American people in education. In many educational pursuits they brought vigorous and creative effort and showed brilliant insight. Americans introduced the concept of universal education on a scale never before practiced in history. They set aside land for educational purposes, even in laws as early as the Ordinance of 1787 or the Northwest Ordinance. They conceived the idea that education in a democracy should be the concern of the local government. They, more than any other nation of people, adhered to the idea that education should be child-centered rather than subject-matter centered.

It is unfortunate that the American people were unwilling to break away from European tradition in one of the most important aspects of education--that of educating teachers. Here they refused to be original; they merely adopted the normal school which was conceived and fostered in Germany. In Europe, the normal schools were especially designed to train elementary teachers; secondary teachers were educated in liberal arts colleges. Normal schools were considered training institutions for the poorer classes, but this idea was distorted when it was transferred to American soil.

Most normal schools grew to four-year state teachers colleges, which are now being converted into state universities. As many as possible of the few remaining teachers colleges are dropping the prefex as fast as possible in order to become respectable state institutions.

The majority of America's classrooms today are conducted by liberal arts graduates. Businessmen graduate from schools of business, lawyers from law schools, physicians from medical schools, engineers from engineering schools, farmers from agricultural schools, but teachers graduate from liberal arts colleges. It is as if the teacher were ashamed of admitting to a degree leading to the most honorable profession of all--a teacher of children. Is it not from the teaching profession that all other professions spring?

A few teacher-education institutions and colleges of education still exist and are proud of their function--that of turning out professional educators who are not only capable and inspiring teachers but are proud of their calling. Although the teacher does not have the Hypocratic oath, the scale of justice, or the cross as a symbol of an honorable profession, he can be duly proud of the fact that he taught the scholars who hold them.

Since the education of American youth is dependent in no small part on the effectiveness of teacher education, this should become one of the most significant problems in higher education today.

Teachers, including supervisors and administrators, must have more than skill in pedagogic methods. They must have a unified background in the liberal arts, science, research, teaching methods, guidance, testing, supervision, theory and philosophy. In this way theory may guide practice, and philosophy may serve, rather than confuse, educational procedure. The teacher needs to be taught how to be a philosopher, not how to become one.

Many prominent leaders in education recommend a 40-30-30 percentage distribution of general, specific, and professional education. The 40 per cent in general education is to provide a good background in the humanities, general sciences, and social studies as well as art and music. 30 per cent should be devoted to specific content in the subject area or grade level to be taught, and the remaining 30 per cent of college work should be taken in professional courses, including methods of teaching and child psychology. This ratio should not be regarded as sacred but should be under constant evaluation in terms of the ultimate product--a well prepared and well qualified teacher.

In as many courses as possible, teachers should be given insights into good teaching techniques. Teachers generally teach as they are taught and need a background so that they may teach children in other ways than the abused lecture system which applies in about 98 per cent of all college classrooms. Realistic experiences such as outdoor education, travel, recreational activities, participation in community affairs and work experience should be a part of every prospective teacher's education.

Northern Illinois University has a unique and very worthwhile program of outdoor education designed to acquaint prospective teachers with the techniques of teaching in the out-of-doors. Students enrolled in the College of Education are required to spend blocks of time during their freshman and sophomore years in an outdoor education center. When they enroll for practice teaching in their senior year, they are required to take their children into the woods for a week of living and learning in the out-of-doors.

New kinds of experiences are needed in the modern era. Mastery of subject matter alone is not enough. This will mean that new methods of learning and teaching may have to be employed. The well-educated teacher will not be afraid to experiment or to break from the present practices.

The teacher education institutions must extend the educational opportunities to include the new kind of experience. In order for teachers to foster wholesome living in the modern world they need to understand what they are about. What is education? Why should children go to school? What is the function of subject matter? What methods should be used in teaching?

Childish arguments and often emotional disagreements between professors in the traditional disciplines and those in the school of education show a lack of ability to solve the problem in preparing well-equipped teachers. True educators seldom need to present their case; they live it. They have been educated both in the liberal arts and in the practical and professional arts. They know subject matter and how to teach. They are at ease in the classroom or at a meeting of factory workers or farmers. They can do things with their hands and are not ashamed of it. They can attend a football game without fear of letting down their bookish and self-styled fellow scholars. In brief, they enjoy good books and read them but they don't have to live inside them. They are not afraid of life.

President Dwight D. Eisenhower, speaking at Pennsylvania State University a few years ago, said: "In this country we emphasize both liberal and practical education. But too often it is a liberal education for one and a practical education for another. What we desperately need is an integrated liberal, practical education for the same person . . . Hand and head and heart were made to work together. They must work together. They should be educated together."

When colleges and universities reach the point that they rest their claim for fame not on the number of their graduates that make honorary academic organizations but count their greatness in terms of the useful citizens they have produced, education will have taken a great step forward.

SUMMARY

In a rapid and fast changing society the educational system, too, must change or the society soon weakens and disintegrates. The educational system of today needs the attention of every good citizen in America--not just the educators and the respected business and professional men of a community, but also the parents who produce the children and pay the taxes.

When a teacher is employed in a public school, today, he has an obligation to the community that reaches far beyond the teaching of the "Three R's." He must become a vital leader in the life of the community; he must be interested in every worth-while undertaking; and he should enter heartily into the activities of the community which he serves. The teacher has many opportunities to bring the school and community together in working toward the betterment of society.

In an honest appraisal of the school curriculum, tradition will be respected but not idolized. It is not whether it is old or new that counts, but whether or not it is useful.

The school curriculum should be designed to stress more cooperation and less competition in the new world. Appreciation and understanding of other people, of other races and nationalities, and of other cultures must be considered. The knowledge of this century, which has seemingly been used for selfish promotion of one nation over another and has been used to destroy rather than build, should be carefully evaluated.

Are the schools teaching the right things? Are they using the right methods of teaching? In a democratic society where the very cornerstone is action and self-government, would it not be better to stress more activity and less listening, more democratic procedures and less formal instruction? These and many other questions must be asked by the citizens of a democracy. They must be unafraid to change, unafraid of ridicule, open-minded and completely objective in the solution of democracy's greatest problems: how shall we care for our bodies, how shall we rear our children, how shall we work together, how shall we live with our fellow man, how shall we play, and for what ends shall we live?

Questions and Projects

1. In your opinion, what is the primary function of general education? Discuss what courses should be required on the high school level. College level.

2. Which do you think would be the best way to teach philosophy in college:
    (a) Through a separate department of Philosophy?
    (b) As a different course in each of the college departments?
    (c) As an inter-departmental course?

3. Discuss the following statements: "The tools of science are observation and experimentation; the tools of philosophy are discussion and contemplation."

4. Spend considerable time thinking, then write briefly (one page) your philosophy of education.

5. To what extent does one's past experience affect his perception? Does an individual see, feel, hear, and think on the basis of his past experience? What does the answer to this question imply for education?

6. Discuss the following statement: "A little philosophy inclineth man's mind to atheism, but depth in philosophy bringeth man's mind about to religion." (Francis Bacon)

7. Discuss the following statement made by Trueblood in *The Predicament of Modern Man:* "Man has been more successful in making engines than in achieving the will and wisdom to use his engines for human purposes."

8. List the kinds of things that can best be taught in the classroom and the kinds of experiences students should have outside the classroom in regard to: (1) conservation, (2) health, (3) healthful living, and (4) leisure time activities.

88

Selected References

American Association of School Administrators, *The Expanding Role of Education*. Washington, D. C. : National Education Association, 1948.

American Association of School Administrators, *Schools For A New World*. Washington, D. C. : National Education Association, 1947.

Brameld, Theodore, *Ends and Means in Ecucation*. New York: Harper and Brothers, 1950.

Butts, R. Freeman and Cremins, Lawrence A. , *A History of Education in American Culture*. New York: Holt, Rinehart and Winston, 1953.

Counts, George S. , *Education and American Civilization*. New York: Bureau of Publications, Teachers College, Columbia University, 1952.

Department of Supervision and Curriculum Development, *Toward a New Curriculum, Extending the Educational Opportunity of Children, Youth and Adults*. Washington, D. C. : National Education Association, 1944.

Dewey, John, *How We Think*. Boston: D. C. Heath and Company, 1933.

Educational Policies Commission, *The Purposes of Education in American Democracy*. Washington, D. C. : National Education Association, 1938.

Good, Harry G. , *A History of Western Education*. New York: The Macmillan Company, 1947.

Gross, Richard E. , Zeleny, Leslie D. and Associates, *Educating Citizens For Democracy*. New York: Oxford University Press, 1958.

Havighurst, Robert J. and Neugarten, Bernice L. , *Society and Education*. Boston: Allyn and Bacon, 1948.

Mort, Paul R. and Vincent, William S. , *Introduction To American Education*. New York: McGraw-Hill Book Company, 1954.

Rugg, Harold, *Culture and Education In America*. New York: Harcourt, Brace and Company, 1931.

Rugg, Harold and Withers, William, *Social Foundations of Education*. New York: Prentice-Hall, Inc., 1955.

Sorenson, Herbert, *Psychology In Education*. New York: McGraw-Hill Book Company, 1954.

Stanley, William O., Smith, B. Othanel, Benne, Kenneth D., Anderson, Archibald W., *Social Foundations of Education*. New York: Holt, Rinehart and Winston, 1956.

Whitehead, Alfred North, *Adventures of Ideas*. New York: The Macmillan Company, 1933.

Chapter 3
OUTDOOR EDUCATION -
A METHOD OF EDUCATION

Nature, School, Life: If there is friendship among these three, a man becomes what he should become but cannot be immediately: gay in childhood, cheerful and eager to learn during his youth, contented and useful as an adult.

—Basedow

Outdoor education is a method of education. It involves intelligent planning by all teachers using nature and real life experiences in interpreting subject matter areas found in the school curriculum. Through direct experiences with nature, people, objects, things, places, and by actually "learning by doing, " there is scientific evidence that "the learning process is faster, what is learned is retained longer, and there is greater appreciation and understanding for those things that are learned firsthand. "[1]

Every subject matter field in our present day curriculum may be enriched through outdoor education experiences. Moreover, subject matter areas tend to lose their bounds and become related and integrated as ideas and facts take on meaning and perspective. Planned programs for all levels of instruction from kindergarten through college have demonstrated the values of the outdoor education method.

Some of the more prevalent outdoor experiences in today's schools are provided through trips and excursions, school gardens, school farms, school forests, park and school plans, day camping, the overnight camp, and more recently, the extended or resident school camp.

[1] L. B. Sharp, "Basic Considerations in Outdoor and Camping Education" The Bulletin of the National Association of Secondary School Principals, May, 1947. p. 43.

Outdoor education is not a separate discipline in the curriculum such as History, English, Arithmetic, and other school subject-matter areas. There are no clearly defined principles and objectives specifically designed for outdoor education. General principles and objectives must be formulated within the framework of education and the school curriculum. Each specific subject matter area must be carefully studied and analyzed to discover how and when direct learning experiences outside the classroom will make textbook learning more meaningful. Outdoor education is not intended to replace textbook learning. It is not a substitute for abstract teaching. Rather, it is a method that can be successfully and intelligently introduced by all teachers, in all subject-matter areas, to supplement and complement written and oral expression.

It is not in conflict with the child-centered, subject matter-centered, or the society-centered approaches to learning. In fact, many rewarding teaching experiences are possible which complement all three approaches.

Every teacher, no matter what grade level he is employed to teach, should be skilled in the outdoor education method.

The attitudes and appreciations, the skills and knowledges, the adventure and enjoyment associated with outdoor education experiences should be an important part of every educational program.

No subject matter area, or no department within a school, should be considered the place or department where outdoor education belongs. All subject matter areas should plan outdoor experiences as a part of their regular classroom work.

It is impossible for any teacher to know all there is to know about the out-of-doors, or about the many experiences they encounter through field trips and other outdoor learning situations. Things are learned together by pupil and teacher as a result of first-hand experiences and as a result of the skillful techniques used by teachers to get the most out of the learning situation. This is a vital contribution that makes outdoor education a real method of acquiring knowledge.

The method by which teachers provide the learning experience is most important; it should be closely associated with and accompanied by adequate library materials, textbooks, classroom lessons, and other aids to learning. Teachers are not required to have all the knowledge necessary to explain and interpret things they study in an outdoor education program. It is more important to provide learning experiences for the students and skillfully guide and direct these experiences so more efficient learning takes place.

Karl Ritter, one of the best known geographers of his time, wrote concerning the outdoor education method used by Pestalozzi:

> Pestalozzi knew less geography than a child in one of the primary schools, yet it was from him that I gained my chief knowledge of this science; for it was in listening to him that I first conceived the idea of the natural method. It was he who opened the way to me, and I take pleasure in attributing whatever value my work may have entirely to him.[2]

The best educational method for any school system is one in which the teachers are not limited to teaching second and third-hand information from a text but one in which the teachers are allowed to plan and direct many outdoor and real life experiences where students have opportunities to learn first-hand.

Second and third-hand information recorded in books and experienced by others is the basis for most classroom teaching. It is far too predominant in our modern day educational procedures. There must be provided a great number of opportunities where textbook material and oral expression are supplemented by direct experiences for students. Many teachers frequently have difficulty in presenting various units in subject-matter fields. They run out of material or can't find enough interesting books and periodicals to keep the students busy. It is almost impossible to run out of interesting and challenging experiences in outdoor

[2]Will S. Monroe, Comenius and The Beginning of Educational Reform. London: W. Heinemann, 1900. pp. 157-158.

education programs that are associated with the same unit of study.

Outdoor education methods involve a summation of many ideas and involves the borrowing of many desirable educational techniques proposed throughout the history of education. Some of these ideas, techniques, and proposals most frequently recommended in education and which are more nearly descriptive of the outdoor education method are:

The mind proceeds from the known to the unknown, from the particular to the general, and from the concrete to the abstract.

Education is a social process.

Experience is the best teacher.

Man learns to do by doing.

Learning is best when information is obtained through all the senses.

Knowledge should be acquired through experience and the written word, not merely through the written word.

It is difficult to teach a person but possible to help him learn.

A skilled teacher must know what to teach as well as how to teach. The "what" and the "how" are inseparable counterparts for good teaching. One is no more important than the other for the learning process is affected by all aspects of the teacher-learner situation. To be a successful teacher requires sound educational methods and techniques as a means of challenging, motivating, and imparting knowledge to students.

Some of the more apparent contributions to learning inherent in well-established outdoor education programs consist of *observation, investigation, cooperation, integration* and *correlation, meditation, informality, creativity,* and *active participation.*

It is very important that all teachers be skilled in the above techniques which are so necessary for successful teaching. These techniques may be used in the classroom, but in outdoor education programs they become more meaningful.

The above mentioned techniques of learning are frequently discussed during teacher training programs in college, but seldom are they demonstrated or are opportunities given to prospective teachers to experience and experiment with them. Often the techniques become educational terms to be committed to memory for some future use. The techniques should become part of the teacher's experience and should be put to practice in all teaching situations.

These techniques become even more important and more essential when outdoor education experiences become an integral part of the total school program. Teachers, as well as children, must learn through experience as well as the written word. Teachers can only learn the techniques of observation and investigation if they have many direct experiences themselves and if they have opportunities to apply these techniques to a directed experience for others.

If the teacher can develop the skills of observation and cultivate the desire and ability to investigate within each learner they will be well on their way toward developing one of education's primary goals; that is the art of thinking.

When students and teachers journey to the woods for studies in nature, the trip is quite frequently made to study one aspect or specialized area of nature such as botany, zoology, or ornithology.

These trips are necessary and important to the understanding of the special subject matter being taught. However, it is very difficult to teach one phase of nature and ignore entirely its other component parts. Teachers may become too specialized in their scientific efforts in one selected phase of nature. We need scientists of this caliber very desperately. We are also in desperate need of teachers who have a general knowledge concerning the biological and natural sciences and who can teach these subject-matter areas in an integrated way while on these field trips.

In a field study program involving nature, it is difficult to separate the zoology from the botany; the geology from the geography, the ornithology from the herpetology; or the entomology from the study of soil.

There are many opportunities for directed experiences associated with the social sciences, language arts, and creative arts. Classes may be organized democratically where leadership responsibilities and self-government are essential disciplines for the successful conduct of the field trip. Experiences associated with history, government, economics and other segments of society are observed and learned. The aesthetic values in education also find their best outlets for expression through studies and observations in nature. Individual interests and creative expression in many forms are innovations and find natural outlets through outdoor education activities.

The outdoor education experiences have been the basis for a great deal of creative work in art, poetry, music, story telling, and writing of various kinds.

These highly desirable results of outdoor education experiences do not just happen simply by taking the students out of the classroom. The goals of outdoor education cannot be realized by haphazard or incidental procedures. The experiences must be planned and planned well. They must be planned in relation to the school curriculum. The results are most successful when teachers, students, parents, and other school personnel plan the outdoor education program in a democratic way.

Most students, when observing or investigating, usually limit their search to those things with which they are acquainted or familiar. To successfully direct and stimulate additional interest in learning involves the scientific approach to the outdoor education method.

An examination of the various techniques used for teaching in outdoor education programs focuses attention on the details necessary for successful results in the outdoor education method.

OBSERVATION

When Louis Agassiz, the internationally renowned naturalist and teacher, was asked what he considered to be his greatest contribution in life, he replied: "I have taught men to observe."

Observation is recognized by educators as the most important and universally available tool of learning. Pestalozzi said:

> If I look back and ask myself what I have really done toward the improvement of methods of elementary instruction, I find that in recognizing observation as the absolute basis of all knowledge, I have established the first and most important principle of instruction.

Many teachers seem to realize the importance of observation as a technique of learning; however, too few teachers know how or will take the time or opportunity to use it. Most teachers tend to teach like they were taught. The methods were primarily based on recitation, question and answer, and reading assignments. There is a feeling of comfort and assurance on the part of the parent and the teacher that as long as the child is in the school building, he is learning.

Observation is an integral part of the outdoor education program. It is the principle factor distinguishing outdoor education from the traditional classroom instruction.

A new skill in teaching and a new concept of learning is shared by students and teachers alike. Together they plan direct experiences related to the subject-matter being studied for the purpose of better understanding.

When the students leave the classroom the teacher begins using techniques that will make skillful observers of the students.

The teacher motivates the students through questions and conversations to help them discover for themselves the importance, functions, and relationships of the thing being studied.

The teacher does not tell the answer but rather helps

the student develop habits of inquiry and discovery, make associations and relationships, and whet the appetites of the students so they will explore the problem in greater detail at their own discretion. The teacher also provides resource materials, sometimes back in the classroom and sometimes through another field trip to make the directed experience complete.

Many phases of education become more neaningful when studied first-hand. When learning situations are observed in their correct setting, students are much more apt to retain their knowledge. They are more likely to see the purpose of their learning.

Most children reach a practical limit of perception by the time they enter the first grade. Most of our senses of hearing, smelling, feeling, seeing, and touching have been developed almost to the maximum at this point. The teacher has an obligation here to provide educational experiences which will call all of the senses into play, for all students learn best when all the senses have an opportunity for exercise. If the teacher does not encourage optimum sensory exercise, students cannot fully develop their capacity to learn.

Outdoor education provides an abundance of opportunities for utilizing the observation method in teaching. Studies in nature and in real life situations require greater skills in observation than reading from the printed page or listening to lectures.

School children and adults alike can walk several blocks to school or home and seldom notice or observe anything but routine movements. Many things are seen or heard but really not observed. So often the things individuals see and hear can only be associated instinctively with movement and things that may impair their safety. This kind of observation might be called instinctive observation; seeing and hearing only what is necessary for physical protection.

How can teachers develop within their students intellectual habits of observation that will stimulate learning? This is the challenge teachers must face outside the classroom.

Intellectual observations involve developing a keen sense of inquiry and concern; a sense of seeing and appreciating details of things observed; a desire to discover facts, relationships, associations, and answers; a desire for complete knowledge concerning things being studied; and practice in technique for discovering truths.

Too many teachers are confined to the classroom and do not have opportunities to develop the powers of observation within their children. Observation is an active process and a good teacher will deliberately create learning situations which will include opportunities for scientific and systematic search for details.

The key to good observation is the purpose which it serves. Dewey points this out very clearly:

> What often makes observation in schools intellectually ineffective is (more than anything else) that it is carried on without a sense of a problem that it helps define and solve. The evil of this isolation is seen through the entire educational system, from the kindergarten through the elementary and high schools to the college. Almost everywhere may be found, at some time, recourse to observations as if they were of complete and final value in themselves, instead of being means for getting the data that test an idea or plan and that make the felt difficulty into a question that guides subsequent thinking.[3]

A good teacher will not consider the accumulation of facts as an educational end in itself. They will use the facts gained from observation through these direct experiences as a means to an end. As facts are observed in the outdoor education program, they usually relate themselves to the understanding of the environment or to the particular living experience under scrutiny. In contrast to this, quite often it is difficult for students to master facts from textbooks or from oral presentations and to comprehend the true meaning of the facts or the relationship of the facts being presented.

---

[3] John Dewey, How We Think. Boston: D. C. Heath and Company, 1933. pp. 250-251.

Observational learning is essential in the educational process in all subjects and in all grades, but it makes its greatest contribution in the outdoor education program. The classroom offers few opportunities for studying nature and its relationships first-hand. Observation is an active process. To get the full benefits of learning, it is necessary to go to the places where life is being lived, where government is in action, where things are being manufactured or made, and where natural areas provide adequate examples of nature. It is far better to "observe" the interesting things referred to in textbooks and see them in context where they have more meaning than to take notes about a vague concept for the purpose of memorization and classification. Both of these may be important but they become more meaningful and better understood when they are based upon observation and experience.

Throughout the history of modern education, many scholars have been encouraging teachers to take their texts from the brooks, the fields, the woods, and real life experiences as a complement to the classroom textbook. Observational learning becomes more basic in the out-of-doors than in the process of reading from books.

The recent International Geophysical Year stands out as an example for high schools and universities as to the importance of outdoor education and its contribution to learning.

In a newspaper article written by Alton Blakeslee of the *Associated Press* on January 6, 1959, the following information was noted:

> ..."We set out traps for nature. Then when nature does something, we often learn her secrets."
>
> To Bartels, Professor of Geomagnetism at the University in Goettingen, this was the essence of the IGY, the 18-month International Geophysical Year which just ended.
>
> It brought the greatest single hunt in history for knowledge--about earth, sun, weather, and the new province of space into which humans are eagerly reaching.
>
> The traps for nature were tended by 30,000 scientists and volunteers from 66 nations in a huge cooperative effort...

In another article written by Mr. Blakeslee on
January 8, the following information was noted:

> IGY brought about the greatest physical checkup in all
> history. The patient--our planet Earth. For 18 months,
> scientists probed and poked at the earth with diagnostic
> instruments ranging from thermometers to orbiting satel-
> lites...
> ...IGY is helping to satisfy man's curiosity about
> his world, and stimulates his curiosity the more. It
> promises to confer great benefits, not only material,
> but far beyond.
> For as Harvard astronomer Dr. Fred Whipple remarked:
> "Securing a better concept of what life means in the
> universe might lead humans to settle their differences."

Education through observation should be the primary
method of teaching for all teachers. It should be encouraged
from kindergarten through college.

Learning through observation in the outdoor education
program has its emphasis in the following ways: All senses
are used to gain knowledge, curiosities are aroused, functional relationships of the thing or things being observed
are noted, the whole object or the entire setting is observed,
and the observer becomes a living part of the environment.

ALL SENSES ARE USED TO GAIN KNOWLEDGE

Observation requires efficiency of use and training of
the sense organs for educational purposes. It is a well
established fact that our senses are the strongest capacities that we possess in acquiring knowledge. The eyes,
ears, and senses of touch and smell are guides to action.
The skillful use of the sense organs is an indispensable
factor towards developing educational achievements. Yet,
the usual classroom learning process limits the use of the
senses and limits experiences which are so essential for
the fulfillment of good educational practices. In most instances, students have not had enough experience to comprehend all of the abstract teachings they encounter in the
modern day curriculum.

When teachers encounter situations where this is apparent, quite frequently a school journey where children

may have direct contact with what is being studied will prove very beneficial. A school camping experience will more nearly insure this. Through direct experiences, all the senses are called into use. Insight and understanding come through actual observing, manipulating, and participating. Children's powers of observation and sense perceptions are improved, and words, objects, people, and relationships are better understood. To see, to touch, to smell, to taste, to lift, and to hear gives real meaning to the textbook, particularly when the teacher is trained in the observation technique.

Comenius said:

> The beginning of wisdom in the sciences consists not in the mere learning of the names of them but in the actual perception of the things themselves. It is after the thing has been grasped by the senses that language should fulfill its function of still further explaining it. The senses are the trusty servants of the memory, leading to permanent retention of the knowledge that has been acquired. Reasoning, also, is conditional and mediated by the experience gained through sense perception. It is evident, therefore, that if we wish to develop a true love and knowledge of science, we must take special care to see that everything is learned by actual observation through sense perception. This should be the golden rule of teachers: Everything should as far as possible be placed before the senses.[4]

The concept of sense perception for learning has application to all subject-matter fields. In the sciences a more direct application is apparent since science concerns itself more with concrete things. However, even in the philosophical offerings and in the language arts where reasoning, poetry, and writing are of primary importance, it is still essential that the poet or artist have real experiences concerned with the poem he is writing or the picture he is committing to canvas. When Joyce Kilmer wrotes *Trees* there is no questions that his attitudes and appreciations and concept of beauty of this tree were actually experienced, and

---

[4] Will S. Monroe, Comenius and The Beginnings of Educational Reform. New York: Charles Scribner's Sons, 1907. p. 98.

probably over quite a number of years. Kilmer's poem is a good example of the results of an individual who has mastered the art of observation.

Many students can recite and sing this poem very beautifully; but no student will be able to write a similar poem until he has observed to the same extent and through all his senses as Kilmer did.

CURIOSITIES ARE AROUSED

As students and teachers make observation trips and as students and teachers learn together through outdoor education experience, there evolves an atmosphere and consciousness of inquiry. Students become aware of the little things in nature and develop a high degree of sensitivity. Curiosity becomes the underlying motivation for discovering new ideas and learning new things about nature, objects, places, and things. As students and teacher explore together there is an inquisitiveness inherent in direct experience which leads to fact finding, analysis and comprehension.

THE WHOLE OBJECT AND ENTIRE SETTING IS OBSERVED

The unique value of outdoor education experiences is that it gives the observer an opportunity to see things in their natural setting, to see things as a whole; to see things as they are and as they live; to see things in relationship to each other; to see the association of things with other environmental factors; and to see how the things being observed relate to the pages in the textbooks that were studied yesterday.

The organization of the school into its many component subject-matter areas is not conducive to learning by the whole method. Seldom does the student have an opportunity to observe, comprehend, or see the relationship of a total subject-matter field at any given period in his schooling.

It is critically important that elementary students be given many opportunities for observing things as they live and function. Objects must be presented in complete and total perspective before they are compartmentalized for special study.

The usual procedure in presenting subject-matter materials in the school consists in separating, isolating, and fragmentizing each specialized area of subject-matter to be learned. It is then studied one part or chapter for each lesson. Quite frequently these assignments must be memorized, classified, and recorded with little concern at the moment as to how it may fit into the total picture or fit into the total subject-matter field. There are not enough opportunities provided for the practical application of the subject-matter being mastered.

Too much of our education today is pulled apart and separated into various areas of learning. Little opportunity is provided to see relationships to the subject-matter or the relationships of the subject-matters, one to each other. As an example, the natural sciences are often broken down into several subject-matter areas such as botany, zoology, geology, and geography. It is important for efficiency of learning to see how one assignment in a special subject-matter area relates to the other and how it relates to the total environment. It is also important to see how closely integrated these studies are when they are applied to nature.

In the out-of-doors a student is not confined to the study of one particular subject-matter area. Here all subject-matter is seen as a whole and in context before it is pulled out for particular study. Consequently, in the outdoor classroom the subject-matter areas become more meaningful, more interesting, and therefore more valuable and useful to the learner.

Practically all instruction today is done by abstract teaching and verbalization. These methods offer very little in the way of real life experiences and in many instances the students do not really understand what they have "learned." In the out-of-doors through the observation technique, the learner is able to see, hear and feel the subject-matter and learn by a meaningful and living experience.

The observation technique of teaching provides a potentially unexcelled laboratory for learning through activity and sense perception.

Learning in the out-of-doors is continuous. Subjects are not kept distinct but fall naturally into interrelated and integrated patterns which may increase the student's understanding of the total environment and how man affects his environment. Through outdoor education experiences, they can visualize and through sense perception actually see how objects fit into their natural setting. They see the influence it has upon the whole or the total environment. Through first-hand observation the relationships of the various things being studied have more meaning because while they are being observed nature is living or functioning, people are working in industries or occupations, vehicles are moving, and the observer is in the midst of an active, on-going life.

THE OBSERVER IS A PART OF HIS ENVIRONMENT

Another valuable contribution that occurs through the observation technique is that the observer is usually standing in the middle or actively becoming a part of the situation or experience he is studying.

Things are happening all about the observer. His influence on what is occurring can be observed. He can more nearly sense his place in the total plan of nature. The observer can also see his relationship and the affect of his association on the object, place, or thing being observed.

When the observer is given an opportunity to have experience associated with industry, government and community life, he feels the importance of being a worker, contributing to government, and becoming a useful citizen.

These experiences give him a better perspective of his place in society and in the world of nature. It gives him a feeling of oneness with the universe and a feeling of belonging. As the poet says it makes him "feel a part of the world and the world a part of him. "

INVESTIGATION

David Starr Jordan, an early president of Stanford University, advised a student who was inquiring about the number of legs a grasshopper had "to go study the grass-hopper." The essential element for investigation is first-hand experience. Investigation is searching and inquiring in order to ascertain facts. It involves a detailed and care-ful examination of things observed.

Investigation also involves the application of reasoning, interpreting, associating, and seeing relationships of the subject being studied.

Outdoor education is filled with experiences that in-volve using, enjoying, and understanding the natural envi-ronment. Students must be taught, encouraged, and stimu-lated to pursue knowledge through investigative techniques.

In almost every individual there is a desire for new experiences and adventure. This desire is satisfied in part by a change from home and school environment to an out-of-doors environment. A challenge to resourcefulness is ex-perienced in many outdoor activities. The search for knowledge, the desire to find answers to questions in the world around us, and a sense of curiosity are urges which must be satisfied and can be satisfied more adequately in an outdoor setting.

Investigation in outdoor education is more likely to take the form of self directed action motivated by interest and curiosity. It is the next step after observation.

Investigation stresses not only the use of many books but many different sources of information. Through scien-tific investigation students get the facts directly from the source. Too many teachers relegate investigation to the science laboratory. A good teacher will teach the techniques of investigation in every subject matter area. Social Studies are concerned not only with the facts of society but with the scientific methods of investigation of these facts. Mathe-matics is concerned with investigating and experimenting with mathematical concepts as well as the abstract formu-las. Wherever possible, first-hand experience is preferred to vicarious textbook learning.

When students are encouraged to observe interesting phenomena, there is a natural urge to investigate. The

degree of this investigation will vary with the individual.
It usually varies from simple questions by the less capable
students to a more detailed scientific approach by others.
This type of investigation requires a great deal in the way
of individual thought, reasoning, and effort. It is quite
obvious that the present educational system does not adequately develop the ability of students to think and reason.
There are few teaching methods now in use which allow for
investigative practice for students. Students are trained
to merely accept the thoughts and opinions of others.

The outdoor education method will more nearly ensure
that the investigative interests and talents of each child will
be developed.

Many worthwhile inventions and much of our scientific
information have been developed through the process of observation and investigation.

Through observation and as a result of direct experiences with nature, there follows that irresistable impulse
for inquiry. The questions of who, what, where, when, and
how become a constant challenge to student and teacher
through most observations and direct experiences. The
intellect is challenged, reasoning is stimulated, facts are
sought out, analyses are made, and comprehension is assured.

As a result of direct experiences and through investigations a chain reaction is usually started which involves
an innate desire to discover other interesting things related
to the subject. When opportunities exist in school camps
and through other outdoor experiences, there is little coercion required to get young people to study; they have a
keen desire to satisfy their curiosity and arrive at some
understanding of the thing being studied. As a result of
experimenting, of testing, of sampling, of smelling, lifting,
touching, crushing, tasting, capturing, searching, seeking,
and merely observing there occurs a learning situation that
needs no motivation but primarily intelligent planning and
direction. It needs an excellent teacher schooled in outdoor
education methods.

COOPERATION

Webster defines cooperation as the association of two or more persons for common benefits or collective action in the pursuit of common well being. Cooperation is the very essence of democracy. Democracy gained its strength on conciliation and compromise, on the give and take of its individuals and groups, and on the cooperation of all those who would rather sacrifice personal gains for the gains of the group.

Although skillful teachers offer many opportunities in the classroom for cooperative experiences for her students, it is sometimes difficult to make such cooperation meaningful in contrived situations.

Outdoor education gives a social flavor to the work of the pupils. They are dependent on each other in most of their outdoor activities. Cooperation becomes a real part of their lives. Each child is called upon to do his part. His failure to carry out his assignment may hamper the learning, fun, or success of his entire group. The spirit of cooperation in the out-of-doors is rewarded by group comradeship and group loyalty.

A democratic camp emphasizes and provides countless opportunities for the development of cooperation among the campers and the staff. Cooperation is closely akin to fellowship, enlightenment, and tolerance of others. Living together twenty-four hours a day provides an ideal laboratory for developing these and other traits. These experiences will provide our students with proper attitudes and appreciations in cooperative living which is so essential to our democratic way of life.

Experience in living together in the out-of-doors tends to give every member of the group a share in planning activities and participating in them. Under the supervision of a teacher skilled in the outdoor education method, each child is made to feel that his contribution is important to the improvement of the group activity. Each child strives to do the best he knows how. When children work together there seems to be a more positive behavior than when they compete with each other for an individual grade, mark, or prize. In working cooperatively toward common goals in the out-of-doors, children tend to forget themselves and act for the good of the group.

When the spirit of cooperation exists, skill and techniques of working together are practiced and tend to become a habit. Children will grow into adults who know how to work together if they have opportunities for the development of good habits in living together cooperatively in their school days.

A student may sit in a classroom and add little or nothing to the discussion; he may even close his ears to the lecture being presented by the instructor, letting his mind wander to something more interesting to him at the moment. As a result, none of the intended material reaches him and thus no learning takes place. This sort of withdrawal is improbable in outdoor education, where students are required to move along with the group and perform tasks necessary to conduct the activity, to observe and investigate, and to manage his affairs in the small group.

Contributions made by members of a class in the out-of-doors will be as varied as the individuals in the class. Since there are so many areas in which contributions may be made--physical tasks, mental deductions, and aesthetic appreciations--each individual may make his contribution according to his abilities and interests.

The opportunities for individual leadership are so frequent and so varied in outdoor education experiences that this in itself tends to unify the small groups. They become dependent upon each other for specialized tasks. Cooperative effort involving individual skills and individual proficiencies is what makes the various learning experiences function successfully.

Because of his spirit of cooperation, each member of the class feels that he "belongs" to the group. He feels that he is needed. Therefore, he is stimulated and motivated to accept his rightful place in all the learning activities which are planned.

Cooperation in the outdoor education program is not limited to experiences for students. The parents are given a new opportunity to cooperate in a school program that directly involves them. Parents seem to be able to interpret the values of outdoor education more readily than they do other educational offerings. This may be due to the fact that they become an important factor in making the program successful.

Successful programs in outdoor education require cooperative participation by parents in planning and conducting the program. Parents have contributed generously in time and effort in problems relating to transportation, supervision, food, health, and public relations. Through these cooperative efforts, the parents become familiar with the methods and purposes of outdoor education.

Cooperation becomes more significant and more meaningful among teachers who are teaching different subject-matter areas.

Since many fields of study may be integrated into one class in outdoor education, classes in different subjects may combine for an outing from which all may profit. This will require a great deal of cooperation from the instructors of the different classes. Instructors who are not making the trip may be asked to prepare the students for the trip by giving special preparation in their respective fields. For example, a geography instructor might be asked to concentrate his teaching on map-reading if that were needed for the tour; a physical education instructor might be called upon to give specific training in water safety if the class were to be on or near a body of water; a home economics teacher could suggest special menus for cookouts and teach the students to prepare them. All of this special instruction could be given immediately prior to the class outdoor meeting. The degree of learning increases as the students appreciate the real meaning and significance of the preparation.

Classes in outdoor education usually require the cooperation and combined efforts of students, parents, and instructors. This has many educational values other than the material learned by the students.

INTEGRATION AND CORRELATION

In a classroom the learning of facts in isolation and without reference to their practical use is almost unavoidable. In many cases it is necessary to teach in this manner.

By leaving the classroom many activities can be planned where the student will observe and study things in their meaningful and natural or normal setting.

Integration and correlation of subject-matter areas under these circumstances are easily taught and observed.

The effectiveness of a well integrated and correlated educational program depends on how well it aids the student in perceiving appropriate relationships and associations of the subject-matter being studied.

The traditional school has taught catalogued knowledge through logically organized subject-matter fields. In recent years, in light of psychological research, there has been a sharp attack upon the teaching of knowledge in compartments and isolated subject-matter areas. Books are now regarded as sources of information and ideas to be used in real life rather than materials to be memorized for their own sake or filed and catalogued for some future use. Whitehead states: "Education is the acquisition of the art of the utilization of knowledge." He expands this thesis by pointing out that schools gather and store knowledge but do not know how to use it. He writes:

> The solution which I am urging is to eradicate the fatal disconnection of subjects which kills the vitality of our modern curriculum. There is only one subject matter for education, and that is life in all its manifestations. Instead of the single unity, we offer children algebra, from which nothing follows; geometry, from which nothing follows; science, from which nothing follows; history, from which nothing follows; a couple of languages never mastered; and lastly, most dreary of all, literature represented by plays of Shakespeare, with philological notes and short analyses of plot and character to be in substances committed to memory. Can such a list be said to represent life, as it is known in the midst of living it? The best that can be said

of it is, that it is a rapid table of contents which a deity might run over in his mind while he was thinking of creating a world and had not yet determined how to put it together.[5]

The scientific thinking of the great philosophers and educators of the past had a virtue that our modern educators seem to lack, and that is the concept of wholeness. The ability to integrate, combine, and see relationships is a much rarer gift than discerning facts. Therefore, why should they be separated? Agassiz states that:

> It cannot be too soon understood that science is one, and that whether we investigate language, philosophy, theology, history, or physics, we are dealing with the same problem, culminating in the knowledge of ourselves. Speech is known only in connection with the organs of man, thought in connection with his brain, religion as the expression of his aspirations, history as the record of his deeds, and physical science as the laws under which he lives.[6]

To take anything out of its context and study it in isolation, completely ignoring its relation to other things, limits the scope and understanding of the student and often distorts final conclusions.

The integration of subject-matter can help the student see the "whole" of a thing before studying its parts. The best place to see the "whole" of anything is in its natural setting and this sometimes dictates that the teacher leave the classroom and go to the out-of-doors.

Integration as found in nature and the out-of-doors before it is isolated and cut up in subject-matter segments for classroom use enhances the use of knowledge and skill in a meaningful whole. Nature is so well planned and things in nature are so inter and intra-dependent that to investigate and study nature leads to observation of the whole. Since most of our special disciplines in school are studies

[5]Alfred North Whitehead, The Aims of Education. New York: Macmillan Company, 1929. p. 19.
[6]Lane Cooper, Louis Agassiz As A Teacher. Ithaca, N. Y.: The Comstock Publishing Company, 1917. p. 67.

of life and its relationship to objects, things, places, and people, it is difficult not to integrate and correlate these special subject-matter areas in order to comprehend the whole.

Lynd states:

> The criticism is frequently made that, instead of helping students to become intelligent builders of democracy in their own communities, college education actually tends to unfit them for community life. A contributing factor is that "coherence" in education has so often been confined to the curriculum while the discontinuity between community and college, between life and letters remains. Field work offers one of the best means of getting beyond this isolation.[7]

All knowledge previously acquired by students from written and oral expression and all knowledge previously gained from experiences are called upon in one stimulating field trip, one school journey, or one camping experience to gather facts, to analyze, and later to comprehend the situation or thing being studied.

Teachers should not use outdoor education as a separate program, but should closely integrate the classroom program with the outdoor education program.

The child should learn in a natural setting those things which have value to him and which he can use for some specific purpose. True learning is "whole-hearted," is fun, and is purposeful. Experience learning tends to fuse subjects, activities, or units of work into a more meaningful whole. In most cases, learning is more effective in activity, in doing or making things rather than abstract study far removed from practical usage. Many schools have profited by making outdoor education an integral part of the total school curriculum.

---

[7]Helen Merrell Lynd, Field Work in College Education. New York: Columbia University Press, 1945. p. 46.

MEDITATION

In the out-of-doors there are numerous opportunities to behold the wonders of God. The story of creation has real meaning when teachers are able to have the world about them as a classroom for learning. Music, literature, and poetry describing nature in all of its glory have little meaning for the person who has never strolled through forests or fields, waded a stream, climbed a mountain, or watched the progress of a rainstorm across a rural landscape. No one can describe the phenomena of nature to the child as clearly as it actually exists, the majestic solitude of the deep woods or the fields of green growing plants with their accompanying sounds and smells. Children cannot help but observe and ponder on these beauties of nature.

For many children, a camping experience is their first extended period away from home. They now have the opportunity to view their home life from a distance and appreciate what it offers them. Camping presents opportunities for expressing ideas through crafts and art activities, participation in campfire programs, skits, stunt nights, etc. All of these go toward developing an appreciation of aesthetic values. Camping also offers opportunities for the development of moral and spiritual values. In everyday camp living the abilities and capacities of each child are challenged. He has a chance to grow in respect for others, in knowledge of himself, and in a realization of his responsibility for the results of his own behavior. Spiritual values accrue from many sources in a camp program. A hike at moonlight, singing by the campfire, grace before meals, meditation at taps, flag ceremonies, a music program, and just being alone out-of-doors can arouse deep inner emotions. A good outdoor education program allows sufficient time for meditation and contemplation so all students may share in this experience.

The aesthetic beauty, the deep appreciation for nature, the feeling of complete humbleness, the wonderment, the pondering, the full trust and belief, the joy, the complete relaxation, the simplicity, the complexity, the magnitude, the relationships, the belongings, all are a part of the intellectual, emotional, and spiritual learning that comes as a result of direct experience with nature. Most of these experiences are not possible in a classroom no matter how skillful a teacher may be. These experiences are a necessary part of life and, with proper direction from the teachers, each student can share in the learning process.

It is surprising how few educators are concerned with giving children time to meditate and "hold communion with nature." Cole shows concern for the lack of time spent in meditation on deeper spiritual learnings. He says:

> Sad, indeed, is it to see how men occupy themselves with trivialities, and are indifferent to the greatest phenomena--care not to understand the architecture of the heavens, but are deeply interested in some contemptible controversy about intrigues of Mary, Queen of Scots!--are learnedly critical over a Greek ode, and pass by without a glance that grand epic written by the finger of God upon the strata of the earth.[8]

Comenius saw education in its true perspective. It must be concerned with the whole man, body and soul, as well as mind. To fail in one is to fail in all. Of what value to educate a man in books if he does not feel a deep sense of feeling and appreciation for the orderliness and harmony of nature. This may come through the discovery of the beauty and balance in nature and through the realization that all plants and animals have a place in the environment, including the observer.

Communion with nature through field trips, school gardens, school forests, and school camping is a contribution that can only be provided through outdoor education programs. A skillful teacher can direct and provide many opportunities for meditation and many opportunities for pondering that will enrich the lives of their students. Nature provides many lessons which a clever teacher can discover, interpret, and apply.

[8]Percival Cole, A History of Educational Thought. London: Oxford University Press, 1931. p. 89.

Due to crowded conditions and administrative practices in our schools there are few opportunities for giving students individual considerations. There are few opportunities when a student can be alone.

In the outdoor education program many chances are available to individuals for self evaluation and meditation. "Know Thyself" is as true a slogan today as it was in the days of Socrates, and no better situation exists today for the pupil to know himself as in the program of outdoor education.

In a serene atmosphere provided in outdoor education, it is not too difficult to guide the pupil into reflective thought about God and nature. It has been said that nature is a representative of God and, hence, to understand nature is to understand God.

How should meditation be introduced into the program? There is no simple formula. Situations vary, and what might prove workable in one instance may not be applicable in another. Many outdoor education programs set aside a few minutes each day in order that the pupil may be by himself in the out-of-doors to think, reflect, and meditate. In the quiet solitude, the pupil frequently discovers that the commonplace things in nature--the sky, the trees, the grass--which were formerly taken for granted assume new proportions. His outlook toward his environment often assumes new dimensions, and he acquires an understanding that permeates his entire life.

The degree to which meditation and Godliness can be infused into an outdoor education program depends in large measure on administrative attitude, as well as type and temperament of personnel. As is frequently the case in anything so abstract, the value emanating from such a program is often intangible, and not immediately perceivable. There will be those who are in favor of discarding meditation for something more concrete, something that can be measured.

Peace of mind and a more stable set of values are but a few of the many benefits that can be derived from using meditation as a method of teaching in outdoor education.

The Biblical injunction, "Be still and know that I am God, " can be just as applicable today as it was twenty centuries ago.

Spiritual values may be felt in moments of solitude, but they also grow out of human experience. Boys and girls will have a deeper appreciation and better understanding of each other, of the culture, and other nationality groups by participating in good fellowship in all activities at camp.

Time of solitude or quiet relaxation is a basic need of every individual. A short respite from the day's activities, problems, and excitement gives a person an opportunity to take stock of himself, his thoughts, his emotions. The fast pace of our society is the cause of much emotional upset. The constant tension of our competitive way of living places a great deal of pressure on an individual. What better way of escaping the sleepless nights, upset stomachs, wrangled nerves, and other symptoms of emotional stress, than to "get away from it all" and spend some time by oneself in the great outdoors?

What a wonderful feeling to be able to say and understand with the poet Sassoon, "How strange we grow when we're alone, and how unlike the selves that meet and talk, And blow the candles out, and say good night. Alone.... The world is life endured and known. It is the stillness where our spirits walk, And all but inmost faith is overthrown. "

INFORMALITY

In the out-of-doors the formality of the classroom is replaced by a feeling of informality and freedom of thought and action. The restraining four walls are gone and the controlled environment disappears and is replaced with relaxed learning in the woods, on the streams, and in the wilderness. The outdoor classroom has little or no limitations in space and time. Bells, whistles, rigid schedules, and other interruptions to learning are absent. The atmosphere of the outdoor class changes as the teacher moves from one location to the other. It is not normal for youngsters to sit for from five to six hours per day in uncomfortable chairs gazing mostly at blackboards or the four walls of a classroom.

There is also a lack of fresh air, good lighting, and other factors which provide a good learning atmosphere.

When the student and teacher leave the classroom to observe and investigate and to experience real life situations, an entirely different relationship exists among students, counselors, and the teacher. The student is placed in a completely new learning situation in the out-of-doors. Teachers are no longer cast in the role of an autocrat but become guides or resource persons. The skillful teacher in an informal setting is able to lead the students on, build up their interests, and help them to see the many relationships and implications of the object under study. Moreover, through interest in and examination of the work of others, students may stimulate each other in one or another of the various outdoor activities.

Social and economic barriers are removed in the outdoor education program. The equality enjoyed by all campers removes inhibitions and stimulates greater interplay among the campers which, in turn, creates a deeper and more desirable group relationship.

Informality is the keynote of outdoor education. Informality does not mean that the class is not organized or well planned or that it lacks discipline. On the contrary, in order to achieve this informal manner the instructor may have to spend more time and thought in preparation for it.

He must be alert to the changing methods in education and the changing behavior of the learner. This involves a totally different kind of lesson plan. It involves a different approach to teaching. Many learnings will take place based on the initiative and curiosity of the student. Learnings will be harder to measure in terms of specific subject-matter areas. It will be difficult to "hold the class" to the lesson. Skillful teaching will be more important because of the cooperative, informal approach to learning which is enjoyed by teacher and student together.

In the relaxed atmosphere of an informal class, the student is at ease and is usually in a frame of mind which is conducive to learning. He is not regimented by strict rules of discipline and routine. Therefore, his mind is freer to grasp the material as it is presented, to associate it with related facts, and even to theorize upon possible effects and results.

Because of the informality of a class in outdoor education, learning may take place because there is a desire for it. Most educators agree this type of learning is best. It then becomes a part of the student's store of knowledge related to real-life experiences rather than a memorized fact to be recited and then forgotten. The student is free, even encouraged, to question the instructor or other students when he desires additional information. Thinking and reasoning may take as many channels as there are members of the class, the possibilities or facets for learning are unlimited.

Because of the informal method of conducting an outdoor education class, each student may progress at his own rate or according to his own capacity. Since the store of material is boundless, the brighter student is constantly challenged to solve more of its mysteries by questioning, by experimentation, and by advanced research and study. On the other hand, since there are no definite requirements, the slower students do not feel that they are lost before they begin but rather each may start at his own level and advance as far as his capabilities will allow. Then, too, since he is dealing with things that may be seen, felt, or heard, things that appeal to his physical senses, he will probably be motivated to a higher degree than he will be by abstract and formalized instruction.

For these reasons, informality is one of the most important advantages of the outdoor education method. Because of it, learning becomes a natural process, almost an involuntary action, rather than a requirement that one struggles to attain.

The outdoor education program is informal in its approach. Rigid and segmented lesson plans are not necessary

when both the students and the teacher learn from nature.
If a child does not choose to follow one line of activity he
may feel complete freedom in following another interest.
Supervision is furnished for all types of learning activities
as the counselors and teacher guide the children into many
enjoyable and worthwhile experiences in the out-of-doors.
Respect, loyalty, companionship, admiration, hero worship, confidence, trust, and sociability are the qualities
of the teacher that receive complete and continuous use in
the outdoor education program.

Artificial means devised to motivate are not so essential; planned rewards for performances become less important. The greatest motivation consists of experience and
the new relationship between student and teacher. The
teacher frequently must say, "I do not know." Students
contribute more to fact finding. The searching, seeking,
and analyzing becomes a matter of teamwork that is skillfully directed and channeled by the teacher.

The key to a good learning climate is a desirable,
healthy atmosphere with excellent teacher-pupil relationships. In a formalized classroom situation, many responses
are stifled for fear of ridicule and criticism. In contrast,
an informal group in the out-of-doors are stimulated toward
freedom of expression and discovery.

The informal situation requires a good teacher. He
bases his teaching on normal behavior and interests of the
students whereby the formal classroom teacher often needs
to be a "disciplinarian." He "teaches the student" rather
than "helps the student learn."

The orderly fashion of classrooms and formal seating
arrangements produces a more stereotyped behavior
scheme. Bring a class with its teacher outside in the
natural setting and the atmosphere of repression is replaced by a feeling of naturalness and open-mindedness.

There seems to be much more rapport between teacher
and pupil. Outdoor education is purposeful without being
dominating; guides without being authoritarian; and is real
fun without artificial stimuli. The experience itself makes
possible the give and take that characterizes good teacher-

pupil relationships. Growth occurs rapidly during such an expedition, and the qualities of self-reliance and self-confidence blossom overnight. The outdoor activity gives opportunity for the exercise of individual resourcefulness that is not possible in an indoor learning situation.

Outdoor experiences serve to fuse all of the other elements of education into workable form. The books that are read and studied in the classroom acquire vitality in the hands of boys and girls who have had direct experiences with the things those books are intended to illuminate.

In the informal situation the teacher is learning right along with the pupil, for more than likely she does not know what is around the next tree or under the clump of bushes. Students and teachers discover together.

Another aspect of simultaneous learning is learning to live better through associations with others. Not only do the pupils have the opportunity to practice social skills in this environment, but the teacher also learns more about them. The informality brings out the best in the shy classroom individual. Emotional problems are more adequately dealt with as they often are more easily recognized by the teacher.

Outdoor education is developed around the democratic processes of group discussion, planning, individual participation, and sharing experiences and responsibilities. These things help toward creating an informal atmosphere, putting the child at ease and opening the way for more facile learning. The outdoor education program provides an opportunity for children and teachers to live and study together. By developing in the child a "sense of belonging," of being accepted by the group, the individual becomes a better socially adjusted individual. Group living activities inspire confidence in the camper and a feeling of independence that cannot be attained in a formalized classroom. Children have a better opportunity to learn and feel that the teacher is interested in them and that all can work, plan, and play together. Informal methods contribute greatly to this accomplishment. The camp offers an opportunity for establishing an atmosphere of related freedom, with a noticeable lack of restraints, rules, and authoritarian

control. Regimentation as known in the formal classroom
is avoided. By having every child participate in the plan-
ing of an activity, the experience will be more complete
and meaningful. Only in an informal atmosphere can the
child be helped to discover himself, his place in the group,
his contribution to it, and his understanding of how people
live together. The informal method allows children to do
for themselves and to solve their own problems. The program is a flexible one to meet changing conditions and the
varying interests of the children, far different from studying a text from front to back in scheduled units and in an
allotted time.

PARTICIPATION

Among other things, outdoor education implies action,
participation, learning by doing, interpreting texts and subject-matter areas through direct experience, observation,
investigation, critical thinking, and physical activity. It
also implies efficiency of learning through active participation in directed experiences by both teacher and student.
Everybody participates in the activities that are planned to
develop skills and increase knowledge.

The act of thinking is a process whereby a student
examines a problem, considers possible solutions, tests
the possible solutions in practice, and evaluates the results
to determine the best possible solution.

The field trip and other outdoor education experiences
offer the best use in the four step thinking process where
both teacher and students participate directly in solving
problems and receive first-hand experiences in dealing
with learning situations. There is opportunity for developing all four phases of the thinking process. Direct participation with responsibility for the outcome is the ideal learning situation. Cantor points out that an active pupil with
ongoing vital interest wants to explore and investigate. He
is full of questions and eager to learn. "Unless pupils
participate in shaping the direction of their learning,

there can be, by definition, no purposeful self-direction. "[9]

Many teachers are over anxious to teach facts and cannot stand to see their students "waste time" by their trial and error methods. They would rather give them the answer. Mistakes should be considered as a part of the learning process. Students are too often robbed of a chance to learn by examining and improving upon their own errors. Great inventors fail hundreds of times before they taste success.

While stressing student participation in learning, teachers need to assume careful leadership and supervision so the experiences will result in desired outcomes. Although student-teacher planning is essential in cases where such procedures are proper, there are also times when independent action by the teacher is essential. Students cannot always, and do not want to, decide for themselves. The teacher, by virtue of more experience and background, sometimes has to set limits for the students. Teachers who are successful in using student participation as an effective teaching technique delegate clearly defined responsibilities which are commensurate with the students' ability to handle them. The teacher does not always expect the students to manage these responsibilities quite as well as she might, but she recognizes that this is a good teaching technique and is willing to let the students get experience in managing and conducting their own affairs.

Group living in the out-of-doors provides many worthwhile activities which may be handled by committee or individual assignment. Among such committees might be work committees, courtesy committees, cleanup committees, safety committees, bulletin board committees, and camp government committees.

CREATIVITY

For centuries philosophers and artists have seen the value of each person being able to express his own unique

---

[9] Nathaniel Cantor, The Teaching Learning Process. New York: Holt, Rinehart and Winston, 1953. p. 289.

self, to create something that is his own interpretation of the world around him. In recent years educators have recognized the social and personal values in creative self expression. Thus music, art, drama, and dance have gradually been added to the curriculum. Unfortunately, however, because of lack of understanding of the somewhat mystic nature of creativity, the traditional schools have restricted their thinking and feel that creative expression is inherent only in such things as music, art, drama, and dance. Opportunities for creativity should be provided in every phase of education. Even the teaching of necessary techniques and skills in all subject-matter areas can be made more enjoyable under the direction of a skilled teacher. This is particularly true if the teacher is skillful enough to allow freedom with control and self-expression with direction.

Creativity should be an integral part of all education. Instructors may pass out knowledge and facts, but the student becomes educated only when he takes these facts for his own, and through creative thinking, associates them with facts already known. He must also realize the relationship of the newly learned material to the whole pattern of life.

An atmosphere that encourages creativity would, therefore, contribute to education. What sort of atmosphere would encourage creativity? The learner would need to find an atmosphere that would be tranquil, relaxed, quiet and informal; an atmosphere that would stimulate, inspire, arouse, and motivate the student by appealing to his aesthetic nature. With a proper atmosphere and an ideal climate for learning the teacher can more readily arouse the creative talent in each student.

There are always possibilities for producing some creative work in outdoor education. There are so many new things to see and so many opportunities for self-expression. It is not necessary for the student to produce a masterpiece or to create things that call for attention. The important thing is that they receive the inner reward that is so enriching when they do something new and different. It is also important that students be encouraged to continue in any creative activity that comes as a result of a directed experience. The major emphasis to the student in this learning situation is upon appreciations, understanding, and self-expression in terms of their relationships to the physical environment. There is less emphasis placed upon mastery of techniques, skills, and factual information. The latter are included, to be sure, but only as a means to an end and not as ends in themsleves. There is a real danger of defeating the purpose of outdoor education if mastery of techniques, skills, and bodies of factual knowledge are made a major aspect of the program. Outdoor education, to accomplish or achieve optimum success in terms of the major objectives of education, must be approached in a creative and enjoyable manner. The aims which guide any educational program are realized only to the extent that each individual reaches his creative potential.

Creativity is conceived not primarily in terms of the product and its intrinsic qualities but in relation to the process through which the individual involves markedly new combinations of factors to help express for him the nature of the situation. Lee and Lee say:

> There must be a seeing of new relationships, a new interpretation of some fact, familiar or not, an approach that gives new meaning before thinking can be creative. This, of course, does not need to be new to humanity, or even to the group, so long as it is truly new to the individual. [10]

The success of developing creativeness within the child is by allowing him to participate in the activity himself, prompted by his own imagination and his own inventiveness.

Everyone has creative potentialities. In the past there was a widely accepted view, both within and without the school, that only the selected few, the elite group of artists, musicians, writers, and actors, are blessed with the possibilities of creative expression. The point of view as to "who is creative?" still persists in the popular mind.

[10] J. Murray Lee and Dorris May Lee, The Child and His Curriculum. New York: D. Appleton-Century Company, 1940. p. 537.

There are indications, however, that the attitudes are
changing and the conception of creativity is being viewed in
broader context. There is ample evidence in educational,
and particularly psychological, literature that creativity is
being seen as a quality of the everyday living of all people,
and not as a privilege for the gifted few. Creativity is not
private property; it belongs to humanity.

Creativity is learning, but all learning is not creative.
The learnings necessary to make skills or techniques automatic are not creative. Creative learning must enable the
child to see new relationships and increase his understanding. Systems of teaching where learnings are in the nature
of rote drill and practice offer little opportunity for creative
self-expression.

In order to give more understanding to the meaning of
creative expression, Hockett[11] contrasts two groups of
words. On the one hand, there is originality, ingenuity,
inventiveness, experimentation, uniqueness, initiative,
freshness, newness, and change; on the other, habit, custom, routine, conformity, rigidity, repetition, memorization, training, and indoctrination. All these words may be
used to describe an activity. An acitivity involves originality or conformity, or some of both. The extent to which the
activity possesses qualities indicated by the first list of
words is a fair indication to the level of creativeness experienced in the activity.

In a broad sense, creativity includes the making of
new interpretations and the seeing of new relationships in
thinking and in learning. In a more restricted sense, it is
the interpretation of an individual's own ideas, thoughts,
and feelings into a tangible form which is original with the
person concerned.

Furthermore, creative expression has a two-way significance, as does all experience. It has meaning to the
individual engaged in the direct experience, and it has meaning to others through vicarious experience.

---

[11]John A. Hockett, "The Significance of Creative Expression, " California Journal of
Education, February, 1941. pp. 159-165.

The out-of-doors with an attractive and stimulating environment, materials and tools, plenty of time, plenty of space, and a permissive, informal atmosphere lends itself to rich and varied creative experience. Through trips and hikes, adventure and explorations, and as a result of interesting observations and investigations, the intellectual stimulation that occurs through outdoor experiences often arouses the creative imagination of all students. This creative imagination is expressed in many different ways and usually according to the dominant capacities of the individual.

Through direct experiences with nature have come attitudes and appreciations of nature expressed beautifully in poetry, paintings, and oral expression. Creativity is also expressed in hobbies, new interests, new inventions and various other media of self expression.

TOTAL FITNESS

Outdoor education programs have all the latent potentials for developing total fitness of the participants. Living twenty-four hours close to nature as children and adults do in camping situations develops all aspects of their personality, and this is the modern conception of education--the development of the whole individual. Fitness involves the total normal, healthy development of people--physically, mentally, socially, and morally.

Modern society with its industrial and technological advances has converted man from a jack-of-all-trades to a specialist. His work has become repetitious and monotonous. The same activity performed day after day in the same old way has reduced the total efficiency and fitness of man. He is rapidly losing his heritage and is often far removed from the soil which sustains him. Living on concrete and asphalt, crowded together in apartments and tenement houses, he is lucky to see the sun rise and set, to see the beauties of nature in a woods, or to see wild flowers and wild life that once was the common heritage of all pioneers.

President Dwight D. Eisenhower recently acknowledged the need for fitness of all Americans by establishing the President's Council on Youth Fitness. The Council set up an eight point program primarily concerned with helping America become and remain physically, mentally, and socially fit for living in the modern age.

President Eisenhower in expressing the reason for the Council said, "National policies will be no more than words if our people are not healthy of body as well as mind, putting dynamism and leadership into the carrying out of major decisions. Our young people must be physically as well as mentally and spiritually prepared for American citizenship."

Some of the most pertinent remarks, quotes, and conclusions which came from the President's Council on Youth Fitness are:

1. In a recent study of 100,000 school children, 79 per cent had defective teeth, 15 per cent were malnourished, 13 per cent had diseased tonsils, 12 per cent had defective vision, 11 per cent had flat feet, and 9 per cent had poor posture. Flabby muscles and poor posture were found in both high and low income groups.

2. Approximately 35 per cent of the young men of the United States are rejected from service because they are physically unfit. Forty per cent of those entering the Armed Services in World War II could not swim fifty feet. Drownings between the ages of five and forty are second only to motor vehicles as the cause of accidental deaths.

3. Less than 50 per cent of boys and girls in high school have physical education. Many of the existing programs are too limited and ineffective.

4. Only 1,200 of our 17,000 communities in the United States have full time recreation leadership.

5. Ninety-one per cent of the elementary schools have no gymnasium and less than the recommended five acres of land for essential play areas.

6. From seven to seventeen, more than 80 per cent of all physical skills essential for sports participation are learned. Those are the "power-building" years also.

7. The objective of an adequate physical fitness program can be summed up in one word--participation; participation on the part of every boy and girl in America in some form of health, recreational, and physical activity.

8. Building fitness is a complex undertaking involving most of the child's health, education, and leisure time experiences during his formative years. It depends upon putting into action a ten to fifteen year plan. We need mental, emotional, and physical fitness.

9. Less than 5 per cent of America's youth have had the opportunity to enjoy the experience of camping and outdoor living.

10. The super-athlete is not our primary concern. He will take care of himself. It is the boy and girl with ordinary physical abilities who should receive the major share of attention.

11. All young people must have things to do that invite active, stimulating but disciplined use of their native capacities for total fitness. In the constant enlargement of these capacities lies the best hope for their individual happiness and the future well-being of the nation.

12. Everyone agrees that the person who has physical fitness enjoys a healthy mental outlook and a general feeling of bodily well-being. Physical activity relieves emotional strain under which people live and relieves the pressure of our highly complicated lives.

Outdoor education experiences provide maximum opportunities for exercising all large and small muscles of the body. Outdoor education is an active program and its success is based upon total participation. Programs range from moderate physical activity to vigorous physical exercise. One of the desirable features of outdoor education programs is that exercise and physical activity often are concomitant values to the learning experiences. Exploring a cave may involve hiking, bending, crawling, pulling up, and jumping. Outdoor education programs usually include waterfront activities, hunting, fishing, and other nature-centered activities. Many worthwhile activities are learned that provide a life-time of leisure time enjoyment.

Mental health, social adjustment, and moral consciousness are basic educational aims that all teachers strive to
accomplish. In outdoor education programs there is a re-
emphasis on these aims.

SUMMARY

The basis of outdoor education includes the emphasis
on the best technique for gaining knowledge. Textbook materials must be supplemented and complemented by adequate
experiences so students may comprehend the written word
more easily. Contact with nature and real life experiences
should be an inherent part of all school curricula. There
should be many opportunities for teachers and students to
leave the classroom to observe, investigate, explore, and
seek adventure in interesting places wherever they may
occur.

Schools need to recognize that all subject matter areas
can be made more meaningful through outdoor education.
There are wonderful opportunities for integrating and corre-
lating the various subject matter fields in the study of nature.

Educationally, there is no difference in a teacher
leaving her classroom with her children to go to the library
or science center--where experiences not afforded by the
classroom can be had--and in their going to the outdoor
laboratory or the camp. There is no more reason for taking
a group of children into the out-of-doors when they have no
specific purposes of their own for going than there is for
taking a class to the library just because the school happens
to have one.

After a student has read about, talked about, and observed an activity or a new concept in action, the next logical step to better enhance his learning is through investigation.

School and outdoor education provides for this experience in what is probably the best possible way. It takes the
student out of the classroom and gives him a chance for
first-hand experience--for learning by actually doing.

For many years, forward looking educators have studied the inherent values of outdoor education and camping with a calculating eye. They wondered how they could incorporate experiences which fostered these values into modern-day education.

In the larger outdoor classrooms, educators have found a unique teaching medium for revitalizing school curriculums. They are using first-hand experience to augment verbal classroom learning.

Outdoor education has opened new doors to enterprising teachers. School subjects, which in the classroom may largely consist of reading the assignments and reciting them to the teacher, take on a new luster when taught in a natural setting. Learning in the out-of-doors is not meant to substitute for classroom learning, but it can be an invaluable supplement to most subject matter.

It has been found that when students experience directly what they have studied in textbooks, they have a better understanding of that material.

In outdoor education, the instruction does not follow the definite lines of a written lesson plan, the pupils are not seated in rows, and the teacher becomes a member of the group equal in stature with the pupils.

In outdoor education, program planning is flexible. Learning is guided by the event as it happens or the actual experiences of the pupils. Nature is not as conveniently categorized as to subject matter as it is in the regular classroom atmosphere. In an outdoor situation the student is surrouned by a wealth of real life experiences. There is music if one will tune his ears to the birds singing, water lapping at the shore line, or the wind rustling through the trees. This is true in art, science, literature or any field the student might wish to explore. The extent of exploration is limited only by the circumstances.

Edgar Lee Masters said, "Out in middle Illinois when I was in high school we eager young found ourselves stifled by the orthodoxy that surrounded us. The unsmoked sky was above us, the fields and woods were around us, yet we needed air......We could not think, speculate, examine

the evidence of things without being emancipated from the
bandages that tied us in. "

Too many of us are acquainted with the bandages of
which Masters speaks--the dull, uninteresting books, the
narrow curriculum, the lesson plan, the seating assignments, the strict discipline and the artificiality of the four
walls, the dusty blackboard, and the lifeless forms of maps
and charts.

Questions and Projects

1. See how many new things you can discover either walking home or through the campus that have been there
   for years, but you have not observed by sight, by sound,
   by odor, by touch, and possibly by taste.

2. Blindfold all members of the class. Place in each person's hand an object not too familiar to the individual.
   Have them describe in detail what they feel, what they
   smell, and possibly what they taste. When they have
   completely described what they feel, smell, and taste,
   have them name the object.

3. Observe a tree. See how many things you can dicover
   about this tree through sight, smell, touch, taste, and
   sound. Study its relationship to other things and objects around the tree. Discuss its value, use and possible future.

4. Discuss the various possible phenomena that would occur in nature if one of the following were totally eliminated: Birds, Fish, Insects.

5. Keep a daily record of lectures you attend this week.
   See how many times second and third-hand information
   is reviewed that students could better learn through
   direct experiences with the things being discussed.

6. Quickly scan through a primary reading text. Observe
   what per cent of the material describes outdoor

experiences or real life situations. Discuss how much of this material could be better learned by direct experience.

7. Select a well known poem. See if the author's creative expressions were based upon direct experiences.

8. How many inventions, great works of art, great books, and great poetry were produced or created that were not based on direct and real experiences of the authors and producers?

9. Discuss the values of the outdoor education program toward the development of total fitness.

Selected References

Beck, Robert H., Cook, Walter W., Kearney, Nolan C., *Curriculum In The Modern Elementary School*. New York: Prentice-Hall, 1953.

Bulletin of the National Association of Secondary School Principals, "Camping and Outdoor Education," Washington, D.C.: National Education Association, May, 1947, vol. 31, no. 147.

Cantor, Nathaniel, *The Teaching-Learning Process*. New York: Holt, Rinehart and Winston, 1953.

Cole, Luella, *A History of Education: Socrates To Montessori*. New York: Rinehart and Company, 1950.

Crow, Lester D. and Crow, Alice, *Readings In Educational Psychology*. Ames, Iowa: Littlefield Adams and Company, 1956.

Cooper, Lane, *Louis Agassiz As A Teacher*. Ithaca, N.Y.: The Comstock Publishing Company, 1917.

Dale, Edgar, *Audio-Visual Methods In Teaching,* New York: The Dryden Press, 1954.

deHuszar, George B., *Practical Applications of Democracy*. New York: Harper and Brothers, 1947.

Dewey, John, *How We Think*. Boston: D. C. Heath and Company, 1933.

Gates, Arthur I., Jersild, Arthur T., McConnell, T. R., and Challman, Robert C., *Educational Psychology*. New York: The Macmillan Company, 1942.

Jones, Arthur J., Grizzell, E. D., and Grinstead, Wren Jones, *Principles of Unit Construction*. New York: McGraw-Hill Book Company, 1939.

Kelly, Earl C., *Education For What Is Real*. New York: Harper and Brothers, 1947.

Kingsley, Howard L. and Garry, Ralph, *The Nature and Conditions of Learning*. Englewood Cliffs, N. J.: Prentice-Hall, 1957.

Lee, J. Murray and Lee, Dorris May, *The Child And His Curriculum*. New York: D. Appleton-Century Company, 1940.

Lee, J. Murray and Lee, Dorris May, *The Child And His Development*. New York: Appleton-Century-Crafts, Inc., 1958.

Monroe, Will S., *Comenius And The Beginning of Educational Reform*. New York: Charles Scribner's Sons, 1907.

Mursell, James L., *Using Your Mind Effectively*. New York: McGraw-Hill Book Company, 1951.

Roucek, Joseph S. and Associates, *Sociological Foundations of Education*. New York: Thomas Y. Crowell Company, 1942.

Rugg, Harold and Shumaker, Ann, *The Child-Centered School*. New York: World Book Company, 1928.

Schoen, Max, *Human Nature In The Making*. New York: D. Van Nostrand Company, 1945.

Sharp, L. B., "Basic Considerations in Outdoor and Camping Education," *The Bulletin of the National Association of Secondary School Principals*. May, 1947.

Swenson, Ester J., Anderson, Lester G., and Stacey, Chalmers L., *Learning Theory In School Situations*. Minneapolis: University of Minnesota, 1949.

Thorndike, Edward L. and Gates, Arthur I., *Elementary Principles of Education*. New York: The Macmillan Company, 1930.

Whitehead, Alfred North, *The Aims of Education*. New York: Macmillan Company, 1929.

Yoakam, Gerald and Simpson, Robert G., *Modern Methods and Techniques of Teaching*. New York: The Macmillan Company, 1948.

Chapter 4

PHILOSOPHICAL AND HISTORICAL FOUNDATIONS OF OUTDOOR EDUCATION

Without a sense of history, no man can truly understand the problems of our time.
—*Winston Churchill*

Man is indebted to his past for many of the present day political, social, educational, moral, and spiritual benefits. Modern culture is built upon the heritage of past civilizations and is a composite of man's achievement from the earliest times. This heritage has been passed from one generation to another through education. Education in its broadest sense is society's chief instrument for recording, analyzing, and disseminating information concerning man's experiences, knowledge, and skills which civilizations have valued most highly.

Education in its many forms is as old as the human race. The early methods of education were rather crude and primarily involved sharing experiences and knowledge among families and tribes. Formal education and public schools are comparatively recent innovations in the history of the development of education.

Historical knowledge concerning various cultures provides facts and experiences which helps man use more intelligent judgments in solving today's problems.

Other things being equal, the more complete understanding and knowledge man has of his past the more likely he is to use correct procedures in solving his problems. In recognition of this fact, practically every field of human endeavor has its historians. Today rather complete histories of music, art, drama, religion, law, education, medicine, politics, and several sciences exist. They provide records, valuable facts, and information upon which their modern application exists. In tracing the history of outdoor education, the primary concern is with the educational methods employed to advance learning through various civilizations. Also this chapter is concerned with the influence of the outdoor education method on the progress of each nation.

Historically, the social, political, religious, and cultural interests of people have determined the character and methods of education in all civilizations of the past. This is also true regarding educational practices in modern day society.

An analysis of the historical developments in education from the beginning of time reveals several significant observations that relate to the outdoor education method. History has shown that nations have progressed most rapidly--politically, socially, morally, and spiritually--when the educational practices had a reasonable balance between textbook learning and direct experiences which consist of observation and investigation of nature and real life situations.

Civilizations progress rapidly when books and adequate records are available for man to study while he continually makes new discoveries in nature. An accumulation of these new findings are then recorded for study and interpretations for more direct and real life experiences. The process is a continuous one.

When man becomes satisfied with his existing literature and stops adding new discoveries and new experiences to them there is evidence of social stagnation and decay. Memorization and acceptance of existing books and literature as final authority caused several civilizations to remain static.

It is also quite evident that where civilizations depended entirely on real life experiences involved with nature, progress was also static because there was no need or no means for accumulating and recording knowledge for others to use.

Another important and significant observation appears in the study of various civilizations; that is, the moral and social behavior of individuals was never successfully taught through textbook learning alone.

For century after century, several nations showed
little change in their social structure and there was little
evidence of any kind of progress beneficial to man. The
social, religious, and educational aims of these nations
were the primary limiting factors which prohibited progress.
In most of these old systems there was an emphasis on the
memorization of texts, laws, and other literature. This
was the only means to educational, religious, and social
acceptability. As long as the right law or text was written,
it was authoritative. Most literature was read and memorized to support a fixed social order. Authority and discipline were more important than observation, investigation,
new discovery, and independent civilizations.

In the most primitive cultures, education came through
direct experience which was related and necessary to sustain life. The experience had to be real because the success
or failure of a man's learning usually determined whether or
not he would survive. Most skills, knowledge, and experience centered around providing food, shelter, clothing, simple tools, and other bare necessities for living. Man was
always in direct contact with nature and real life experience.
There were no texts, no written words. There was no need
for learning how to read or write. Today some of these
civilizations still exist and have not progressed even slight-
ly from the primitive existence of thousands and thousands
of years ago.

History shows that education appears to fail most, and
social and scientific progress suffers its worst setback,
when the only emphasis, and too often the primary source
of all learning, originates and ends in the textbook. The
written experiences of others provide little incentive for
new discoveries and independent thinking. Butts points up
a very real and grave danger of education today when he
says that:

> The invention of writing must be considered one of
> the most illuminating steps that was ever taken by
> human beings, but it must also be recognized that grave
> educational problems were created in the process. A
> slavish devotion to the mastery of reading and writing
> could change education; for example, from an informal

and direct induction into a culture to a formal and
bookish dealing with written materials of the past
that had little meaning for the present. These gains
and losses must be properly assessed as one looks at
the amazing achievements of human culture.[1]

Social changes, religious emphasis, scientific improvements, and political ideals all have a tremendous impact on the emphasis or course of educational methods.
Today, the world is in the midst of one of the periods of
most noticeable change in all of the above mentioned factors.
Educators, business executives, parents, civic leaders, and
all citizens seem concerned today about what should be taught
and how it should be taught.

Recognition should be given to all of the factors included in necessary curriculum revisions and changes in
educational method. Recognition of the success and failure
of educational experiences of past civilizations should likewise be evaluated.

Outdoor educational methods can make a generous contribution to present day educational programs when the techniques are scientifically used by teachers who have proper
qualifications and training.

EDUCATION IN THE ANCIENT WORLD

PREHISTORIC MAN

In the millennia which preceded the period of recorded
history, culture, life, and education were one and the same.
There were no schools--no formal education. Prehistoric
man did not have the capacities nor the incentive to study or
attempt to understand and control his environment. His
existence was not a great deal superior to the plight of
animals.

It was improbable that man would remain in this lower
level of life and living forever. Man was endowed with a
brain and a mind that soon lifted him to his rightful heritage

[1]R. Freeman Butts, A Cultural History of Western Education. New York: McGraw-Hill
Book Company, 1955. p. 12.

in the world. His culture began to develop when he turned his attention to intellectively solving problems concerning his environment.

Education started when man began teaching his off-spring and family the accumulated cultural knowledge of this era.

There were no schools and no consciously recognized methods of education among the prehistoric tribes. Yet, their youth were fitted to the physical and social environment through informal teachings handed down from father to son, from mother to daughter, and from the older to the younger generation. Mulhern describes a typical example of such education as found among the Arunta tribe of Central Australia:

> Boys and girls under the age of twelve or thirteen live in the women's part of the camp and accompany their mothers into the scrub, where, with their toy digging sticks, they mimic the operations of the women as they dig for roots and small animals. The children help the women to carry back to camp a collection of lizards, rats, frogs, etc., as well as grass seed which the women bake into flat cakes. Thus, while civilized children are in school getting their experience from books, the savage child is reading the book of nature and learning by actually doing in play the things which will later become a serious life activity. He soon learns, by this informal and playful method, where and how to find tasty bulbs and nuts. He is taught to note the tracks of animals, large and small, and the habits of all animal life in his region.....
>
> At about the age of twelve, boys pass into the charge of the men, whom henceforth they live with and accompany on hunting expeditions. The boy now makes and carries his mimic weapons as, indeed, he did even while he was in the charge of the women. With these mimic weapons he performs all the actions of the hunter, but as yet only by way of play. By this method of playful imitation of the activities of their elders.... boys and girls acquire those skills upon the perfection of which their physical life depends![2]

[2]James Mulhern, A History of Education. New York: The Ronald Press Company, 1959. pp. 43-44.

The control of the educational process was the responsibility of the family. The family frequently called on the
tribal medicine man when they felt additional help was
needed. Their education consisted primarily in learning
ways and means to sustain life by obtaining food, clothing,
and shelter. The chief means of education were by observation, imitation, oral expression, demonstration, crude
drawings, and self-activity. The approach to education was
through participation. Almost everything was learned
through real life experience.

Prehistoric man found a close relationship between
himself and his environment. He tried to explain nature by
developing magical and religious beliefs for what he saw
about him. He bestowed mysterious powers on every forest,
mountain, cave, stream or lake. If harm came to an individual from a falling limb or rock, a bolt of lightening, or a
swollen stream, it was considered as an act of an angry
demon or spirit and sacrifices had to be made to keep the
demon under control. Through the centuries these beliefs
were developed into taboos and folklore that controlled the
thinking of man for a countless number of years.

The prehistoric period of man represented one facet of
the outdoor education program--the emphasis on direct and
real life experiences. Education and culture cannot progress without it, neither can they advance with this technique
alone. There must be a combination of recorded knowledge
to supplement and guide experiences. There must also be a
teacher to direct, supervise, and stimulate thinking.

During the long prehistoric period prior to the invention of writing, the human voice was the most important
means of communication. Other methods were added as
time progressed. Signs and symbols were developed and
given meaning until a method or system of writing was
slowly evolved. An alphabet, in which a sign was to stand
for a sound, was far in the future.

The most noticeable and most limiting educational
features of prehistoric man were the absence of reading and
writing. He also lacked a method for collecting, recording,
testing, and analyzing facts that are essential to social and
scientific progress. An example of what happens to a society

which does not have the above techniques of education may be seen by studying any one of the primitive tribes of the world today. They have made very little scientific, social or educational progress from the earliest dawn of history.

Without written facts, without written records and reports, without skills and knowledge to read and write, without other recorded media of expression in the classical and fine arts, man would never have progressed educationally, culturally, religiously, and socially beyond that of prehistoric man.

EARLY CIVILIZATIONS

Some of the earliest recordings of Western civilization indicate its beginning was either in the valley of the Nile or in the valley of the Tigris and Euphrates. The beginnings of recorded history in Eastern civilizations appear rather vague, but traces of early culture of the Orient still belong to the periods of antiquity.

The foundations for modern civilizations have their basis in the contributions made by the cultures of antiquity. Some nations contributed a great deal more than others to the successful social progress, scientific progress, and educational progress of man.

The educational methods of this historical period are quite interesting, particularly as they relate to educational progress and the outdoor education method.

Cultures were in some instances blended together through trade, explorations, wars, and treaties. Each nation had some contribution to make to progress, particularly those in the Western hemisphere.

EGYPTIANS

Early Egyptian education was handled by the family. The father instructed his children in the ways of righteousness, piety and obedience to the pharaoh. The aim of education was to develop religion and morality.

As Egyptian civilization advanced, three types of schools were developed--the temple schools, the court schools, and government schools. The temple schools were supervised by priests, and children were given religious training and taught the elements of writing. The court schools were established to train the successors to the throne and therefore were very exclusive. The third type of schools were supervised by the various governmental departments and stressed political and social knowledge.

Throughout Egyptian history, education stressed vocational arts and neglected the liberal arts. A few scholars were concerned with the liberal but the masses were always given a more practical training.

The Egyptians are usually credited with being the first to introduce formal and organized writings. It was a common custom for those engaged in trades and business to use hieroglyphics with reed pen and papyrus as early as 3,000 B.C.

The introduction of writing and the dependence on records and reports soon made this skill a necessary part of the Egyptian culture in order to sustain government and industry and to impart knowledge for daily living.

Immediately, the ability to write and to read became of paramount importance throughout the civilized world. To those who were skilled writers and skilled readers, there were unlimited opportunities for positions of responsibility and dignity, for advancements, and for social prestige.

Promising youngsters were sent to school to learn the three R's. They copied the many symbols, and the primary concern of the teachers was that the student learn the correct written forms.

Here then, is the beginning of the use of so-called textbook education with formal instruction by a teacher. Eby and Arrowood comment:

> The symbols of writing were learned and recognized by writing them. The youth also learned arithmetic, geometry, astronomy, and other branches by learning to write the symbols of each science. So it was also with the literature and the moral philosophy or wisdom of the ancients. These were acquired by laboriously copying

the ancient writings. In ancient times, the learned man was the scribe, because through practice of writing he had acquired the funded wisdom of his forefathers.[3]

For the first time in history, man began writing his experiences for others to share; man began recording facts as he discovered them; man began a formal system of language that was simple and understandable to the masses; man began recording descriptive materials of his environment, his culture, his religions; and man began using writing as a tool for business, education, religion, and everyday life.

There is no doubt but what the discovery of writing and its skillful use throughout the history of mankind has been one of the most outstanding contributions to the progress of civilization. Without the invention of writing, man would still probably be in the same cultural climate as prehistoric man.

There is one caution regarding the use of writing for education purposes that originated when these early books and writings were introduced as a means for formal education. This caution is still being voiced today by educators who are continually advocating that textbook knowledge be supplemented by real life experience. The emphasis on the use of the written word for educational purposes as a sole means of learning was immediately criticized when Thamus, a renowned king in the Egyptian kingdom said:

> This discovery of yours will create a forgetfulness in the learners' souls, because they will not use their memories; they will trust to the external written characters and not remember themselves. The specific which you have discovered is an aid not to memory but to reminiscence, and you give your disciples not truth, but only semblance of truth; they will be hearers of many things and will have learned nothing.[4]

The caution voiced by Thamus unfortunately proved to be more of a prediction of educational methods that were

---

[3]Frederick Eby and Charles Flinn Arrowood, The History And Philosophy of Education Ancient and Medieval. New York: Prentice-Hall, 1940. pp. 79-80.
[4]Ibid. p. 80.

soon to become practice throughout the history of educational developments.

The history of educational development of such countries as India, China, the Semitic nations, and other known countries at this time was extremely static. Almost every principle now advocated for outdoor education learning was ignored. One of the interesting things about the ancient educational methods is that there are some traces of the same kinds of educational teachings and emphasis found in some modern schools. The practice of memorizing volumes of poetry, laws, and other literature as a means to acquire social prestige or for the sake of being considered cultured is quite apparent in some schools and in common use by too many teachers.

A brief summary of some of the educational patterns in these countries will help to show why progress has been so slow in these countries and why the mass of people are still illiterate.

INDIA

The Indian educational system and religious beliefs account for their caste social system and the limited opportunities for the masses. The majority of the people in India are deemed unworthy of education and therefore are illiterate. They are not recognized as individuals with important contributions to make to society. The educational system teaches each person his place in society and teaches him to keep his place.

Man is subordinated to his society and the individual ego is obliterated or absorbed in the larger social order. Life, according to most Indian leaders, is only an interlude in a vast cosmic process which eliminates individuality and personality. Indian education stresses the cultivation of spirit, harmony and cosmic values which are manifested in the existing universe. Success or progress is not measured by the accumulation of material wealth, fame, or physical power. Therefore, their education emphasizes the life of the spirit and neglects the life of the senses. The life of the spirit leads to true happiness and contentment, according to most Indian educators, while the life of the senses brings only superficiality, animal pleasure, and personal or physical gratification. Personal or social improvement is subordinate to spiritual betterment; thus, the many centuries of a caste social order in India. India has tended to reject scientific and technological improvements, since they improve social conditions but contribute little to the ideal of cosmic supremacy. Scientific conclusions are not accepted as absolute for science is replaced by mysticism.

The highest state of knowledge in India is intuition, through which man may achieve a oneness with the universe. There is unity in education, religion, science, faith, and philosophy. The Indian educator is a holy man as well as a man of wisdom. It is impossible for him to separate his religion, philosophy, and education.

It is too early to predict the effect that the modern exchange of ideas and the new concepts scholars may have on India. It can be said, however, that India has much to give to the rest of the world and to education in her creative approach toward unity of knowledge, spirituality, tolerance, and religious freedom, morality, and the need for meditation and quiet reflection in helping man evolve an education for a fuller and more abiding life.

CHINA

China's cultural development was doomed for stagnation for centuries because of the dedicated belief of the Chinese in a fixed social order. Chinese education emphasized the past, rather than the present, the family rather than society. Occupational skill was handed down from generation to generation. Only a few arts and professions were taught.

Centuries ago, the great Chinese patriot, Confucius, formulated a system of laws, moral principles, and a code of living which was to influence Chinese civilizations for thousands of years.

The social system advocated by Confucious recognized but one form of social order, which was based upon and demanded worship and respect for the past. Learning meant memorizing the content of a few books, laws, and other literature. These sources were considered the supreme authority for government, education, and social organization. The learning of this system provided the only opportunity for appointments in government and other closely allied positions. The entire government was, and to a large extent still is, organized to conform to this cultural heritage. This type of education, considered the longest experiment in the history of education, lasted over 4,000 years. It should prove without a doubt that education must consist of more than memorization of old books and past laws.

Chinese citizens studied these voluminous laws and codes primarily to win social prestige and governmental posts. The system was not concerned with the education of a man for man's sake but as a means of developing the man for the benefit of the social order.

The educational system advocated by Confucius is based upon his doctrine of the superior man--the teacher or the scholar. The ideal man has a practical education. He does not live in an ivory tower but tries to reform society.

The object of the superior man who represents the best of education, according to Confucius, is truth. Although food may become secondary in seeking the truth, Confucius did not believe anything could be gained by self-denial or through mortification of the flesh. The educated man is respectful, righteous, and always sincere.

The educational system of China was in direct contrast to Western civilization. It allowed no opportunity for independent thinking or for the educational techniques advocated in the outdoor education method. The educated class was bound by tradition and filial piety. Innovations were regarded as dangerous and social reformers were ignored.

Since 1905, China has removed to a large extent the traditional philosophy of Confucius. A modern system of public education patterned after Western educational methods has been introduced. China is progressing rapidly socially, scientifically, and educationally. Education in China today has definite social consequences and stresses change and application to daily existence. Chinese scholars are making

146

education a living process. The new educational program in
China is based on knowledge and learning associated with
living and community needs. Their scientific progress is
far ahead of their social progress. Much of this progress
can be contributed to a re-awakening of the Chinese leader
for a need for public education.

China's new approach to education is significant in that
it has changed from the dedication and memorization of Con-
fuscian law and ideologies to a dedicated and determined effort to learn of things real and significant to improve present day living. China made a worthwhile contribution to
civilization in stressing the role of the teacher, for the
scholar in China even today is respected and held in high
esteem.

SEMITIC NATIONS

The system of education in the Semitic Nations was to
a large extent similar to that found in the Oriental nations.
It lacked many essentials of good educational methods. Their
system of education was very formal and consisted mainly in
memorizing rules and doctrines for the conduct of life.
Originality was discouraged. The primary emphasis was
to learn the many laws and moral codes to fit individuals
into the proper social order. There was not much encouragement for critical thinking, inquiry, and new discoveries.

Hebrew education made its greatest contribution to
education in law through moral and religious emphasis. The
training of the Hebrews was divided into four periods. Children up to the age of six were educated in the home. They
were taught basic moral attitudes and were introduced to
the basic Hebrew ritual.

The second period of education was conducted in the
synagogue under the supervision of the scribe. Religious
instruction was intensified and the basic rudiments of the
three R's were taught.

When the child reached ten and until he was sixteen,
his education was concentrated on the mastery of Hebrew
law. The student was in close contact with the rabbi, the
spiritual leader of the community.

At the age of sixteen the more intelligent students went into the fourth phase of education. They learned the intricacies of law and Hebrew religion and through an intellectual interchange of ideas with their teacher, became challenged with ideas and wisdom.

Although orthodox religious dogma hindered creativity, the Hebrew educational system was intensely interested in the betterment of children and, through the exchange of ideas between student and teacher, brought a new respect for education. Kemp states:

> When its fundamental conceptions of God, man, righteousness, and duty are considered, and the moral dignity and earnestness it put into human life, it does not seem unreasonable to say that Hebrew education was the noblest of all Antiquity.[5]

WESTERN CIVILIZATIONS

In Western cultures the individual was exalted. Society was dynamic and changing. Man turned his mind outward to his environment and to nature. He was investigative. The purpose of education was to develop the individual and help him make his place in society rather than to take the place assigned to him by birth. Traditions and ancestoral worship had a comparatively small hold upon the man of western cultures.

The content of education was more than literature and folkways of past experiences and ideals. It included science, nature study and practical social, economic, and political problems of the day. The method of education was not rote memory and imitation, but observation and investigation. The past traditions and customs of society were taught not for the purpose of conforming to them but that man should use them for his own improvement and progress.

GREECE

Anaragoras said, "All things were in chaos when Mind arose and made order."

[5]E. L. Kemp, History of Education, Philadelphia: J. B. Lippincott Company, 1912. pp. 51-52.

The Greeks were one of the first, if not the first, culture to introduce order into the universe and man's life. Western culture is considered as beginning with the Greeks. Probably for the first time in the history of mankind, the Greeks developed a systematic practice of criticizing their traditional beliefs and institutions. They wrote the beginning chapters of man's long history. Almost entirely within their own realm they began from a very simple, primitive life and developed a very high degree of civilization. The Greeks made impressive contributions to philosophy, history, science, art, and literature. They produced great philosophers, poets, artists, and statesmen, whose works are studied today for ideas of modern application.

The Greeks became profoundly interested in the primary essence or substance of which things are made. The greatest contribution of the Greeks was their critical, inquiring spirit. They were limited in the kinds of books that were of interest to them and so they went directly to nature for their learning. As they discovered nature, they discovered man. These discoveries and learnings were recorded and became the basis for many books and writings of this era. Many of these discoveries are the basis for materials in present day textbooks.

It was Athens which presented the best of Greece and it is to Athens that the modern world is most indebted for the valuable heritage of Greek culture. An entirely new spirit appeared among the Athenians. They probably reached the greatest heights of practical and effective education in the early history of any nation or city of the world. Education to them was life. Knowledge was sought for a purpose. Knowledge became wisdom and wisdom was used in the great institutions of the state. Citizens proposed, debated, and made laws in the assembly; they enforced the laws as members of the juries; they witnessed or performed the great tragedies of their day in the theater; and they attended the Olympian games en masse from all parts of Greece. The citizen was a part of his government and did not fear it or mistrust it as an alien power. His government gave him opportunity and incentive to develop and express his individuality.

The education of the Greeks was deeply rooted in the life

of the community. They did not separate their major interests from their everyday life. They considered learning, art, music, poetry, religion, sports, and politics as inseparable from life. Their great poets and scholars were active public citizens.

The excellence of Greek civilization was enhanced by her great thinkers, scholars and nature philosophers. Higher thinking is said to have originated with Thales, an Ionian Greek of the seventh century before Christ. Living by the sea and observing the mist rising in clouds, he concluded that rainfall was caused by a natural process of evaporation and precipitation and not by some god. In this way he substituted science for mythology. Henceforth, the Greeks turned to a closer observation of nature.

Thales was interested in astronomy, cosmology, geometry, and physics. He traveled widely and is reputed to have taught the Egyptians how to calculate the heighth of a Pyramid by its shadow, foretell the eclipse of the sun, and calculate the distance of ships at sea. Thales was the first man in recorded history to make scientific deductions from general principles. In his measurement of the heights of pyramids and the distance of ships at sea, Thales was the first to apply theoretical geometry to practical use.

This abstract and deductive thinking was a new phenomenon in the realm of human culture, one of the most revolutionary steps in the history of education. Several other Greek philosophers made contribution to our civilization as a result of observation and investigation of nature.

Pythagoras (584 to 500 B. C.) taught that number is the origin, or essence, of all things. He accordingly laid great stress on mathematics. He discovered that the square of the hypotenuse of a right-angled triangle is equal to the sum of the squares of the other two sides. Pythagoras is said to have placed a movable bridge under a cord stretched over a resounding board, and by moving the board from one end to the other he demonstrated that tones are governed by definite mathematical laws. Pythagoras' ideas in mathematics eventually led to the application of mathematics to all the fields of physical science.

Democritus (460 B. C.), one of the early nature philosophers of Greece, propounded the atomic theory of matter which is the foundation of modern physical science. Democritus, Thales, and other Greek leaders of this time substituted science for supernaturalism. They rejected animism as an explanation of the phenomena of everyday experience and substituted natural causes. Matter, said Democritus, had physical properties adequate to account for the nature of all things and to explain all events. It was not angry gods that were responsible for lost battles but a stronger enemy, not angry gods that caused a ship to sink but poor weight distribution.

Socrates (469-399 B. C.), unlike Democritus, was uninterested in scientific philosophy. He was primarily a moralist and considered the problems of man more important than science or nature. If man does not find himself, of what value is knowledge of science and nature?

"Know thyself" was the foundation of the philosophy of Socrates. It was the keynote to his great educational contribution. The beginning of education is the recognition of limitations and prejudices. Truth is absolute and man should not live by pretension. The teacher, according to Socrates, must pursue truth even though he is opposed by his society for he is the leader of civilization.

Socrates lived according to his educational ideals. He believed in universal education and the function of education to him was to awaken the average man who lives in a world of ignorance, half-truths and prejudices.

Socrates was not a specialist. He believed that education, religion, ethics, and philosophy are all basically one and man through education can unify his life through virtue and knowledge.

Socrates believed that education did not require a formal school or an organized student body. He taught in the market place, at banquets, and in the out-of-doors. The world was his classroom. He saw the aim of education as knowledge arising from power of thought and analysis of experience. Experience was found in the everyday life of the citizen and not in the classroom.

Although prehistoric tribes used first-hand direct experience as their only means for teaching, Socrates was probably the first to use the outdoor education technique consisting of skillful questions and thoughtful answers, and forming concepts from precepts--as a method of teaching. Socrates' method of education has survived throughout man's long history and is still accepted by educators as a valid and important method of teaching. Socrates tried to show that the greatest of all arts was the art of living a good life.

Plato (429-348 B. C.), was a student of Socrates and was responsible for handing down to posterity the works and aims of his teacher. Plato's great weakness was his contempt for the masses and his tendency toward totalitarianism.

One of his greatest contributions was his belief in the unity of theory and practice. Plato stressed the interrelatedness of life and saw education, philosophy, politics, ethics, and economics as an indissoluble unit and not specialized areas for study. His integrative approach to life and the whole method of teaching is consistent with the modern concept of outdoor education.

Plato was probably the forerunner among educators recognizing the importance of individual differences in talent. He realized that all children were not capable of pursuing the same course of study and he made special arrangements for superior students to continue their education.

The present day school system is often credited to Plato. He started the early Greek academy and organized grammar schools, music schools, and gymnasiums. His ideal of the importance of training the body as well as the mind is universally recognized today as an important tenet in education. Both intellectual and physical prowess are essential to a complete education--for what would it profit a man to have a high degree of intelligence in an unsound body. Learning should involve both mind and body when possible.

Aristotle (384-322 B. C.), a man of genuinely scientific mind, was perhaps the greatest of all the Greek nature phi-

losophers. His chief interest was in natural science. He
believed the cultivation of the intellect was man's most important mission in life. Leisure, to Aristotle, was the
most important aspect of man's life because it gave him
time to contemplate, meditate, and speculate. Labor deprived man of this opportunity and was of secondary value
although a necessity to survival.

Aristotle was far advanced of his age and in many
respects would be a pioneer in educational thought today.
He taught that mind proceeds from the specific to the universal, from the particular to the general. He believed
that without a correct method, education would not progress.
Other basic concepts of modern education which were taught
by Aristotle are (1) education is concerned with the whole
child--physical, mental and moral, (2) the educated man
combines theory with practice, intuition with scientific
data, (3) study of the past should enhance the creative possibilities of the present, (4) experience is the guide to
learning, and (5) interest alone is not enough for real learning and real creativity; discipline is essential.

Aristotle rejected Plato's theory of ideas and abstractions for the more practical theory that education is a life
activity. He believed that truth and divine intelligence are
revealed in nature. Aristotle was probably the greatest
systematizer of knowledge, the greatest scientist, of all
time. He wrote treatises on nearly all departments of human
endeavor. He is often called the father of modern science
as he used the objective, inductive method and thus founded
practically all the sciences.

The Greeks had most of the essentials recommended
today for sound educational practices. The elementary and
secondary schools and even universities were an important
part of Greek culture. They amassed a tremendous amount
of experience and knowledge because of their strong belief
in observation, inquiry, critical thinking and analysis of
nature and life about them. They recorded these findings
in appropriate volumes for the use of future civilizations.

Outdoor education was a primary educational technique
of the Greek era.

THE ROMANS

Most historians agree that as Greece gave content to education, the Romans gave it organization. It was Rome that brought form to the schools and shaped them into our modern concept of elementary, secondary and higher divisions. The history of Roman education is largely a continuation of that of the Greeks, with their own modification and practical translation.

Before the Roman empire entered its period of decline, it had the most extensive and highly organized system of education that the world had ever known. The Romans learned everything from the Greeks except their inquiring spirit. Where the Greeks were imaginative, the Romans were practical and concrete. Where the Greeks made their great contribution to modern civilization in philosophy, art and literature, the Romans gave law and order and government. The Greeks and Romans supplemented each other perfectly in laying the foundation on which modern civilization is built. Greece created the aesthetic, the beauty, and the intellectual ideals while Rome organized and unified the Greek heritage and added her own practical skills. Rome bequeathed to posterity a rich heritage in governmental forms, legal codes, and engineering science.

Rome's greatest intellectual and moral achievement and her chief contribution to civilization was her system of law and justice. Although the empire was born of military conquest it was won by law and order. Rome, to her everlasting credit, enjoyed the longest period of continuous peace that the world has ever known. For nearly two hundred years the Mediterranean world enjoyed a relative quiet that has yet to be achieved in world history. The great rulers of Rome were interested in the welfare of their subjects. Even the earlier countries which were added to the Empire by conquest were eventually grateful for it. An example of the tributes paid to the Roman Empire may be found in the oration of Aristeides:

> You Romans are the only rulers known to History who have reigned over free man...The lustre of your rule is unsullied by any breath of ungenerous hostility; and the reason is that you yourselves set the example of gener-

osity by sharing all your power and privileges with
your subjects...with the result that in your day a
combination has been achieved which previously appeared
quite impossible--the combination of consummate power
with consummate benevolence...Rome is a citadel which
has all the peoples of the Earth for its villagers.
And Rome has never failed those who have looked to her.

Another contribution that Rome made to modern civilization was her language and alphabet. The English language has incorporated so many words and phrases from the Latin language that scarcely a sentence is spoken without using a word once used by the ancient Romans. Traces of their language also are apparent in Spain, Portugal, and France.

The Romans left no outstanding heritage to philosophy, art, medicine, geography, or astronomy. They did leave to posterity certain practical knowledges in road building, agriculture, sewer construction and baths, central heating and engineering, and architectural methods and styles still found in modern civilization. Many historians see important parallels in the development of Roman and American education. Both systems grew from puritanical beginnings and both stressed practical and utilitarian endeavors as they developed. Both systems were outstanding in technological development and both were cursed with social ills such as crime and juvenile delinquency. Compared to Greek education, the Roman schools, as they developed, became too practical and were under too much state control. "As to liberty, " said Plutarch, "we have that which the government leaves us. "

Another important contribution which Rome indirectly made to world culture was that of Christianity. Rome consolidated the barbarian tribes of the Mediterranean in an empire of law and order and thus laid the foundation on which Christianity was built.

The Romans were eager and anxious to capitalize on all the Greeks had to offer in the way of education. The experience and scientific progress accomplished by the Greeks were a matter of well recorded discoveries and progress. The school systems that Rome created and the literature compiled by them was the greatest in the world. Their ability to organize existing knowledge and to disseminate it through elementary, secondary, and university school systems has not been matched. In most respects their methods of education were good, but reliance upon existing knowledge and ideas soon retarded progress.

Probably the greatest educator of the Romans was Quintilian (35 A.D.). Unlike Plato, Quintilian considered the experienced statesman superior to the scholar and philosopher. He regarded life as action and excess contemplation and philosophizing was an escape from reality. Quintilian pointed out that philosophers failed in their attempt to reform whereas the most famous men of history were practical men close to life. He regarded public speaking and oratory among the foundations of education. Quintilian was ahead of his time in much of his educational method. He did not believe in corporal punishment but encouraged the teacher to appeal to the idealism of their students. Quintilian held that all parts of the curriculum were interrelated and should be presented to the students at the proper stage of emotional and intellectual development.

Among the many reasons cited for the decay of the Roman empire might be added the failure of their educational system to perpetrate the methods that made Greece rise so prominently. The Romans failed to recognize the value of the educational methods of observation, inquiry, investigation, and critical thinking regarding nature and the life of man. They were so concerned with practical matters that they lost sight of the real purpose of education. To the Romans, education was involved too much with methodology and too little with intellectual and moral qualities.

THE MEDIEVAL WORLD

The period usually considered to be the Middle Ages lasted from the decline of the Roman Empire, around 300 A.D., up until the beginning of the Renaissance about 1300 A.D. Many historians regard the Middle Ages as a period of intellectual decay and barbarism. They refer to this period as the "Dark Ages." Following, as it did, the glorious realms of Greek and Roman civilizations, the Middle Ages seemed to be an era of confusion, hopelessness, and anarchy. It was a period marked by wandering tribes and barbaric kingdoms, no fixed boundaries or armed frontiers, few outstanding scholars, and primarily church dominated. During the Middle Ages the monasteries or church offered with few exceptions the only means to an education, and the only type of career for which learning was needed. Education throughout the world was in a deplorable condition. Cole states that:

> A small amount of learning was disseminated among members of the priesthood. Noblemen and princes acquired at best only the rudiments of elementary schoolwork. The common people as a whole were taught the dogmas of the church by word of mouth but little more, although individual boys from peasant families did sometimes go as far along the road of learning as anyone else. The minds of people were fixed upon the next world, and education at all could be defended only because through reading Christian writings might help the soul on its journey through life...

> These centuries bequeathed to posterity two features that remained characteristic of education for a long time. From the Greek and Roman world came the main content of the Medieval curriculum and most of the elementary school books. From the Christian world came the objectives of instruction, the more advanced reading materials, and the new kind of schools.[6]

Christianity, largely through Christ and his disciples, laid a foundation just prior to Medieval times that contained the seed of democracy. It is to the everlasting credit of the relatively few outstanding scholars of Medieval times that the groundwork for modern Christian culture was preserved. For Christianity stressed brotherhood and equal rights of all mankind.

Jesus Christ, the greatest teacher of all, had used the outdoor education methods in presenting the gospel. His parables were simple and were taken from the familiar objects of nature. The universe was his classroom and his

[6]Luella Cole, _A History of Education Socrates to Montessori_, New York: Rinehart and Company, 1950. p. 109.

textbook was the open field and the market place. In His teachings, birds of the air and lilies of the fields were used to present the most sublime truths. He was embodied in all that He taught. He lived what He taught. Christ was a master in the art of asking questions and much that He taught required critical thinking and interpretation by His pupils. Because He stressed the power of love instead of force, of cooperation instead of bigotry and selfishness, Christ and His disciples created a new influence which laid the foundation for a new method of education, that of leading and directing children as opposed to forceful coercion, and that of stressing understanding and compassion as opposed to knowledge of facts.

The leaders of the Medieval Ages, as leaders of any age are prone to do, made an honest attempt to foster and preserve Christianity but were confused about how to do it. They accepted the teachings of Christ and protested against the prevailing worldliness. Monasticism developed as a protest to worldliness. Scholars entered the monastery and vowed poverty, chastity and obedience as they withdrew from civic life. St. Benedict issued codes which were adapted by monasteries throughout the civilized world which prescribed seven hours work and two hours of reading. The monasteries, thus, made social and educational contributions by furnishing leaders for an ignorant population.

Civilization was already on the decline at the beginning of the Middle Ages. It was not enhanced by the deluge of barbarism which sprang up in this era. Invading, barbaric tribes descended on many nations in different parts of the civilized world. The atmosphere was not conducive to producing great scholars and as a result the Middle Ages contributed very few. One of the ancient poets of Toulouse, when asked why he no longer produced anything of value answered, "How can I write six foot hexameters when I am surrounded by seven foot barbarians?"[7]

About midway between the two dates encompassing the Medieval Ages, Charlemagne, one of the most distinguished

[7]J. Sandys, A History of Classical Scholarship, London: Cambridge University Press, Vol. I. p. 246.

and capable rulers of all time, came to the throne of the
Frankish nation. At this time, learning and schools had
degenerated into a sad state due to the turbulent conditions
and lack of direction. Charlemagne established a strong
government and restored and extended education throughout
his kingdom. With the help of Alcuin whom he appointed
head of the Palace School in Frankland, he was responsible
for a wonderful revival of learning which placed a vital
role in saving ancient civilization from complete loss.

Charlemagne might very well be credited with laying
the foundation of modern education. His capitulary of 789
A.D. reads: "Let every monastery and every abbey have
its school, where boys may be taught the Psalms, the system of musical notation, singing, arithmetic, and grammar;
and let the books which are given them be free from faults,
and let care be taken that the boys do not spoil them either
when reading or writing." Alcuin, Charlemagne's chief aid,
is regarded by most historians as the greatest educator of
the Middle Ages. Although Alcuin actually created or originated nothing new, he deserves great tribute for preserving the heritage of the past for the ages which followed him.
Charlemagne and Alcuin were forerunners of scholasticism
which maintained the rights of human reason. Authority
was subjected to reason by the scholastic teachers bringing
about reconciliation of faith and reason.

The history of educational thought during the Middle
Ages would not be complete if it included only a discussion
of monasticism. Other educational forces which added to
the intellectual and moral activity of the Middle Ages were
Mohammedan learning, chivalry, and the rise of the universities.

When the Saracens conquered and plundered the Western world, Christendom feared that it might lose its very
existence. The reverse proved to be true. The conquerors
took the best that the Greeks had to offer and merged it
with the best of the Eastern culture to stimulate a remarkable intellectual activity. The scientific activity of the modern world took roots in their schools. They combined the
best of the Greeks and Hindus to produce algebra in its modern form. They founded a new trigonometry and gave the

Hindu arithmetical notation to the West. In their laboratories they made original and noteworthy contributions in their effort to discover the real nature and relationship of things. They made important discoveries in chemistry and physics. They discovered nitric acid, alcohol and sulphuric acid. Their chemists laid the foundation for modern chemistry. They were far advanced in medicine and surgery and knew the properties of many medical drugs.

The spread of chivalry was a natural outgrowth of the changing and turbulent times. Nations were conquered and re-conquered by first one tribe and then another until they lost their identity. Boundary lines disappeared and merchants, students, pilgrims, scribes, teachers, peddlers and beggars wandered freely from place to place. Groups of common interest banded together in their castles and the age of knighthood was in vogue. The world of chivalry owed its existence to the hard work of the serf. The noblemen were primarily concerned that their sons become knights.

"The University was the best product of all that was best in the Middle Ages. It was at once the crowning achievement of the age and one of its noblest bequests."[8] The seven Liberal Arts were expanded in the twelfth century leading to professional faculties of medicine, law, and theology. Universities grew up in cities throughout the Western world and were attended by scholars from all countries. The universities, by gathering together hundreds of young men from all over the civilized world, broke down prejudices and aided in spreading tolerance and understanding as well as learning on a universal scale.

The tremendous progress civilizations had made for centuries almost came to an abrupt end during the earlier centuries of the Middle Ages. It is a period in history that most individuals view with regret and wonderment. Man and societies sunk to an all time low in social, moral, and educational achievement. The basis for education to a large extent focused on the supernatural. Education was primarily concerned with preparation for life in the next world. There

[8]E. L. Kemp, History of Education. Philadelphia: J. B. Lippincott Company, 1912. p. 138.

was little emphasis upon or recognition of things real, and little attention was given to necessities for improving the present social system for the benefit of man. Educational practices lacked most of the essentials that we recognize as desirable today.

Education was almost directly opposite to what is recommended in outdoor educational methods.

The few scholars of this period have been recognized as being some of the world's greatest teachers. Although there were too few scholars, they were able to maintain enough educational stability in various societies to lead civilizations partly out of the Dark Ages.

THE RENAISSANCE AND REFORMATION

The Renaissance and Reformation periods in history were the threshold to modern times. It was the beginning of the intellectual awakening of the world society and here over the closing centuries were planted many ideas that found their development in modern society.

The Renaissance in the early centuries turned their thoughts back to the classics whereas the Reformation began to free man from the book, from ancient dogma and from institutional rule.

The Reformation is important for the many martyrs who gave their lives to begin the battle for enlightenment and freedom of mankind, a battle which is still being fought today in many parts of the world.

THE RENAISSANCE

For ten centuries man lived in the shadow of the monastery. He was submerged in society; he was denied all worldly pleasures; he was rebuked and even condemned by the medieval institutions stressing the "other worldly" aim of life.

The period known as the Renaissance, usually considered to represent the fourteenth, fifteenth, and sixteenth centuries, brought about a break from the church. Its break with the Middle Ages was gradual but opened a new period of man's culture; a new world view.

The crusaders discovered that the people of the East were more intelligent and lived a better life. Man became more and more interested in life of the present world. "Otherworldliness" began to give way to the interests of this world. The status of man changed. The artist glorified his body and educators made him complete. It was a revival of the old long-forgotten way of looking at life. Attention was directed to the literature of Greece and Rome as man began to enjoy life on earth and became interested in the beauties of nature. Things human rather than things divine were stressed. Thus the term humanities. Humanism spread quite rapidly throughout the western world. Medieval ecclesiasticism gave way to a broad concept and study of ancient literature for content and "borrowed experiences" in living a richer and fuller life.

The invention of the printing press about 1450 spread the new learning throughout the world and brought about a broader foundation for universal education. Ancient manuscripts were searched from old monasteries and printed. Libraries arose in the cities and the book became the chief instrument of education. Women, who were without status in the Middle Ages, played a prominent role in the advancement of learning during the Renaissance.

The chief scholars of the Renaissance were Petrarch and Erasmus.

Petrarch (1304-1372), often referred to as the first modern scholar, was the embodiment of the early Renaissance. He repudiated the otherworldly ideals and scholasticism of his day and recovered the ancient spirit of the Greeks. Petrarch urged the cultivation of the arts and sciences.

Erasmus (1467-1536), if not the first scholar, was the most influential in outdoor education methods. He criticized the empty verbalism of the humanistic approach to learning and tried to substitute true learning. He ridiculed those who substituted form and linguistics for the real spirit

of classical culture. Erasmus held that learning, morality
and religion could not be separated and education must be
open to everyone according to each individual's ability. He
urged the importance of practical experience to help clarify
the classics and advocated study of science, geography, and
history. The aim of education proposed by Erasmus was the
development of innate capacities and independent judgment.
Wisdom to Erasmus was applied knowledge. He did not rely
on the ancients for education but stressed the intelligent application of knowledge to the problems of his day.

Soon the humanist movement became formalized, fixed,
and narrow. Since the scholars of the Renaissance looked to
ancient Greece and Rome for their learnings, the term,
humanities, came to mean the literature and language of the
ancients. "Consequently, the aim of education was thought
of in terms of language and literature instead of in terms of
life."[9] Education became the mastery of ancient literature.
Thus the content or literary value of the ancient writings
were dominated, or even lost, in the narrow linguistic education that came to control the European schools. School
children became involved in laborious and formal drills and
most universities adapted the narrow humanistic approach to
learning. All emphasis was placed upon language, grammar
and style. Form became more important than content and
the educational method again became memorization and imitation.

Although ancient literature contained much of nature
and science, few contemporary scholars of this era had any
experience or shared any interest in the scientific approach.
Few educators considered science equal to language and
literature, and interest in science gave way as linguistic
formalism advanced. By the seventeenth century the study
of the humanities became almost as formal and profitless
as the narrow routine of scholasticism of the Middle Ages.

Educational methods during the Renaissance were experiencing a reluctant change to the progressive concepts
of the Greeks. Memorization of laws, moral codes, bibles,
and other literature for preparation in the next world was

[9]Paul Monroe, A Brief Course in the History of Education. New York: The MacMillan
Company, 1935. p. 170.

being replaced by educational methods which recognized a
need for improved living immediately. The change was
slow and did not gain momentum until sometime during the
seventeenth century. The outdoor education method did
not have much recognition during this period.

THE REFORMATION

The Reformation period overlapped the Renaissance
period both in time and accomplishment as it was part of the
general intellectual awakening throughout Europe. The Reformation period is generally considered the fifteenth and
sixteenth century. The big difference between the Renaissance and the Reformation was that the former looked back-
ward and the latter looked forward. Whereas the Renaissance was a revival of ancient literature, and a return to
an earlier type of thinking and education, the scholars of
the Reformation period used the ancient writings only as
source material to supplement their own experiences. The
Reformation completed the work began by the Renaissance
in exalting the intrinsic worth of the individual.

The seventeenth century became known as the Age of
Science. A Franciscan monk, Roger Bacon, challenged the
narrow humanistic teachings of the church and through his
many writings popularized the value of "useful knowledge. "
He pointed out that men could study nature because they,
hereby, were studying the work of God. The contributions
of the "Age of Science" and "Age of Enlightenment" were
realized by Alexander Pope when he wrote:

Nature and Nature's laws lay hid in night,
God said, Let Newton be! And all was light.

In 1609, Galileo first turned a telescope to the heavens
and about the same time Kepler worked out the law of plan-
etary movements. Modern physics were born in this century with the invention of the barometer, thermometer, air
pump, and pendulum clock. Boyle formulated his famous
law of gases, and Gilbert made important contributions in
magnetism and electricity. The development of decimals
and logarithms and other improvements in mathematics
came during the Reformation. A long series of geographical

discoveries extended the horizons and brought about an age of colonization and increased commercial activity.

The real contribution to knowledge came as a result of the discoveries of many men who turned to nature for observation, investigation, and learning.

The Reformation period saw large scale revolt within the Church. Dishonest and unfaithful Church officials used their authority to collect wealth and power. Disillusioned people joined the reformers who launched attacks against the Church. Mystics, like Joachin of Fiore, believed in a personal approach to God; they favored the abandonment of all material desires and temporal powers of the church. William of Ockham placed emphasis on the individual worshiper and challenged the Church organization; he pleaded for a return to the Scriptures as the final source of knowledge. He was joined by rebels like Hues and Wycliffe who urged that the Church return to the simplicity of Christ and substitute the Bible for the Church. The humanists joined the revolt and criticized the material desires of the Church; they tried to make the Church organization more democratic and were critical of the Church doctrines and translations of the Scripture. The works of these early scholars prepared the way for the most renowned reformer of the Reformation. It remained for Martin Luther to make the first substantial break with the authority of the Church in 1515.

Martin Luther (1438-1546), an Augustinian monk, was convinced that salvation is a gift from God to man and is gained by faith alone. He attacked the sale of indulgences by the Church and repudiated the belief that the merit of the saints can make up for the sins of mankind. He further critized the Church in his famous ninety-five theses published in 1517.

Luther's writings and teachings established the Protestant Reformation as a great religious movement. He translated the Bible into the German language and insisted upon universal education and government by the state. He appealed to the writing of St. Augustine who taught that each soul is unique and that each is capable of learning the truth. "Each man," said Luther, " is his own priest."

Luther formed a new religion, the Lutheran Church, and brought about further revolt within the Catholic Church. Revolt within the ranks of the Lutheran Church followed and new churches were established by John Calvin and other religious dissenters of the Reformation.

No history of outdoor education would be complete without mention of John Amos Comenius (1592-1670). Comenius believed that knowledge was power. He was dedicated to his religious faith and was interested in education primarily to further Christian teaching. He taught children to read and write, so that as many as possible could read the Scripture for personal salvation

Comenius emphasized man's goodness and was convinced that the good in man would triumph over the evil. He had a dedicated faith in education and believed universal learning would lead to an ideal society. He held that Christianity was not an abstract ideal, but a practical way of life that could be realized if only man were educated enough to find his salvation. Comenius, although well versed in Greek classics, believed in progress through science rather than through the humanities. He stressed useful subjects.

The beginning of modern educational theory may be found in his writings. He was the outstanding writer of educational literature during the Reformation and paved the way for widening the aims of education from the narrow religious concept to the application of sense realism for all of life. Comenius insisted that knowledge is not innate and all learning must come through the senses:

> To the rational soul, that dwells within us, organs of sense have been supplied...These are sight, hearing, smell, sound, and touch, and there is nothing whatever that can escape their notice. For, since there is nothing in the visible universe which cannot be seen, heard, smelt, tasted, or touched, and the kind and quality of which cannot in this way be discerned, it follows that there is nothing in the universe which cannot be compassed by a man endowed with sense and reason.

> From this (fact) a golden rule for teachers may be derived. Everything should, as far as is possible, be

placed before the senses. Everything visible should be
brought before the organ of sight, everything audible
before that of hearing. Odours should be placed before
the sense of smell, and things that are tastable and
tangible before the sense of taste and touch respec-
tively. If an object can make an impression on several
senses at once, it should be brought into contact with
several...Surely, then, the beginning of wisdom should
consist, not in the mere learning the name of things,
but in the actual perception of the things themselves!
It is when the things have been grasped by the senses
that language should fulfill its function of explaining
it still further...[10]

Comenius proposed four types of educational institutions. The training of the child should be in the home at the
School of The Mother's Knee. Here the parents were the
teachers and the child would learn by their example. Religious and moral ideas were to be emphasized.

When the child was ready--and Comenius was the fore-
runner among educators to emphasize all phases of learning
--he would be sent to a *Vernacular School* or the *Latin
School.* The vernacular school would stress the mother
tongue, arts and science with little emphasis on the classics.

The fourth school, *University and Travel,* was to create
the leaders of society. Comenius himself was a tireless
traveler and believed that much could be gained by scholars
exploring the ideals and morals of various nations.

Modern educators echo the past with their recommendations that all should not be taught in the classroom.
Comenius said:

The school itself should be a pleasant place, and attractive to the eye both within and without. Within
the room should be bright and clean, and its walls
should be ornamented by pictures...without, there should
be an open space to walk or play in...and there should
also be a garden attached, into which the scholars may
be allowed to go from time to time and where they may
feast their eyes on trees, flowers, and plants.[11]

[10] M. W. Keatings, The Great Didactic of John Amos Comenius. London: A. and C.
Black, 1910. pp. 184-185.
[11] Ibid. p. 130.

The accumulation of mass information was not the aim of education, according to Comenius. The important thing in the educative process was to stir the creative urge and imagination of the pupil. His was a school of action. We learn to write by writing and we learn to read by reading. We learn by doing. More than any thinker of his time, Comenius stressed the interrelatedness of reason and emotion. The scholar who strives for intellectual and bookish pursuits can never have an impact upon life. His formal education is wasted unless he can cultivate compassion and humility.

Comenius believed that education is related to life and learning and is best accomplished by direct experience:

> What object is there in learning subjects that are of no use to those who know them and the lack of which is not felt by those who do not know them? Subjects that are certain to be forgotten as time passes on and the business of life becomes more engrossing? This short life of ours has more than enough to occupy it, even if we do not waste it on worthless studies. Schools must therefore be organized in such a way that the scholars learn nothing but what is of value.

> Truly it has been said, that nothing is more useless than to learn and to know much, if such knowledge be of no avail for practical purposes; and again, that not he who knows much is wise, but he who knows what is useful.

> Whatever is taught should be taught as being of practical application in everyday life and of some definite use. That is to say, the pupil should understand that what he learns is not taken out of some Utopia or borrowed from Platonic Ideas, but is one of the facts which surround us, and that a fitting acquaintance with it will be of great value in life.[12]

Sensory learning was fundamental in Comenius' scheme of primary education. Nature studies--plants, animals, and minerals--were introduced from the first that the child might early cultivate his powers of observation and form the habit of acquiring knowledge.

[12]M. W. Keatings, The Great Didactic of John Amos Comenius, London: A. and C. Black, 1910. p. 189.

Educators like Montaigne thought that "lessons should be practiced rather than recited." Hobbes taught that man learns through the senses of seeing, hearing, touching, tasting, and smelling. Bacon contended that the study of nature was basic to all scientific progress. Ratke believed that the order of nature should be sought and followed. Children should not be forced to memorize but should be led to understand through questioning. Comenius said that children should study things before reading words about things. He believed that the teacher must make a constant appeal through sense perception to understanding nature and the child.

Thus, the thinking of some of the great educational leaders of the Reformation indicates the change in thinking which occurred during this period in regard to the importance of outdoor education principles as proposed today.

MODERN TIMES

The Renaissance and the Reformation brought forth one wave of rebellion after another against authority and enslavement of the individual. Each new awakening or revival of learning that sprung up in various parts of the world promised emancipation of man from institutions, but the idea gradually was lost to another movement or hardened into a new formalism not much better than the one it replaced. Yet in this early period the seeds were sown for the Modern Age.

Despotism and ecclesiasticism which had for over a thousand years controlled the lives of man had grown intolerable. Scholars of the Renaissance and Reformation, with persistent gnawing at its structure, had it ready to topple at the beginning of the eighteenth century. Institutional barriers were here and there swept away. Individualism ran rampant; the French Revolution, although extreme, was an example of the revolt against institutions and authority.

The new freedom of the individual was won in the eighteenth century but it was given direction in the nineteenth and twentieth centuries. For many years the new won freedom was without guidance and social control. Anarchy sprang up as a result of a lack of knowledge of living as free men.

The modern age provided movement after movement in education, the influence of which can be felt in our schools of today. Some of the outstanding movements and educational theories may best be discussed by considering their authors.

NATURALISM IN EDUCATION

No one in history has given more emphasis to the principle of individualism than Jean Jacques Rousseau (1712-1788). He expounded the social philosophy of the rights of man in his *Social Contract* and the rights of the child in *Emile*.

In his long discourse, part novel and part didactic exposition, Rousseau in *Emile* explained his theory of education according to nature. In his opening statement he says, "Everything is good as it comes from the hands of man." Rousseau objected to intellectual formalism and its pretentious and narrow aristocracy. He advocated the return to a simple and natural state where men are by nature unequal physically and mentally but are socially equal to live in happiness and contentment, free from domination by their fellowmen.

Emile is the first important book on child study, the forerunner of modern psychology. It dealt with individual differences, growth and development, laws of learning and the educational implications.

Rousseau trumpeted the cause of modern concepts in educational practice such as education is life not a preparation for life; that education is best obtained from direct experience through the senses; and democratic education concerns--liberty, equality, and fraternity. He emphasized the importance of play in education; the importance of interest in learning; and the ideas that the child must learn, develop and grow from within.

Johann Bernard Basedow (1723-1790), was one of the

world's greatest teachers. He concurred in the philosophy
of Rousseau and applied it to his teaching in Germany. He
wrote textbooks appropriate to various grade levels as a
supplement to the teachings of nature. He, like Rousseau,
objected to education becoming too formalized and too verbal. His rebellion to giving too much authority to the
printed word and his adaptation of Rousseau's "natural way"
of learning and living sowed the seed of modern education.
Basedow's method of teaching nature study by means of excursions in the neighborhood and teaching arithmetic, geography, and physics as practically as possible by relating
them to the interests and comprehensions of his pupils is
still advocated today by outstanding proponents of outdoor
education.

Rousseau and Basedow contributed a great deal towards
making education more meaningful to the student. Their emphasis on naturalism in education is still stressed in educational methods today. However, they did fail to consider
man as a member of society and ignored the important relationships of man to society. The social function of education was left to later educators.

"PSYCHOLOGIZING 'EDUCATION'"

The influences exerted by Pestalozzi, Herbart, and
Froebel are so interwoven in the educational practice of today that it is difficult to trace any one practice directly to
its founder.

Johann Heinrich Pestalozzi (1746-1827) was the first
of Rousseau's disciples to attempt to "psychologize education." He is credited for the beginning of modern pedagogy
in substituting experimentation for tradition in educational
practice. His advocacy of universal education was due to
the belief that it was the only way the masses could improve
their wretched position. He considered sense perception to
be the real foundation of knowledge and observation to be the
basis of all instruction. Pestalozzi contended that studying
from a textbook filled the child's mind with hazy ideas and
meaningless words, whereas teaching through observation
and direct experience gave him clear ideas, greater knowledge, and more natural experience in oral expression.

Pestalozzi tried to make his teaching as dramatic as possible. He started with concrete objects to teach concepts in arithmetic and tried to show how arithmetic is involved in daily living. He had a model bank in the classroom where the children acted out the roles of bank president, the tellers, and the customers.

Pestalozzi used clay models to portray mountains and rivers and taught future teachers a new and dramatic concept of geography. He would often take children on walks and nature hikes in order to make them conscious of their environment. In his *Diary* he beseeched teachers to get the children out of the classroom:

> Lead your child out into nature, teach him on the hill-tops and in the valleys. There he will listen better, and the sense of freedom will give him more strength to overcome difficulties. But in these hours of freedom let him be taught by nature rather than by you. Let him fully realize that she is the real teacher and that you, with your art, do nothing more than walk quietly at her side. Should a bird sing or an insect hum on a leaf, at once stop your walk; bird and insect are teaching him; you may be silent.

The teacher, according to Pestalozzi, was an active participant in the teaching-learning process, an organizer of materials of instruction and a guide, not a passive hearer of recitations. Pestalozzi tried to organize instruction materials in each subject into its simplest terms and proceed to the more complex. In the study of geography, for instance, he began in the school yard, the village, the local river-side and the community, where the children learned by personal observation and then were led to a study of the world and its relation to man. He believed that the teacher-pupil relationship should be one of mutual love and friendliness, and the school room should be a pleasant environment not unlike the child's home.

Johann Friedrich Herbart (1776-1841), a German professor, was an educator, an admirer and supporter of Pestalozzi whom he often visited. However, where Pestalozzi stressed perception of the physical world and knowledge in geography, nature, drawing, and oral expression, Herbart emphasized history and literature and aimed his emphasis on personal character and social morality. Herbart held that character is the aim of education. Since the individual is destined to live in a society, then education must enable the individual in developing moral character without sacrificing individuality. Herbart taught that knowledge comes from two sources, nature and society. He contended that nature, including science and physical knowledge, was important but could not offer an opportunity for learning human relations and the moral aspect of education. Herbart believed that instruction must have four phases. It must be (1) concrete, (2) continuous, (3) elevating, and (4) must have application to life situations. Then he outlined the steps in teaching which were modified and extended by his disciples and came to be known as the five formal steps of method of the Herbartians: preparation, presentation, comparison, generalization, and application.

Friedrich Froebel (1782-1852) originated and advocated the introduction of the kindergarten. He believed in the principle of self activity in children and education through play, and he was especially concerned with the problem of creativity. Froebel was a strong advocate of learning by doing. He encouraged manual work, construction, games, songs, and dramatics in the learning process as a means of expression and development of creative powers. To become truly educated, Froebel believed that the senses, especially hearing and vision, had to be developed. Froebel's three great principles of education were: child development as the aim, motor expression as the method, and social cooperation as the means. These principles are as valid today as in his early kindergartens.

"SCIENTIFIC" EDUCATION

The seventeenth century witnessed a remarkable development in emphasis on scientific knowledge. Modern civilization probably has been influenced most strongly by the development of science. The sense-realists demanded a new content and a new method in education based on the study of nature and things real. The sense realist movement, initiated by Francis Bacon and best represented by

Comenius, met with vigorous opposition from the classicists and made limited progress during the seventeenth and eighteenth centuries. Bacon thought that science could be combined with theology to strengthen the dogma of the church, but church leaders were opposed to the experimental approach to education.

The development of science during the nineteenth century was remarkable. Many inventions and discoveries were made that revolutionized the lives of men. Such inventions as the cotton gin, the steamboat, the locomotive engine, the automobile, the telegraph, and the telephone changed man's working conditions and improved his transportation and communication. Discoveries such as antiseptics, chloroform, and vaccinations improved medicine and surgery. While all these inventions and discoveries were making history in the world about them, the schools and universities continued their formal, academic intellectualism in a world of their own, ignorant of the changes brought about by scientific advancements. This state of affairs led Herbert Spencer to publish his *Education* in 1861.

Herbert Spencer (1820-1903) formulated a new concept of culture which emphasized scientific and practical knowledge. He attacked the conventional curriculum with its classical emphasis and its stress upon the past and believed the study of history to be almost a waste of time. Sociology, and a study of how social factors affect society, were seen by Spencer to be more important than the study of past events. He did not believe that a subject was cultural in proportion to its remoteness from direct relationship to life. He could not see the schools and universities sticking to abstract, impractical classics oblivious to the changes in man's thinking due to the discoveries of science and the revolutions in political and social life. Spencer, in his essay *What Knowledge Is Most Worth,* lists five areas or activities which best prepare man for complete living. They are:

1. Activities related to preserving life and health.

2. Vocational activities related to earning a living.

3. Domestic activities related to family living.

4. Social and political activities related to citizenship.

5. Leisure activities related to gratification of tastes and feelings.

Spencer trumpeted the claims of science and scientific learning and demanded a place for them in the curriculum. By the end of the nineteenth century, largely due to his accomplishments, science was introduced into the curriculum on a level with the classics. Spencer's effects were especially felt in the United States where Harvard University introduced science--astronomy, natural philosophy, natural history--into the curriculum and began to supplement textbooks with laboratories. In 1825, Renssalaer Polytechnic Institute was established at Troy, New York, as a school for higher education in applied science and technology. Spencer's treatise, *Education*, became the best selling textbook for teacher training both in England and the United States.

SOCIALIZING EDUCATION

The sociologist regards the purpose of education as a preparation of man for successful participation in his society. They tend to minimize the humanistic and classic subjects and stress the social studies and sciences. Late in the nineteenth century, education was fairly well socialized and educators were pondering the problem of what should be taught just as in the century before they were concerned with how it should be taught. Educators began to ask what knowledge is of most worth in aiding the individual to take his place in society. The Church obviously had failed in fitting man to society and eighteenth century schools were doing little better.

The twentieth century schools began to make rapid strides towards socializing their curriculum. Professor John Dewey and his disciples had a profound effect upon the thinking of educators throughout the world. Scientific methods were applied to education. The state became conscious of the purpose of education, and universal and free public education became an established principle of a democratic government.

John Dewey succeeded in bringing the psychologist and

the sociologist, the individual and his society, together through his idea of *progressive education* which is based upon the spontaneous activity of the child and his social participation with other children. Dewey contended that education is life and not a preparation for life and the chief function of the school is to help children in cooperative and community living. Today's curriculum with its emphasis on memorization of facts, language, literature, form and other content subject matter is no longer a sacred method of education which must be learned in order for the child to be labeled "cultured." The education process is concerned both with the child and society. Dewey says, "the psychological and social sides are organically related, and that education cannot be regarded as a compromise between the two, or a super-imposition of one upon the other."[13]

Education, today, shows the cumulative influence of thinking men throughout the ages. It utilizes the concept and findings, as well as the methods, of psychology and sociology, in blending the rights of man with the laws of society. Educational programs change frequently and are sensitive to the needs and interests of children as well as being sensitive to the demands of society. This is education for real life and the real education that includes feeling as well as reason.

One of the movements which is emerging as a potential force in the motivation of sound education practice in today's schools is outdoor education and school camping. Although the roots of outdoor education go far back in history, the modern concept of using outdoor experience to supplement classroom learning rises out of the artificial and highly technical nature of society. Man has been separated from his heritage--the land.

This separation has come about so quickly and unconsciously that it has practically been unnoticed by the public. Only two generations ago formal schooling was planned to supplement the various activities of farm and home with a three or four month period of "book learning" during the winter months. The one room little red school house was

[13]John Dewey, My Pedagogic Creed. p. 6.

an adequate building for teaching reading, writing, and arithmetic. Here were all the required education tools that were needed. Training in initiative, resourcefulness, and thrift came in meeting the varied circumstances of their relatively simple environment.

They had no need for formal schooling in nature study as their lives were close to nature. Knowledge of nature and her workings became a part of the endowment of every man, woman, and child. They had no apparent need for such subjects as manual training, home economics, or physical education. Many things taught in the schools of today were common to the daily lives of children less than fifty years ago.

Within the past generation a great social change has come about. Educators can speak of respect for the individual and a more democratic and spiritual education, but must be too much concerned with buildings and equipment. The physical plant of the modern school receives more time and attention than the welfare of the children and the goals of education. Progress has come to be measured by large auditoriums, stadiums, and laboratories--all of which may hide a poorly organized and aimless educational program. Children once born on the farm and who spent their childhood in thé woods and open fields today are born in hospitals and reared in the cities. In the transition children have lost contact with nature. Consequently, larger school buildings are necessary to teach crafts, social science, natural science, home economics, physical education, and other subjects that were normal living situations two or three generations ago. Yet the education provided by consolidated schools and expensive buildings cannot satisfy the nature of children. They need experience in living, exploring, adventuring, and learning in the open space. Outdoor education can help fill this void.

SUMMARY

The history of educational practices and methods used by various civilizations prove interesting as they relate to the success and failure of each nation's progress.

Those nations which failed to progress socially, scientifically, morally, and educationally were dedicated to memorization of laws and other literature to perpetuate a fixed social order. New discoveries and new observations were not encouraged or recorded since all that was important in the minds of national leaders in the various countries had already been written.

In early primitive societies there was likewise very little progress noted. Man lived almost entirely from the earth and all his experiences and education concerned itself with the basic necessities for the maintenance of their families in providing food, clothing, and shelter. There was no literature or books for reading or gaining knowledge, and all education was handed down orally from one generation to another.

Good educational methods, including proper emphasis on outdoor educational methods, were inherent in the culture of those nations whose progress was most rapid and successful.

It is also quite obvious that when civilizations reverted back to memorization and near worship of existing written materials, and refused to explore nature and observe new things in life, there was invariably produced a static and decaying society.

The world's great philosophers and educators are continually cautioning school teachers in all countries that first-hand experience and direct experiences with nature and real life situations are most essential to understanding and improving existing texts and literature.

The outdoor education method is more urgently needed in today's schools in the United States because of the obvious lack of opportunities provided modern day youngsters for direct learning experiences of any kind.

Questions and Projects

1. What value for educational purposes may students gain from a year of travel *(das wanderjahr)* which is customary in Germany?

2. What conditions in colonial America existed which influenced their type of eduction? What are the conditioning forces affecting education today?

3. Name five natural tendencies of the child upon which education builds today.

4. What is character? To what extent is character building the goal of education?

5. Discuss the following as aims of education:
     a. to give culture
     b. to discipline the mind
     c. to fit into society

6. Discuss the dictum, "Things before words, " as a tenet of realism in education.

7. In every period of history man has sought new knowledge. Is new knowledge what is needed for a generation to progress?

8. List ten of the greatest educators of all time in your opinion. Under each educator list his contributions to the history of education.

9. Who were the educators in history that favored the outdoor education method of instruction?

10. Did the philosophy of education of the various civilizations in history affect their social and political welfare? What were the characteristics of the educational systems of those civilizations which prospered? Those which failed?

Selected References

Butts, R. Freeman, *A Cultural History of Western Education*. New York: McGraw-Hill Book Company, 1955.

Cole, Luella, *A History of Education*. New York: Rinehart and Company, 1950.

Cubberley, Ellwood P., *The History of Education*. Boston: Houghton Mifflin Company, 1920.

Dewey, John, *Philosophy and Civilization*. New York: Minton Balch and Company, 1931.

Duggan, Stephen, *A Student's Textbook in the History of Education*. New York: D. Appleton-Century Company, 1936.

Eby, Frederick, and Arrowood, Charles Flinn, *The History and Philosophy of Education Ancient and Medieval*. New York: Prentice-Hall, 1940.

Frank, Lawrence K., *Society as the Patient*. New Brunswick: Rutgers University Press, 1950.

Graves, Frank Pierreport, *A History of Education During the Middle Ages*. New York: The Macmillan Company, 1914.

_____*A History of Education in Modern Times*. New York: The Macmillan Company, 1914.

_____*A History of Education Before the Middle Ages*. New York: The Macmillan Company, 1915.

_____*A Student's History of Education*. New York: The Macmillan Company, 1922.

Kemp, E. L., *History of Education*. Philadelphia: J. B. Lippincott Company, 1912.

McCormick, Patrick.J., *History of Education*. Washington, D.C.: The Catholic Education Press, 1953.

Mayer, Frederick, *A History of Ancient and Medieval Philosophy*. New York: American Book Company, 1950.

Monroe, Paul, *A Brief Course in the History of Education*. New York: The Macmillan Company, 1935.

Morrow, H. I., *A History of Education in Antiquity*. New York: Sheed and Ward, 1956.

Mulhern, James, *A History of Education*. New York:
The Ronald Press Company, 1946.
Northrop, F. S. C., *The Meeting of East and West*. New
York: The Macmillan Company, 1947.
Taylor, F. Sherwood, *A Short History of Science and
Scientific Thought*. New York: W. W. Norton and
Company, 1951.
Thut, I. N., *The Story of Education, Philosophical and
Historical Foundations*. New York: McGraw-Hill
Book Company, 1957.

Chapter 5

THE DEVELOPMENT OF CAMPING IN THE UNITED STATES

Organized camping is the most significant contribution to education that America has given to the world.

—*Charles W. Eliot*

Progress in the acceptance of outdoor education as a learning technique has been hampered and retarded by incorrect assumptions and interpretations by parents and many educators. Until recently, the acceptance of outdoor education in many public schools has been restricted because of these false notions.

First, many parents and educators regard outdoor education as a camping program. The terms, *outdoor education* and *camping* are used synonymously. Many teachers and administrators hesitate to include outdoor education in their curriculum because they feel that they cannot afford the money required to develop a campsite and provide operating expenses year after year.

The truth is that outdoor education is the most inexpensive and most universally available method of education known. The classroom with all its appurtenances have been provided free by nature. Opportunities for good teaching and learning situations are just outside the classroom, across the street in the city part, outside the city limits with a sympathetic farmer, or down the street on a vacant lot which may become the school garden.

Starting on a small scale the teacher may introduce her children to the informal settings of learning in the out-of-doors through short nature hikes, longer field trips, a day on the farm, or an extended experience working in a school garden, operating a school forest, or cooking the noon meal in a day-camp situation.

Many public schools and youth serving agencies have bought land for educational purposes which is the next step after the above mentioned outdoor education experiences. If land is not available through public parks or other lands near-by which can be used for educational purposes, schools should consider purchasing land for this use.

School boards hesitate to buy land because of the fear of great expense in operating a camp--a second erroneous assumption. Too many educators regard a camp as many fine buildings with modern plumbing, power lines, athletic fields, swimming pools, and an expensive duplication of the physical plant in the city which has been transplanted to the woods.

This conception of a camp is not only expensive, but destroys the purpose for getting into the woods. When the woods are cleared away, the lands are leveled by the bull dozer, modern buildings are constructed, and the area sprayed for insects, the reason for moving to the woods has been eliminated.

A good camping program need not be expensive. Shelters can be provided by inexpensive tents; make-shift and temporary campsites can be built by the campers themselves. The basic needs can be improvised. Latrines can be constructed, drinking water can be hauled if necessary, an inexpensive well may be dug, or a chlorinating unit can be purchased very inexpensively. Generally speaking, the best camp is the one that requires the least amount of cash especially when that cash is unwisely used to improve on nature.

The third misconception concerning outdoor education is that camping is purely recreation; that it is fun and therefore cannot be education; and that recreation is not a worthy reason for spending taxpayers' money.

Camping can be educational as well as recreational; furthermore, the modern age has made recreational skills almost as important as educational skills. Early pioneers in camping kept both in mind. They did not spend time trying to decide which activities were educational and which were recreational. Many camps, both private and public, have set a good example for modern educators to follow.

The contributions made by the better camps are too important not to be considered in any discussion of outdoor education.

Camping is older than history. To the early prehistoric
tribes, camping and outdoor life was a year-round proposi-
tion; it was a part of their very existence, a way of life. Prehistoric man had to know the skills of camping because his
very life depended upon his ability to provide food, clothing,
shelter, and protection for himself and his family.

Down through the long centuries, history shows that
the greater part of man's existence on earth has been spent
in camping and living in the out-of-doors. The Bible speaks
of Moses and his people camping on the banks of streams,
by the shores of lakes, and in the mountains.

Centuries later, the Pilgrim Fathers landed on the
shores of America and found the Red Man living a primitive
existence and camping three hundred and sixty-five days a
year. Indians maintained life by learning the ways of wildlife in order to secure food, by utilizing herbs and roots for
medicinal purposes, by using the skins of animals for clothing and shelter, and, in short, sustaining life from nature's supply. Camping was the way of living of the Red
Man.

The Pilgrims themselves were forced to camp and
live in the out-of-doors for many years as they slowly
gained in their long quest in wresting a living from the
wilderness of the new continent.

As America developed and the frontier pushed to new
lands over and across the Alleghenies, the pioneers had to
develop skills in campcraft and in camping. The gold rush,
the Oregon Trail, the Santa Fe Trail and other events and
routes were rich in tradition and folklore of the early frontiersmen and explorers. As the early settlers made their
way across the continent during the middle years of the
nineteenth century, they camped along the way depending
upon slim rations and upon nature for food to carry them
over the long perilous trek. In those early days men knew
the out-of-doors because their very existence depended upon it and they lived the kind of life in which they were on

their own. These early pioneers were skilled in procuring food from the wilds, in outdoor cooking, in pitching camp, and all other skills in campcraft and living as comfortable as possible in the out-of-doors.

From the pages of early American history, many great scouts and famous frontiersmen learned the lessons of the wilderness so thoroughly that they made great contributions not only to history, but left to modern America a rich heritage in the folklore of their accomplishments. Among those who became famous for their knowledge and skill in campcraft and their exploits in the wilderness are Daniel Boone, Kit Carson, Davey Crockett, Adirondack Murray, Dan Beard and others who learned to live with nature.

At the time of the signing of the Constitution about 98 per cent of the country's population lived in rural areas, while today more than 60 per cent of the population live in cities. Since the days of the great pioneers and outdoorsmen the wilderness has been all but destroyed. Rural life has been largely supplanted by urban living. Camping, as a way of life, is no longer necessary. It has gone with the frontier, the wilderness, the open fields, and the rapidly diminishing forest lands.

Modern camping is an effort to re-create the life of the primitive man or the way of the pioneer during the early days of the country. Many parents, educators and business and professional men have realized the emptiness caused by the machine age, by industrialization, and urbanization, and have tried to revive camp life to enrich the highly sophisticated and artificial life of the modern age. Supporters of camping can see many basic values for developing character traits so essential in the preservation of a democracy. The work of various individuals and agencies in an attempt to recapture the traditions of the outdoor man and the heritage of the pioneers has resulted in the modern institution of organized camping.

The first campers did not have to get "back to nature" or to "head for the woods." They were already there. But as our nation became more industrialized and families moved to the cities, many far-seeing leaders could foresee the danger of boys and girls growing up without experience in the out-of-doors. This is especially true for those being reared on the concrete and asphalt of the cities in an artificial and highly congested life.

It is significant to note that the first three camps for children were established by men from three different professions--an educator, a minister, and a physician. An examination of the writing of these and other early pioneers in camping reveals that they were all educators in the best sense of the word. Their philosophy was sound and their objectives are, by and large, the objectives of the better camps today.

Gibson summarizes the objectives of camps of sixty years ago as follows:

1. To restore those values of life which come from living in the great out-of-doors.
2. To find joy in the simplicity of living.
3. To develop a love of nature and a study of all that God created for our enjoyment.
4. To play the game for the fun of playing and not for awards given or public recognition.
5. To rationalize the recreative impulse so that it may be a carry-over into later life.
6. To enrich life through healthful and simple pleasures.
7. To expose boys to the sound principle of work being the law of life and the love of work being the joy of life.
8. To invest boys with responsibility, personally, for others and with others.
9. To show boys that honor cannot be bought but must be won; that manliness, justice, truth, conscientiousness, have their own reward.
10. To reach boys through teaching; to mould them into men of stamina and character; to create in them a definite aim in life; to give them a conception of their Maker through an understanding of nature.
11. To lay foundations for loyalty, integrity, and respect for the rights of others.[1]

[1]H. W. Gibson, Camp Management, A Manual of Organized Camping. Cambridge, Mass.: The Murray Printing Co., 1923. pp. 1-5.

Today, organized camping is sponsored by many different
agencies and institutions, both public and private, and is
conducted for many different purposes. Many camp programs, although highly desirable and continuing to expand
and grow, have lost the basic objectives set up by the early
pioneers. Camp programs, in many cases, have fallen into
the rigid schedules, the blocks of time, the bells and whistles, and the formal classes because this is the accepted
way of handling youngsters.

Many other camps have come to mean a vacation, 100
per cent fun and recreation, a highly organized program of
competitive sports, a resort with caterers and servants,
and a place for the wealthy to get baby sitting service for
the summer.

Fortunately, these camps do not enjoy the prestige of
those camps that combine education with recreation, work
with play, and practice with theory. The better camps today provide for the needs and interest of all children, and
especially those needs that cannot be met in the city, in the
classroom, and in the home.

A look at the development and growth of the camping
movement in the United States reveals the work of many men
of vision. It is a history of a people becoming modern and
again re-discovering the tradition of the past, the joys and
the heritage of the pioneers, and a return to nature and a
life in the out-of-doors.

The summer camps originated in this country in the
last decades of the nineteenth century as private ventures
on the part of a few idealistic individuals who took boys off
the streets of cities and into the woods.

In addition to private camps, agencies, institutions and
organizations soon got into the camping business. Groups
sponsoring camps today include: church and welfare organizations, public and private schools, Boy Scouts, Girl Scouts,
Camp-fire Girls, Young Men's Christian Association, Young
Women's Christian Association, Boys Club of America, Salvation Army, 4-H Clubs, special interest agencies, families,
and many others.

THE PRIVATE CAMP

Today, many private camps have been established for twenty to fifty years. The older established camps which have done a good job, which are serving the real needs of children, and which have built up a faithful clientele through good will and service have become recognized institutions and continue to improve and set standards which other camps strive for.

In 1890, there were only two organized private camps. By 1900, there were twenty; by 1910, one-hundred and fifty. Today there are close to 15,000 camps. Each decade and each new year brings new camps, new developments and new experiments in the camping movement.

THE NORTH MOUNTAIN SCHOOL OF PHYSICAL CULTURE

The first private camp was established in 1876 at North Mountain, Pennsylvania, by Dr. Joseph Rothrock.

Dr. Rothrock, a physician, was very much interested in forestry, conservation, and boys. In an autobiographical sketch Dr. Rothrock writes:

> In 1876 I had the happy idea of taking weakly boys in summer out into camp life in the woods and under competent instruction, mingling exercises and study, so that pursuit of health could be combined with acquisition of practical knowledge outside the usual academic lines. I founded the school on North Mountain Luzerne County, Pennsylvania, and designated it a School of Physical Culture. There had been, I think, but a single attempt to do this work at an earlier period . . . . The multitude of such camps now (about 1913) shows that the seed fell into good ground.[2]

The North Mountain School of Physical Culture was located adjacent to the North Mountain House, a hotel thirty-three miles northeast of Wilkes-Barre. In the first camp there were twenty campers, twelve years of age or older, and five teachers who served as counselors. The campers

[2] Porter Sargent, Summer Camps. Boston: Porter Sargent, 1934. p. 45.

lived in tents, two boys to each, and they slept on rough beds. Meals were served in a large tent which was used as the dining room. The camp had several rowboats, a buckboard and two horses. Most of the boys brought rifles and shotguns which they used for target practice under supervision of the counselors. Other activities included deer drives, nature study, lariat throwing, swimming, boating, fishing, sketching, engineering, and Indian club swinging.

Dr. Rothrock's camping enterprise did not pay expenses and he turned the venture over to a Wilkes-Barre teacher the next summer and went on an Alaskan exploration. The teacher, a Mr. Taylor, with Herr Frank, an artist, conducted the camp during the summer of 1877 with a few boys and a narrower range of activities. That summer, Mr. Taylor met a Mr. Kelly at the North Mountain House and these two men joined together with plans for a large camp in 1878. They advertised in the *Philadelphia Bulletin* and in the *Wilkes-Barre Times* and again had a camp the next summer of about twenty boys. At the end of the season, the camp was disbanded, the bills and the counselors were paid "and as to profit, there wasn't any."

CAMP CHOCOURUA - 1881

One of the most significant figures in the development of camping was Ernest Balch. He developed a standard camp practice, set up the ideals, worked out the routine, developed the methods, and achieved a degree of success that was an inspiration to all those who knew him.

In July, 1880, Henry Blair and Stephen Balch hiked from Plymouth to Asquam Lake near Holderness, New Hampshire, and were impressed at the scenic beauty. They returned the following summer and camped on Burnt Island which they purchased for forty dollars. Here they established a boys' camp and named it Chocorua because of the excellent view of Chocorua Mountain, thirty miles away. There were only five boys in residence at the camp the first summer, ranging in age from twelve to sixteen years of age. Mr. Balch wrote, "This is the golden age of man . . . . prior to this period his ego is too plastic . . . .

later, too rigid. The life of a boys' camp was designed for this period. "3

Camp Chocorua lasted from 1881 to 1889. Its great success was due to its many pleasant features and its emphasis on reality. There was nothing artificial. It developed a sense of responsibility in the boys, both personally and for others, and gave everyone a share in carrying out the work of the camp. The boys were encouraged in everything that would tend to develop them physically, mentally, and morally. Working in the out-of-doors, they became strong and healthy both in body and mind. They built up their own world, their own high standard of honor, and worked face to face in a primary social group in which the laws governing conflicting interests were recognized and obeyed.

Members of the camp staff were in charge of camp improvements and the boys could put themselves under contract to do the work required for the accomplishment of the improvements and, in this way, earn credit to buy desired articles at the camp store. Thus, the boys were taught the value and use of money. Swimming and diving tests had to be passed before the boys were allowed to use the lake. The campers were divided into four groups which alternated on camp jobs. Every fourth day they were free of special duty. The camp had a chapel and published a camp newspaper--the *Golden Rod*.

CAMP HARVARD - 1882

Mr. William Ford Nichols and a fellow student of the Cambridge Theological Seminary started their camp in 1882 near Stow, Massachusetts. An article entitled "A Boy's Camp: Camp Harvard," which appeared in the *St. Nicholas Magazine* June, 1886, locates the camp "on the shore of one of New Hampshire's most picturesque lakes, about equi-distance from Winchenden, Massachusetts, and Rindge, New Hampshire." The camp operated a program similar to Camp Chocorua and stressed moral, mental, and physical

---

[3]H. W. Gibson, "History of Organized Camping" Camping Magazine,VII, February, 1936. p. 19.

development. Each camper was identified by a uniform with
"high red stockings" and a "stout red belt." In 1884, the
camp was taken over by Dr. Winthrop Talbot, son of the
dean of the Boston University Medical School, Dr. J. T.
Talbot. Dr. Talbot moved the camp to Lake Asquam and
renamed it Camp Asquam. It was through the efforts of
Dr. Talbot that the first Camp Conference and Leadership
Institute was held in Boston in April of 1903.

CAMP ALGONQUIN - 1886

Camp Algonquin was founded by Edwin DeMerritte in
1886 and continued under his leadership until 1929. At the
time of its closing after forty years it was the oldest existing private camp for boys. Dr. DeMerritte established
high standards and Camp Algonquin became well known for
its emphasis upon the study of nature. The camp was well
equipped with a nature library, microscopes, museum,
herbarium and a flower garden. One hour a day was devoted
to nature study. The boys worked eagerly and enthusiastically compiling lists of nature flora and fauna. Dr. DeMerritte said, "A camp should be educational, not only in the
development of character, but also in a close study of all
that God created for our enjoyment."

The early camps which sprang up in New England were
built around personalities rather than around fine buildings
and expensive equipment. The founders were men of unselfish motives, sympathetic understanding, tactful leadership, and employed sound principles of work, play, and
study. They were professional men, men of influence and
importance, and men possessing a creative and restless
spirit and a vision for better things for youth through outdoor education in a camping environment.

NATURE SCIENCE CAMP - 1890

Professor Albert L. Fontaine, head of the Department
of Science of the Rochester Free Academy, founded the
Nature Science Camp. The aims of the camp were to provide a good time for the camper, an opportunity for healthful activities in the out-of-doors, and cultivation of the love
of nature. The boys were charged nine dollars a week and

the camp period covered eight weeks in the month of July and August. Girls were accepted for a four-week period.

CAMP IDLEWILD - 1891

Camp Idlewild, established on the banks of Silver Lake, Massachusetts, was moved to its present location at Lake Winnipesaukee, New Hampshire, in 1894. It is the oldest private camp for boys that has been in continuous existence.

KEEWAYDIN CAMPS - 1893

Keewaydin Camp was founded by Judge A. S. Gregg, who got his inspiration for camp while a student at Gunnery School. The permanent camp site was chosen in 1897 when Camp Kahkow was established at Cancomgon Lake, some forty miles north of Moosehead Lake, Maine.

Other early New England private camps include Camp Shoconuit established in 1895 by Dr. Roland J. Mulford, former headmaster of the Ridgefield School, in the mountains of northern Pennsylvania; Pine Bluff Camp established by Dr. Henry S. Pettit on Long Island, New York; Camp Pasquaney founded by Dr. Edward S. Wilson on Newfoundland Lake, New Hampshire, in 1885; Camp Marienfeld founded by Dr. C. Hanford Henderson in 1896 at Chesham, New Hampshire; and Norway Pines Camp established in 1898 by Dr. W. A. Keyes at West Point, Maine.

Camp Greenbrier was the first camp established in the South. It is still in existence, at Alderson, West Virginia. Camp Greenbrier was established by Dr. Walter Hullehen.

Pioneers in western camps were Dr. William Monilaw's Camp Highland and Dr. John Spragne's Camp Minocqua, both established in Michigan in 1904. Indianola, the first camp in Wisconsin, was opened in 1907, and Mishawka, the first camp in Minnesota, in 1909.

Private camps started in New England but quickly spread to the South and West until today thousands of private camps are spread throughout the United States.

As early as 1910, attempts were made to organize camp personnel. In this year, the Camp Directors Associa-

tion of America was organized with Charles R. Scott elected
as the first president. In 1916, the National Association of
Directors of Girls Camps was organized with Charlotte
Gulick as president. In 1924, these two associations merged
into the Camp Directors Association and elected George Mey-
lan as President.

Two of the largest camp associations today are the
American Camping Association formed in 1935 with headquarters in Bradford Woods, Indiana, and The Association
of Private Camps, Inc. with headquarters in New York City.
These associations are dedicated to the betterment of camping through conferences, workshops, formulation of standards and assimilation of materials and exchange of ideas.

CHURCH CAMPS

Although one of the earliest attempts at camping was
under the auspices of a church, church leaders have been
slow to recognize the values inherent in a good camping
program. It was not until recent years that the church began to give serious attention to the use of land for the purpose of fostering Christian education.

The first church camp was established in 1880 by
Reverend H. H. Murray, pastor of the Park Street Church
in Boston. Reverend Murray wrote many excellent books
and articles on camping and outdoor life in the 1870's and
is regarded by many as the father of the great outdoor movement from which the camping movement sprang. He wrote:
"To such as are afflicted with that dire parent of ills,
dyspepsia, or have lurking in their system consumptive
tendencies . . . . I most earnestly recommend a month's
experience among the pines. " Many of Reverend Murray's
contemporaries knew that he also took healthy people on
excursions and used the guise of health cures as an excuse
to get to the woods.

GOOD WILL CAMPS - 1880

Reverend George W. Hinckley established the Good
Will Camps at Hinckley, Maine, in 1880. Reverend

Hinckley was greatly influenced by the writings of Reverend Murray, and when he became pastor of a church in West Hartford, Connecticut, he established a camp for boys for "moral and religious purposes." Reverend Hinckley writes of his camp.

> I cannot give much detailed information about the two camps on Gardiner's Island in 1880 and 1881, for I did not keep a journal or make any records at the time. My impression is that the first year there were seven boys in camp, including the three Chinese high school students who went with me from Connecticut. There were other boys in camp, former pupils of mine in the Kingston Public Schools where I had taught, but I did not regard them a part of my camping company.
>
> The equipment consisted of two or three tents, two rented towboats and a sail-boat of which we had the use on several occasions. Our cooking was done in the open and our dining facilities consisted of a long table built near the camp fire.
>
> We had in camp a regular daily program, such religious observances as seemed to me adapted to the group, story telling, swimming, boating, fishing, and an evening service. I thought that I had reached the height of dignity and had crowned my program with success when the Kingston Brass Band of about 20 pieces, as I remember it, spent a day in camp and gave a concert as a part of the program.[4]

The Good Will Camp program consisted of "religious and educational study, swimming, athletics, and evening entertainment."

SAINT ANN'S CAMP - 1882

The first Catholic boys' camp was founded in 1882 by the Marist Brothers of Saint Ann's Academy, New York City. The camp is located on Lake Champlain.

These three pioneer church camps were established by churchmen who were also statesmen and educators. The profit motive did not enter into the reason for founding the

[4]Porter Sargent, Summer Camps. Boston: Porter Sargent, 1934. p. 48.

camps. The unselfish devotion, sympathetic understanding, tactful leadership, and sound philosophy and principles of camping gave the first efforts at church camping high standards from the very beginning. Unfortunately, many church camps which followed became camp meetings, revivals, and conference meetings. This is not to say that such is not good, but a camp setting may be wasted for such activities that could just as well be carried out in the city or in the church building. Many church leaders, too, became academic in their approach and refused to see God except through the Bible. Although Jesus Christ, the master teacher, used the out-of-doors to teach his greatest parables, many church leaders today have to rely completely on the printed word of the Bible.

Today, the church camp is turning to the techniques of the Great Master Teacher. The camp serves a wide range of purposes but more and more is returning to the objectives of the first church camps and is placing emphasis on Christian living, fellowship, and closer communion with God and nature through living in the out-of-doors.

Outstanding church leaders throughout the nation are using camps to extend their program of Christian Education.

Today the best estimates place the number of church camps in the nation at around 5,000. During the past few years, practically all the major church denominations have developed some type of camping program. Camping as a means for broadening the base of Christian education is probably the newest and fastest growing trend or phase in Christian education.

SCHOOL CAMPS

School camping is not new to the American schools. The newness today comes as a matter of emphasis.

The school camp movement has grown most rapidly in the decade, 1949-1959. In 1949, there was a very limited number of school camps in operation. Today, school camping is found in at least thirty-five states. It is estimated that well over 300 school districts throughout the United

States are conducting either day camps of one week duration or resident camps for two days to two weeks.

Two approaches to school camping are found in the
United States--those that are school-centered and those that
are camp-centered. R. P. Brimm has outlined his concept
of the two approaches as follows:

SCHOOL-CENTERED

1. Camping experiences are evaluated on their contribution to the work of the classroom.
2. Experiences are planned in the classroom. Practical
   applications are possible in the camp so the experiences are more meaningful.
3. The program is centered around "classes" in mathematics, science, English, art, and other classroom
   subjects of the school. Time is given to recreational activities but this is not stressed.
4. The classroom teacher operates the program with the
   help of resource persons in much the same manner as
   a resource person is brought into the classroom.
5. Pupils are housed in comfortable cabins and their
   food is prepared by hired personnel. Occasional
   "cook-outs" give limited experiences in living in
   the open but this aspect of the camp is not considered highly important.

CAMP-CENTERED

1. Camping experiences supplement the school curriculum
   with new and different experiences which are not directly connected with the classroom work.
2. Experiences are not planned to bring out specific
   learnings but valuable concepts are gained by incidental experiences.
3. Recreation type activities dominate the program with
   "nature study" groups, "crafts" groups, and other
   activities which contribute to academic learnings
   but are not named to parallel the course offered in
   school.
4. A trained staff in outdoor education operates the
   program with the pupils and teachers participating.
5. Much time is devoted to living. Primitive living,
   including out-of-door cooking and building shelters,
   take a large portion of the time. One of the major

objectives of the camping experiences is recapturing some of the aspects of our pioneer ancestry.[5]

There is some controversy in determining which of the earliest camps was the first organized as a project in education. Most studies dealing with school camping give Frederick Williams Gunn, the founder of the Gunnery School for Boys in Washington, Connecticut, credit for establishing the first school camp. In the summer of 1861, Mr. and Mrs. Gunn took the entire student body of Gunnery School on a camping venture for two weeks. Mary Gunn Brinsmade gives an account of the first school camp:

> The School year was divided into two parts--the summer term from the middle of May to the end of September, and the winter term from the middle of November to the end of March.
>
> When the Civil War began, the boys were eager to be soldiers, to march, and especially to sleep in tents. They were given opportunity to roll up in blankets and sleep outdoors on the ground, and sometimes the whole school would camp for a night or two in this way at a lovely lake near by. In the summer of 1861, Mr. and Mrs. Gunn took the whole school on a hike, or gypsy trip, as it was called, about four miles to Milford, on the Sound, near New Haven. This trip took two days. The tents, baggage, supplies, etc., were carried in a large market wagon. There were also a few comfortable carriages and two donkeys, but many walked much, and some of the boys all of the way. Camp was established on the beach at Welch's Point and named Camp Comfort. Here two happy weeks were spent boating, sailing, fishing and tramping. This proved such a helpful and delightful experience that Mr. Gunn repeated it in the years of 1863 and 1865. Old boys came back to join the merry troop, and with friends of the school, some of them ladies, made up a party of sixty or more in the following trips.
>
> At a later period this seaside jaunt gave place to a Gunnery Camp at Point Beautiful on Lake Waramaug, seven miles from the school, and for twelve years the school spent two weeks in August, camping in this picturesque and delightful spot. The Gunnery was one of the latest

[5]R. P. Brimm, "What Are the Issues in Camping and Outdoor Education?" Camping Magazine, January, 1959. pp. 14-15.

schools to adopt the long summer vacation and this
change eliminated the summer camp.[6]

In 1893, a Judge Clark established the Keewaydin
Camps and gave credit to his old schoolmaster for the origin of the camping idea. Judge Clark writes,

> In 1872, the year of my birth, Mr. Frederick William
> Gunn, the Master of the Gunnery School in Washington,
> Connecticut, came to the conclusion that the summer
> vacation was too long for the average school boy. Mr.
> Gunn thought it would be better to have the boys occu-
> pied during the summer time; and so in that year he es-
> tablished the Gunnery Camp on the shores of Lake Wara-
> maug in Washington, Conn., and took practically all of
> his pupils with him to this camp for the summer. This
> camp was in no way a summer school. It was a regular
> camp, in which the time was spent, not in studies, but
> in recreation and general training. This camp was con-
> tinued for many years. In the fall of 1880, when I was
> eight years old, I became a pupil of Mr. Gunn's at the
> Gunnery School. Mr. Gunn died a few years afterwards
> and the Gunnery Camp was discontinued at the time of
> his death.[7]

Although one of the earliest camps, if not the very
first one, was established for educational purposes, the
public schools have been exceedingly slow to develop school
camping.

One of the first public school ventures in camping was
in 1912 when the Board of Education in Dubuque, Iowa, co-
operated with the visiting Nurse Association in establishing
a summer camp for mal-nourished school children.

In 1917, J. Madison Taylor of Temple University proposed that "each state provide, as part of its education system, a vacation camp for boys." He proposed a program
for thirteen to fifteen year old boys in the out-of-doors and
in a camping environment which would aid the boys in knowledges, skills, and appreciations in health, growth, character, teamwork, patriotic citizenship, group spirit, leadership, nature and the development of knowledge and skill.

[6]Porter Sargent, Summer Camps. Boston, 1934. p. 44.
[7]Ibid. p. 45.

In 1919, the Chicago Public schools established a camp for normal boys in cooperation with the War Department and Association of Business Men. It was primarily a R. O. T. C. camp but activities such as sports, lectures, campfire programs and crafts were included in the program. The camp, known as Camp Roosevelt, was directed by Major F. L. Beals.

In 1925, the Irvington Health Camp was established at Irvington, New Jersey, and was partially financed and supported by the Board of Education. The camp, still in existence, has a recreational program for one-hundred undernourished and underprivileged children between the ages of seven and fourteen who spend four weeks at camp.

Clear Creek Camp of the Los Angeles City school system has provided school camp programs supported by the public schools beginning as early as 1925. Each year educators of the Los Angeles school system, impressed with the educational values of camping, improve and expand camping opportunities for their children. Outdoor education study groups and curriculum committees have developed valuable guides for conducting school camping programs.

By the early 1930's, at least seven cities in the United States had camps maintained or directed by Boards of Education. These cities were Chicago, Dallas, Dearborn, Jersey City, and Lacrosse, Oshkosh, and West Allis, Wisconsin.

One of the most noteworthy projects in school camping is the community school camp program organized by the Kellogg Foundation in the communities of Lakeview, Otsego, and Decatur, Michigan. Each community organized a camp committee composed of parents, teachers, and campers to work out the purposes and details of the camp sessions. During the pre-camp period, counselors and teachers worked with the students in preparation for a two-week camp session. The program was planned in terms of developing work experience, healthful living, leisure pursuits, and social living.

New York City, with backing from Superintendent

Jansen, has conducted camp programs for public school children for several years. Dr. L. B. Sharp, working closely with school personnel of New York City, conducted an experiment in school camping which proved the educational value of camping in a scientific study with two control groups. Dr. Sharp wrote of the story of New York City's research in outdoor education in his book, *Extending Education Through School Camping*.

Many other school systems in all parts of the United States are seeing the educational value of outdoor education programs. The states of Michigan, California, Illinois, Texas, New Jersey, Wisconsin and Indiana are leading the way in getting children out of the classroom for first-hand and meaningful experience in the out-of-doors. Michigan, with over a hundred school systems participating in school camping, has over three times that number engaging in field trips, day camps, school forests and a variety of other outdoor education activities.

Educational literature contains an increasing volume of materials on the value of camping experience. Numerous educational leaders have advocated the establishment of camping programs as a part of the public school system and there are some predictions that the movement will expand rapidly. This point of view was expressed in an article appearing in a national magazine as follows:

> "All signs suggest that the extension of public school camping will be the next major development in American education. This, say the educators, is as it should be if we really care about eliminating the great disparity in educational opportunity for children of high income and low income families.[8]

Colleges and universities are operating camps for developing leaders in outdoor education, providing laboratories for many subject matter areas, and providing facilities for the development of true concepts of democratic group living, conservation education, healthful outdoor living, and leisure-time education.

[8]Amy Porter, "Open-air Schools", Collier's, 120:23 March 1, 1947.

Over fifty colleges and universities own or lease camp property and approximately three-hundred more include camp leadership courses in the college curriculum.

AGENCY CAMPS

Many agencies, institutions, and civic organizations are conducting camps for their members as an aid to carrying out their many and varied objectives. It is practically impossible to develop the history and growth of camping for all groups, but some of the organizations better known for their use of camping are described. In addition to these, camps are conducted by the Audubon Society, Catholic Youth Organization, Community Chests and Welfare Boards, Four-H Clubs, Jewish Welfare Board, Settlement Houses, Woodcraft Rangers, Young Men's Hebrew Associations, Young Women's Hebrew Associations, Lionist Youth Commission, and many other organizations and agencies, both private and public.

YOUNG MEN'S CHRISTIAN ASSOCIATION CAMPS

One of the first organizations to utilize camping as an activity was the Y. M. C. A. In the summer of 1885, Sumner F. Dudley, a young businessman associated with his father and brother in the manufacture of surgical instruments, borrowed a tent, hired a boat and traveled with seven boys belonging to the Y. M. C. A. to Pine Point on Orange Lake, about six miles from Newburgh. This was probably the first camping venture held by the Young Men's Christian Association. Mr. Dudley had an ardent love for outdoor life and his genial personality and unbounded enthusiasm permeated the camp. The boys had a wonderful time and the camp grew.

The next summer, Mr. Dudleys' camping party grew to twenty-three boys and was moved to Lake Wawayanda, New Jersey. In 1891, the camp had increased to eighty-three and a new location was found on Lake Champlain near Westport, New York. The location was owned by a Mr. J. H. Worman, editor of *Outing* magazine, and a good friend of Mr. Dudley. It was on this site that the camp was permanently established.

From this early beginning in 1885 with seven campers and an enthusiastic young businessman who loved boys and loved the outdoors, the Young Men's Christian Association has developed a world-wide camping movement serving many thousands of boys in all parts of the world.

FRESH AIR CAMPS

Probably the earliest camps developed primarily for the promotion of health of children were started as a part of the social service of New York City. The Children's Fresh Air Society of New York established a camp on Staten Island as early as 1872 to get the children off the congested streets of New York City and out where the air was fresh, thus, the fresh air camp. The *New York Times* and the *New York Tribune* gave the camp much publicity and money was donated in sufficient sums to carry out the project.

Since this early beginning many fresh-air camps are sponsored throughout the United States by municipalities, by newspapers, and by many and varied groups both public and private.

New Britain, Connecticut, every year operates a fresh air camp, taking several children into the beautiful Connecticut woods. The school principals of the city schools help select children who would not otherwise be able to attend a camp and who would be most likely to benefit from such an experience. Many other municipalities operate fresh air and health camps for children who need outdoor experience for health care.

BOYS CLUB CAMPS

In 1900, the first Boys Club camp was organized by the Boys' Club Fraternity in Salem, Massachusetts. During July and August of that year, seventy-six boys joined a seven-week camp which was held at Towley, Massachusetts, and Hampton Falls, New Hampshire.

The literature of the Boys Club organization today

202

reveals that many thousands of boys are given camping experience each summer by the Boys Club.

BOY SCOUT CAMPS

Although the activities of the Boy Scouts are not confined to camping, many of the scouting activities are built around out-of-door life.

The Boy Scouts of America was incorporated in February 8, 1910, and headquarters were established in New York City. The men who met that February day were Dan Beard, Ernest Seton-Thompson, James E. West, Colin H. Livingston, George Pratt, Mortimer Schiff and others.

It did not take long for the Boy Scouts to become highly organized. The first council camps began to operate as early as 1911 in many cities, including New York, Philadelphia, Boston, and Columbus.

The Boy Scouts have several good publications on camp standards, and program guides. As they stress nature and the out-of-doors, many of their merit badge pamphlets assist the leaders in guiding their scouts to more knowledge and understanding in outdoor cooking, knowledge of botany, astronomy, campcraft and practically every area of outdoor life.

Today the Boy Scouts probably operate more camps and serve more boys each summer than any other one agency in America.

GIRL SCOUT CAMPS

Girl Scouting in the United States was first organized in 1912 at Savannah, Georgia, by Juliette Low. She founded the first Girl Scout Camp near Savannah during that year. Mrs. Low's purpose was to provide simple living under camp conditions for as many girls as possible.

The growth of Girl Scout Camping since World War II is nothing short of phenomenal. The Girl Scouts have set up camp standards and held a nation-wide training program at their summer camps each year to assure leadership for their camping programs. They insist on small-unit camping and discourage mass participation.

The Girl Scouts publish many excellent materials to assist their leaders in conducting a camp. Their philosophy is good, their camps are as close to nature and primitive camping as they can get them, and they stress educational as well as recreational objectives.

The Girl Scouts report more and more the use of their campsites for winter use during weekends and holidays.

Other organizations and agencies sponsoring camps include the Young Women's Christian Association.

SUMMARY

Camping today is conducted by many different agencies for many different purposes, including health, character, recreation, education, and citizenship. Every organization and agency has set up a list of general and specific objectives which they wish to carry out in their camping programs. Camps are sponsored by social agencies, public and private philanthropic agencies, by local, state, and national government agencies, by municipal departments of health and recreation, by state boards of health, by many religious and church groups, by boards of education of city public schools, by teachers colleges, by state departments of education, and by public and privately supported colleges and universities.

Although Mr. and Mrs. F. W. Gunn are credited with the establishment of the first organized camp in the United States, Ernest Balch is recognized as the founder of the movement. It was through his efforts and his writings that the present pattern of organized camping was established.

The present number of organized camps in the United States is unknown because of the absence of any agency serving as a clearing house for the reports of all the varieties and types of camps.

The Camp-School Research Bureau reported that there were some 10,000 camps in the United States in 1947.

Robert McBride in his study for the American Camping Association--*Camping At The Mid-Century*--estimated that there were approximately 14,300 camps in the United States in 1952 which served at least 4,000,000 campers.

Camp facilities in the United States are grossly inadequate. Camping opportunities today are not reaching all the children who may profit from their program. Private camps, for the most part, provide opportunities to children of wealthy families and a small percentage of underprivileged children are provided camp experience by various charity organizations. A small number of the middle class youth may go camping if they belong to an organization that provides camping programs to its members.

Public support to offer camping for all children has not yet been provided. This seems to be the next major emphasis in curriculum development in the public schools of America.

Questions and Projects

1. How do the objectives of church camping differ from those of school camping?

2. How do the objectives listed by Gibson for the camps of 60 years ago differ from those of today?

3. Committees or individuals in class may be appointed to do further research into the historical development of:
   church camping,   Y. W. C. A. camps,
   school camping,   Boy Scout Camping,
   private camping,   Girl Scout camping,
   Y. M. C. A. camping,   Other assigned camps.

4. What has been the influence of current educational philosophy upon camping programs?

5. Write for more information on the history and development of some of the better known and older private camps such as camp Idlewild.

6. Read the recent literature on school camping to determine what leading educators think of the future of camping in the public schools.

7. How do you account for the fact that school camping was established as early as 1861 but has developed very little excepting in recent years?

8. Camping has been fostered for many purposes by many groups. What are the chief purposes of church camping? School camping?

9. Visit camps in your area. Do the type of buildings, the amount and kind of services and facilities, and the general lay-out of the camp tell you anything as to the philosophy and purposes of the camp?

Selected References

Department of Supervision and Curriculum Development, *Toward a New Curriculum*. Washington, D. C. : National Education Association, 1944.

Ledlie, John A. and Roehm, Ralph D. *Handbook of Y. M. C. A., Camp Administration*. New York: Association Press, 1949.

McBride, Robert, *Camping at The Mid-Century*. Bradford Woods, Indiana: American Camping Association, 1953.

Rubin, Robert, *The Book of Camping*. New York: Association Press, 1949.

Sargent, Porter, *Summer Camps*. Boston: Porter Sargent, 1934.

Sheeder, Franklin I., "Church Camping", *International Journal of Religious Education*. March, 1958.

Chapter 6

MODERN CONCEPTS OF OUTDOOR EDUCATION

WE LEARN WHAT WE LIVE

An outdoor education program is not to be regarded as a panacea for all the weaknesses in education. It is not a substitute for any existing subject matter curricula. It cannot replace the many course offerings now provided to students. Outdoor education should not be considered as an additional subject or an additional requirement of an already crowded curricula. It should not be regarded as being more important than one or another department either in high school or college. Outdoor education is not an extra-curricular activity.

Outdoor education is the means by which each teacher at every grade level uses nature and outdoor experiences to make the subject matter being taught more meaningful. It is a method, an environment, and it applies to all areas of learning and at all levels of instruction.

Social and economic conditions today make it more imperative than ever that youth be provided with adequate experiences and enjoyment of the out-of-doors.

It is an accepted fact that most textbooks now used in schools are based on experiences of the individual writers. Without these experiences they would not have been able to write their books.

One of the concepts of outdoor education is to allow students to share some of the experiences that were lived by the author and were the foundations for the facts and principles of the texts.

Another modern concept of outdoor education consists in an appeal to take the student out of the classroom and plan activities wherein they may live and learn first-hand what is being taught in the classroom. These experiences may be necessary only in a few instances in some subject matter areas. They might involve frequent trips in other subjects. Some areas of the curriculum might benefit from an extended program of one week's duration or more.

Many educators feel that students develop interests in problems and experiences from reading and class discussions that cannot be satisfied in the classroom. The teacher whets the appetite but it is too soon shut off because of classroom limitations or when the bell signals the next class.

In many classes students are required to memorize many outstanding pieces of literature and a great deal of subject matter content. The actual value of this work to the student and the usable knowledge is based on the results of experiences the learner has had in relation to what is memorized. Here is where many teachers have an opportunity to provide experience for the students which are directly related or closely related to the subject matters taught.

The most noted national leader in developing the modern day philosophy and school programs in outdoor education is Dr. L. B. Sharp. Dr. Sharp has frequently spelled out the aims and objectives of outdoor education. He conducted the only research of note in outdoor education when he, in cooperation with the public schools of New York City, set up a control group to test whether a three and one-half week session in school camping contributed as much as the classroom in the education of children. The results of these tests, says Dr. Sharp, is why he is still working in and promoting outdoor education. Most of the literature appearing in various states can be traced back to philosophical statements made by Dr. Sharp. School men, church leaders, and agency directors from all parts of the country have learned the theory behind and the objectives of outdoor education by putting them into practice at National Camp. Under the direction of Dr. Sharp, workshops are conducted every summer at National Camp for Church groups, for teachers, and for agency leaders.

Some of the principles set forth by Dr. Sharp are:

1. Those things which should be learned and can best be learned through direct experience in life situations outside the classroom should be learned there.

2. We learn faster, we retain longer and we have a deeper appreciation and understanding of those things we get first-hand.

3. Outdoor education comprises all the learning that can be attained in the out-of-doors.

4. The philosophy of outdoor education applies in any situation, in any organization, in any group, wherever learning takes place, because it deals directly with how well we learn and how much appreciation and understanding comes as a result of that learning.

5. In order to understand their dependence on natural resources--in order to learn to use them fully and wisely --our young citizens must have first-hand experiences with them.

6. Outdoor education, offered under competent leadership, adds to the strength and wisdom of our citizenry and thereby to our national security.

7. Man is fundamentally dependent on the out-of-doors. This dependence has, through the ages, shaped the development of all his cultures. Only through an understanding of his relationship to his non-artificial environment can he properly distinguish those things which are truly essential to his survival and progress.

8. For modern man, the knowledge of his ultimate dependence on the out-of-doors is often obscure. Removed from close contact with natural resources, he becomes less and less aware of them. He is increasingly separated from the fundamental experiences of mankind.

A preliminary survey just completed by the authors reveal that some type of outdoor education is practiced in every state in the country. Innumerable schools throughout the nation are conducting nature hikes, field trips, and activities outside the school to emphasize or motivate classroom learning. Others have acquired land for sanctuaries, school farms, school gardens, school forests, school camps and other educational uses. Information concerning these programs were made available through the state departments of public instruction, state departments of conservation, state departments of parks and state departments of forestry.

Many of the programs in outdoor education now in existence throughout the United States have developed into sizable and well recognized educational contributions. A brief survey of the philosophy and objectives of some of these public school programs in various parts of the country might indicate what the basic concepts of outdoor education programs are.

ATLANTA (GEORGIA) OUTDOOR EDUCATION PROGRAM[1]

The Atlanta Public Schools pioneered in the field of outdoor education during the years prior to World War II. The war stopped the program until recently. Yet, educators in Atlanta proved that a day or week in the outdoors can be of equal or greater value than the same time spent in a classroom.

Moving the classroom into a camp environment for outdoor education is proving to be one of the most promising extensions of the American school program. Most cities entering this phase of education start by using existing state, agency, or private camps. About a dozen camps have indicated willingness to cooperate with the schools of Atlanta. During the year 1954-55, four schools participated in the program. In 1955-56, seventeen schools sent groups to camp for three to five days. Several others made field trips to farms for one day's time.

[1] Board of Education, Atlanta Public Schools, "Let's Go Camping", (mimeographed bulletin) Atlanta, Georgia, 1956.

PHILOSOPHY

The basic philosophy must be in agreement with the overall educational objectives in Atlanta. Procedure must be made on the assumption that education is the chief aim of the outdoor program, with enjoyment on the part of the camper as a means toward this end. The intention, and this is a basic objective, is to provide the essential real-life situations in an outdoor camp and farm environment which could not be accomplished as well, or not at all, in a school room. Experiences must grow out of the class-room into the broader horizon of the outdoors, yet be integrated as a part of the continuing education of a child in the Atlanta schools' program. Outdoor education is to be the concern of the whole educational program. Every resource must be used to enable pupils to have real acquaintance with the wild outdoors, agriculture, rural life and industry.

As a means to achieve the goals or objectives of education, outdoor education in a camp or farm environment is most effective. The outdoors offers a splendid laboratory for learning. It brings youth into first-hand contact with natural and human resources in pleasant situations. In the woods, by a lake or stream, on a farm and at rural industries, children can smell, hear, see, and feel reality.

In the wide open spaces about the camp and farm, on silent friendly trails deep in the woods there are endless varieties of nature to be examined. Opportunities exist for meaningful work experiences. These satisfying situations, growing out of the classroom in the city into country environment, do much to develop wholesome attitudes (values) which result in improved patterns of behavior as well as adding to knowledge and understanding.

The natural environment undergirds civilization. A society which is rapidly becoming urban can easily lose sight of this basic reality. Outdoor education makes use of:

1. Wildlife in its natural environment
2. Man-made controls (dams and other conservation controls)
3. Agriculture
4. Rural Industry
5. Recreation skills for the outdoors

With continued approach to more leisure time for adults, children must be prepared for recreation in the great outdoors. This program provides an ideal laboratory for teaching and the learning of skills, attitudes and appreciations necessary for maximum use of the outdoors for better living.

Camping stands high on the roster of desirable activities. It is a pastime in which the individual, family, or group can become participants.

OBJECTIVES

The objectives of camping as formulated by the schools of Atlanta are listed in terms of the opportunities provided teachers and students in the out-of-doors:

1. Enriching the curriculum by providing real-life experience in the outdoors and better acquaintance with agriculture and rural industry.
2. Practicing democratic procedures.
3. Developing leadership, followership and the spirit and practice of successful cooperative endeavor.
4. Developing an attitude of social responsibility and an insight into the nature of a social group.
5. Fun, wholesome recreation, and the making of new desirable friendships.
6. Helping children see that educational standards of conduct based upon commonly accepted religious principles are valid guides to personal-conduct and result in better relations.
7. Allowing children to try out new situations and develop new worthwhile interests.
8. Understanding themselves as worthwhile individuals.
9. Learning how to get along with their peers and adults.
10. Better pupil-teacher relations through understanding (not likely to be possible in a regular school day.)
11. To make sound plans and carry them out.
12. To take responsibility based upon their maturity.
13. To face new problems with intelligence and fortitude.
14. To be a worthy citizen in a free society.

PROGRAM

It is impossible to say just when outdoor education first came into the Atlanta school program. Like many other subject matter areas and activities, it started with an occasional field trip by a class or club taking off to the woods, farm, or camp. Along with several other elementary and junior high schools, the Atlanta Superintendent, Dr. Ira Jarrell then principal, took her seventh grade class camping for a school week each spring. This program was dropped at the outbreak of World War II.

Since 1952, West Fulton High and Inman Park School have each spring provided a three to five day camp experience for pupils. In 1954, the Department of Club Activities was formed and the Director was instructed to begin establishing a pilot outdoor educational program as soon as possible after establishing an adequate program of organized group activities in schools.

It is intended that all schools shall eventually participate in the program. A grade level is to be determined both for the elementary and the high schools.

BATTLE CREEK (MICHIGAN) OUTDOOR EDUCATION PROGRAM[2]

The justification of a school camp program rests on certain basic tenets of present day education. These are:

1. The modern curriculum is developmental, based on real experiences that meet the needs of children and change their behavior patterns toward good citizenship and full individual life.
2. General education is aimed at a common core of learning necessary for each individual in a democratic society.
3. The modern school is concerned with the growth and development of the whole child in all areas of his living.

[2] Battle Creek Public Schools, A Camping We Will Go. Battle Creek, Michigan: Division of Instruction 1957.

With these objectives in mind, it is logical to assume that the function of the classroom is changing and that educational experience must extend outward from the classroom as needs and experiences indicate, into areas where appropriate learning can take place more naturally, more efficiently, and more effectively.

The modern school is doing this in various ways such as field trips, community studies, supervised play and recreation, school farms and camps. The camp, then, should serve basically as a laboratory of the classroom group to meet some of the aims which are difficult to meet within the four walls of the school.

Camping at Clear Lake Michigan is viewed as an extension of the classroom as well as the home and the immediate neighborhood. Parents, teachers and counselors search out almost unlimited opportunities for learning which are especially evident in this particularly "raw" environment.

Middle grade boys and girls welcome becoming better and more richly acquainted with the many factors in their physical environment. These years can be particularly fruitful ones for capitalizing upon and setting the circumstances to build seeking behavior--forward-reaching and out-reaching behavior. Because boys and girls are able to cope with the ideas, their interests center mainly around investigating more intensively the "why" and "what" of the here and now. They seem to feel a need to find out how these things come to be and begin dreaming of what they can become. They are working at the task of figuring out their places in the cosmos. They are growing up. They are differentiating more clearly between reality and fantasy.

The Clear Lake Camp, when it is skillfully and thoughtfully utilized, can contribute uniquely to the following:

A. To the development of intellectual powers toward which middle graders are reaching.

B. To the building of awarenesses within children of the values, skills, and understandings which constitute these intellectual powers.

The following are some intellectual abilities which can be developed in varying degrees:

1. To perceive more fully and clearly.
2. To verbalize what is perceived.
3. To analyze factors in a simply structured situation.
4. To recall related learnings from past experiences.
5. To know what constitutes a pertinent problem.
6. To define a pertinent problem.
7. To compare and to contrast.
8. To find similarities and differences.
9. To recognize cause and effect.
10. To understand and to experience a complete process.
11. To see relationships and interrelationships within system in nature.
12. To know the process of problem-solving.
13. To arrive at generalizations from enough real specifics.
14. To find relevant questions and information.
15. To sort out the irrelevant from the relevant.

The descriptions of learning experiences which follow are offered as resources to teachers to aid them in planning for children's learning and in planning with children for their learning.

The camp counselors are resource people available as co-leaders who have most of the technical knowledge suggested in many of these experiences. Counselors work upon request in classrooms previous to the camp period, during the camp period, and are available for work with interested parent groups.

WESTERN NEW YORK STATE OUTDOOR EDUCATION PROGRAM[3]

A definition of outdoor education would include activities and experiences ranging from short field trips in the

---

[3] Western New York School Study Council, A Guide To School Camping and Outdoor Education. (mimeographed bulletin) Buffalo, New York: The University of Buffalo, 1959.

environment of the school to attending a school camp. Such activities and experiences are directed towards learning to live at one's best level within the cultural and natural environment. The use of the out-of-doors as a living laboratory for the study of many subjects of the curriculum, such as science, social studies, agriculture, health and physical education has been a practice for many years.

That this approach is considered important is indicated in the following statement, found in the pamphlet *Exploring the Environment,* published by the New York State Department of Education in 1943: "The immediate environment is one of the first areas to be utilized in any educational program. This is true whether we are experiencing our first lessons in geography, studying the background of community life, or attempting to learn something regarding our responsibilities as citizens. No matter how far from home lessons may lead, one always returns to the local environment for any realistic interpretation as to the impact of these factors on one's daily life and living."

Camping experiences ranging from day camping to resident camping have been provided by many school districts over the country. Camps conducted by private and civic organizations during the summer months have gained wide public acceptance. Such experiences are viewed as a most valuable contribution to the development and education of boys and girls.

In communities where schools have provided some camp experiences for pupils during the school year, membership in voluntary organizations which have a summer camp program has increased. In other words, experience in the school's camp gave the child the fundamentals of outdoor living. This, in turn, increased his appetite for participation during the summer months in camps conducted by private and voluntary agencies.

Some of the objectives of outdoor education have been stated as follows:

1. An appreciation and understanding of the natural environment through the use of the out-of-doors as a living laboratory.

2. The development of desirable traits of character and citizenship.
3. The development and maintenance of physical fitness and the practice of healthful living.
4. Knowledge and appreciation of the conservation and wise use of natural resources.
5. The development of outdoor living skills, knowledge and attitudes for the worthy use of leisure.
6. The acceptance of responsibility for one's share of the work in connection with outdoor education projects and camp chores.

Outdoor education, particularly school camping, provides on-the-land experiences for the education of boys and girls in the conservation and wise use of natural resources. The New York State Departments of Conservation and Education, as well as similar departments in other states, have been working together to improve the conservation education program in schools and colleges. One tangible evidence of such cooperation is the 1956 bulletin, *Using Natural Resources Wisely*, issued by the Bureaus of Elementary and Secondary Curriculum Development. The foreword in this bulletin includes the following statement - "It has long been recognized that the continued strength and prosperity of our people rests upon the wise use of natural resources; that intelligent resource management and national and international conditions affecting resources require sound conservation education."

"Demands upon our national resources, however, have been increasing in recent years due to repeated wars and to rising living standards for an expanding population. Now we must add aid for other countries and the drain of long-term national resource-use have become acute. Never has conservation education been of more far-reaching importance to the people of our State and Nation."

State and national conservation departments have issued many bulletins and materials which are available to school districts and colleges concerned with programs of conservation education.

Outdoor education thus provides a unity of living experiences for the child. In the surroundings of nature, teachers and other professional personnel work together as a

unit in guiding the well-rounded development and education
of boys and girls. Today's students will be tomorrow's
citizens; how they learn and what they learn are important.

THE SCOPE OF OUTDOOR EDUCATION

For many children, summer has been the time for
outdoor living: in the street, on the playground, in the park,
on farms, or at camp. Now that outdoor education is taking
its place in the school curriculum, the child may look forward to the integration of more of his interests into his
formal education. Besides enjoying outdoor living in the
summer, he may find that it can also be a year-round
activity.

Outdoor education consists of those learning experiences which are dependent upon, and grow out of, the natural environment. Varying with local situations, many different persons may direct these outdoor learning experiences of the child.

Often the first group to introduce the natural environment to the youngster is the family. Family camping has
become increasingly popular during the past few years, with
the result that many agencies are now opening camps for
such family activity. While this introduction to the out-of-
doors gives the child the protection and companionship of
his family, it may not permit him to explore and develop
skills on his own.

Many children have their first glimpse of outdoor life
through outings with various organizations, such as Boy
Scouts, Campfire Girls, Girl Scouts, and Y groups. All of
these give the child first-hand experiences with nature but
limitations of funds, facilities, and adult leadership restrict
the number of children who can profit from the camping
activities of these organizations.

Private camps, also, can be a means for some children
to attain a knowledge of the out-of-doors; but the expense of
private camping is often a deterring factor. Another dis-
advantage for the child is the possibility that few of his
friends may be with him.

Therefore, the introduction of outdoor education into the school curriculum means that for the first time nearly every child, together with his friends and his teachers, may enjoy the education provided by the natural environment, free from classroom restrictions.

The success and the value of outdoor education activities in the school depend on their integration into the regular curriculum. The program of outdoor education should not be conducted as an extra day, week or month attached to the school year, but on school time during the regular school year. Camping and outdoor education activities which fall outside of these times are extra-curricular activities and are perhaps better left to agencies outside of the school.

The school camp and other outdoor education activities are directed, not by full-time specialists, but by the individual classroom teachers, who take their own classes out for their mutual benefit. They may call upon others to assist them in their program, but the direction of the program is in the hands of the teacher and the class. This time in the out-of-doors is not something isolated from the day-to-day work of the classroom but is an integral part of the curriculum, from a new and exciting vantage point.

Outdoor education programs are usually presented in a progression designed to help the student adapt to the new setting. It may begin with a few hours spent on a field trip, develop into a series of day camp trips, and culminate in a camping experience of five or ten days and nights. This progression may be accomplished within one school year, or several.

A class may undertake no more than a nature study at a local park and still achieve many of the objectives of outdoor education. Day camping will involve many more elements, including meal planning, cooking, and health and safety problems. After this, the exciting experience of being totally away from the school environment for a number of days will follow as a natural sequence, with the added adventures of exploration and discovery. In each case, discoveries made out-of-doors can be taken back to the classroom for further investigation and study.

SCHOOL CAMPING

School camping is outdoor education in a remote natural setting for a period of more than one day. It may be as civilized or as primitive as the group itself is ready for, but it must embody the elements of the natural setting in order to promote those attitudes, ideals, and objectives which give school camping its unique position.

In this age of television, two-car families, indirect lighting, school buses, and push-button power, many children have never spent twenty-four continuous hours away from these things. A trip to a campsite, however primitive, is sure to be different from ordinary life. At a time when nothing at circuses, theaters, concerts, or assemblies is meaningful because "I saw something better on T. V. last night", the fascinating world of nature--be it human or otherwise--can at last begin to be of interest to the student. Here is one world where the child's curiosity and enthusiasm are not in competition with professional producers.

Outdoor living--cooking, clean-up, tents, health, safety, planning--and the skills related to it are not work but fun when done in the companionship of friends. The song of a bird, the field mouse with her babies, the rock formation, the weather--all these become a source of adventure, and for some children, a completely new experience.

Outdoor education is one way in which schools help the child grow in accordance with the general aims of education, and the specific aims of subject matter. Through this medium, the school can help the child live his today to the fullest, and prepare to meet an unknown tomorrow with knowledge, skill and flexibility. In this manner, the objectives of education are effectively attained by taking the children and teachers out of school and placing them in a new environment so that they can learn and grow together.

Activities out of doors may seem to be entirely unrelated to anything the school is supposed to do for children. A critical look at the outdoor idea, the camp program, and particularly at children in the out-of-doors in terms of the objectives of education will reveal that the outdoor program contributes in a real way to the child, the school, and the teacher. The wonder is not that some schools are doing some camping, but that more schools are not doing more camping.

The school camp is a laboratory for learning. If the purpose of education is to contribute to the growth of the child in terms of himself, and in terms of his relationships with others and with his environment, the camp is an ideal learning situation. In camp the child lives with others and with his environment from dressing to eating, to working, to playing. He lives with himself, with other children, and with adults who offer him help with no strings attached, and guidance with no ulterior motives.

HUMAN RELATIONS

In the wonder world of the out-of-doors, the framework of human relationships begins, either consciously or unconsciously, to become meaningful to the child. Here he can no longer return home at the end of the day to the familiar orbit of family and friends. At camp, he lives with and observes the habits of children from other environments, cultures, and up-bringing. He learns to live with his schoolmates, with his teacher, and with other adults. He learns to help himself, to see the needs of others, and, it is hoped, to help others. For many children, the first time that the Golden Rule becomes a practical reality is at camp. The association of individuals from many homes, with their common classroom experience plus the new and exciting vistas of the camp experience, gives a firm background for the development of group solidarity. Here the child who has not excelled as a scholar has the chance to show proficiency in music, campcraft, homemaking, or any of the unlimited list of skills. At the other extreme, the child who is an excellent classroom scholar may also have an opportunity to develop a mastery of outdoor living skills.

In the learning situation of school camp, the child has a chance to demonstrate his initiative and resourcefulness in ways that are important to himself and significant to the group. His sense of worth may be enhanced by something as simple as knowing where to look for salamanders, or as complicated as chairmanship of the cook-out committee.

More than just living outdoors, camping is living out-doors with other people. There are people to work with and people to share discoveries with. Camp involves living, working and sharing, so that one child and all children are a part of a whole new world that they themselves helped make.

Democracy thrives in this situation. Camp society is, as much as possible, similar to those early communities in which the members made their own codes for action. The outdoor environment is such that textbook autocracy is re-placed by living democracy. The need for democratic or-ganization and government is clear; there is no refuge in authoritarian control. The adult members of the camp com-munity act as resources, with organization and leadership developing from the children themselves.

Cooperation is a necessity in camp. Food, fire, fuel, sanitation, and recreation have to be planned, and someone must work to make the plans reality. The individual child has an important and meaningful place in the camp society. The consequences are clear-cut if one of the group fails to do his job; there is no room for spectators in camp.

If, on the other hand, each camper contributes his share, the needs of food and shelter will not occupy a camp-er's full-time. With places to go, things to do, and things to see, camp offers the child a whole new world to explore, to know, to keep and to share.

NEW EXPERIENCES FOR STUDENTS

Camp is life surrounded by life. There are small things hiding under rocks and logs, big things leaving tracks in the soft mud, inanimate things to be picked up and pock-eted. The earth is covered with growing things; stars are uncurtained by roof-tops. Camp is a small bit of the uni-verse--there for a child to discover.

At camp, then, students can begin to understand the environment in which they live. The camp is remote enough from home and school so that the study of an environment is heightened by the simplicity of the situation, and principles are accented over the details of the ordinary social environment.

Camp life is primitive enough so that students can begin to acquire understanding of how people lived and worked in frontier America. They can begin to identify themselves with the pioneers who laid foundations of the American ideal of democracy.

In this relatively simple environment, students can also begin to gain insight into the problems of people who still live in agricultural economies with undeveloped technologies. School time in camp helps children put themselves in the place of others less materially endowed than they.

School out of school--school in camp--contributes to the growth of the individual child, the children's group, and the curriculum. At the same time, contributions of as great value are being realized by the teacher who goes camping with his class.

TEACHER BENEFITS

At camp the teacher can gain new knowledge of his children in an entirely different situation. The children are isolated from the outside influences which affect their in-school behavior. This isolation can help the teacher discover and identify problems which may trouble the child: problems of family, friends, possessions, or activities. The teacher has the opportunity to observe the child in continuous activities in many areas of living. This continuous observation and association may well result in new attitudes, approaches, or techniques. Because both teacher and child are in a changed situation, the teacher can help the child find his own strengths and weaknesses. Together they can discover means of making new contributions to the group and can strengthen areas of weakness.

The unique situation in which the teacher and child find themselves release the teacher from the customary role of an expert. There is fun in sharing knowledge; there is fun in learning and growing together. For the child, there is a wonderful feeling in being able to offer some of his skills

and knowledge to an adult who needs it and who will accept
it graciously. And there is excitement in a new relationship
with people, regardless of age, who have shared in discoveries.

SCHOOL COMMUNITY BENEFITS

The camp program of any organization is an attempt to
carry out the basic objectives of the group in an outdoor setting. The basic objective of all youth organizations is to
help the child grow in harmony with his society. These
organizations differ only in their approaches to the attainment of this aim, and in their particular emphases.

As do other organizations, schools use camp as a
means of furthering their over-all objectives. School camp
programs are neither substitutes nor competition for the
camp programs of other agencies. Because private and
agency camps serve only a small part of the school-age
population, camp experiences are not available to all children. The American Camping Association, an organization
of professional camp people, is doing extensive work at the
regional and national levels to help promote school camping.
Its publication, *Camping Magazine,* has devoted many articles to this subject. School camping exists only because
camp offers unique benefits to the school program, helping
the schools do a better job, and for no other reason.

Cooperation between schools and organizations operating camps can result in mutual strengthening of programs.
Organizations benefit through increased membership, and a
new source of leaders and counselors. Children who have
attended camp will want to return, and adults who have seen
what camp means to the children will help school and organizational camp programs expand.

The use of established camps by schools will facilitate
development of the school camp program, since this will
reduce the initial cost. Besides supplying the specialized
personnel necessary for a camp, organizations with which
the school cooperates are a source of experienced help and
leadership for in-service education of school camp personnel.

School and organization cooperation in the use of camp facilities results in a better camp program for both agencies. While a school camp project in erosion control, for example, aids the school's objectives, the camp benefits from an improved site at the same time. If summer fees for the use of an organization camp are used to fit the camp for winter school camping, both groups can expand their programs.

The public school is only one of many agencies working for the improved education of youth. Cooperation between the schools and various youth agencies such as the Boy Scouts, Girl Scouts, Y. M. C. A., and church groups will improve all education and most especially outdoor education.

LOS ANGELES (CALIFORNIA) OUTDOOR EDUCATION PROGRAM[4]

Educators for years have been alert to discover ways and means of providing meaningful learning experiences that contribute significantly to the total growth and development of children and to their adjustment to their living environment.

Some administrators and teachers feel that the classroom is confining, that the instructional program that is carried on in such a setting is not adequate to fully prepare children to meet the many exigencies of a twentieth century society. It is felt by many that to meet these needs children should have adequate preparation through joyful learning experiences that will help enable them to:

1. Live together harmoniously, understanding and experiencing the democratic way of life in action, and
2. Understand and utilize wisely the great natural environment that is the heritage of this nation.

---

[4]Los Angeles County Schools, Outdoor Education, A Handbook For School Districts. (mimeographed bulletin) Los Angeles: Office of the County Superintendent of Schools, 1954.

Outdoor education has become an integral part of the school experience in many school districts within recent years. The setting for these educational experiences has been the out-of-doors.

In this setting a typical classroom situation is transplanted with some modifications to outdoor surroundings which may be located on the school grounds, within the immediate neighborhood, or some distance away from the school district at the seashore, a ranch, a farm or in the mountains.

However, in the Southern California area most of these outdoor education programs are conducted in the natural setting of the mountains for a period of one week during the school year. This is due, in part at least, to the many opportunities in such an environment to provide valuable learning experiences that contribute to a child's understanding and appreciation of the conservation of natural and animal resources.

In outdoor education programs the out-of-doors serves as a laboratory for learning in the areas of:

1. Democratic living.
2. Community work experiences.
3. Healthful living.
4. Outdoor science understanding and appreciations.
5. Recreational skills.
6. Spiritual values.

In addition to the above listed areas of the outdoor education program, many opportunities for experiences in other aspects of the traditional classroom curriculum exist, but with different techniques and different emphases from those employed in the classroom.

Outdoor education under competent leadership provides children with experiences that are direct, first-hand, and realistic. Such experiences are not a mere duplication of previously experienced classroom activities, but are supplementary and complementary to the child's classroom activities. In this setting, under competent leadership learning becomes vital, interesting, meaningful and joyful. Under such conditions, learning occurs through all the senses a child possesses.

Attempts are made through wise and constructive guidance to improve the quality of living of the child in a democratic setting in a twenty-four hour situation. This is in contrast to the educational and personal guidance in a six or seven hour traditional classroom environment. The child's whole personality is displayed during an around-the-clock day and week long experience with his peers and teacher in a natural location. This makes for greater understanding among children and between pupils and teacher. The development of such understanding of the natural environment is a basic aim of outdoor education programs. Learning thrives in an atmosphere where children have the adventure of discovering fundamental principles relating to man's dependence upon his environment and the satisfactions of understanding the factors relating to the natural heritage.

Through guided experiences in the out-of-doors, children are stimulated to seek, discover, and maintain an active interest in the natural processes relating to the trees, plants, animals, birds, geological formations, and astronomy.

Children learn the realities of human relations by having opportunities to plan, conduct, and evaluate their experiences.

NEED FOR OUTDOOR EDUCATION

There is a genuine need in our complex twentieth century society to provide boys and girls with experiences which are real and fundamental to the problems that our civilization faces in an atomic age. This means children need to learn to live cooperatively, to plan together, to think and to evaluate, to realize the importance of nature to man and man's dependence upon natural and wildlife resources. It means children need to understand the environment in which they live, and they need to appreciate opportunities to contribute toward the conservation of its resources. Children need to learn self-dependence and reliance in order to be better equipped to meet any eventuality.

It is evident that there is a need for strong programs in outdoor education in mountainous environments when it is realized that devastating forest fires each year denude thousands of acres of valuable forest land in our own state. Cities have become great centers of industrial business and congested residential areas which means that many children seldom if ever get an opportunity to visit and enjoy the mountains or the seashore. Children need opportunities for meaningful experiences to help them understand their environment and meet the problems inherent in present day civilization.

The need for increased conservation of our country's natural and animal resources becomes more evident in times of war or other crisis. Extraordinary demands are made upon them for war and defense purposes. The development of attitudes of wise and constructive use of natural and wildlife resources contributes much toward the general welfare of our country.

FREDERICK COUNTY (MARYLAND) OUTDOOR EDUCATION PROGRAM[5]

The Frederick County Outdoor School is a part of the school system and can make unique and worthwhile contributions to our total school curriculum. Modern conditions of living have increased the need for outdoor education and we need to assume our responsibility in this very important area.

Educational goals and procedures continue to change in our dynamic society and school camping and other outdoor educational activities are among the most promising frontiers of curriculum improvement.

A school camp is a place and an instrument through which children can have worthwhile educational experiences otherwise difficult to obtain. It provides opportunities for vital and meaningful learnings in science, conservation and outdoor living which cannot be gained effectively in a formal classroom situation.

[5]Frederick County Board of Education, Teachers Guide Frederick County Outdoor School. (mimeographed bulletin) Frederick, Maryland: Board of Education of Frederick County, 1958.

SOME GENERAL PRINCIPLES

1. All activities should be related as much as possible to the regular curriculum.
2. Those things should be done at camp which cannot be done at school.
3. Children learn best by doing.
4. Pupils and teacher should plan cooperatively as much as possible.
5. Some things can be learned better outdoors; they should be taught outdoors whenever possible.
6. Many outdoor situations are highly motivating to children; these should be exploited.
7. All available resources possible should be used in developing and operating the program.
8. Emphasis should be educational and not primarily recreational.

PROGRAM AREAS

Social Living
Healthful Living
Purposeful Work Activities
Outdoor Recreation
Nature Interpretation and Conservation
Related Educational Activities
   (mathematics, science, social studies, language arts, music, art, dramatics, shop, homemaking, etc.)

SOME OF THE EDUCATIONAL OBJECTIVES

A. <u>General</u>

1. To recognize the value of our natural resources and to learn to use them wisely.
2. To increase our emphasis on science education and to give every student a chance to develop increased knowledge and interest in several areas of science.
3. To make classroom learnings more meaningful through the application of knowledge to practical outdoor situations.
4. To learn to live democratically with other children and with adults through experiences in outdoor living.

5. To develop skills and interests in outdoor recreation which will carry over into later life.

B. Specific

1. Democratic Social Living

a. To have children know teachers and teachers know children better.
b. To have children make new friends in their own class and in other classes from other schools.
c. To have children gain independence apart from their families.
d. To give some children a chance to excel who may not have had a chance before.
e. To give children a chance to work cooperatively and democratically with other children and adults in operating the camp and its program.
f. To have children understand the problems caused by bad outdoor manners such as dumping, defacing signs, damaging trees, picking flowers and being a litterbug.

CRITERIA FOR A GOOD SCHOOL CAMP[6]

The National Education Association Department of Supervision and Curricular Director have outlined these evaluations on the criteria of school camping.

The following criteria for a good school camp are proposed for the consideration of schools that follow the pioneers into extending educational opportunities through camp experience.

SCHOOL CAMP PURPOSES AND PHILOSOPHY

The school camp should have as its central objective helping young people understand the democratic way of life and practice it in their relationships with others.

[6]Department of Supervision and Curriculum Development, _Toward a New Curriculum_. Washington, D.C.: National Education Association, 1944. pp. 102-104.

1. The school camp should treat each youngster as an individual. It should guide him, help him to face his problems, help him develop his potentialities, open up new interests to him.

2. The school camp should help youngsters to live with others, giving and taking, sharing and accepting responsibilities, constantly learning to widen the area of shared interests through partaking in enterprises with others for objectives commonly agreed upon by the participants.

3. The school camp should stress problem solving, using the method of intelligence.

4. The school camp should help youngsters to be concerned for human welfare, in and outside the camp.

PROGRAMS TO ACHIEVE PURPOSES

1. The school camp should fully utilize its environment for educative ends whether that setting be the field, forest, and stars of the organized out-of-doors summer camp, or the community setting of the work camp.

2. The school camp should teach social living and citizenship through using as the raw materials of education those situations and problems which arise in the everyday life of the camp. (Democratic values should be applied not only to the present camp problem which serves as the source but also to larger social issues related to the immediate problem.)

3. The school camp should involve camper and staff planning, and cooperative conduct of the program.

4. The school camp should be an informal experience where fun and joy are cherished and promoted.

5. The school camp should be a place where health and vigor are improved, and where health, nutrition, and safety practices are learned through the demands of camp living, and expanded upon by educationally alert adults.

6. The school camp should encourage and develop work experiences of a variety of kinds through which campers come to understand the dignity of labor, and the significance of shared responsibility in democratic living.

7. The school camp should continuously evaluate and appraise its program in the light of its values and periodically report its findings to interested groups.

8. While the school camp should fully utilize work experience, forest living, crafts, hikes, athletics, dramatics, and similar activities, it should not conceive its function to be that of a noneducative, nonintellectual agency devoted simply to recreation and physical culture.

9. While the school camp should fully utilize such activities as discussion, reading, forms of self-government, community visitation and study, speakers, radio, and movies, it should not conceive its function to be that of a non-social, nonemotional agency concerned with developing the mind of the child through the traditional curriculum centered on assuring college entrance for the few.

In short, the school camp may well become an integral part of the youngster's year-round educational experience, which blends what is best in schooling to foster democratic living.

An examination of outdoor education programs in a score or more of schools including the five representative schools discussed in this chapter has resulted in the emergence of many basic concepts in outdoor education. It is interesting to note that outdoor education programs growing up in all parts of the country have so many concepts in common, are striving for the same objectives, are so close in their stated philosophy, and are using similar methods and techniques.

GENERAL CONSIDERATIONS

Will Durant said, "Our knowledge is dangerous today and our culture superficial because we are rich in mechanisms and poor in purposes." Educators seem to be more concerned today about which courses should be required, how much mathematics is necessary, and various and sundry other problems relating to curriculum. Committees are appointed to study and revise the curriculum. It is the thing to do apparently, for every school and university is doing it. Committees are appointed to take a close look at the General Education programs.

It is very seldom that administrators select committees to examine the philosophy of education and of democracy. Without a thorough understanding of the goals of democracy and therefore the ends of education, curriculum study is a waste of time. A football player must know the direction of his goal before he can decide which way to run.

Educators who, with their teachers and parents, have taken time to examine the goals of education are stepping out in new directions and are using new techniques and devices in order to implement and supplement education. One of the most prominent and fastest growing techniques in modern education is the emphasis placed on learning things first-hand through outdoor education. General considerations regarding outdoor education are:

1. The outdoor education program throughout the United States has been accepted by many State Departments of Education.

2. The state administrators endorse the program primarily because of the stated purposes of the program--more efficient learning, improved teaching methods, relating subject matter to experience, and contribution to the total educational program.

3. Many states have introduced special legislation for outdoor education programs.

4. State educational leaders from other states feel that existing school legislation is adequate for schools to include outdoor education programs.

5. Professional educators have repeatedly recommended the use of outdoor education as a teaching method.

6. Many professional people other than educators have publicly recognized and proclaimed the educational importance of learning in the out-of-doors.

7. Many state education departments have published teaching guides and other materials to assist schools in the development of outdoor education programs.

8. Colleges and universities are now offering courses in outdoor education. In some colleges, a student may pursue a major program at the master's and doctor's level in outdoor education.

9. Universities, colleges and many public schools are acquiring land and facilities for the conduct of their outdoor education programs.

10. National and state conferences are being conducted throughout the United States for the purpose of interpreting outdoor education programs.

11. Many workshops and in-service training programs are being held on a state and local basis.

12. Several states have organized State Outdoor Education Associations. Some states have State Advisory Councils working with the State Department of Public Instruction.

13. There is one national organization devoted entirely to the development of outdoor education--The Outdoor Education Association, Inc., under the direction of Dr. L. B. Sharp.

14. Several national organizations are developing programs related to outdoor education--American Camping Association, National Recreation Association, the Isaak Walton League, National Education Association, National Audubon Society, and the American Association of Health, Physical Education, and Recreation.

15. Historically, the public schools were encouraged to use the out-of-doors for educational purposes. In the Northwest Ordinance of 1787, each 16th section of land was set aside for school purposes.

16. Many church organizations are using outdoor education to further Christian education. The results have been so tremendous that church camping is probably the fastest growing aspect of outdoor education.

17. State departments of conservation are more and more bringing their program to the schools and are enlisting the help of teachers on all levels to make conservation a way of life.

18. The claims for outdoor education (more efficient learning, etc.) has been substantiated in an experiment with New York City children by Dr. L. B. Sharp, director of the Outdoor Education Association.

CONCEPTS REGARDING OUTDOOR EDUCATION

Outdoor education is too often confused with outdoor recreation; camping is likewise confused with a vacation. Educators have not yet realized the importance of recreation enough to support camping merely for the sake of developing leisure time skills. Those educators who do support programs in outdoor education see the development of recreation as only one of many reasons for its acceptance.

Camping has come to mean many things to many people. Most educators who are openly opposed to outdoor education have not taken time to think it through; those against school camping have more than likely never visited a school camp. While they approach the academic field very scientifically, weigh evidence on both sides of every issue and visit and investigate school matters very carefully before supporting or speaking against their adoption, they dismiss outdoor education as a waste of time.

Educators, and their number is rapidly increasing, who have experimented with using the outdoor education method for teaching their particular subject-matter area are enthusiastic over the results. Parents who visit a school camp are usually even more impressed at what can be learned outside the classroom. The day that education meant classrooms, textbooks, and schools has gone. Education today has gone beyond the walls of the classroom and has become associated with the life and activities of the community. In a democratic society it can afford no other choice. The church, the Y.M.C.A., the public library, the police, the home, the woods and the streams are all powerful agents in the education of youth.

GENERAL CONCEPTS

The basic concepts of outdoor education are as old as organized education. Their special plea to educators is to use nature and directed experiences as an important part of the instructional program.

1. The modern plea for outdoor education is merely a renewed effort on the part of educators for teachers to again return to nature and to outdoor experiences as a basic educational necessity in the modern school curricula.

2. The underlying concepts of outdoor education include: efficiency in learning; first-hand experiences with subject matter taught; integrated and correlated learnings resulting from a study of nature; personal discoveries, investigations, and reasoning involved in nature study; application of facts to principles derived from experiences to develop the art of critical thinking through direct experience and through relationships; aesthetic appreciations and inspirations derived from nature; development of good physical and mental health through active learning situations; development of group cooperation and human relationship; and enjoyment of challenging learning and recreational activities.

3. The outdoor education program should be an inherent part of all school philosophy, policies and curricula. It should blend into school programs in the same manner as all other educational methods.

4. The outdoor education program fulfills and meets the highest standards of educational psychology. It fulfills the educational requirements for youth as stated in the cardinal principles of education. It recognizes and makes meaningful the laws of learning. It stimulates and motivates reasoning and critical thinking.

5. The American public has highly endorsed and accepted the values of modern summer camping programs. The outdoor education directions of the schools are not intended to duplicate or eliminate these programs. The traditional summer camp is one of the greatest complements to our educational system.

In the outdoor education program, the emphasis is

still on the subject matter areas of the curriculum; the emphasis is not so much on camping but on the educational significance of the experience; all children receive continuous experience in outdoor education from kindergarten through high school when the need arises. Finally, the purpose of the outdoor education program of the schools is much different than that in the typical recreational camp.

ADMINISTRATIVE CONCEPTS

School systems that are known for an excellent program in outdoor education in most cases are known to be fine institutions in all phases of instruction and educational service. An administrator concerned enough to keep up with developments in one phase of the curriculum usually is concerned with all facets of the school program.

This does not mean that the administrator has to personally administer the program. He will usually find a man with a good background in educational philosophy and outdoor education to assume this responsibility. Colleges and universities are beginning to add courses and work out patterns within their existing curricula to enable students to meet the requirements of administrators for outdoor education, including school camping. Administrative concepts in outdoor education include:

1. Outdoor education has proven to be a valuable method of learning. It should be considered as a normal and proper function of all educational systems.

2. It should not be necessary to view outdoor education programs as something new or different. There should be no need to seek new legislation to permit its acceptance. Legislation should not be necessary that dictates to the classroom teacher or the schools in general how they are to teach.

3. Local school boards and school administrators should have, and in most cases do have, authority to develop programs in outdoor education.

4. One of the most valuable contributions outdoor education makes to the administrative structure of the school is

found in its unique camp program when there is complete dependence upon harmonious relationships between the schools, community, parents and citizens. In extended outdoor education programs there is teamwork in planning, supervision, instruction, and evaluation of the program.

5. Some school laws are restrictive enough in content to prohibit various desirable offerings in outdoor education. Originally the purpose of the law was not specifically directed to limit outdoor education programs but were enacted for other reasons.

6. There are school laws which need to be amended to permit school programs to function more efficiently. Amendments to present laws which allow more freedom of education are in many cases more valuable than laws which require certain subject matter be taught.

School board members and school administrators need to review some of these restrictive laws with the purpose of correcting them for the proper function of education. Some current inflexible laws include: length of school day, length of school week, transportation limitations, insurance coverage and limitations, liability responsibilities, land use and purchases, and child labor laws.

7. Several states have comprehensive legislation permitting outdoor education and school camping. These laws are very helpful to the schools in those states, but in many instances the school administrator experiences conflict with other established school law. It would be much better to recognize the important contribution various school programs make to education and amend present legislation rather than establish new codes for new programs.

8. Administrators encounter little difficulty in traditional programs when the teacher takes her class on short field trips within the time limits and locations necessary for compliance with school schedules and regulations. These programs are valuable but need further encouragement and motivation.

9. Recognition is given to many outdoor education programs functioning successfully in many schools in special

subject matter fields. Those departments which most frequently conduct their instructional programs outside the classroom include: agriculture, botany, biology, and sociology.

10. The outdoor education program provides experience and learning activities that have the same educational values for 7th graders as for 5th graders. They frequently learn together. According to many educators, there is nothing sacred or scientifically satisfactory with the grade placement system. The outdoor education program offers opportunities for educational experiments in this administrative practice.

11. The values of outdoor education do not always coincide with sequential offerings of subject matter areas back at school. Discoveries, observations, and reasoning by 4th and 5th graders in the outdoors involve subject matter content that will not appear in textbooks until the 8th grade. Similar experiences may be related to high school students. More experimental work and research needs to be done to assure students of the best opportunities for acquiring knowledge in various subject matter fields.

12. The outdoor education program infringes in a constructive manner on traditional class schedules of most schools.

The proven values of outdoor education to the total educational program should cause school administrators to sacrifice administrative procedures in behalf of more efficient learning.

Administrative practices should be determined on the basis of how well they provide the best educational opportunities for teacher and students.

13. The outdoor education program infringes in a constructive manner on the administrative structure of the school. The lines of authority are not always entirely broken but they frequently become indistinguishable. Teachers assume new responsibilities in policy planning, administration and supervision. Administrators have an opportunity to share their problems with teachers, parents, and students

in order to make extended outdoor education experiences possible.

14. The outdoor education program offers a release to teachers and students from the highly organized routine of schools. The bells are gone, the clocks are missing, the frequent march down the hall is not necessary, the clanging of lockers is gone, the chalk dust and dingy blackboards are not needed, the hard seats in formal rows are useless, the stuffy room is left behind, and the four painted walls disappear.

15. The outdoor education program provides opportunities for new class structures. The rigid formality of the classroom disappears. It becomes necessary to reorganize the class. The most efficient organization of classes for an outdoor education experience consists in a democratic structure of small groups where the emphasis is placed on self-discipline, teamwork, self-government, and group cooperation.

16. The classroom educational program relies heavily upon knowledge secured from recitations, discussions, problem solving and textbook learning. The outdoor education program relies upon other resources for its maximum value. Some of these resources include an adequate library both at school and at the school camp, miscellaneous equipment and supplies necessary for a high standard of learning in the program, leadership from sources other than the school, and facilities and land to conduct programs.

17. The outdoor education program provides new opportunities for teachers and administrators in guidance and counseling. The very nature of the program requires more knowledge and information concerning each child.

The program offers the teacher and guidance counselor an opportunity to understand students better since in many cases the students live together for several days at a time. Interests, attitudes, abilities and conduct quite frequently change when students leave the classroom for their learning.

18. The outdoor education program offers new opportunities in program evaluation. The techniques of research

applicable to formal education and textbook knowledge will
not measure educational success in the out-of-doors. New
methods of research will be needed to scientifically evaluate
the outdoor education programs.

19. The philosophy and program values of outdoor education should be acknowledged by all public schools. It
should become an inherent part of school policy and program.
It should become a topic of teacher meetings, workshops,
and in-service training programs.

20. The outdoor education program has caused a re-
awakening and a new educational challenge to teachers and
administrators in many schools. Teachers are discovering
that subject matter becomes more interesting to students;
that teachers become interested in other subject matter areas
because of the integrated learning experiences that occur;
that classroom and even school morale is improved; and
that discipline has been replaced by sincere interest in
learning and motivation for further learning.

CURRICULUM AND PROGRAM CONCEPTS

Before outdoor education can be justified in a school
situation, it must be accepted as a part of the curriculum.
It is not extra-curricular. It is a vital and worthwhile
technique of education which can be used in conjunction
with every subject matter area.

Some concepts emerging in curriculum and program
throughout the country are:

1. The outdoor education program supplements the
subject matter curriculum by providing planned experiences
relating to the subject matter taught.

2. The outdoor education project provides realistic
learning experience in many areas of the curriculum not
possible to develop within the classroom.

3. The outdoor education program makes classroom
learning more meaningful when students have opportunities
to discover and investigate specific things and facts so well
written in the text books.

4. The outdoor education program fills a vacuum

created when the classroom and school building became the seat of learning." Schools which permit students to have direct and planned experience in the out-of-doors are recognizing once again a basic educational need.

5. The art of critical thinking can be scientifically developed in an outdoor education program because all the elements necessary for successful motivation are available to the teacher. Nature's laboratory provides the resources and the teacher provides the leadership. Students discover, observe, and investigate things and learn first-hand. They are stimulated and motivated from these interesting experiences to discover more facts, principles, theories, and philosophies regarding places and things.

6. The outdoor education program provides a better climate for the practice of psychological principles and methods of teaching regarding the development of attitudes, knowledges and practices.

7. In outdoor education programs, learning of the subject matter takes place faster, is comprehended more fully, is more easily related to the fact and subject matter, is retained longer, and is more meaningful. First-hand experience relating to subject matter should always improve learning.

8. Nature's laboratory provides the one basic educational resource where integration and correlation of all subject matter areas is a reality. In studying nature it is difficult for the learner to isolate and pull nature apart and place it into many specialized subject matter areas. Things in nature are too related and inter-dependent. Only in advaned specialized curricula involving scientific discovery and research is this feasible.

9. The outdoor education program serves as a means of motivation to many students (both academically and socially) who frequently appear uninterested or incompetent in regular classroom procedures.

10. The outdoor education program provides new and different opportunites for developing proper attitudes and new appreciations concerning--the students themselves, the

students' classmates, the teacher, the principles of democracy, conservation, health, physical fitness, nature and God.

11. The outdoor education program introduces students to new and useful skills and broadens their knowledge in all areas of the present day curriculum.

12. In many instances where outdoor education programs are conducted for high school and university students, it has been most helpful to students in selecting their vocational and professional careers.

Many high schools and college students have opportunities to work with younger students and serve as junior or senior counselors. They also are privileged to have teachers who are well-trained in working with small groups in outdoor education. These experiences serve to orientate and acquaint students with many specialized fields of employment. Many discover that they enjoy working with youngsters and become interested in teaching. Others discover quite the opposite. Many learn of the many and varied job opportunities related to the biological and natural science. Some learn, for the first time, just where the poets and artists received their inspirations and knowlege for writing poetry and painting pictures. Others discover the need and opportunites in social work, mental and physical health, and other types of vocational and technical employment.

13. Outdoor education programs for college students further knowledge and research in chosen areas of specialization, education, forestry, geology, geography, music, and other areas.

14. The outdoor education programs provide opportunities for gaining new skills and knowledge in activities that involve constructive use of leisure time.

15. The outdoor education program can be a vital source of educational research in such areas as--grade placement, sequential learning, group living, efficiency of learning, educational methods, child psychology, and other related educational practices.

16. The outdoor education program introduces new

techniques in evaluation of curricula. It also broadens the scope of those evaluating to include students, parents, resource people, teachers, and administrators.

17. In the outdoor education program you cannot "take the next 12 pages." Learning cannot be fed or planned in this manner. Learning may involve 12 partial pages from 12 different texts. Knowledge and skills are acquired through discovery, observation, investigation and reason from many sources in nature.

18. The outdoor education program should extend from kindergarten through college. Concentration of outdoor education programs through school camp experiences at selected grade levels is not sufficient.

Outdoor education programs should be planned to meet the needs of the program at each grade level.

LEADERSHIP CONCEPTS

The leader in the basic outdoor education program is the classroom teacher. It is impossible for a specialist to take over an educational program with little or no background as to the needs, wants, abilities and previous education of the children. However, a good specialist, well-educated in the techniques of outdoor education, can be of invaluable assistance to the teacher.

Since the use of nature and direct experience is an essential part of our educational program for students from kindergarten through college--it becomes all the more important that teachers receive adequate education in this area.

Some of the major leadership concepts include:

1. The primary responsibility for leadership in outdoor education programs rests with existing school personnel. Outdoor education programs should be given the same considerations in terms of personnel and leadership that exist for other school-centered programs.

2. It is imperative that leadership for outdoor education programs receive the same sanctions, supports and

encouragement from school boards, school administrators and teachers as any other important school program.

3. The classroom teacher has most of the skills and knowledge necessary to conduct outdoor education programs. It would be desirable if teachers had more preparation and experience in conducting classes informally in small group leadership techniques; in stimulating and motivating students towards discoveries and reasoning about nature; in outdoor living skills; and in knowledge concerning the out-of-doors.

4. Leadership in an outdoor education program assumes a different perspective from the traditional concepts of classroom leadership. In a well-planned program every student at one time or another is the leader. The success of the learning process is dependent upon the leadership responsibilities assumed by each individual student. Teachers have unlimited opportunities for encouraging and supervising directed leadership duties for students.

5. True and worthwhile education consisting of the school, the community, and the family are brought together more significantly and all are engaged in cooperative leadership responsibilities.

6. The teachers lose authoritative position and learning takes place among all of the groups together. No one teacher could be expected to have answers to all the new discoveries made and to factual questions raised in the learning experiences of the students. They seek the answers together through library resources and through reason.

7. The strict formality and formal structure of the classroom disintegrates. The class is organized democratically into small groups. The emphasis shifts to self-discipline and student leadership.

8. Supervisory responsibilities are frequently assumed by parents and often by older high school students. This is true particularly for extended outdoor education experiences. Parents have opportunities to learn more about school problems, curriculum content and teaching methods.

9. In reading, investigating, conversing, and debating

the values of camping with educators, camp administrators, counselors, campers' parents, and many professional and lay leaders there are many concepts and many objectives inherent in teaching Americanism and democracy in camp. Many individuals would isolate specific camp objectives and experiences as separate entities and special areas in the total education picture. It seems most logical to classify the main objectives derived from camping under four distinct major headings, namely: Democracy or Democratic Group Living, Conservation Education, Healthful Outdoor Living, and Leisure Time Education.

CURRICULA

Most school curricula include the subject matters of art, music and literature.

Many of the great masterpiece of art, many of the famous musical compositions of the world, and most of the finer writings in poetry and literature are expressions of beauty and aesthetical interpretations of nature.

The schools spend a great deal of time reading and discussing good poetry. Additional time is spent analyzing poetry in terms of the metrical systems and composition. More emphasis is given to discussions and analysis of free verse. Poems are memorized and interpreted. All of these efforts are necessary and essential to fuller appreciation, understanding and knowledge of literature and poetry. The outdoor education program can supplement this learning by taking the students to the out-of-doors and provide them with some of the same experiences, inspirations, and aesthetic appreciations the writer lived. Inspiration for creative writing is a valuable contribution of direct experiences in nature.

In art, there is study and attention focused on color, symmetry, design, and the techniques necessary for proper artistic accomplishments. There is also a considerable amount of emphasis given to interpretations and appreciations of art.

Art is based on experience and the quality of that experience is determined by the skill possessed by the individual. Too many individuals spend their days on earth in a very shallow and meager existence. They have not been taught to observe or to become aware of life around them. They need to develop a sensitivity toward things, toward people, and toward their relationship with each other. This is art in its highest form--the art of living, of being aware, of being sensitive, of observing and understanding, of imagination, manipulation, and participation and of expression, in significant and beautiful common everyday living.

Music instruction has the same educational requirements for understanding, appreciation, enjoyment, and competences as other similar subject matter areas. Teaching of these fundamental processes concerning music is an absolute essential. Improvements can be made in music programs if supervised experiences are made available to students along the same lines as those enjoyed by the great men and women who contributed so much to the music world. These experiences should start in early life and be a continuous part of living throughout life.

Instruction in the fields of mathematics and physical sciences receive a considerable amount of emphasis in the modern schools--increasingly so because of concern in America for maintaining world leadership in science and research. Instruction in the elementary grades concentrates on addition, subtraction, division, fractions, percentages and various kinds of measurement. Learning is centered in memorization of tables, charts, and cards. These simple mathematic teachings and all forms of measurement take on real meaning in the experiences prevalent in outdoor education programs.

Most mathematical concepts developed as a result of the dedication of learned men who spent years in investigating nature and the laws of nature. Modern day scientists find the exploration and observation of nature to be the most challenging place to develop critical thinking about many things. Civilizations have regressed when educators and political leaders have rejected and de-emphasized the emphasis or study and research of the world and the universe.

Social science refers to those courses in the school curriculum which deal with the student's understanding of his social world: his home, community, nation, other countries and past history of all these which affect present social developments. The Social sciences comprise the focal points around which the experiences of children are organized.

In the past teachers have stressed book knowledge. If a student could relate dates and historical facts, name the states and capitals, and diagram the structure of government, he was considered socially educated. Today educators realize that a child may remember facts and even understand all things necessary to get good marks in the social sciences and still be a social misfit. Outdoor education provides a very real laboratory for the social sciences where children may gain experience in democratic group living. Students participate in the government of the camp and assume civic leadership and responsibility as they develop these social skills.

Natural science teachers have probably used, or need to use, the outdoors more than any other. It is hard to visualize a science teacher teaching entirely from a textbook inside a classroom away from living things. Field trips to the outdoors to study the environment in context results in greater interest and understanding in the sciences. Opportunities abound in all phases of science in the out-of-doors, beginning just outside the classroom door.

The communication arts, especially writing and speaking, is based on experience. The more experience a student has the broader the base on which he may build further creative expression. The outdoor setting can provide the permissive and inspirational setting needed for self-expression. Talks, essays, and writings based on first-hand experience make for better compositions than unreal and irrelevant topics assigned from the textbook. Good literature is based on the first-hand experience of great authors. The best novels are lived by the author.

Physical education was added to the school curriculum when technological developments replaced human effort in production. Physical education is an outdoor subject. One of its objectives is healthful exercise and the outdoors contributes more to healthful living than the indoors.

SUMMARY

Today, educators and national leaders are aware, as never before in history, of the necessity for a sound and workable philosophy of education. Several years ago, H. G. Wells said that "civilization is a race between education and catastrophe." Every year that passes makes his statement more real and meaningful. For the first time in the history of mankind, the destiny of the world lies in the hands of men. One road may lead to peace, prosperity, productivity, and a golden age of leisure beyond brightest expectations. The other road leads to war and the certain destruction of all life on earth.

The atomic bombs that fell on Japan closed the door to an age. Man is living in a new age which is vastly different than the one only twenty-five years ago. If he survives this age, it too, will probably change beyond recognition twenty-five years hence. Change and revolution--politically, socially, economically and scientifically--are the characteristics of modern civilization. There is a widespread feeling of dissatisfaction among educators concerning the role philosophy has played (or not played) in the recent changing civilization. John Dewey has already warned us that we cannot substitute a book for civilization. Alfred Whitehead warns of divorcing education from life. Many other great thinkers and philosophers, even though differing in educational viewpoints, express their concern that philosophy has become too divorced from reality. They point out that a true philosophy is one that serves its society, one that is functional, and one that springs from the patterns and relationships of community living. Isolated facts and pure abstractions are of little real use. Only when abstractions are embodied in reality do they help in dealing with real problems.

Outdoor education is an attempt to deal with realities. Instead of dealing with second, third, or fourth-hand information, wherever possible children should be given an opportunity to learn from direct first-hand experience. Direct experience can make learning more meaningful and therefore insure longer retention. It can provide integrated learning in four areas of living which every educator would agree, at least to a degree, are of utmost importance in living in our modern society--democratic group living, healthful outdoor living, conservation education, and development of leisure time skills.

Questions and Projects

1. Search through books on educational psychology and list the most prevalent laws of learning. Why are programs in outdoor education particularly suited to the observation of these laws in learning?

2. Four committees may be appointed to develop a yardstick or criteria for a good program in each of the following areas of learning:

    1. Democratic group living
    2. Healthful outdoor living
    3. Leisure time education
    4. Conservation education

3. The class, committees or individuals may be interested in developing attitude inventories in conservation education, healthful living, leisure time and recreation, and democracy and human relations.

4. The class should visit a near-by school camp and evaluate it as to type and location of buildings, program, and leadership.

5. Write several schools which are conducting programs in outdoor education to determine the type, the extent and the success of their programs.

6. What are the chief objectives of outdoor education? How

do they relate to the broad general objectives of education?

7. The class may as a project visit a nearby farm or area which might be suitable for a potential school camp and draw up a master plan.

8. Do you agree with the four concepts of outdoor education presented by the authors?

Selected References

Bathurst, Effie G., *Conservation Excursions*. (Bulletin no. 13) Washington, D. C.: U. S. Government Printing Office, 1940.

Bathurst, Effie G., *Curriculum Content in Conservation For Elementary Schools*. (Bulletin no. 14) Washington, D. C.: U. S. Government Printing Office, 1940.

Clarke, James Mitchell, *Public School Camping*. Stanford California: Stanford University Press, 1951.

Department of Public Instruction, *Guide To School Camping For Wisconsin*. (mimeographed bulletin) Madison, Wisconsin: Department of Public Instruction 1956.

Department of Public Instruction, *School Experiences In Camp*. (Bulletin no. 420) Lansing, Michigan: Department of Public Instruction, 1948.

Department of Supervision and Curriculum Development, *Toward a New Curriculum*. Washington, D. C.: National Education Association, 1944.

Macmillan, Dorothy Lou, *School Camping and Outdoor Education*. Dubuque, Iowa: Wm. C. Brown Company, 1956.

National Recreation Association, Recreation Magazine, *Camping and Outdoor Education*. March, 1961.

Smith, Julian W., *Outdoor Education For American Youth*. Washington, D. C.: American Association For Health, Physical Education, and Recreation, 1957.

Western New York School Study Council, *Education Beyond Four Walls*. (mimeographed bulletin) Buffalo: University of Buffalo, 1959.

Chapter 7
DEMOCRATIC GROUP LIVING

Our nation is composed of no one race, faith or cultural heritage. It is a grouping of some thirty peoples possessing varying religious concepts, philosophies and historical backgrounds. They are linked together by their confidence in our democratic institutions as expressed in the Declaration of Independence and guaranteed by the Constitution for themselves and for their children.

—Wendell L. Wilkie

The present day American democracy has its basis in the documents and teachings of many great scholars from many different countries dating from antiquity to modern civilization.

Democracy is sometimes considered a way of life, an ideology, a form of government, or a social and moral philosophy.

Religious teachers of antiquity provided the world with scripture, law, documents, and bibles that advocate many basic Christian ideas, values, and institutions inherent in American democracy. Such leaders as Jesus, Buddah, and Confucius spelled out clearly the necessity of developing proper attitudes and behavior in human relationships. They pointed out the importance and dignity of man as an individual and the values of recognizing the brotherhood of man. Many more democratic principles can be traced to these great religious teachers.

The early Greek nature philosophers, such as Plato, Socrates, and Aristotle contributed greatly to the present democratic ideals. Their teachings emphasized the dignity and capacity of man and his need to achieve the good life through humane means. They advocated the necessity for reason in solving problems and the need for justice in dealing with mankind.

The American democratic faith and ideals are based on the works of many scholars, including philosophers,

lawyers, teachers, and poets of various historical periods
of modern civilization. Concepts have been drawn from
legal documents, poems, speeches, constitutions, pream-
bles, and other scholarly works.

A few of the more recent leaders who helped establish
American democracy are Thomas Paine, Thomas Jefferson,
George Washington, Oliver Wendell Holmes, Patrick Henry,
Andrew Jackson, Theodore Roosevelt, Woodrow Wilson,
Abraham Lincoln, and Walt Whitman. The influence of the
earlier leaders together with many others helped establish
the Constitution of the United States and other important
documents governing American life.

George S. Counts has summarized the American conception of democracy into seven categories. These seven
areas most nearly represent the thinking of most writers
concerning the ideologies and meaning of democracy.

> First of all, democracy affirms the worth and dignity of
> the individual. It declares that every human being is
> precious in his own right and is always to be regarded
> as an end, never as a means merely.

> Second, democracy declares that in a most profound sense
> all men are created equal. This declaration flows in-
> evitably from the idea of the worth of the individual.
> If every individual is uniquely precious, the very foun-
> dation of unequal treatment and consideration collapses.

> Third, democracy regards political and civil liberty as
> the only dependable guardian of individual worth and
> equality. It therefore proclaims a profound faith in
> the abilities of common people--the people who do the
> work of the world--provided they have full access to the
> heritage of knowledge and thought. It declares that in
> the long run the masses of the people are the best judges
> of their own interests, that they and they alone can be
> trusted with both liberty and power, that they can and
> should manage their common affairs, that, in a word, they
> can and should rule themselves.

> Fourth, democracy rests on law and orderly process. It
> places its faith in the methods of enlightenment, persua-
> sion, and peace in the adjustment of differences among
> men, in the formulation of policies great and small, and
> even in the transformation of the structure and basic
> institutions of society.

Fifth, democracy rests on basic morality. It can thrive only if elementary standards of decency and humanity in all public relations and in the conduct of all public affairs are observed. In the political process, if democracy is to endure and prosper, men must be guided by the canons of simple honesty, truthfulness, and intellectual integrity; in the exercise of power they must be just, humane, and merciful.

Sixth, democracy rests on individual opportunity. Historically, our democracy grew and flourished in a land of unparalleled opportunity for the common man. If America should ever lose this quality, the very foundations of our freedom would be destroyed.

Seventh, democracy rests on individual responsibility. In a free society all men must be disciplined by a sense of common brotherhood, a love of truth and justice, and a devotion to the general welfare. If they employ their liberties merely to further their own selfish interests, if they are callous to wrongs and injustices, if they permit the basic supports of liberty to be destroyed, if they care not how the "other half lives," if they neglect their civic duties, if they are indifferent to the fortunes of the Republic, they will surely sink back into bondage.[1]

There exists in this country a great controversy on interpretations and concepts of democracy. There is also controversy on how the ideals of democracy can best be served. Democracy means many things to many people. Some of these differences are in many cases detrimental to the principles of democracy itself.

Some individuals feel the government should be organized and administered to promote the economic and social welfare of the masses. Others feel that government should limit itself chiefly to maintaining law and order in a free, competitive society.

Many differences arise in interpreting democracy because of conflicting thoughts individuals possess regarding the nature of man and the nature of society.

In many respects these conflicting views may be a healthy stimuli to the democratic form of government so

[1]George S. Counts, _Education and American Civilization_. New York: Bureau of Publications, Teachers College, Columbia University, 1952. pp. 281-284.

long as the differences of opinion are not detrimental to the principles of democracy itself.

It is more important for the citizenry to distinguish clearly between democracy and authoritarian concepts of government.

Authoritarian concepts of government are characterized by dictatorship, by glorification of one or few men who have all the answers, by coercion, force, indoctrination and slavery, and by suppression of thought, communication and religion.

There are many common beliefs and behavior patterns by which the majority of our American citizens support the ideals of democracy. Unfortunately, there are still some Americans whose views and actions are inclined toward other ideologies. There is a great danger that some of these subsidiary beliefs could be increasingly detrimental to the American way of life.

Although democracy and democratic government are difficult terms to define, there is evidence that the American public agree almost unanimously on the common principles and ideologies inherent in democracy. Most of these principles and ideologies have been spelled out clearly in books, documents, and periodicals and have been read and frequently memorized by all school children.

There is probably more unanimity in accepting a definition of democracy by the American people when word descriptions are presented for clarification of its meaning. In word descriptions democracy finds almost complete harmony of acceptance by all American citizens. Some of the more descriptive words include liberty, justice, reason, equality, freedom, dignity, peace, responsibility, honesty, opportunity, and fairness.

Some of the other concepts which appear to have general acceptance as being essential to a democracy include: belief in God, dignity of man, human relationships or brotherhood, four freedoms, self government, use of reason in resolving social differences and seeking greater knowledge, respect for rights and property, and basic American traditions concerning work and leisure.

There are many common beliefs and behaviors by which the majority of American citizens support the ideals of democracy. However, there are still many Americans who have conflicting views which are more inclined to other ideologies. There is great danger in modern democracy that these subsidiary beliefs might become increasingly detrimental to the American way of life.

It is difficult to find a group, and in some cases two individuals in America with like definitions and interpretations of democracy. Many educated men have wide differences of opinion on their concepts of democracy.

There is a great need today to re-emphasize the necessity for all citizens to take a more active part in making democracy work. This can be done through voting and by openly defending the ideals and freedoms granted through the Constitution and the Declaration of Independence.

There is also a critical need for the right kind of education for youth so they may more fully learn through formal instruction and particularly through experience in the democratic ideals. Fortunately, there are many common areas of agreement prevalent among the ideals of democracy. These agreements can be discovered in the volumes of materials in books, magazines, pamphlets, and other periodicals concerning American democracy.

There is general agreement among most educators that the schools are not doing a successful job in teaching students the real meaning and true principles of democracy.

Many indications have clearly shown that efforts to teach democracy in the schools have not been completely satisfactory. There are too many recent discouraging signs which indicate that there needs to be a considerable amount of improvement in teaching democracy.

Too many Americans are refusing and abusing their voting privileges. There is too much apathy and not enough dedicated support in upholding the basic principles of democracy as outlined in the Declaration of Independence and other early American documents.

There is still a great deal of animosity toward minority

groups in the United States. There is also an increasing amount of unrest and lack of understanding within the minority groups. There appears to be an increased amount of religious intolerance and misunderstanding still much too prevalent throughout the country. Certain polls have indicated that more than one-third of the American people still show strong prejudices against minority groups.

Some other indications of failure in the democratic process are the increased amounts of activity by various minority groups to organize and spend large amounts of money for education programs and legislative programs to protect their interests. This type of activity should not be necessary if the principles of democracy are adequately being taught to the youth of the country. Organizations now actively engaged in this type of work include the Civil Liberties Union, the National Association for the Advancement of Colored People, National Conference for Christians and Jews, Bureau for Intercultural Education, the National Urban League, the League of Women Voters, the Human Rights Commission, and many others.

Failure in teaching democracy is also demonstrated in the increased amount of legislation that is being passed to eliminate discrimination of various kinds throughout the country. Again, if the educational program is functioning and developing proper attitudes toward democracy, this type of legislation would not be necessary. Fifteen states have new equality of opportunity statutes and at least thirty-two major cities have passed legislation of a similar nature.[2]

In the state of New York, legislation passed only in 1945 was a pioneer law concerned with anti-discrimination. This law is a fore-runner to many of the recent state laws regarding protection of minority interests.

Another indication that a poor job is being done in teaching democracy in the schools occurs in the everyday living and conversation. It is true that to define democracy is a very difficult task, and there are varying concepts of democracy, but too frequently the public is not even fairly

[2]Robert Rienow, American Problems Today. Boston: D. C. Heath Co., 1958. pp. 68-69.

well informed about the principles and future of American democracy. In comparison to citizens of most any European country, the American citizen is almost totally ignorant of the principles and ideals of his government.

There are indications that Americans are becoming apathetic and negligent in their responsibilities toward conserving natural resources. There appears to be an increased amount of destruction and mutilation of public properties, including buildings, parks, playgrounds, scenic areas, forests, rivers, streams, and lakes.

Some church groups feel that a large number of Americans are turning away from the church and the ideologies for which they stand. There are also indications that many Americans are disavowing their belief in God.

Some American leaders feel that the strong moral code and the high ethical standards of conduct inherent in democracy are not being continuously and properly respected by our citizenry. Movies, books, periodicals, and in some cases general conduct, frequently fall below the high standards required of democracy. There is also some indication that the American public is becoming more materialistic than a successful democratic society allows.

Many interested citizens and many organizations and associations have attempted to force schools to teach democracy through legislation, by requiring various courses. Practically all states require that schools teach some history course or some other related course in the Social Sciences with the primary thought in mind that this will assure the lay citizens that the American way of life and democracy are being taught to young people. Not too much consideration is given, however, to the method or the amount of emphasis being devoted to teaching principles of democracy.

Reading and recitations alone will not suffice at any grade level or in any area of the curriculum to insure the continuance of our democratic ideals. Applegate states that:

> American children, while born into a democratic society,
> unluckily do not come equipped with the democratic
> skills...If the democratic process is to improve or
> even continue, the skill of living together must be
> taught children with their pablum and practiced, until,
> as old men and women, they become again as little chil-
> dren.[3]

Educators and interested citizens have been advocating a new approach to teaching democracy for at least the past fifteen years. Historically, attempts have been made by schools to "get democracy across" to the students. The methods used by most schools have been very unsatisfactory. Democracy has been taught primarily through lectures, read-ings, discussions, and typical memorization and recital of facts.

Most educators believe that democracy can be most successfully taught through the experience method.

> The true end of democratic education is not book knowl-
> edge. It is not even the ability to speak and write ex-
> cellently. Democratic education looks to the control of
> experience. Whose experience? That of the person who
> is being educated.

> The need for training boys and girls in democratic ways
> of living has now been recognized and is bringing changes.
> The more progressive schools emphasize activities in
> which students may practice the techniques of group
> action.[4]

Many schools are making progress in teaching demo-cracy. Some of the more progressive schools are now em-phasizing activities in which students may practice the tech-niques of group action and self government. These schools plan democratic experiences as part of classroom activities. Yet, the majority of schools which emphasize experiences in democratic group living confine these experiences to the so-called extra-curricular activities. Some of these activ-ities are noteworthy, however, and involve student partici-

[3]Maurice Applegate, Everybody's Business--Our Children. Evanston: Row, Peterson and Company, 1952. p. 60.
[4]Gavian, Ruth Wood, Gray, A. A., and Groves, Ernest R., Our Changing Social Order. Boston: D. C. Heath and Company, 1953. pp. 576-577.

pation in cooperative school stores, banks, and cafeterias, assembly programs organized and conducted by students, special interest organizations such as athletic clubs, camera clubs, dramatic clubs, and music clubs, organizations devoted to cooperative planning and work with community interests, and student government.

Extra-curricular activities in which students are given real and meaningful experiences in the democratic processes should be encouraged in the schools. These activities are most valuable when they allow students the maximum amount of opportunity in experiencing democratic methods of planning, organization and action under trained leadership.

Unfortunately, the American public schools are not organized or administered in a manner which permits opportunities for experiences in democracy as part of classroom work. The rigid code and pattern of administration; the layout and design of building and classroom; the schedule and planning of curricula; the formal organization of classes and classrooms; the authority and discipline characteristic of teachers; the esteem and honor enjoyed by the textbooks; legislative limitations; and many other school procedures almost eliminate the concept of planned experiences for students in democratic group living.

One of the most promising ways in which democracy can be properly taught through direct experience is through outdoor education, particularly the school camp program. The teacher has the privilege of taking her students away from the bonds of rigid formality and the disciplines imposed upon learning in the classroom. They may go to the woods and organize themselves, establish self-government and live the principles of democracy. The learning process continues in all areas of the curriculum and recognition is given to the fundamental psychological concepts of learning. The Association for Supervision and Curriculum Development points out the value of experience in learning efficiency:

> The destruction of the sanctions through which some disciplines had justified the study of content unrelated to life and learners opened the way for understanding the learning process. A more tenable psychological theory

recognized the importance of experience in learning. Aided by this insight, educators increasingly helped young people to remember through meaningful experiences in remembering, to think logically through facing real problems to which logical thought was applied. Increasingly educators recognized that learners learn best what is part of their own experience. Thus motivation became a matter of high importance. Unless content really matters to a learner, he does not learn efficiently. The phrase "we learn what we live" succinctly sums up a major psychological insight which is of great significance for education.[5]

AMERICAN DEMOCRACY

There are so many principles involved in the democratic form of government that are compatible and in many instances similar to the many other ideologies of foreign governments that it is easier to point out the distinguishing differences that make democracy the best form of government. The principles and objectives regarding democracy, which most nearly distinguishes between democracy and other less desirable forms of government, consist in the emphasis on aesthetic values and belief in God, human relationships, self government, the four freedoms, American traditions of work, opportunities for the common man, and political freedoms.

Some of the everyday activities in camp allow a great deal of practice in the above American democratic ideals.

AESTHETIC APPRECIATIONS AND BELIEF IN GOD

The outdoor education program provides direct experiences with nature. Many of the basic ideas, values, and concepts of democracy originated through scholars whose basic philosophy emanated from their close contact with nature. Democracy is also the product of the writing concerning early colonial hardships and experiences of the

[5]Association For Supervision and Curriculum Development, Forces Affecting American Education. (1953 Yearbook) Washington, D.C., National Education Association, 1953. p. 5.

basically rural population whose toil and labor were re-warded from products of the woods, water, and soil. Early Americans lived close to nature; they developed a deep and sincere appreciation for nature. Nature, in turn, taught them to respect and appreciate their place in the universe and the integrity of their fellowman. An examination of the literature and the great works of art coming from the early settlers and from noted American scholars reveal that most of the poetry and art is the expression of experiences the poets and artists had in observing, investigating, and living close to nature.

The tremendous respect and appreciation resulting from man's contact with nature, the deep seated conviction in his belief in God, and the necessity for recognizing God through worship is displayed in the written volumes and documents. The most important ideals of democracy seem to be the recognition of God as a Supreme Being, freedom of worship and freedom of religious belief. Each man to his own choice.

In the Bill of Rights the first amendment granted to the people was freedom of religion. Man's constant contact with nature also revealed to him the important place he has in the whole of nature--the most important being, the most digni-fied, the only living thing provided with the power of reason-ing. These ideologies are an inherent part of the teachers methods when they turn to the out-of-doors and use nature for a classroom. The thought behind many present day democratic ideals and the writings for them came as the result of man's aesthetic respect and feeling for nature--the belief in the dignity of man; the emphasis on the impor-tance of reason and investigation to discover the laws and hidden secrets of nature, man's relationship to nature, and man's relationship to man.

Contact with nature revealed to the early advocates of democracy and to many modern proponents of democracy the necessity for recognizing a Supreme Being. Recognition of God can be considered as a basic concept of American Democracy. It is one of the beliefs that distinguishes it from many of the other world ideologies.

An examination of our famous American documents reveals the great emphasis placed upon this belief.

SALUTE TO THE FLAG

I pledge allegiance to the flag of the United States of America
And to the Republic for which it stands
One nation, Under God, indivisible,
With liberty and justice for all

DECLARATION OF INDEPENDENCE

When in the course of human events, it becomes necessary for one people to dissolve the political bands.....the separate and equal stations to which the laws of nature and of nature's God entitles them....

...That all men are created equal; that they are endowed by their Creator with certain unalienable rights....

...We, therefore, the Representatives of the United States of America, in General Congress assembled, appealing to the Supreme Judge of the world for the rectitude of our intentions do, in the name and by the authority of the good people of these colonies, solemnly publish and declare, that these United Colonies are, and of right ought to be free and independent states....

...And, for the support of this declaration, with a firm reliance on the protection of Divine Providence, we mutually pledge to each other our lives, our fortunes, and our sacred honor.

TYPICAL AMERICAN SONGS

AMERICA

Our fathers' God, to thee
Author of liberty,
To thee we sing.
Long may our land be bright
With freedoms holy light;
Protect us by thy might
Great God, our King!

THE STAR SPANGLED BANNER

Oh, thus be it ever when free man shall stand
Between their loved homes and the war's desolation!
Blest with victory and peace, may the heaven resued land
Praise the power that hath made and preserved us a nation!
Then conquer we must, when our cause it is just,
And this be our motto: "In God is our trust!"
And the Star-spangled Banner in triumph shall wave
O'er the land of the free and the home of the brave!

AMERICA THE BEAUTIFUL

O beautiful for spacious skies,
For amber waves of grain,
For purple mountain majesties
Above the fruited plain.
America! America!
God shed his grace on thee,
And crown thy good with brotherhood
From sea to shing sea

BATTLE HYMN OF THE REPUBLIC

In the beauty of the lilies   .
Christ was born across the sea,
What a glory in His bosom
That transfigures you and me;
As He died to make men holy
Let us die to make men free,
While God is marching on.

TYPICAL AMERICAN POEMS

I will make the most splendid race the sun ever
    shone upon,
I will make divine magnetic lands with the love
    of comrades,
With the life-long love of comrades.

I will plant companionship thick as trees...

Walt Whitman

This land is mine, for I am part of it.
I am the land, for it is part of me---
We are akin and thus our kinship be!
It would make me a brother to the tree!
And far as eyes can see this land is mine.
Not for one foot of it I have a deed---
To own this land I do not need a deed---
They all belong to me---gum, oak, and pine.

> Jesse Stuart

Go where he will, the wise man is at home,
His hearth the earth,--his hall the azure dome;
Where his clear spirit leads him, there's his
    road
By God's own light illumined and foreshowed.

> Ralph Waldo Emerson

He who, from zone to zone,
Guides through the boundless sky they certain
    flight,
In the long way that I must tread alone,
Will lead my steps aright.

> William Cullen Bryant

Our Lord and Master of us all!
Whate'er our name or sign,
We owe thy sway, we hear thy call,
We test our lives by thine.

> John Greenleaf Whittier

Trust no Future, howe'er pleasant!
Let the dead Past bury its dead!
Act, --act in the living Present!
Heart within, and God o'erhead!

> Henry W. Longfellow

Poems are made by fools like me,
But only God can make a tree.

> Joyce Kilmer

We grant no dukedoms to the few,
     We hold like rights and shall;
Equal on Sunday in the pew,
     On Monday in the mall.
For what avail the plow or sail,
Or land, or life, if freedom fail?

                    Ralph Waldo Emerson

For better or for worse, it's Freedom's hour---
     A shining contrast in a troubled world;
For here no despotism wields its pow'r,
     Here, under God, is Freedoms' flag unfurled!

                    Robert Frost

THE PRESIDENTIAL OATH

Before he enters on the execution of his office, he shall take the following oath of affirmation:

"I do solemnly swear (or affirm) that I will faithfully execute the office of President of the United States, and will to the best of my ability, preserve, protect, and defend the Constitution of the United States." (Recent presidents have added the phrase "so help me God.")

STATEMENTS FROM AMERICAN LEADERS

"There can be no prescription old enough to supersede the Law of Nature and the grant of God Almighty, who has given to all men a natural right to be free, and they have it ordinarily in their power to make themselves so, if they please."

                    James Otis

"Then let us pray unto that merciful and tender God... that it would please him to bless and water these feeble beginnings, and...so to nourish this grain of seed, that it may spread till all people of the earth admire the greatness and seek the shades and fruit thereof..."

                    John Smith

"Is life so dear or peace so sweet as to be purchased at the price of chains and slavery? Forbid it, Almighty God! I know not what course others take, but as for me, give me liberty or give me death!"

                    Patrick Henry

"I have sworn upon the Altar of God eternal hostility against every form of tyranny over the mind of man."

Thomas Jefferson

"The God that gave us life gave us liberty at the same time."

Thomas Jefferson

"God grants liberty only to those who love it, and are always ready to guard and defend it."

Daniel Webster

"I thank God my life has been spent in a land of liberty."

Andrew Jackson

"With malice toward none; with charity for all; with firmness in the right, as God gives us to see the right, let us strive on to finish the work we are in."

Abraham Lincoln

"Christ was the first true democrat that ever breathed, as the old dramatist Dekkar said he was the first true gentleman."

James Russell Lowell

"The world must be made safe for democracy...we shall fight for the things which we have always carried nearest our hearts---for democracy, for the right of those who submit to authority to have a voice in their own governments, for the rights and liberties of small nations, for a universal dominion of right by such a concert of free peoples as shall bring peace and safety to all nations and make the world itself at last free.

"To such a task we can dedicate our lives and our fortune ...the day has come when America is privileged to spend her blood and her might for the principles that gave her birth and happiness and the peace which she has treasured.

"God helping her, she can do no other."

Woodrow Wilson

"We do not distrust the future of essential democracy. The people of the United States have not failed. In their need they have registered a mandate that they want direct, vigorous action. They have asked for discipline and direction under leadership. They have made me the present instrument of their wishes. In the spirit of the gift I take it.

"In this dedication of a Nation, we humbly ask the blessing of God. May He protect each and every one of us. May he guide me in the days to come."

Franklin D. Roosevelt

"While resolutely pursuing the aims of democracy, which are the products of our faith in God and in the peoples of the earth, we shall eagerly grasp any genuine opportunity to free mankind of the pall of fear and insecurity which now obscures what can and should be a glorious future.

Dwight D. Eisenhower

"Whether you are citizens of America or citizens of the world, ask of us here the same high standards of strength and sacrifice which we ask of you. With a good conscience our only sure reward, with history the final judge of our deeds, let us go forth to lead the land we love, asking His blessing and His help, but, knowing that here on earth God's work must truly be our own."

John F. Kennedy

A recent survey reported in the *Psychological Digest,* a journal of the Psychology Club of the City College of New York, revealed that 45% of a sampling of Liberal Arts and Science students at the school did not believe in God. The pioneers of this country growing up close to nature, developed a democratic form of government and a firm belief in God.

Children, today, growing up in cities surrounded by man-made structures and living on an artificial man-made stage seldom get a chance to meditate or turn their thoughts inward. They are so removed from the "good earth," from the soil, from trees and streams, and from God's creation that they lose contact with the out-of-doors. Getting all their knowledge second, third, and fourth hand from books, magazines, newspapers, and television, it is not hard to understand how they may become narrow in their views, often without a heart or spirit and as mechanical as the machines and carbon civilization which surrounds them.

Could it be that students of the large cities have lost complete contact with nature and with God?

So engrossed in books, especially old books, and anything academic, many professional educators are guilty of becoming "desk men" surrounded by libraries and fortified by "canned knowledge" that their educational system comes about as near meeting the demands of a democratic society as a horse and buggy meets the demands of the American diplomat.

Becoming a slave to the printed word has tended to sidetrack the educational system in another way. If the printed word is important, then the more words and passages committed to memory the better educated a person becomes. Reasoning, meditation, moral and spiritual education often become secondary objectives to the zest for collecting knowledge. On many campuses throughout the nation, students belong to young communist organizations, free love socities, Godless and atheistic organizations because they have learned scientific facts but not scientific principles.

There is a too popular belief that it is not possible for a true and scholarly scientist to believe in a Supreme Being. Science teachers are so engrossed in turning out scientists that they neglect to teach or point out that science strengthens rather than refutes the belief in a Supreme Being. Too many scientists are educated in the college laboratory. It is alarming how little college classes in the sciences get out into the outdoors even in studying such subjects as botany and zoology.

Morrison, one of the great modern scientists, points out seven reasons why he believes in God. Most of these beliefs are the result of his contact with and his knowledge of nature. The reasons are:

1. By unwavering mathematical law we can prove that our universe was designed and executed by a great engineering intelligence.

2. The resourcefulness of life to accomplish its purpose is a manifestation of all-pervading Intelligence.
3. Animal wisdom speaks irresistibly of a good Creator who infused instinct into otherwise helpless little creatures.
4. Man has something more than animal instinct--the power of reason.
5. Provision for all living is revealed in phenomena which we know today but which Darwin did not know--such as the wonder of genes.
6. By the economy of nature, we are forced to realize the only infinite wisdom could have foreseen and prepared with such astute husbandy.
7. The fact that man can conceive the idea of God is in itself a unique proof.[5]

It is quite clear that the recognition of God and the freedom of worship are as much a part of democracy as freedom of speech. Central to the Christian faith is the dignity of the common man and his sense of responsibility for his fellowman. This is democracy; this is Christianity.

Living together in the out-of-doors in a camping situation affords one of the most enriching experiences in helping youth become aware of God and in providing an atmosphere for the most impressive spiritual setting available. Outdoor education tends to break down the exaggerated importance of man as it emphasizes the creation of God and develops a reverence for nature and all living things.

HUMAN RELATIONSHIPS

One of the greatest threats facing the democratic form of government and the world-wide prestige for which America has been noted is the breakdown of good human relationship. The failure of the American people to demonstrate to themselves and to people of other countries the democratic ideals of good human relationships does not further the cause of freedom and liberty in a world where both are on the defensive.

---

[5] A. Cressy Morrison, "Seven Reasons Why A Scientist Believes In God." Adapted from "Man Does Not Stand Alone," published by Fleming H. Revell Co., Copyright 1946 by The Reader's Digest Association, Inc.

Until the past quarter of a century, the lack of communication and transportation among states and among countries pretty well suppressed America's shortcomings in the broad fields of intergroup and human relations. The actual treatment of minority groups throughout the United States and the conduct of various individuals and groups who frequently violate the American code of human relationships once had more local and state influence than national or world attention.

Historically, America was settled by rugged individualists who left their foreign lands because of intolerance of varying kinds. America's early population consisted primarily of people often classified as the common man. Because of these factors it was quite logical and less difficult to organize a democracy. Democracy is often referred to as government of the common people or government of the masses.

The American forefathers were quick to draft declarations, constitutions, and legislation in an attempt to insure equality, to insure the recognition and dignity of every individual, and to insure justice and tranquility for all.

The sum of these efforts did not eliminate bigotry and intolerance in American society. Today, the lack of acceptance and compliance with these noble ideals is tearing at the core of democracy. For one of the most important and basic ideals of the democratic form of government is the belief in the unqualified worth and dignity of the human being. No longer can America hide or even tolerate the inadequacies now existent in this country in the field of human relations. The strength of economic and social systems depend on an intelligent approach to a quick and equitable solution to the problem confronting minority groups. This is essential in a democracy.

The world today has shrunk to the point where all nations regardless of race, color, or creed must be recognized as brothers of equal stature in a world community.

Because of recent advances and changes in technology, transportation, communications, education, economic and social adjustments, and health, the world has developed into

a large community of many nations with various cultures,
ideologies, colors, and ambitions. There are very few laws
thus far established to govern this community. The world
community must look to the laws of democracy for action
and government.

Compiling laws, codifying them, and interpreting
them for a world community is almost prohibitive. The
world community will have to rely on the ideological principles of democracy in order to sustain itself peacefully in
economic, social, and ideological compatibility and growth.
All nations must come to the conference tables as equal
members of a body politic to solve problems that will mutually benefit their representative constituents.

Most of the great American leaders, from the areas
of education, government, religion, and business have recognized the urgency of this problem. Franklin Delano
Roosevelt summed up the feeling of most of these leaders
when he said, "Today we are faced with the pre-eminent
fact that, if civilization is to survive, we must cultivate
the science of human relationships--the ability of all people
of all kinds, to live together and work together, in the same
world, at peace."

The American Association for the United Nations in
their "Declaration of Human Rights" list a simplified unof-
ficial version of the thirty human rights of man:

1. Since all people are brothers and sisters in the
human family, you should treat everyone with respect.
2. Your rights have nothing to do with your back account, family ancestry, religion, sex, color, or
political beliefs.
3. You have the right to be alive and to stay that way.
4. No one can make you a slave.
5. You cannot be tortured or punished in any degrading
way.
6. Your rights belong to you wherever you go.
7. You are as important as anyone else in the eyes of
the law.
8. If anyone takes away any of your basic rights, you
can ask court action to get them back.
9. You can't be arrested or exiled unless you've done
something wrong.

10. If charged with a crime, you will get a fair, public trial in an impartial court.

11. You must be considered innocent until proven guilty. You can't be punished for any act that was not considered a crime when you did it.

12. No one, without lawful reason, can read your mail, enter your home without your permission, or butt into your personal and family affairs.

13. You can come and go freely in your own country, leave and return as you please.

14. If you are persecuted in your own country, you can seek refuge in another.

15. You have the right to a nationality. No one can take it away or prevent you from changing it if you want to.

16. Once you're of age, you can marry whomever you choose and raise a family. You can't be forced to marry against your will.

17. You may own property, either by yourself or with others. It can't be taken away from you illegally.

18. You have freedom of religion and the right to express your religious convictions.

19. You may say, write and read whatever you choose.

20. You may form organizations and attend any public gathering. But you can't be forced to go to meetings or join any association.

21. You have the right to take part in your government by voting in free elections. And you're entitled to all the services which your government provides.

22. You have the right to social security benefits and, according to the available facilities, to live in dignity.

23. You may go after any job you can handle, and you are entitled to a living wage. You may join a trade union.

24. You have the right to rest and leisure, reasonable working hours and paid holidays.

25. You are entitled to decent food, clothing, housing, medical care, and pensions for sickness, disability and old age. Mothers and children deserve special care.

26. You have the right to a free elementary education, and to as much higher schooling as your abilities merit.

27. You may share in the enjoyment of art and science, receiving any profit that results from your own talent.

28. You deserve to live in a peaceful world where all these rights can be realized.
29. You must shoulder your own responsibilities to society, making sure you don't step on the rights of other.
30. Neither you nor any other person, nor any nation, has the right to destroy any rights listed in this Declaration.

The educational programs of a democracy obligates every family and every community to renew efforts in preparing youth for citizenship in the world community.

The field of human relations means experiencing, understanding, and compliance with the basic fundamental ideals comprising successful citizenship in the field of democratic group living.

Education for human relations involves knowledge and directed experiences in the democratic principles concerned with the dignity of man; in providing equal opportunities for living, work, play, and social progress within the capabilities of each person; in recognizing and ever defending the rights and freedoms of individuals to worship, speak, assemble, and write within the rights of the democratic structure; in seeing the values of peaceful methods for solving differences as opposed to belligerence, bigotry, and even war; in knowing the limits of tolerance when minorities or other groups attempt to undermine or destroy their liberties; in developing a dedicated faith and willingness to defend the principles of democracy when other ideologies attempt to sap its strength through various subversive techniques.

Unfortunately, organized education is not doing a completely satisfactory job of "education for democracy" in spite of the dedicated confidence the public has in its school system. The schools are not accomplishing a satisfactory job of teaching democracy and citizenship even though various organizations and citizens have demanded such teaching through legislation and other coercive methods. School administrators have not identified themselves with the fight against prejudice and discrimination. Many have not been oriented in terms of intergroup education and too often give passive support or pay mere lip service to the ideals of democratic education. The isolated knowledge and facts which they teach to accomplish a democratic way of life often becomes more important than the end for which it is taught.

When educators lose sight of the goals of education or confuse the objectives with the ends, memorization of codes, rules, and declarations necessary for a democratic way of life become more important than living democratically. Human relations and democratic living, thus, are often taught from a textbook by a dictatorial or autocratic teacher. Small wonder that democracy has to fight so hard to stay alive when even the schools have failed to support it!

Educators are becoming more and more concerned about the problem of teaching democracy and are beginning to recognize the need for improving methods for accomplishing these goals. The importance of teaching human relations so vital to the success of a democratic form of government cannot be magnified too much. Instead of trying to avoid community and school problems in human relations, administrators should welcome them.

> ...Democracy is a vast and complex cultural achievement in the sphere of human relations and social values. Like all of man's finest achievements, it is extremely delicate and fragile, difficult to maintain at the highest level of excellence and easy to let follow a course of gradual degradation. Democracy exists only in the patterns of behavior, feeling, and thought of a people. Let these patterns be destroyed and democracy itself is destroyed. And they will be destroyed if they are not acquired anew by each generation, acquired by the complicated process of teaching and learning. Much attention is devoted in the schools to insure the mastery by the young of reading, writing, and arithmetic, of technical skills and processes, of the arts and the sciences. This is all very good and necessary. But the mastery of the ways of democracy is a far more difficult task of teaching and learning and certainly quite as important to free men. The doctrine that children will learn these ways, if left to themselves, is as unsound as the thought that they would master geometry without the help of their elders...

> ...The American people should pass their entire system of theory and practice under careful scrutiny with a

view to bringing it into more complete and direct harmony with the articles of the democratic faith...More
particularly they should fashion an education frankly
and systematically designed to give to the rising generation the loyalties, the knowledge, the discipline
of free men. In a word, the American public school,
through its life and program, should proceed deliberately to foster and strengthen all those physical,
intellectual, and moral traits which are the substance
of democracy--to incorporate into the behavior of boys
and girls and youth the great patterns of democratic
living and faith.[6]

Most individuals are overwhelmed when considering
the magnitude of human relationship in a world community.
The thought of many countries assembling together to discuss problems with individuals of varying cultures, language, laws, ideologies, social organizations, economic
structure, and physical differences appears to encompass
phenomenal barriers seemingly incapable of solution.

An examination of the social and economic structure
of the citizenry of the United States reveals a very similar
problem. The people of the United States are 60 million
Anglo-Saxons, 15 million Teutons, 15 million Negroes,
10 million Irish, 9 million Slavs, 5 million Italians, 4 million Scandinavians, 3 million Latin-Americans, 2 million
French, 1 million Lithuanians, 1 million Greeks, and several thousand Orientals and American Indians.

The people of the United States are: 56 million Pro-
testants, 30 million Roman Catholics, 5 million Jewish,
2 million Eastern Orthodox Catholics, nearly 2 million
Mormons, a half million Christian Scientists, and many
thousand Quakers. Herein lies the root or the foundation
for education in the democratic principle of human relations.

Educators know that the first and only place for world,
national, state, or local education for human relationships
begins with the individual. In the case of the school, community, and family it begins with the individual child.

[6]Educational Policies Commission, Policies For Education In American Democracy,
Washington, D.C.: National Education Association, 1946. pp. 110-111.

Through this media and this alone can world problems be solved.

Human relationships should signify to youth cooperation, respect, good-will, equality, brotherhood, understanding, kindness, tolerance to all individuals and firmness, dedication, compliance, and defense of all democratic principles.

In the choice of method for teaching youth these principles, it appears that schools are seeking more satisfactory means to accomplish their objectives. Never before in history have more facts and knowledge concerning the physiological, sociological, ideological, and psychological attributes of all races of people been made more available to teaching and individuals concerned with the taching and developing of proper attitudes and appreciations of human relations in the world community. Never before in the history of the country has knowledge concerning all neighbors, both within and without the country, been more essential.

Knowledge concerning neighbors, memorization of American historical facts and documents, oral explanation of democratic principles, assigned reading materials concerning democracy, and required courses related to democracy are only the beginnings for youth in accomplishing complete understanding of American democracy, particularly as it concerns the field of human relationship.

Knowledge without appropriate experience does not produce the desired results. Leading educators have been consistent in proclaiming that democracy cannot be taught by formal classroom procedures. It needs many complimentary and supplementary educational methods to be realistic and of lasting value to youth.

It must be recognized that the chief deterrents of the American democratic ideologies in interpersonal dealings are prejudice and discrimination. The evils of prejudice cannot be taught realistically by class discussions or through the history and plight of minority groups. Nor can it be successfully attacked where community pressure and, in some instances, the teachers themselves are not willing to take democratic action to tackle the problem.

Discrimination can quite frequently be solved through enforcement of existing legislation or drafting of new legislation. Neither method should be necessary with a well educated public. It is necessary that American get "her own house in order" before she can realistically sit in assembly with a world community in the hope of solving world problems peacefully.

Eliminating prejudices of all kinds depends almost entirely on the educational program. The school, community, and family are all involved. Finding and accepting the best educational methods for teaching human relationships is one of the primary functions of the school.

The majority of the public schools have not recognized the importance of providing directed experiences in democratic group living. Most schools have taught the traditional history and social science courses concerning democracy as required by state law. Most schools have required memorization of documents and historical facts concerning the development of democracy. Comparatively few schools have provided experiences in democratic group living during school time or have attempted to correlate it to community and family living situations. Herein lies the value of an outdoor education and school camp program. The school camp program offers the greatest opportunity for teaching democratic group living through first-hand experience.

Living and learning in a modern camp where students participate in planning and learning together in small groups provide the most desirable atmosphere and organization for learning the democratic processes.

Historically, the camp has been used to indoctrinate various ideologies into youth from antiquity to our present civilization. The Spartans and Greeks took the youngsters from the home at a very early age and indoctrinated them into a way of life advocated by a political despot. In recent years, the youth camps of the Nazis and Communists are well known to citizens of the world. The success of these youth camps toward indoctrinating the youth of these countries into ideologies quite contrary to the American ideologies is still being felt today. Many educators feel that it will be impossible to change the deep rooted concepts of

Nazism and Communism installed in the youth at that time. Today these same individuals are the mature citizens of these countries and there is every indication that their early training to a large extent still influences their thinking and actions.

The ideologies of democracy can also be deeply entrenched in the minds of youth through camping programs which could very well supplement the traditional classroom teachings to a great advantage.

The school camp has some very unique offerings to make, particularly as it relates to the school's responsibility in teaching democratic group living. This implies more specifically the democratic principles involved in human relationships.

In a camping program, one of the most desirable features of the camp is the atmosphere and actual dependence upon close cooperative living experience where students learn to work, study, and play harmoniously together. The teacher becomes a part of the total family living situation. She becomes more of a parent or leader rather than a master or dictator. When students are camping there are many cooperative work, study, and other living situations that cannot be fun or successful unless each and every person assumes responsibility for their fair share of the tasks.

All are important members of a team or a small society where race and religion have no prejudice. A spirit of mutual trust and confidence, respect for each other, and dependence on each other is an inherent part of camp living.

In the planning and preparation of food, religious understandings become a part of the learning situation. Differences in food selections by various religious groups have a real meaning since each member of the small group has opportunites to explain fully the ideals behind their actions. These opportunities seldom are experienced in a classroom. Proper attitudes and appreciations for the brotherhood of man are inherent in well supervised school camp programs.

Children living in small decentralized families of eight to twelve under skilled leadership establish a democratic unit in the woods. These small groups, in turn, belong to a camp community. They manage their own affairs and are responsible for the welfare of each member of their group. In addition they carry on numerous projects in cooperation with the larger camp community.

In this setting children learn to:

Work effectively with others
 Willingly taking suggestions from others
 Thinking of the needs and desires of others
 Respecting the opinions of others
Cooperate for the good of the group as a whole
 (no stress upon competition)
 Willingness to go along with group decisions
  enthusiastically
 Encouraging others to go along with group
  decisions
Gain recognition through acceptable social endeavors
 Success in constructive actions
 Commending constructive acts by other members
  of the group
 Encouraging weaker members and helping them
  to be successful
Effective interaction with others

SELF GOVERNMENT

One of the distinguishing features of a democracy is that it is a government of, by, and for the people. American democracy is a system of representative self-government; that is, the people govern themselves by electing representatives by majority vote. The representatives are responsible to the people electing them and must account to them. In a democracy, the majority rules, but the majority's right to govern is limited by the right of the minority to criticize and oppose the majority.

In a democratic government it is essential that the citizenry is educated to the ideals of democracy among which are freedom, equality, liberty, and respect for the individual. Since democratic government is by the people, it is important that the people know what they are doing. They must be able to think for themselves. The truism that a chain is as strong as its weakest link applies equally to a democracy. Uneducated and ill-informed citizens may be swayed by promises and by crooked political bosses to vote against the best interests of themselves and others. It is the duty of the school to graduate informed citizens who have had practice in democratic living as well as the tools of learning and reasoning.

Thomas Jefferson pointed up the importance of education when he said: "I know no safety depository of the ultimate powers of society but the people themselves; and if we think them not enlightened enough to exercise their control with a wholesome discretion the remedy is not to take it from them, but to inform them their discretion by education."

The school systems today practice a much different concept of education than that proposed by Jefferson. There are still too many schools which maintain formalized classes where the teacher is the supreme authority and where the teacher feels that her job is to make the students learn.

The American school systems are structured so as to discourage self-government or at best to almost prohibit it. Most larger schools start with the supreme authority, the administrative personnel, superintendents, and assistants. The next level or class consists of the departmental chairman who must hold to certain disciplinary functions in order to hold their prestige and position. Next comes the large group of teachers who in many cases have rank classifications which are prized and sought after. Many high school systems and even grade school systems are developing and many already have similar despotic structure. In the smaller schools the structures do not always exist but the authority, dominance, and subordination are present.

Among the administrators, department chairmen, and teacher groups can be found many social cliques, small groups organized for personal improvement purposes, and other groups organized for developing internal improvements in curricula, facilities, and personnel.

The students likewise have specific class assignments according to age and in many cases according to sex, intelligence, and special interest. In extra-curricular activities the students are further organized into social gangs, teams, and clubs which are often based on economic status, social status, political choice, and in many cases academic interest.

The American school is not conducive to demonstrating self-government nor is it likely to modify its structure so self-government may be taught.

Quite frequently where students have opportunities in leadership responsibilities through extra-curricular activities and in some instances in the classroom, the student leaders will behave and pattern their leadership after the classroom teachers. Allowances are often made for discussions so long as it does not conflict with pre-determined decisions.

The typical American school, including all levels and types of schools, have a despotic political structure where self-government is something talked about but very seldom practiced. Such schools are characterized by unlimited authority, dominance, subordination. Self-government is rarely real. It is often structured and dominated by the administration and often becomes a governmental body to carry out the dictates of the administrator.

Education for democracy cannot be found in the classroom of the typical school today where discipline is brought about by rewards, punishment, external pressure, compulsion, coercion, and control is superimposed by the teacher. True democratic education is based upon attitudes, knowledges, and appreciations of right and wrong and respect for others. The student behaves properly not because he is ordered to do so but because it is the right thing to do. This system of self-government removes the police function of the teacher and makes the student a member of a democratic group. He is taught to give as well as receive; to follow as well as lead. Education, thus, is useful to the child while in school and will enable him to bridge the gap between school and society and between the student and the citizen.

Too many administrators have the idea that democratic school government means that the students should run the school. Instead the administration of the school is the re-

sponsibility of the administrator. He can administer the
school democratically or as a totalitarian. Too many choose
the latter method. A school is a democratic society should
provide opportunity for children to participate jointly in the
solution of problems affecting the school community. School
government through student councils, home rooms, and appointed or elected committees should encourage student
participation with teachers and administrators so that they
may better understand their function in a democratic society.

Nobody questions the schools function in teaching history or American government. Most state laws require
that they be taught. These courses, however, do not provide the necessary learning experiences in self-government.
Without an opportunity to practice democracy, book learning
becomes meaningless. Children cannot be expected to think
independently if they are required to follow blindly; they
cannot be expected to live democratically if they are trained
autocratically. Too many citizens blindly follow self-appointed political bosses because they were taught in the
classroom to obey without question.

The school camp provides an ideal laboratory for the
practice of self-government. In the small tent or cabin
group the democratic processes are continually experienced
in making decisions concerning studies, work, play, and
living.

Living together in small face to face groups, differences must be resolved and cooperation become essential to
every member of the group. In a camp, the welfare of the
individual and the welfare of the group to which he belongs
is dependent upon mutual respect and acceptance of responsibility.

Camping programs open with flag raising and the
salute to the flag. The story of the flag and its meaning are
thoroughly understood and appreciated. Respect for God,
country, and the traditions of democracy are stressed in
a functional way.

Each camper has an opportunity to fully express himself on each and every issue and finally must act as the

majority of the group decides. The campers have experiences in dealing with their peers as well as teachers or authorities who in many cases are older counselors or adults.

In many camps, the counselors have their counselor meetings and policy making sessions. The wishes and desires of all campers are carefully analyzed and most decisions are based on the choice of the majority. The teacher also is more inclined to rely on the democratic practices of listening to the discussions of the small camper groups, counselor meetings, and administrative councils. Here in camp is democracy in action. In too many instances, it is the children's first experience with democratic action. In camp, democracy has to be practiced or camping loses its most important contribution.

AMERICAN TRADITION OF WORK

Another characteristic of American life is the emphasis placed on the value and importance of work. There is a universal feeling in America that because of her democratic form of government it is possible for every person to succeed if he will work long and hard at a given job or task. All youth idolize the great American heroes and their struggle for fame, because most of them came from modest homes and were able to achieve fame through hard work. Such men as Abraham Lincoln, Thomas Edison, and Henry Ford are examples of American success.

Hard and dedicated work has held amost as high in esteem in American tradition as religion. The emphasis and importance placed on work by our forefathers has made a lasting impression on American culture.

Historically, the word "work" had a very significant meaning in the cultural development of America. Work meant survival and existence, cooperation between families and groups. It was a symbol of prestige and personal progress in a democratic society. Work signified creativity, the making and building of products in the whole, such as clothing, equipment, and supplies. It indicated status in the family group and community. It meant freedom from social disgrace and, in some instances, freedom from jail. It meant reward and approval, both social and monetary. It meant the American way of doing things.

Work was the kind that required both mental and physical prowess. However, there was more emphasis on the physical aspects of work since at this time in history the nation was predominantly an agricultural nation.

This concept of physical work is still considered the basis for success and accomplishment in America.

Early Americans looked upon work as a way of life where hard labor was exalted and leisure was frowned upon or held in contempt. Leisure was regarded as a form of idleness and was considered by the colonists as undesirable and sinful. Even young children who loved to play were criticized for wasting time. Play was considered a worldly amusement and was time poorly spent in preparation for the higher goals of life.

The early concepts of work were given support and impetus through various religious organizations during colonial times. The church lent strong support to the dignity of work, but clergymen were especially critical of leisure time pursuits because they were considered sinful and useless diversions.

The importance of work in our American democratic philosophy of life is still inherent in the minds and thinking of many American people today. Some of the concepts regarding work and play have changed considerably. However there is still a thread of the old Colonial, the Puritan, and the Quaker concept of work extant in modern day thinking.

The concepts regarding work, such as necessity, dignity, dedication, enjoyment, and social and economic rewards are truly traditions of American democracy.

American leaders, historically, have indoctrinated citizens to a concept of work that was and still is a guiding discipline for youth. This has been accomplished through actions, writings, and speeches, beginning during early Colonial times and continuing through the present day. Some famous quotes by American leaders include the following:

"No man needs sympathy because he has to work...Far
and away the best price that life offers is the chance
to work hard at work worth doing."

Thomas Alva Edison

"Genius is one per cent inspiration and ninety-nine
per cent perspiration."

Thomas Alva Edison

"Plough deep while sluggards sleep."

Benjamin Franklin

"No man is born into the world whose work is not born
with him. There is always work, and tools to work
withal, for those who will; and blessed are the horny
hands of toil."

James Russell Lowell

"Work is my recreation, the play of faculty; a delight
like that which a bird feels in flying, or a fish in
darting through the water, --nothing more."

Henry Wadsworth Longfellow

"I look on that man as happy, who when there is question of success, looks into his work for a reply."

Ralph Waldo Emerson

Some authorities feel that youth are now being deprived of valuable work experiences because of recent social
and economic changes in the American democratic society.

American youth still have a strong desire and willingness to work, but social and economic developments in recent years have dictated against including youth as an important segment of economic growth and development.
Attitudes also are changing among most Americans concerning work as it applies to society today. Some of these atti-
tudinal changes are not too desirable.

People used to "hunt for work;" later they "looked for
a job;" more recently they are seeking employment, a position, or a good deal. In earlier years a person looking for
work was primarily interested in finding some thing, some
place where he could use his skills and strength at physical
labor to the satisfaction of his employer and expect to receive

some kind of remuneration. Quite frequently the reward
consisted of pride and satisfaction of accomplishment in the
complete production of goods, as well as a nominal remuneration. The individual was interested in finding and doing
work to conform to his own self-satisfaction, to fulfill society's requirements, and to be reimbursed monetarily so he
could maintain himself and his family.

When individuals seek employment today, too frequently they first ask: What is the salary; how much vacation and
time off will I get; what are your social insurance plans;
what are my advancement possibilities; and what are other
concomitant benefits? The enthusiasm for the work itself,
the creative potentials, and the production or finished product are usually of secondary importance. They have for
the most part a one-sided approach--"what can I get, not
what can I give?".

Some of the social and technological factors that are
depriving youth of work experience and causing change of
attitude toward work include social and welfare legislation
and scientific and medical advancement.

In recent decades, laws concerned with child labor,
social insurance, fixing of liability responsibilities, union
regulations and practices, and contemporary school, military, and governmental qualifications and regulations have
almost eliminated work opportunities for youth. At best,
youth are allowed only seasonal work opportunities and even
these opportunities are gradually being eliminated through
child labor laws because of their "hazardous" classification.
Employment for youth in business and industry is more and
more difficult because of recent innovations in regulatory
laws concerned with liability, workmen's compensation,
social security, and health and accident. Unions are becoming more selective and age conscious in considering
youth for apprenticeship employment. The influence of
unionism is encompassing many more heretofore non-union
employment opportunities. Schools and other governmental
agencies are increasing their regulation and supervisory
control over youth through various welfare programs.

Automation has deprived youth of the unlimited number
of "chores around the house" that were part of every child's

growth and development. Automation has increased job opportunities for the mass of American people--all but the
youth. The work emphasis is shifting from heavy physical
labor with its accompanying muscle power and perspiration
to agility, skill, comprehension, and reasoning.

Progress in the social and economic phase of American
democracy has been phenomenal and most of it very good.
However, in depriving youth of work opportunities and work
experiences, it is gnawing at the thread of one of the basic
American traditions that must be preserved--the right,
opportunity, and encouragement of youth to work.

It is more of a moral and idealistic necessity in today's society rather than one of economics that we find ways
and opportunities of providing work experiences and work
opportunities for young people.

Educators are very much aware of this basic need and
are attempting in a meager way to do something about it.
Thus far, most of their efforts have been only in writings
and speeches. The educational opportunities in this area
are found only in a very few school systems. They are usually not included as part of the regular school curriculum.
There are also very few extra-curricular organizations
giving any thought or practice to this program.

Schools should assume a major responsibility in upholding and continuing this basic concept of the American
way of life. The camp, because of its simple society, returns to children the right to do useful work which is necessary to the welfare of his group and the camp community.
The school camp affords a very desirable location and atmosphere for a variety of purposeful work experiences.

The outdoor education and school camping program in
the schools provides the best and most desirable place for
these teachings.

Some of the values of work experience inherent in an
outdoor education program include development of pride and
satisfaction in accomplished tasks; skill and knowledge concerning the use and care of tools; physical growth and mental health; a sense of responsibility for conserving the natural resources; a feeling of importance to a small tent or

cabin group; spirit of cooperation in completing projects; an appreciation and respect for the work of other people; proper attitudes and appreciations toward work; and a basis for interpreting many items of course content in the curricula.

Many school districts which conduct outdoor education and camping programs have found the work experience program to be one of the more enjoyable and educational for both student and teacher. Work experience usually cuts across all areas of learning at camp or on a field excursion. Work experiences are planned and practiced in the living units at camp, in the preparation and service of meals, in cleaning and repair of the general camp layout, in conservation projects, in camp beautification, in preparation and participation for trips and tours, in setting up and breaking camp, and in many other opportunities that exist for interpretive work connected with program.

A list of work experiences which most typifies those now being conducted by schools throughout the United States in their outdoor education programs is shown below. It includes samplings from printed programs distributed by various state departments including education, conservation, and agriculture and outdoor education materials from public schools.

LIST OF WORK EXPERIENCES

1. Responsibility for government of the camp community.
2. Operation and management of the camp post office.
3. Operation and management of the foodstore and trading post.
4. Housekeeping duties (sweeping, dusting, making beds) involved in keeping the cabin or tent clean.
5. Raking and cleaning the grounds around the campsite.
6. Gathering wood and kindling and keeping the woodpile in ample supply.
7. Keeping the latrines and showers clean and disinfected.

8. Building fires for outdoor cooking.
9. Duties involved in preparing the meal.
10. Washing dishes, pots, and pans.
11. Raising and lowering the flag.
12. Empty trash cans and dispose of garbage daily.
13. Mapping the camp.
14. Improving walks and trails in camp.
15. Raking leaves to lessen fire hazards.
16. Planting, cultivating and harvesting in a camp garden.
17. Making camp tools, furniture, and equipment.
18. Planting trees.
19. Building bridges over streams.
20. Constructing mechanical erosion controls.
21. Seeding bare soil to prevent erosion.
22. Washing clothing and towels and hanging them to dry.
23. Pitching a tent and setting up a campsite for over night camping.
24. Care and feeding of horses and other camp animals.
25. Building campfires, totem poles, bulletin boards, and other program aids.
26. Care for waterfront equipment.

Providing meaningful and constructive experiences for all American youth should be an inherent part of their early training. The important educational aspect of these experiences is primarily to develop proper attitudes and appreciations toward work. As the youth progresses through school, he should be eager to seek and find constructive opportunities for employment with remuneration even on a part time basis. Youngsters are not getting these opportunities through the usual sources available to early and recent generations of Americans.

If the schools are to educate the "total child" then work experiences must become another facet in the educational programs. Curricula, legislation, facilities, teachers, administrators, and money must all be made available and dedicated to preserving another democratic ideal by providing educational work experiences for the youth of the country.

THE ABILITY TO THINK CRITICALLY

The only real alternative to autocratic government is an education that equips people so that they are capable of solving their own problems. The Educational Policies Commission points out that "Democracy places its faith in the inquiring mind which applies the method of intelligence."[7] Education is the heart and sould of democracy.

For many decades the schools have not been teaching effectively for the propagation of democracy. The American school system borrowed its philosophy from Germany, a country ranking high in literacy, but nevertheless dominated by militaristic and rigid discipline. German schools poured out information for memorization and emphasized the tools of learning, vocational concentration and physical development which met the needs of a totalitarian government. This type of education, much too prevalent in America, falls far short of the needs of a democracy.

The schools train children to follow blindly but society expects them to think independently. Slaves of facts and knowledge, expected to believe the printed textbook without questions, disciplined and coerced by a teacher whose education was the same, children become men and women who believe what they read and what they hear without question. How can children become good citizens of a democratic society when they have been trained to live in a totalitarian society of the school?

The schools of America have a gigantic job before them and it is a job that can no longer be put off. Every child in America must be educated, and many adults must be re-educated, not only to know, but to understand and be able to think for themselves. Ignorance is the greatest enemy of democracy and not until it is wiped out can America enjoy true democracy. For democracy is built upon understanding and understanding will dictate thinking, working, and voting for the betterment of the country and for the support of democratic ideals. The child must be freed from the autocratic teacher so that he may be able to work inde-

[7]Educational Policies Commission, Forces Affecting American Education. Washington, D. C.: National Education Association, 1952. p. 2.

pendently under the guidance of a teacher who knows and understands democratic procedures. The school will not only have to teach the tools of learning but must teach children how to use them and provide opportunities and problem-solving situations for their application. The schools will have to re-examine the needs of society and the objectives of education in order to get away from cramming facts and memorization of materials which are irrelevant to life and the living of it.

Too often citizens of a democracy assume the attitude that "I am as good as you" rather than "you are as good as I. " They believe that liberty gives them the privilege of promoting their own welfare rather than acting for the well being of all. Instead, real democracy is based on some personal sacrifice for the good of all. Schools do not emphasize this enough. Children's general behavior patterns are too often made secondary to the cramming, memorization, and testing of factual materials. Children need to be taught to cooperate with their teachers, with their classmates, with other classes, and with the administration in sharing their responsibility for a democratic, functional, and happy school environment. With experience in cooperation and sharing responsibilities in the school, children may well carry these attitudes, appreciations, and understandings over into their home and civic life.

This type of education should not be a choice for educators; it should be a must for every school in the land-- for more than most of us realize it is the very life blood of the democratic way of life.

Countries that have non-democratic political ideals which prohibit learning experiences and knowledge concerning anything but that which contributes to thinking and belief of a political faith or deity may well be taken as an alternative to democratic education. Books are destroyed that propose other beliefs; radio and television stations are rigidly controlled; public meetings are prohibited, and market place conversations are restricted and are frequently monitored. Death or imprisonment are the punishment for offenders.

In America the ideal situation is to provide all the

challenges possible for the school child. As Smith says:

> The obvious conclusion for the schools is that every
> effort possible should be made to advance any kind of
> local, social, economic, institutional, or cultural
> organization that will give to the boy and girl prac-
> tice in cooperation, a sense of fellowship, or a feel-
> ing of community responsibility. To aid in these
> things, every school insofar as possible should be a
> social and community center.[8]

Mme. Sun Yat Sen said, "Progress toward democracy
is like learning to swim--one learns, not by talking about it,
but by getting into the water."

Too often discipline assumes a more important role
than learning. The many characteristic traits which are so
essential to democracy--cooperation, respect, tolerance,
leadership, fellowship, loyalty, honesty, and responsibility
--cannot be taught by a mere memorization of facts. To
educate children for living in a democratic society the spirit
in which materials are taught is equally as important as the
materials themselves. Modern education is beginning to
differentiate between memorization of facts and the ability
to use these facts creatively. Facts are regarded as a
means to an end, merely tools of education, but not education.

Programs that take the child away from the classroom
where direct experiences compliment textbook learning are
becoming more difficult to negotiate because of the above
mentioned problem. Democracy is a way of life and must
be experienced in all its forms in order to develop attitudes
and appreciations toward the living of it.

It is an excellent teacher who can stimulate students
to this desirable climate in a classroom and more specifically behind a fixed desk. In a school camp program the
fresh air, sunrise, nature atmosphere, enjoyment and
eagerness of the youngsters to learn is always there. In
the out-of-doors children are called upon to practice democratic living if their camp stay is to be successful. Learn-

---

[8]Walter Robinson Smith, Principles of Educational Psychology. Boston: Houghton
Mifflin Company, 1928. p. 110.

ing what democracy means through direct experiences with it will give individuals a sense of appreciation for the democratic way of life.

THE IDEALS OF FREEDOM AND LIBERTY

The struggle for liberty and freedom is as old as mankind. This fight against slavery and bondage, tyranny and despotism is still going on. In order to win, citizens of the world must be guaranteed civil liberties or civil rights which include freedom of speech, freedom of the press, freedom of assembly, freedom of conscience, and freedom from false arrest and imprisonment.

In a democracy the government is the servant of the people. The citizen may criticize it and may take part in meetings of protest against it. The government is his and its success or failure is his doing. If he is arrested, he is entitled to a trial by jury.

Freedom in a democracy is universal, for the weak as well as the strong, for the minority as well as the majority. Any citizen regardless of race, creed, or religion is entitled to express his freedom so long as he does not prevent others from exercising theirs.

In his annual message to congress in 1941, President Franklin D. Roosevelt broadened the concept of civil rights when he said:

> In the future days, which we seek to make secure, we look forward to a world founded upon fair essential human freedoms.
>
> The first is freedom of speech and expression--everywhere in the world.
>
> The second is freedom of every person to worship God in his own way--everywhere in the world.
>
> The third is freedom from want--which, translated into world terms, means economic understandings which will secure to every nation a healthy peacetime life for its inhabitants--everywhere in the world.
>
> The fourth is freedom from fear--which, translated into world terms, means a world-wide reduction of armaments to such a point and in such a thorough fashion that no

nation will be in a position to commit an act of physical aggression against any neighbor--anywhere in the world.

In 1946, President Harry Truman appointed fifteen prominent citizens to serve as his special committee on civil rights. After a year of study and gathering information on the conditions of civil liberties throughout the nation and of holding public hearings, the committee submitted its report in a pamphlet, *To Secure These Rights.*

They set forth four basic rights as essential to the well-being of the individual: (1) the right to safety and security of person; (2) the right to citizenship and its privileges; (3) the right to freedom of conscience and expression; and (4) the right to equality of opportunity.

The Commission recommended twenty-three specific measures to be taken to safeguard these rights. Among them were: the enactment of anti-poll tax legislation; providing self-government and the right to vote to citizens of Washington, D.C.; enactment of federal legislation that would eliminate discrimination and segregation in Washington, D.C. and the Armed Forces; strengthening the civil rights code and providing specific punishment for police brutality and related crimes; enactment of federal and state fair-employment-practices legislation; eliminate segregation in schools; housing projects; and public and private health facilities.

Fighting for the rights of the individual and his freedom has brought about a new threat which Mark Ethridge, publisher of the Louisville *Courier-Journal,* in an address at Kentucky State College points out:

> The danger is that in our hysteria to achieve what we regard as security, we tear out the very roots of security--man's confidence in himself and in other men; in our hunt for subversives, defined to those who have arrogated to themselves the right to judge what is subversive and what is 100% American, we create real subversives. Those who would whittle away ancient and hard won liberties; and we set in motion forces so dangerous that frequently they can be

stopped only after they have left deep scars upon all of us...[9]

America's hatred of Communism and fear of subversives has brought about new threats to civil liberties. Many people are afraid to exercise their political rights or to disagree with a popular belief concerning government because of the tendency of some people to call anyone who disagrees with their point of view a "Communist." Self-appointed guardians of the "American Way" would deny freedom of speech, press, and assembly to those who differ with their opinion. Denial of civil liberties to any one citizen threatens the civil liberties of the entire nation of people.

Living democratically in a camp provides many attitudes, appreciations, and direct experiences where the basic freedoms are put to use.

Camp newspapers, counselor meetings, camper councils, tent and cabin meetings, and campfire programs all provide freedoms of press and expression.

DEMOCRACY IN THE MODERN CAMP

Various camping organizations in America point with pride to the recent development and progress of the modern camp. This pride results in the outstanding achievements attained in education, particularly character development, social adjustment, and recreational enjoyment.

The acclamation and approval of these modern camps stems primarily from their structure and leadership. The schools can profit greatly from the experience of organizational camps.

The distinguishing inherent characteristics of the modern camp consist primarily in the democratic way in which it is organized and conducted. Proper selection of the leaders makes the program function successfully.

The modern camp is usually divided into small units

[9]Mark Ethridge, "Danger From Inside: A Study of National Fear," San Francisco Chronicle, July 26, 1953. p. 14.

or villages for living and program purposes. Experience has proved that best program results are obtained and campers are much happier and relaxed in small group participation. The small groups are divided usually on the basis of age, maturity, sex, skill and knowledge, previous experience, home backgrounds, and desires of the campers.

In the small groups, attention is focused on the individual. Consideration is focused on the individual's needs and desires, his place in the living unit, his capacities and interest in activity groups, his relationship to his unit, the total family camp, and his need for counsel, companionship, and instruction by the leader.

The emphasis in camp administration and supervision is freedom. It focuses responsibility for planning and conducting programs back in the small decentralized units and on the individual campers and camp leaders. Freedom does not imply chaos in any sense of the word. It implies well-planned programs with self-disciplined action by each unit. It indicates freedom of choices and opportunities and freedom of governing themselves according to the highest camp standards as proposed by the overall representative and democratic camp government.

The program consists of everything that happens at camp. The planning, living, camp activities, ideas, discoveries, and evaluations all comprise the total camp experience.

HOW SCHOOL CAMPS FUNCTION

The class as a whole agrees on various rules and regulations that all campers are expected to follow. These rules and regulations are suggested and spelled out by the entire group in a democratic way. The teacher assists in arriving at standards compatible with school policies.

The rules and regulations are usually concerned with student behavior, academic activity, participation, and living while at camp.

The school curricula is discussed in terms of important contributions that may be learned from a school camp experience.

Various committees are elected to perform the many functions necessary for a rewarding living and learning experience at camp. Committees such as transportation, food, recreation, publicity, entertainment, and many others give the children a share in managing their own affairs.

The class is usually divided into small living groups. This is done partially on the basis of choice and partially on the basis of assignments. Frequently students are assigned to living units when the teacher feels it will benefit individual students. Assignments of living quarters are usually made to improve a student's social and education needs.

The leaders of each group are chosen by the members of the group. The leader may be a different person for each day and is usually a different person for each activity.

This small group organization affords an opportunity for the practice of democracy at its best. Every member of the group has many opportunities to elect a leader for the various activities, and many will themselves be elected to assume responsibilities for the entire group. In a closely-knit group, such as a decentralized unit of eight to twelve children in a camping situation, the importance of selecting the best and most qualified leadership for specific responsibility assumes its true perspective. No amount of promises or electioneering will be substituted for skill and ability.

Frequently older high school students or parents are selected to serve as counselors in the camp village or small unit. High school students may in this manner be given an opportunity for experience in democratic leadership so often denied them in the rigid and formalized school structure.

By using parents in the outdoor education program, two purposes may be served. In the first place many parents are qualified and can offer much in the way of constructive leadership and assistance to the teachers. Secondly, much in the way of good public relations can be accomplished by having the parents close to the program. On the scene, the parent may be able to recognize the value of children learning through first-hand direct experience.

The units usually elect representatives to an all-camp council which in turn helps plan events in which the entire camp takes part. This council becomes the representative government and usually acts on all matters which affects the entire camp.

The well integrated program emphasizes several areas in the school curriculum. They may not be taught as separate and individual subject matter areas as in the classroom but are woven into the everyday fabric of living at camp. Subject matter becomes a tool and not an end in itself, as it is used in first one pattern and then in another as children live and learn together in the out-of-doors.

Knowledge and skills often found buried in social studies, arithmetic, civics, or other textbooks are put to use on the spot as they are needed by the children. In this way they become integrated with life and become a functional part of the children's living--not facts and knowledge to be stored for future use.

The emphasis on several areas of the school curriculum is not a limiting factor in camp since the basis of success of the camp program lies in its freedom of discovery, investigation, and learning.

Experience in democracy and experience in the full use of democratic principles has its best opportunities for teaching in the school camp. In the camp setting, there is established a real living situation, a small community, a twenty-four hour per day relationship, an informal approach to discovery and problem solving, a new and constructive relationship between teacher and pupil new opportunities for individual adjustments and progress, and opportunities for full and complete use of democratic principles by actually practicing them under skillful guidance and leadership.

The thousands of American camps conducted each summer by private, semi-private, and public agencies have long proclaimed the educational value inherent in their programs. One of the most significant contributions the camp director claims is the teaching of democracy through camping.

It would be most desirable if more schools would

recognize the teaching potentials a camping program affords in democratic group living. Mursell states that:

> Even though a child in the elementary schools or in some cases the high school cannot clearly understand the constitution and comprehend its meaning like the National Bar Association would like, and even though the same youngsters cannot understand the many history courses for all levels that the American Legion likes, the experience that camping affords these youngsters in democratic group living will give the youngsters experiences in democracy that will enable them to better understand the constitution and the reasons for the importance of American history and the principles that our fighting men defended with their lives.[10]

The modern camp should be studied by all educators to determine what educational experiences and what learning can take place best through supervised laboratory experiences in camp.

DEMOCRACY IN ACTION AT CAMP

Many schools throughout the United States have been conducting school camp programs for several years. In recent years several states, through their State Department of Instruction or State Education Agenices, have published "Guides to School Camping." Other guides to school camping are being circulated by universities and local school districts.

Below are some sample statements selected from approximately twenty of these guides, which indicate the actual democratic experiences derived from school camping:

1. Small group living allows campers to adjust more easily to one another and to the leader.
2. Small group living provides opportunities for personal growth and limits the strain and over-stimulation resulting from the tight organization with its rules and regulations necessary to control a large group.

---

[10] James Mursell, Principles of Democratic Education. New York: W. W. Norton and Company, 1943. p. 175.

3. Students learn how democracy works as they participate in planning and carrying out their programs.
4. Students learn that freedom is possible only under self discipline that respects the rights of others.
5. They learn that individuals who try to impose their will by force in small or large groups cannot succeed.
6. Students learn the art of compromise, understanding, and good will.
7. Students learn discovery, observation, reason, and aesthetic appreciations through direct experience with nature.
8. Practicing good citizenship through care of the campsite.
9. Learning to get along with others by more experienced campers helping the less experienced ones.
10. Understanding pioneers by setting up a simple pioneer campsite.
11. Discussing ways to improve future camp programs.
12. Cooperating and helping each other.
13. Respecting others' opinions, ideas, beliefs, in order to live happily together.
14. Learning to enjoy new experiences such as foods, ideas, scenes, and activities.
15. Learning to be alert by seeing, hearing, moving quietly.
16. Sacrificing pleasures of the city for this period without complaint.
17. Learning to accept pleasantly the hardships of a more simple life.
18. Experience of living in a group.
19. Learning self-reliance.
20. Becoming better acquainted with staff.
21. Respect for the flag.
22. Care of camp property.
23. Comparing the camp community with the local community.
24. Exploring the farm community as a community and discovering how it ties in with the urban community.
25. Operating bank, store, and post office.
26. How to maintain friendly relations with neighbors.
27. How to plan a work project: How to divide and share responsibility.
28. Racial and religious food habits.
29. Food habits in relation to economic status.
30. Group work and fair division of labor in cooperative endeavor.

31. Understanding and appreciating folk life and music as they relate to inter-cultural relations.
32. Opening up possibilities for enjoyment and for building group solidarity.
33. Sympathy and understanding of various types of people are engendered.
34. Recognition of abilities, values, expectations of others may be learned.
35. Development and application of imagination.
36. Development and application of reasoning powers.
37. How to be a good sport.

Personnel available for working in camp have read about democracy and have a general idea of what it is about. But since they have never had opportunities to practice it, they cannot do a good job leading children in a democratic climate. The U. S. Office of Education published a guide to indicate all the aspects of a democratic camp. They call the following twelve points the foot rule for a democratic camp:

1. Evidence that the director and the staff members, as individuals, have a sincere interest in and respect for everyone on the campsite, as people, entirely irrespective of their contribution to the camp.
2. Evidence of mutual confidence among all members of the camp--directors, counselors, campers, employed help.
3. Evidence of the right of self-expression--of the tendency of counselors and campers to criticise constructively the camp procedures and to offer suggestions for improvement.
4. Evidence of the tendency on the part of all members to accept all others as equals, regardless of race, religion, and economic and social status.
5. Evidence of the delegation of responsibility to counselors and campers to the extent of their capacities.
6. Evidence of lack of many rules, restraints, and rigid controls; lack of fear of those in authority.
7. Evidence of participation in the formulation of rules by all those who are expected to live under them.
8. Evidence of participation in the planning of their own programs and the making of decisions by the campers.

9. Evidence of strong intrinsic motivations rather than those arising from coercions and administrative authority.
10. Evidence of initiative on the part of campers.
11. Evidence of free group discussions and frequent meetings of counselors and campers.
12. Evidence of the use by those in authority of the terms "we" and "our" instead of "I" and "mine."[11]

SUMMARY

Education is a powerful tool that may serve many masters. Communism and Nazism use education to mold the minds of children to follow blindly the dictates of their leaders.

Education alone will not save democracy. Nor does the fact that education in America is universal, and is free to every child, guarantee that democracy will survive. Education must be of the right kind. It must start with the individual and not the textbook.

It is generally agreed among educators that the primary purpose of today's educational system is to educate youth to become better citizens of a democratic society. In a democracy it is important that youth become useful, mature citizens who will be able to face life situations, think them through logically, and arrive at the best possible decisions.

In an everchanging and complex society, it is often necessary to change educational methods and to try out new ideas to meet the needs of individuals, groups, and society. The needs of modern day society call for knowledge and skill that could not be seen by the curriculum designers of twenty-five years ago. For example, new opportunities in leisure time have developed within recent years for which the schools of twenty-five years ago were not adequately equipped to provide. The same may be said for changes in industry and technology, political affairs, and many other areas.

[11]U. S. Office of Education, Democracy In The Summer Camp. Washington, D.C.: United States Government Printing Office, 1941. p. 3.

In the out-of-doors life is changing; life is moving. Printed facts of the textbook are supplanted by up-to-date realities. In a camp setting, children, too, are learning many traits so important to living in a democracy that cannot be learned in a stiff, formal classroom-cooperation, tolerance, leadership, "followship", loyalty, fellowship, respect for others, sense of responsibility and honesty.

In outdoor education, the child finds the fullest expression of his personality needs. It is his desire for acceptance by the group that motivates much of his behavior. The child must learn to be independent and be emotionally mature in order to carry his share of the responsibilities. Each person is treated as an individual, not as a group, and achievement is based on the individual, not absolute standards.

Outdoor education provides an unexcelled laboratory while learning through practice the attitudes and skills of democratic living. The child is placed in situations which will provide worthwhile experience and an opportunity to make decisions and regulate himself to the group. One learns to live the democratic life only by living the democratic way of life.

In an educational environment, the camp community is governed by the children. Camp problems are discussed and solved by the campers. Living in small decentralized groups, managing their own affairs individually and collectively, representing their group at all-camp councils, and participating in planning and evaluating their program, children may get first-hand experience so important to living in a democracy, yet so difficult to teach in the classroom.

Questions and Projects

1. Each member of the class may take a few minutes to write the definition of democracy. Compare the definitions. Organize committees to write a definition suitable to each member of the committee.

2. What is meant by a minority group? Have any of you, or do you now, belong to a minority?

3. Discuss the pros and cons of decentralized camping and centralized camping as it relates to teaching democracy.

4. A committee may want to do some research to determine the nature and function of the Civil Liberties Union. The National Conference of Christians and Jews.

5. A committee may want to investigate the organizations of the community to determine if any have programs that include the question of minorities.

6. What is the difference between special interest and general or national interest? Give examples.

7. Should labor unions or corporations be allowed to spend money to promote political causes favorable to them?

8. A class member may interview a local officer and report to the class on the activities of the League of Women Voters.

9. A committee may make an extensive study of lobbies, collect samples of appeals, talk to legislatures, read articles and then report to the class on the findings.

Selected References

Association For Supervision and Curriculum Development, *Forces Affecting American Education.* (1953 Yearbook) Washington, D. C.: Association For Supervision and Curriculum Development, 1953.

Callahan, Raymond E., *An Introduction To Education In American Society.* (2nd ed.) New York: Alfred A. Knopf, 1960.

Educational Policies Commission, *Policies For Education In American Democracy.* Washington, D. C.: National Education Association, 1946.

Gilcrest, Robert S., Dutton, Wilbur H. and Wrinkle, William L., *Secondary Education For American Democracy*. New York: Rinehart and Company, 1958.

Lee, Gordon C., *An Introduction To Education In Modern America*. (Rev. Ed.) New York: Henry Holt and Company, 1957.

Lee, J. Murray and Lee, Dorris May, *The Child and His Curriculum*. New York: Appleton-Century-Crofts, Inc., 1960.

Mursell, James, *Principles of Democratic Education*. New York: W. W. Norton and Company, 1943.

Rugg, Harold and Withers, William, *Social Foundations of Education*. New York: Prentice-Hall, 1955.

Stanley, William O., Smith, B. Othanel, Benne, Kenneth D. and Anderson, Archibald W., *Social Foundations of Education*. New York: The Dryden Press, 1957.

Chapter 8

CONSERVATION EDUCATION

The story of our nation in the last century as regards the use of forests, grasslands, wildlife and water resources is the most violent and the most destructive of any written in the long history of civilization.

—Fairfield Osborn

Conservation of natural and human resources must be an immediate concern of all American people. For natural resources, both physical and human, more than any other factor determines the well-being of the nation and the standard of living of its citizens.

When the pilgrims came to this country in the early 1600's, they found a land rich in fertile soil, forests, grasslands and a seemingly unlimited supply of natural resources. The land supported them as it did the Indians for centuries with game, fish, nuts, berries and maize.

With the great immigration from all parts of Europe, the early settlers began to push out across the Allaeghenies. In little more than 100 years they had raced across the continent. In order to feed the growing migration, land was cleared, virgin forests were burned, and the grasslands were turned over by the plow.

The improvements made on the plow and other agricultural implements made it possible to feed America's ever increasing population. But the two world wars in recent decades put such a demand on food crops that much land was cultivated that should have been left to grassland. America, in order to get a quick dollar, has robbed herself of millions of acres of land and forests that can never be recovered.

Even more damaging to the economic and moral fiber of American life is the lack of interest, understanding, and appreciation for natural and human resources. Too many citizens have been led to believe that America's natural resources are inexhaustible. America has always been a nation blessed with an abundance of resources and because of this her citizens have been wasteful and destructive. They have not developed a reverence, appreciation, and understanding for the land that sustains all life on the earth. America has not attached the same importance to conserving resources which other nations, less plentifully endowed, have recognized as essential to life. The great reserve bank of natural resources appeared to be impregnable against use and abuse. Too many Americans acted accordingly, only to find that now there is a great need for conservation practices.

Historically, conservation education cannot be recognized as important factors in the development of the American way of life and in the development of the United States. The long centuries of wanton waste and destruction will not be halted overnight, for deep seated habits and attitudes dating back to the Mayflower will not be changed without exerted and continuous effort of every educational institution and agency in the country.

CONSERVATION AND DEMOCRACY

Conservation as a way of life is fundamental to American Democracy. The very survival of the nation depends upon principles of conservation. Democracy is based on freedom from want and freedom is concomitant with plenty.

In other lands, there is a very definite and continuous educational program for conservation. Within each family there is a demonstrated need, because of shortages, to conserve resources. Attitudes, understanding, appreciations and practices in conservation education have been handed down from generation to generation. Schools also have emphasized its importance through well-established programs.

Many countries have experienced the same cycle in terms of natural resources that we have--from abundance and waste to shortages, then conservation or starvation.

Fortunately, the United States is still blessed with enough natural resources, with prudent conservation to adequately sustain the growing population.

Many ideals of democracy have been handed down from generation to generation and parents and relatives have thus had a substantial influence for good on the youth of the nation. The schools have furthered these ideals through the educational system. Unfortunately, conservation might be regarded as one of the weakest areas of concentration in education for American democracy.

The need for conservation education did not appear of importance in the early years of the nation's development, but today it is just as vital as the four freedoms. Without one, the other is of little use.

In a democracy the people are free and privileged to develop the natural resources of their country in any manner which seems advantageous to them. Any citizen or group of citizens can propose and help to establish any conservation practice which the democratic process approves. A lazy or indifferent citizen takes a chance of losing his heritage and impoverishing his nation by not conserving the many fine resources, just as he gambles with his freedom and liberty by not exercising his right to vote.

Democracy calls for intelligence and critical thinking, individual responsibility, energetic action and cooperation. These same qualities are necessary if America is to face the problems of saving her natural resources. These qualities are important to survival, not only for the freedom, the integrity of man and the democratic way of life, but for his heritage--the land, the forests and the beautiful rivers and enchanting lakes which have provided the setting for man's noblest experiment in self-government.

THE SCHOOL'S RESPONSBILITY FOR
CONSERVATION EDUCATION

Just as the public school is responsible to a democratic society to teach the skills of self-government and the duties of citizenship, it is equally responsible for developing concepts, attitudes and appreciations in the conservation of resources.

The best method for conserving natural and human resources is to have a well educated public; no other method will succeed. If the citizens of the United States are not prudent, if they do not protect what resources still remain, the United States may well join the ranks of those countries which have perished. Osborn states:

> The issue might as well be clearly drawn. The problem is how to conserve the remaining good natural soils that exist on the earth, together with the complimentary resources of forests, water resources and the myriads of beneficial forms of animal life there is no other problem. If that is not solved the threat to human life will grow in intensity and the present conditions of starvation that are already apparent in various parts of the earth will seem as nothing in the years that lie ahead.[1]

Conservation education and good conservation practices must be the task of all private, semi-private, and governmental agencies. The major responsibility for mass education, however, will rest with the nation's schools. They are confronted with a major task in building a public conscience toward the vital problem.

School administrators have recently renewed their efforts to make conservation education an important part of the public school curriculum.

Many leaders of the movement and many organized conservation groups are challenging and encouraging the schools to become more concerned. Fink states that:

[1] Fairfield Osborn, Our Plundered Planet. Boston: Little, Brown and Company, 1948. pp. 75-76.

Conservation must exist in the mind before it exists
on the land. The number one problem in the establishment of conservation lies before the educators of the
nation. The causes of destruction and depletion are
deeply fixed in the American way of life, in the habits, attitudes, and beliefs. Thus the superintendent
of schools is the key leader in educating the apathetic
citizen. Our schools should make the citizen aware of
the resources upon which he depends for survival, the
role they play in the rise and decline of civilizations,
and how they are to be regarded as to their abundance
and exhaustibility. Translating conservation into
school terms, the ultimate issue is hunger, squalor,
poverty, ignorance, destruction of physical and social
vitality, depopulation, and finally disappearance of
the civilization. Every teacher, in every grade, in
every subject, must share this responsibility of teaching conservation, the primary duty of our schools. Conservation being a matter for education, the schools
must accept the major responsibility of relating it
to ordinary life.[2]

Many educators have accepted the challenge of providing learning experiences and extensive curriculum and
library literature related to conservation. Yet many organized groups and lay citizens do not feel the schools are moving fast enough in this direction. These groups are in many
cases disappointed with the way conservation education is
being taught. When educators are slow to accept public
opinion in regard to their wishes, there inevitably follows
a host of state school legislation which adds required subjects to the curriculum.

LEGISLATION FOR CONSERVATION

Conservation education legislation is cropping up in
many states and may become common to the fifty states in
the immediate future.

Legislation is often regarded by school administrators
as one of the least desirable means for introducing subject
matter into the school program. If all subject matter fields

---

[2]Ollie E. Fink, The Gateway to Conservation. Friends of the Land, 1638 North High
Street, Columbus, Ohio. pp. 9-10. (Mimeo.)

were legislated into the curriculum, there would be little
opportunity for change and selection of courses in terms of
student needs. Other desirable school programs now being
conducted would be stymied and possibly eliminated. Some
legislation goes so far as to indicate how conservation education must be taught. In Montana the school law states:

> The state board of education shall determine the type
> of conservation education to be taught in the public
> schools of the state and shall also determine the type
> of services in this general conservation program to be
> given by the above named agencies at the various units
> at the greater university of Montana; provided that
> conservation education shall not be taught as a speci-
> fic subject in the elementary and secondary schools
> but rather shall be taught as a part of and integrated
> with all other related subjects and courses.[3]

It must be recognized that the public school systems
in general have not been doing an adequate job of teaching
conservation education. The record of school curricula
content and offerings is highly inadequate. The performance
of students and their parents in public parks, on playgrounds,
and in public buildings is poor. Many municipal budgets supporting these programs must spend 25 per cent of their monies to repair buildings and equipment and replace equipment
and supplies because of vandalism or improper use. There
is still a strong tendency on the part of too many Americans
to view the resources of this country only in terms of economic returns with little or no ethical consideration in regard to conservation. On the farm, the situation is improving. However, there are still too many who have the attitude: "You can't tell me anything about farming, I've already
worn out two of them. "

The same public sentiment and pressure which have
caused schools to take a new look at teaching conservation
education have prompted government agencies into action.

There has been a noted increase in activity and constructive planning through several thousand agricultural
conservation districts in the United States. Many Federal
Bureaus, including those responsible for the national parks

[3]School Laws of Montana, 75-2015.

and national forests, are showing more active concern about this problem. The same is true of regulatory agencies dealing with mines and minerals.

There have been several White House Conferences and other similar meetings devoted to the problem of conservation. Numerous public and semi-public organizations have been formed to safeguard America's natural and human resources. New legislation and action programs have been introduced. Laws dealing with child labor, social security, old age, food and drugs, unemployment, and health have been instituted toward this end.

Considering the vast amount of money, the voluminous and complicated legislation, and the diligent work of groups and organizations toward developing conservation practices and attitudes it becomes a little disheartening when the results are examined.

EDUCATION FOR CONSERVATION

Money and legislation are ineffective alone. Public education and acceptance is the real answer. This area has not been entirely neglected as many efforts along these lines have been excellent. Recognition must be given to all organizations who publish magazines and circulars; who conduct national, state, and local conferences; who provide other kinds of resource materials; and who dedicate their full efforts to the cause of conserving natural and human resources.

It is quite apparent that the schools could do a more effective job. A recent survey of educational methods and educational offerings in public schools clearly bring out the failures of the school systems in developing proper attitudes and appreciation of the problem.

Because of the teachers inability or because of the apparent lack of written materials or methods of teaching conservation, many teachers are reluctant to teach conservation. Few teachers, especially on the elementary school level, have adequate backgrounds in conservation education. Because of its imperative importance in a democratic society, teachers and administrators must be made to realize their obligation to teach conservation.

Actually, conservation is one of the easiest areas to approach, because it deals with the natural environment in which the child lives and thus, is of real interest to the children.

"Traditionally, both elementary and secondary schools have turned to textbooks as the leading type of instructional material. Perhaps this fact explains, partially at least, the seemingly slowness with which schools have accepted their responsibility for education in the conservation of natural resources. Altogether too many texts reflect an obvious disregard for this vital problem on the part of both textbook writers and publishers, a fact which can be demonstrated and illustrated with the textbooks used in the sciences and in the social studies."[4]

This study showed only scant attention given to the study of conservation in social study textbooks in both elementary and secondary schools. Until recently history texts, geography texts, and other books wherein one would expect to find the conservation problem discussed give but meager attention to the waste of natural resources.

Too few textbooks emphasize realistic problem-solving techniques. Most of the answers to important scientific problems are in the books. Many students are provided with laboratory manuals which add experimental work to the text. Answers to the problems are gleaned from the texts or from ready reference material. Yet, limited or no experience is provided with the local community or the local environment so students may relate and interpret facts and principles to day-by-day living.

Some of the more recent texts are examples of a more sound approach to teaching conservation education. Many of these are recommending and outlining the use of problems in developing basic scientific principles. Problems related to everyday living are studied and examined in relation to basic principles and generalizations learned from the text.

[4] American Association of School Administrators. Conservation Education in American Schools. (29th Yearbook), Washington, D.C.: National Education Association, 1951. pp. 76-77.

Direct, first-hand experiences concerning these studies are provided to make the lessons more meaningful.

Teaching conservation means teaching attitudes, appreciations, and understanding of the natural and human resources. Conservation education is not to be regarded as a special course of study; nor should it be considered as a curriculum offering of a special educational department. It should be considered as a way of life.

Teaching and living conservation is everybody's business in the school. It should be an inherent and continuous offering in all subject matter areas and all extra-curricular activities.

Teachers need to re-evaluate their methods of teaching conservation education. They must also re-evaluate the emphasis now being placed on this important subject.

Olsen states that:

> A number of different ways can be used to learn about resources. Direct, first-hand experience in seeing and solving problems of resource - use in perhaps the most vivid. But that direct experience must be supplemented by other types of experience - documentary materials, audio-visual aide, constructing activities, and community experiences - if learning is to be fully effective.[5]

The present day outdoor education program fulfills most of the basic requirements for learning conservation education.

It is true that any change in concept for learning and any new subject matter introduced into the present school curricula creates problems of administration, presentation, and source material. Solutions to these problems must be solved so that the best educational opportunities for students will prevail. Many school administrators and teachers measure the value of subject matter content and the emphasis placed on this subject matter on the basis of the

---

[5]Association for Supervision and Curriculum Development, Large Was Our Bounty. Washington, D.C.: National Education Association, 1948. (Yearbook) p. 138.

texts and printed literature available. The primary resources for learning conservation education lie in the vast
warehouse of discoveries, observation, and investigations
of nature, community resources and uses, and day-to-day
living. Students are limited only by their ability and knowledge to interpret these in light of their accumulated teachings.

It is quite obvious that: "The best materials and facilities for the study of conservation are those found in the
child's immediate environment. No vicarious experience is
as effective as direct experience. No textbook, pamphlet,
or flat picture, or slide, or movie can take the place of actually seeing the problem of conservation as it exists in the
immediate environment."[6]

Many observations and discoveries which take place by
students in outdoor education programs cannot fully be described in books. They do not always occur in chapter 10,
page 120 of the text. They can only be meaningful to the
observer. From these experiences and discoveries may
come other texts, inventions, or new mathematical formu-
las. Directed experiences for students by capable teachers
will insure these results.

CONSERVATION EDUCATION CONCEPTS

A great deal of planning and study has gone into the
problems of the teaching of conservation education in the
schools. Leading educators have searched for answers and
consulted with leading authorities in the conservation fields.
As a result of these investigations educators have outlined a
number of scientific and social concepts that should be a part
of the teachings of conservation education in the public
schools.

The scientific and social concepts which follow seem
important in every sound program of conservation education.
These concepts have been compiled with the assistance of
several widely known writers and thinkers in the field of
conservation. The order in which they are listed should

---

[6]American Association of School Administrators, Conservation Education in American
Schools, Washington, D.C.: National Education Association, 1951. p. 95.

not be regarded as the order of their importance. Instead
it is an arbitrary arrangement, dictated by an apparent
logic rather than by the significance of the items.

1. Conservation of natural resources means the wise
   use of natural resources for the greatest good of
   the largest number of people for the longest time.

2. The broad categories of natural resources commonly
   used include (a) <u>renewable</u> resources such as water,
   soil, animals, forests, grasses, and other vegeta-
   tion, and (b) <u>nonrenewable</u> resources such as minerals. Each of these terms, however, carries
   numerous shades of meaning, and for the various
   resources there are varying degrees of renewabil-
   ity or nonrenewability.

3. The most serious problem related to natural resources is how to conserve the remaining good natural soils that exist on the earth, together with
   the complementary resources of forests and other
   plants, water, and the myriads of beneficial forms
   of animal life.

4. Natural resources must be thought of as having an
   essential unity rather than as separate categories.
   They are inter-related and interdependent. This
   unity, the closely linked interdependence of soil,
   water, minerals, plants, animals, and man, constitutes the seamless web of life and matter.

5. In planning for the wise use of natural resources
   one cannot think of man apart from either his social environment, or culture, or his natural environment. Each culture develops its own ways of
   using natural resources.

6. In its broadest sense conservation is a way of
   life, involving processes that are social and ethical as well as material. It is not alone something
   to do; it is something to feel, to live.

7. No conservation program can succeed unless those
   who control natural resources accept the obligation
   of trusteeship for the general good. Posterity is
   entitled to a share of the resource heritage to
   which we have become heir.

8. The tide of the earth's population is rising and
   that of the earth's natural resource base is falling. No one yet knows the ultimate efficiency of
   man's resource use or, therefore, the eventual
   population-supporting capacity of the earth or any
   of its parts. Nevertheless, unless ways can be

found to provide subsistence for rapidly increasing populations, we face a dark future.

9. At the present rate of resource use, neither the United States nor most other nations can support even their present populations indefinitely on a high plane of civilized living.

10. Conservation applies to all people, rural and urban, and to be effective must be practiced universally.

11. The wealth of a nation depends upon both its available natural resources and upon the courage and resourcefulness of its people.

12. A given civilization, with its institutions and order, rests upon certain natural resources. Destroy those resources, in any case, and you destroy that civilization.

13. The seeds of resource destruction are present in every manner of resource use.

14. Our existence depends basically upon the living matter, whether plant or animal, that is produced by the earth's fertility, including the products of inland waters and the oceans.

15. Our energy and well-being, physical and mental, are dependent in the main upon the composition and quality of the diet. All of it, except fish and other food taken from the ocean and inland waters, is derived from the soil, whether in the form of grains, fruits, or vegetables, or in the form of meat and milk of animals which, in turn, live upon plant life.

16. Man must know and respect nature.

17. Science can aid and abet natural processes, but it cannot replace them. However, dependence upon the processes of nature does not, in any sense, exclude science and its vast benefits.

18. An important objective in all conservation efforts should be to bring about the maximum integration among such pursuits as farming, ranching, fishing, mining, manufacturing, and lumbering. Until the efforts to integrate these activities become more extensive and more effective, there will be dust bowls, silted reservoirs, polluted streams, and other consequences of exploitation and waste.[7]

[7]American Association of School Administrators, Conservation Education in American Schools. Washington, D.C.: National Education Association, 1951. pp. 72-74.

Concepts existing in the minds of men or in printed textbooks are of little value unless they are put into actual practice. It is not enough to know; there needs to be attitudes and appreciations developed. Children need to experience conservation; like democracy, it must become a way of life.

Most teachers understand and are willing to accept the basic concepts for teaching conservation education. Authority for the conduct of such programs usually rests in the decision and policy of the local board or the school administration. Local boards and administrators, then, must be made to see the imperative need for supporting conservation education and assisting in making it a part of every subject matter or school activity possible.

Until recently, too few books contained information about conservation based on the interests, needs and experiences of children. Books were written for adults. Now that conservationists and educators have realized that the public schools can and must play a vital role in saving natural resources, much progress is being made in the collection of material on conservation and in its preparation for school use. Even more important, children are being introduced to conservation problems on the school ground, on field trips and in school camps. In this manner they develop correct attitudes and appreciations and develop a clearer conception of their responsibilities and opportunities in conserving land, forests, wildlife, water and mineral resources.

Teachers colleges and teacher education institutions are now offering courses and workshops in conservation education for both prospective teachers and in-service teachers.

BASIC PRINCIPLES FOR TEACHING CONSERVATION

Many of the leading educators and leaders in conservation education have agreed upon seven basic principles for introducing the study of the subject into the schools. The most significant program in the modern day school which fulfills their requirements is the outdoor education program and, more specifically, the school camp. These seven basic principles are:

1. Conservation cannot be adequately taught through single unit or a series of single units in this field. While for purposes of emphasis it may be desirable to develop such units, it is only as the concepts of conservation are made a fundamental part of curriculum planning that the subject can be adequately treated.

2. The materials of conservation education lend themselves effectively to curriculum planning. Conservation forms one of the major themes which may appropriately be considered in curriculum construction.

3. The materials available in the field of conservation from both private and governmental sources provide basic material to be developed and organized for instructional purposes.

4. In developing a program of conservation education, it is important to consider the various aspects of conservation, but such consideration should by no means narrow the view of this subject for the pupils.

5. Conservation education cannot appropriately be confined to any one subject or field. Its understanding and appreciation come best through a knowledge of materials in several fields including economics, science, civics, agriculture, home economics, and geography.

6. The primary concepts of conservation can be understood and appreciated in their elementary form by very young children.

7. In developing a curriculum in conservation education, its larger concepts should be dominant and such aspects as the study of wild flowers, the protection of game, the proper utilization of mineral resources should be presented as elements in the development of a complete program.

Conservation education should not be the concern of any one teacher or any one department, but the business of the entire school staff. A careful survey of school and community conservation education resources which may provide areas for conservation experience should be made by the teachers. Pupils with teachers should survey and should have experiences in conservation practices through field trips and work experiences.

Most teachers realize today that learning is more effective if the children are involved in the learning process. Cooperative planning with the children will help in developing the concepts of conservation and in the acquisition of broader and broader understandings of their responsibility in a democratic society.

OUTDOOR EDUCATION AND CONSERVATION

Since it is desirable to make learning experience as direct and concrete as possible, outdoor education is a natural setting for developing conservation concepts. Teachers need not depend upon the textbook for materials, nor upon the blackboard to draw contours when just outside the classroom the groundskeeper is working to keep the school grounds from eroding, the trees healthy, and the plants beautiful. Just down the street the city park is likewise a laboratory for teaching good conservation concepts. Some schools own a school farm which all classes may visit throughout the school year in order to investigate and explore first-hand those things they study in the classroom.

More and more school systems are developing school camps where children may have an extended experience in a camp setting where they gain experience in conservation. By living close to nature conservation becomes more meaningful. Children understand their relationship with their environment and their responsibility in cooperating with nature to preserve this environment.

Outdoor education can have a tremendous impact on the students' understanding of the conservation of human resources. More discussions concerning this problem will be found in the next chapter. In the field of conservation education, students should be cognizant of the importance of the relationships of land and natural resources to their well-being. It is quite evident that in the few inches of top soil lie the essential mineral salt requirements necessary to sustain life. From direct observations by students and from knowledge gained from textbooks, they can easily see how acres of top soil are being lost each year because of poor conservation practices.

Many civilizations and many countries have degenerated and collapsed because of their continuous abuse of natural resources.

Osborn made this provocative statement:

> The supposition cannot be dismissed that the alarming increase of degenerative diseases, including psychological and neurological illnesses, may be related, in a manner yet to be defined, to the steady deterioration and wastage of top soil, the precious sensitive earth cover through which life flows.[9]

Man has always been conditioned by his environment. Modern science and experimentation with nuclear and atomic matters have shown that man is tied closer to his setting than previously supposed. Children can develop this concept by living and learning together for an extended period in camp. A camp program may be justified for the sake of conservation alone because of the previous failure of schools to develop a conscience toward the problem.

Concepts in healthful outdoor living, leisure time education, democratic group living can be developed around the concepts of conservation. All are very closely related. Camp administration and staff must be ever mindful of developing attitudes, appreciations, and wise use of natural resources as an important function of outdoor education. The interrelatedness of soil, water, air, plant life, animal life and the children themselves should be one important concept which children appreciate and understand at the end of their camping sessions.

CONSERVATION ACTIVITIES IN OUTDOOR EDUCATION

Much of the recent materials published by governmental and private agencies and organizations break the

[9] Fairfield Osborn, Our Plundered Planet. Boston: Little, Brown and Company, 1948. p. 86.

conservation education program down into several main
fields, subdivisions, or areas. Areas listed by the various
conservation groups include:

> Water Conservation
> Soil Conservation
> Wildlife Conservation
> Forests and Plant Life
> Mineral Resources
> Human Resources, and
> Recreational areas.

This breakdown patterned after the subject matter
classification of the public shools, is not conducive to
teaching the proper approach to conservation. Conservation is related and interrelated with all aspects of nature
and man. To discuss one aspect of the total problem of
conservation in isolation works against the proper conception of conservation as an intricate balance of nature. Teaching conservation in the out-of-doors and pointing out how
one phase is affected by another, or several others, will
produce much more effective results in understanding conservation problems and the responsibilities of citizenship.

It is best to approach conservation in its entirety--to
study it as a whole. After the essence of the subject has
been thoroughly established in children's minds, then the
individual areas may be studied more in detail through research and further exploration. It is doubtful that children
of the elementary grades are ready to approach the problem through the study of isolated segments.

Proper practices in camp can serve to make the life
at camp more comfortable and beneficial. Likewise, poor
practices can have a reverse effect and be detrimental to
enjoyable camp life. Every activity in camp should be conditioned to the extent that it become illustrative of the balance of nature.

Following are some of the unlimited activities in outdoor education which directly or indirectly affect conservation:

1. Selection of overnight camp sites so that plant life
    and forest growth will not be extensively damaged.

2. Using edible plants in outdoor meals.
3. Selection of site for campfire and taking all precautions to prevent fire from spreading.
4. Use of good forestry practice in gathering of firewood.
5. Cleaning camp area and disposing of garbage.
6. Using good forestry practices in selection of wood for construction purposes.
7. Care and protection of trees, soil, and wildlife.
8. Practice in correct land usages.
9. Correct procedures in extinguishing fires.
10. Construction and maintenance of latrines, refuse pits, and garbage disposals so that they will not pollute streams or disturb or be offensive to the camp site.
11. Use lashing techniques where trees are involved in camp construction so that nails are not driven into trees.
12. Get acquainted with state fishing regulations and know the various kinds of fish.
13. Instruction in wise use of camp tools and equipment.
14. Set up a weather station and learn how to operate it. Study the effect of weather on animals and plants.
15. Plant and cultivate trees.
16. Know and avoid noxious and poisonous plants.
17. Study the relationship of birds, snakes, toads, and other insect eaters to conservation.
18. Plant, cultivate, and harvest garden produce.
19. Work with Fish and Wildlife Department in banding birds and game bird census.
20. Prepare bare ground for fertilization or mulching and seeding.
21. Construction of check-dams and other mechanical means to prevent serious erosion of soil.
22. Study the history of the area, look over abandoned farms and open fields.
23. Lay out nature trails or riding trails using conservation practices.
24. Observe gullies and measure the amount of erosion.
25. Practice in contour planting of hillsides.

26. Visit a saw mill or pulp mill and seek information as to good or poor conservation practices.
27. Examine the source of the camp water supply.
28. Explore the campsite for possible recreational and historic places.
29. Practice in use of the compass and map-making.
30. Planned field trips by foot or by canoe to study the ecology of the area.
31. Explore the camp area to determine extent and type of action needed to help nature regain her balance.
32. Interview old settlers of the area to determine what changes have occurred in forest, cropland, and wildlife in the past fifty years.
33. Visit conservation agencies and resource people to learn more about specific problems in conservation of natural resources.

SUMMARY

America has been a nation of exploiters, wasters and plunderers, who have been unscrupulous in regard to her natural resources. The attitude and appreciation of the American people regarding conservation has been generally poor. The schools have given little recognition to its importance, and conservationists have depended upon schools very little to promote their cause.

In recent years there has been some indication of good school programming and dedicated concern by the teacher for the importance of conservation education. The gradual depletion of natural resources, the alarming rapidity with which public lands for recreation and wildlife are disappearing have brought conservation to the forefront and has made it a problem of every citizen and all educational agencies.

At first, the schools taught conservation as they taught all other subjects, in the only way they knew how--as an academic discipline with textbook assignments and question and answer sessions. While the teacher was teaching from charts and the blackboard, the school ground and other near-by community grounds were eroding away. It was hard for the early teachers to unite conservation facts with conservavation practice. It was more important to get an "A" in conservation on the report card than to put such knowledge into practice.

Today, most teachers are getting a background in conservation through field experiences and in-service workshops. Colleges and universities have added courses in conservation education to their curricula.

Good teachers realize that in conservation children learn by doing, by getting first-hand experience working and practicing conservation. Important concepts becomes meaningful attitudes, appreciations are developed, and conservation becomes a part of their everyday life.

Living close to the natural environment in a camp situation where the benefits of good conservation practices, or the consequences of poor conservation practices, can be experienced on the spot is the ideal approach to conservation education.

Furthermore, away from the world of a man-made civilization with its skyscrapers, modern conveniences and other modern evidences of man's conquest of his environment, children get a better perspective of man's true relationship and his complete dependence of nature. Man is usually regarded as outside of nature--separate and apart from his environment, the lord over all, the master of his culture and in many cases above his own social order. Because he has the ability to think and because he has seemingly mastered his environment, man has endowed himself with a false sense of power and has set himself up as the most important of all living organisms.

Living close to nature the children are brought to a realization of the true picture--man is just another link in the wonderful balance of nature. He uses the same environment and utilizes the same basic biological, chemical, and physical process. The air he breathes is also being used and reused by other organisms. The oxygen he needs for life has just been released by the surrounding plants. The food and clothing he needs are derived from plants and animals. Heat and light from the sun is used by all living organisms, not just man.

Conservation education approached in this manner brings a new insight into the relationship of man and nature and develops a reverence for those things beyond man's power to control.

Questions and Projects

1. Interview a local farmer, a miner, and a businessman, and find out what conservation means to him.

2. Make a survey of the natural resources in your community. Are they being used wisely?

3. Invite a Soil Conservation Service man in from your county to discuss with you the role his organization is playing in the conservation of soil.

4. Search current newspapers for articles on floods, water pollution, and the development of irrigation and water power.

5. Discuss the waste of human resources.

6. What relationship do city planners and landscape architects have to the conservation problem?

7. A member of the class may read Fairfield Osborn's *Our Plundered Planet* and make the book report to the class.

Selected References

American Association of School Administrators, *Conservation Education In American Schools*. (29th yearbook) Washington, D. C. : American Association of School Administrators, 1951.

Association for Supervision and Curriculum Development, *Large Was Our Bounty*. Washington, D. C. : Department For Supervision and Curriculum Development, 1948.

Coyle, David Cushman, *Conservation: An American Story of Conflict and Accomplishment*. New Brunswick, N. J. : Rutgers University Press, 1957.

Dale, Tom and Carter, Vernon Gill, *Topsoil and Civilization*. Norman: University of Oklahoma Press, 1955.

Dasmann, Raymond F. , *Environmental Conservation*. New York: John Wiley and Sons, 1959.

Hogner, Dorothy Childs, *Conservation In America*. Philadelphia: J. B. Lippincott Company, 1958.

McNall, P. E. , *Our Natural Resources*. Danville, Illinois: The Interstate Printers, 1954.

National Association of Biology Teachers, *Handbook For Teaching of Conservation and Resource - Use*. Danvill, Illinois: The Interstate Printers and Publishers, 1958.

Osborn, Fairfield, *Our Plundered Planet*. Boston: Little, Brown and Company, 1948.

Renner, George T. , and Hartley, William H. , *Conservation and Citizenship*. Boston: D. C. Heath and Company, 1940.

Chapter 9

HEALTHFUL OUTDOOR LIVING

Whether or not a teacher is conscious of the fact, he is responsible for the life of the children in his care. A child may get through life if he does not know all the facts of history and geography, or if he cannot do all the arithmetic problems in the course of study. But a child cannot get the most out of life if his body has been allowed to deteriorate and wear away through carelessness or ignorance.

Frasier and Armentrout[1]

Health has been defined many ways by many authorities. One of the most quoted definitions in the last decade is that of the World Health Organization of the United Nations. Their definition which is almost a cliche phrase among health educators state that health is "a state of complete physical, mental and social well-being, not merely the absence of disease and infirmity."

Health is a quality of physical, mental and emotional well-being which enables a person to live effectively, and enjoyably. President Dwight D. Eisenhower called a Conference on Fitness of American Youth in 1956. At this conference the Secretary of the Department of Health, Education, and Welfare said, "There is a third dimension to fitness, and that is the capacity to function in every way at one's own best physically, mentally and spiritually. I wonder if we are not moving toward a concept of well-being that involves, not only physical powers but also the whole of man's capacity for expression."

This statement seems to sum up the recent attitude of leading authorities in health education. Health, today, is considered as a vital part of the total fitness of man; it is

---

[1] George Willard Frasier and Winfield D. Armentrout, An Introduction To Education. Chicago: Scott, Foresman and Company, 1927. p. 70.

his capacity for living in all its aspects; his capacity for entering the activities required of a happy and successful life.

NEW THREATS TO MAN'S HEALTH

As the activities of man's life change from one generation to another, the threats and challenges to his physical, mental, social, and emotional well-being also change. Modern medical science has practically eliminated many of the dreaded diseases of just fifty years ago, but new threats have taken their place. Norman Cousins, speaking before a Washington Conference on *Personnel Policies for Schools of the Future* in 1957, points out a real threat to modern mankind:

> It is the real issue--not solely human life but the nature of human life today--that is threatened. The neutrons released by these explosions can twist man's genes all out of shape and leave their hideous mark on generations to come. In this way unborn generations will be punished for our failure--principally for our inability to understand what is important in our time and what is not.

Another real threat to the health of the nation is the stress and strain of the modern competitive social order. Millions of people are unable to adjust to the rigors of modern life and suffer emotional disorders such as anxiety, depression, hysteria, lack of confidence and chronic worry. Americans, in order to stand the pressures of modern living, have become consumers of aspirins, tranquilizers, and sleeping pills. As discussed earlier in this book, mental institutions are being expanded and built at a rate as never before, and yet the number needing treatment far exceeds the available facilities. Mental disorders have increased so fast that the latest statistics show that one person in ten will enter a mental institution or receive psychiatric care before he dies. Approximately, 50 per cent of all hospital beds in the United States are occupied by mental patients. Dean Quillen of Stanford University summarizes the mental health problems of the future as follows:

I think that the problems in the future will be increasingly in the area of mental hygiene and mental
health, that the development of anxiety and boredom
in our culture means that there needs to be more emphasis on individuality and creativity. I think that we
may be overstressing socialization because of the hold-
over of our memory of conditions in the 30's. What we
may need to be concerned about with many children is a
greater sense of privacy, a greater sense of concern for
their individuality and for the development of that individuality in terms of uniqueness in creativeness.[2]

The third threat to the health of man in the twentieth
century, is the lack of exercise and therefore poor physical
tone. There is reason to believe that many of the modern
health problems are due to inactivity. American youth are
physically softer than their fathers were at their age. The
more complex civilization becomes, the less man is required to exercise his body. Muscular weakness and lack
of physical fitness is due to machines replacing manual labor, labor saving devices, bus and automobile transportation,
sitting long hours in front of the television set, spectator
sports, lack of play space, and a diet of rich food eaten in
too great a quantity. Dr. Paul Dudley White, the eminent
heart specialist recommends walking and bicycling as simple and practical exercises that should be a part of everyone's plan of normal living. Since 1940, the Selective Service Administration has examined millions of young men.
Approximately 40 per cent of all those examined were rejected for medical reasons and one out of every eight rejected for some form of mental disorder.

Heart disease and cancer are two modern threats to
health that require much more research and greater health
information for all citizens, both youth and adults. Heart
disease is the nations number one killer, with approximately
a million deaths per year. According to latest statistics
Cancer may be expected to strike one in four women and
more than one in five men.

Dental defects heads the list of health needs among the

[2]I. James Quillen, "Current Changes in Community Life and Their Implications for
Health Education, " Los Angeles, University of California, 1958 Workshop in Health
Education. p. 10 (Mimeographed)

American population. It is estimated that American dentists are working with a backlog of 1,000,000,000 untreated carious lesions in teeth in America. Modern diet which includes rich food and a great amount of sweets have made the dental problem an increasingly perplexing one.

The environment of modern man is one of dynamic change and action. Because of the speed of transportation, the network of highways, the congestion of humanity in cities, and the many other physical hazards brought by moddern industrialization the prevention of accidents and the promotion of safety has become an important function of the schools. The number of lives lost, the number of injured, and the staggering property loss due to accidents reported each year by the National Safety Council, Inc., is almost unbelievable. Most of these accidents are due to carelessness.

HEALTH EDUCATION

Because the American concept of education has changed from a classical and bookish schooling to a functional process of living which deals in terms of life requirements, health has become the concern of the public schools.

In a broad sense, health education refers to all instruction (both direct and indirect) which may help the individual to acquire wholesome attitudes, understandings, and health practices.

More and more educators have concluded that health cannot be separated from the process of education and therefore, a school system is responsible for the health of the children in its care. The health program is an integral phase of the general school program. Health activities are correlated and integrated with all phases of the school program in order to make it a functional part of the child's life. It is no longer possible for the teacher to say "my job is to teach English, or Social Science. I am not responsible for the health of the child. "

In 1918, in defining the Seven Cardinal Principles of Secondary Education, health was stated first on the list.

Since that time, particularly in recent years, health has been given a more and more prominent place in the school curriculum. The school has rightfully assume its responsibility in cooperation with parents and community groups for attending the health needs of children.

The American Council on Education listed ten objectives of general education in 1941 and again the health objective was listed first. "General education should lead the student to improve and maintain his own health and take his share of responsibility for protecting the health of others." The Council further elaborated in the implementation of the health objective when it stated:

In order to accomplish this purpose, the student should acquire the following:

A. Knowledge and understanding

1. Of normal body functions in relation to sound health practice.
2. Of the major health hazards, their prevention and control
3. Of the interrelation of mental and physical processes in health
4. Of reliable sources of health information
5. Of scientific methods in evaluating health concepts
6. Of the effect of socio-economic conditions on health
7. Of community health problems, such as problems related to sanitation, industrial hygiene, and school hygiene
8. Of community organization and services for health maintenance and improvement.

B. Skills and abilities

1. The ability to organize time to include planning for food, work, recreation, rest and sleep
2. The ability to improve and maintain good nutrition
3. The ability to attain and maintain good emotional adjustment

    4. The ability to select and engage in recreative activities and healthful exercises suitable to individual needs

    5. The ability to avoid unnecessary exposure to disease and infection

    6. The ability to utilize medical and dental services intelligently

    7. The ability to participate in measures for the protection and improvement of community health

    8. The ability to evaluate popular beliefs critically.

C. Attitudes and appreciations

    1. Desire to attain optimum health

    2. Personal satisfaction in carrying out sound health practices

    3. Acceptance of responsibility for his own health and for the protection of the health of others

    4. Willingness to make personal sacrifices for the health of others

    5. Williness to comply with health regulations and to work for their improvement. [3]

It is the responsibility of the schools today to help each child reach and maintain the optimum level of physical and mental development within the range of individual hereditary possibilities.

The Joint Committee on Health Problems in Education of the National Education Association of the United States and the American Medical Association has presented the aims of health education:

1. *To instruct* children and young people so that they may conserve and improve their own health, and thus be more able to secure that abundant vigor and vitality which are a foundation for the greatest possible happiness and service in personality, family, and community life.

[3]American Council on Education, A Design for General Education. Washington, D.C., American Council on Education, 1944.

2. *To promote* satisfactory understandings, attitudes, and ways of behaving among parents and other adults so that they may maintain and improve the health of the home and community.

3. *To improve* the individual and community life of the future; to work toward a better second generation, and a still better third generation; to build a healthier and fitter nation and world.

Many modern day schools are in the process of developing some very desirable school health programs.

Unfortunately, most school health programs fall far short of minimum standards as recommended by leading authorities in this field.

The success of a good school health program encompasses the cooperative effort and cooperative planning of every individual connected with the school. It involves cooperation from parents, citizens and local, county and state legislative organizations. It involves adequate planning, care, and management of school land, facilities and equipment.

In those schools where good health curricula function, there are three distinct but closely related and interrelated areas of concentration on good health programming. These three phases consist of health services, health instruction, and providing a healthful environment. Numerous texts have been written in each area for the guidance and direction of the schools. Many schools have put into practice the recommendations of the medical authorities and professional educators in these areas.

Legislation is one of the least desirable ways to introduce courses of study into the school curriculum. However, several states have felt this necessary and have established precedents in health legislation. A rapidly growing population and the need for social progress led public sentiment and public pressures to develop legislation which seemed to be the answer for developing school health programs to fulfill the demands of health service, health instruction, and healthful environment for schools.

A number of legal enactments occurred in the United States around the turn of the century. By 1890, all states required instruction about alcohol and narcotics. In 1899, Connecticut legislation required teachers to test the vision of their pupils. Several states required the teaching of physical education before 1900. Today, many states require the teaching of physical education both in the elementary and secondary schools. Some states require physical education to be taught on the college level. In some states where there is a mandatory law requiring the teaching of physical education, the schools are allowed to substitute health education for a portion of the hours required for this program.

In the 1930's, the Nebraska State Supreme Court had decreed that the state's public schools were responsible for the control of the pupils health during school hours. In Utah, the school code requires the classroom teacher to be responsible for the health of her students. They must see that their students receive certain kinds of physical examinations and must notify the parents or guardians if any medical attention is needed. [4]

Many state and local laws and regulations are designed to safeguard citizens from environmental hazards and poor health practices. Many of their laws are not specifically directed at schools but because of the nature and function of the schools, they do have application. Laws and state health department regulations have application to such things as schools cafeterias, buildings, grounds, personnel, transportation, and equipment. Most states also have state health laws and regulations governing school camps. Many of their laws are specifically directed at camps and need to be understood by teachers and students.

Local ordinances and regulations concerning health are also intended to cover both schools and school camps in most areas. Many schools have drafted their own health and safety standards which in many cases are more specific and detailed than the laws.

Legislation has meaningful interpretations to students who participate in the outdoor education program because

[4]Utah Code Annotated; Volume 5: 593-94, 1953.

they become the doers and managers of their own living situations.

Health education is concerned with helping children and adults to live to the maximum of their capacity. Methods change as new threats and new ways of living become present in the ever-changing social order. In earlier years legislation became necessary because schools were concerned only with teaching the "three R's." In modern times, legislation becomes less necessary because schools are beginning to take the lead in adding those areas to the school curriculum that affect the welfare of the child in society. The responsibility of the schools has expanded to include many phases of life which can no longer be left to the home or community.

OUTDOOR EDUCATION AND HEALTH

One of the most noticeable and measurable contributions of outdoor education to the total educational program is its contribution to the physical and mental health of the participants - both teachers and students. No other school program can compare with the broad educational values of outdoor education in terms of healthful environment, health instruction, and health service. These three aspects of the health program become very meaningful because the success of outdoor experiences rely heavily upon proper health attitudes, knowledge, and practice. They are directly related to the success and enjoyment of the experiences and become an inherent part of the educational contributions in all activities. The above observations are particularly true of the school camp but to a varying degree they also apply to almost all of the other facets of the outdoor education program.

Outdoor education provides an ideal atmosphere for combining mental and physical activities. The learner is obtaining physical exercise as he wanders through woods, over hills, across plains, making first-hand discoveries and observations. He is back to nature and in his natural environment. His mind and body are functioning together.

In many cases the physical exercise is incidental to the learning situation but this is all the more significant.

This kind of activity is most conducive to the development of total fitness by the student. It is what is meant by total fitness--the mental, social, physical, and psychological development of the individual. In many programs there is an emphasis on leisure time education. Here the physical development of the child is further enhanced by learning many new skills in an atmosphere conducive to good mental health that will be enjoyed for a lifetime.

A camp program provides many healthy boy and girl relationships as they actively participate in learning experiences that cut across all subject matter areas. Furthermore, the boys and girls are at camp on a 24 hour basis. Practically all learning and all recreational activities are co-educational. Under the guidance of skilled leaders who are on the job 24 hours a day, the camp affords a greater opportunity than the classroom for a continuous laboratory in human behavior and group guidance.

The program develops large and small muscles; it develops strength and endurance; it also develops agility and improves organic efficiency.

Physical and mental health becomes important because an active learning program demands the best of an individual to produce its fullest reward and enjoyment.

THE CLASSROOM TEACHER AND HEALTH

Teaching of health attitudes, appreciations, knowledge, and habits starts in the home and is a continuous responsibility of the parents until the child matures. Since many parents have a limited knowledge concerning desirable health programs for their youngsters, the school has had to assume a major responsibility for the welfare of the students.

It has been pointed out in previous discussions the many ways and means that legislators and school administrators have used to ensure good health programs. Attempts are being made to strengthen health programs through legislation, by creating desirable environments, by providing health service programs, through adult education, and through other means of public relations.

In the final analysis, the interpretations and teachings of good health is the primary responsibility of the classroom teacher. No one can make a more significant contribution to the health of the school children than the classroom teacher. With her interest, enthusiasm and professional understanding of each child, the teacher can weave health instruction into every subject matter and every activity of the school day.

The teacher in daily contact with her pupils know the children and can detect health abnormalities that would not appear to one who had less contact with them. Through an intimate and friendly approach the teacher can prepare children for their visit to the school doctor or their periodic physical examinations.

The teacher is also in a key position because she more than any other person affects their physical environment and mental well-being. The classroom can be made more inviting and comfortable through attention to proper lighting, temperature, ventilation and seating arrangement. The teachers attitude toward life and toward the students has much to do with the mental health and happiness of the class. Most teachers are not equipped with the knowledge and skills regarding health education to accomplish the objectives of health education. In the formalized classroom the need does not always appear to be great. The health service department is close at hand and becomes a source of security.

Many teachers depend almost solely upon a textbook to teach health. Not only is this the established way of teaching in a classroom but this is the way in which the teacher has been prepared to teach. Fortunately, many of the better teachers realize that facts and knowledge concerning health are of little value unless the correct attitudes and appreciations concerning health are developed along with health practice.

The alert classroom teacher seldom misses an opportunity to correlate health topics with suitable materials regardless of the subject being studied at the time.

Health instruction may be carried on in a variety of situations including:

1. Teacher example,
2. Opportune or teachable moments,
3. Daily healthful living,
4. Correlation with other subject areas,
5. Direct planned teaching, and
6. Individual guidance.

Health education results from the experiences that a child has in school which affect his knowledge about, his attitude toward, and his behavior related to health practice. Such experiences are limited in the formal atmosphere of the school plant. Even at best very few schools are provided with real life-like learning situations. Much of the materials learned from books must be left to chance or to the parents to see that it is put into practice during the eighteen hours a day and over the week-ends when children are not in school. In camp, children are guided in their experience twenty-four hours a day. Teachers can see that the facts learned by instruction is put into practice.

When teachers know they are going to leave the classroom for out-door experiences the importance of knowledge and skill concerning the health of their students must be realistically faced. Teachers who have had many experiences in outdoor education have "arisen to the occasion" and have equipped themselves with the necessary knowledge and skills to feel confident in providing adequate instruction and adequate learning experiences to meet the students needs.

HEALTHFUL ENVIRONMENT

The school plant at best is an artificial and unreal setting designed for formal classroom teaching. Although the classroom may be a pleasant place where children have many satisfying experiences, it is only used about six hours a day for five days a week. The other eighteen hours (and the two day week-end) are spent in an entirely different setting--at home, on the playground, in church, and at various other community agencies and institutions. This makes it imperative that parents, schools, churches, and all youth serving groups in the community work together to provide a healthy climate for living.

Teachers often set up contrived experiences in the classroom to give children an opportunity to put health concepts into practice. These make-believe or role playing situations often have a dull ring; they are not real as in a camp setting.

The camping program provides the teacher with her own real laboratory for teaching health. Camp life is a healthy life and an excellent place to practice health habits in a controlled environment. Factors contributing to healthful environment are: living in the open with plenty of fresh air and sunshine, plenty of physical exercise, well-balanced meals, a free and relaxed atmosphere, regular sleeping hours, lots of fun and recreation, periods of rest and relaxation and few if any external pressures. The students may learn and practice day after day the teachings according to accepted standards concerning health attitudes, health knowledge, and health practice.

The school camp also offers a very desirable atmosphere for learning. The psychological principles for learning are an inherent part of the program. The program itself contains many desirable qualities that are conducive to good mental health. Some of the more descriptive words often used to describe a school camp program in terms of learning include: need, interest, readiness, repetition, fun, motivation, proper direction, reward, and self learning. Each of these desirable learning qualities have application to the teaching of health in outdoor education. There will also be fresh air, physical exercise, relaxation, enjoyment in learning and a new teacher-pupil relationship. Children will relax in an informal setting free from bells, clocks, marching from class to class, shouts of orders, dodging traffic, rigid schedules, lockers clanging, clothes consciousness, and other annoying school routines. Personalities of teachers and students quite frequently change and blend into the atmosphere provided by nature. Life becomes challenging, alive, interesting, calm, changing, and inspirational as children live close to nature away from man-made civilization.

HEALTH SERVICE

The required medical examination becomes more meaningful in an out-door education and camping program. Instead of the student record resting in the files of the nurse's office for reference it becomes an important instrument of information and guidance for the classroom teacher. The students physical condition becomes an important item and important factor in the total plans for an outdoor experience. In too many instances in the schools, the physical condition of the child is only the concern of the physical education teacher, the nurse, or the coach.

New meanings concerning the child's health are revealed to classroom teachers. Teachers become aware of the necessity for preventive medicines and vaccination against contagious disease. Through direct contact with the environment and through active participation in the health inspection and health appraisal program, it becomes necessary for intelligent action and closer association in living together on a 24 hour basis. The entire class comes face to face with problems that must be worked out. What are the physical limitations of each child? What must be done for protection against poisonous insects, snakes, and plants? What about climate, food, shelter? These and many other meaningful problems must be resolved in preparation for real living and learning experiences in the out-of-doors.

The medical service program in the school becomes an important part of the planning and administration of the outdoor education program. The physical examination, the periodical health inspections and other health services at camp are educational experiences in a friendly atmosphere along with other campers. In this way each child becomes more conscious of his health and its importance.

A great deal is learned by all participants in the outdoor education program as teachers, nurse, doctor and students discuss the need, the importance, the individual affect, the group affect, and the values in terms of conservation of human resources.

In the better school camping programs, the nurse is

not only the health service consultant, but is also the health educator. Working in cooperation with the camp director and every member of the staff, the nurse coordinates the entire health and welfare program of the camp. This includes the daily healthful living of the children and camp personnel, health inspection, first aid, safety, sanitation, food preparation, health instruction, knowledge and understanding.

Although the nurse has separate quarters in the infirmary building, she is a part of the entire camp program and as often as feasible she becomes a member of groups at campfires, on cookouts and at parties at the waterfront. She should know the conditions of the sleeping quarters, the kitchen, the dining room or cook-out facilities, the garbage disposal area, and other facilities relating to the general health and welfare of the campers and staff.

Medical service also assumes a more important role in the school program. Plans must be made to provide medical care of the groups who leave the classroom for education experiences. Contracts for emergency care of the students must be planned. A close liason is usually established between camp and the school medical service or provision is made for hospital facilities and medical care close to the area.

Teachers and students plan and pack the large first-aid kits for their trips and tours. They have opportunities to learn first-hand the necessity, values and dangers concerning the case of various items comprising the first-aid kit. Students are made aware of but not afraid of the many experiences in camp that are challenging, hazardous, interesting, and perilous.

Many schools which conduct camping programs feel that the health aspects of their educational offerings are quite rewarding. Teachers discover many new and different things about their students that make classroom teaching easier to plan and in many cases more effective for each individual.

Teachers have discovered things about their students that have in many instances been the reason for slow learning, inattentiveness, restlessness, drowsiness, and indifference. In living with their students they observe and have a chance to study in more detail the total personality and character of the child. Some of the more common discoveries and learnings teachers find in regard to their students are - poor eyesight, hearing difficulties, physical deformities, nasal stoppages, teeth troubles, and extreme posture difficulties. Other significant findings consist of asthma, allergies, sinus, skin disease, bed wetting and infections. A great deal is learned about the emotional, psychological, and sociological adjustments of the students. All of these observations make the teacher more cognizant of the importance of the health of the students and more appreciative of the importance of the health service in helping to solve health problems. The students are also made much more conscious of the need for health service and they learn a great deal more about their own bodies.

The school camp programs provide teaching and learning opportunities in health practices that occur through day by day living experiences.

The entire teachings of good health practices may be stressed and practiced in the living and activity programs at camp. Such things as body cleanliness; diet planning; food care, service, preparation, and disposal; sanitation; insect, rodent, and weed control; first aid; climate and weather protection; necessity for rest, relaxation, and sleep; necessity for body eliminations, body care, and body protection; and the relationships of disease, body fatigue, and illness to poor health practices are the inherent educational experiences and learnings which continuously occur in the outdoor education program. The program involves health practices from the simple kinds regarding the brushing of teeth to the more advanced kinds of dealing with diet planning and general camp sanitary practices. The opportunities for good leadership, teaching, guidance, and self learning in developing proper attitudes and skills regarding health practices are unlimited.

Health practices allowing for the development of good mental health also are stressed in the outdoor education programs.

When school camps are organized and planned in a democratic manner, the results of the educational experience are conducive to good mental health. The very nature of the program allows for so many different kinds of associations and so many different kinds of experiences that most individuals find opportunities for leadership, work, self-expression, and accomplishment.

Some of the more desirable health practices inherent in the outdoor education program which are conducive to good mental health include experience and opportunities in companionship, belonging to a group, receiving and accepting responsibilities, opportunities for leadership and excelling in some camp experiences, sharing in decisions, meditation, helping others, constructive work experiences, new leisure time learnings, feeling of importance as an individual, and feeling of equality in a living and learning atmosphere.

HEALTH INSTRUCTION

The health instruction program in outdoor education requires a variety of teaching methods. Many of the techniques now being used by the classroom teacher are retained. There are three other new opportunities for teaching health and safety which are directly related to outdoor experiences. First, some comprehensive planning sessions take place between the medical service director, teacher, students, and parents in preparation for living and learning in a new environment. The interest is high, the motivating factors for learning are meaningful, and the lessons are made to have significant purposes for each individual. The second phase of the health instruction involves the actual participation of activities at camp where additional opportunities exist for learning good health habits and good health practices.

Health instruction becomes meaningful at camp because health habits can be lived under the twenty-four hour supervision of teachers and assistants. Children can put health knowledge to practice in: their personal hygiene, planning balanced meals for cook-outs, sanitary food preparation, sanitary dish washing, dressing properly for changing weather conditions, keeping living quarters clean, cleaning the camp grounds, and observing other health and safety practices needed in the out-of-doors for themselves and others.

A comparison of learning environments show quite obvious changes in the relationships between teacher to student and student to student. The mental health aspects of the new experience in terms of environment, personnel, and learning can provide many teaching opportunities.

The third phase of the instructional program occurs when the students return to class. The learning is related to the many direct experiences the students and teachers have received while attending camp. An evaluation and an appraisal of experience related to health service, healthful environment, and health instruction are critically analyzed in terms of how they affected each individual in camp.

As a result of the new health education techniques there is a better understanding, there is greater appreciation, and there is a closer working relationship between the teacher, the medical service, and administrative personnel concerned with the health program.

Another significant contribution to health education instruction provided through these experiences is that the teacher has an opportunity to discover how health education relates to all subject matter areas. In living and learning with nature in small group shelters the curriculum becomes integrated and health education becomes associated with the total program.

Oberteuffer states the objectives of school health instruction as:

1. To secure behavior (action, conduct, habits) favorable to a high quality of living, and to point the way to those acts which, if performed, will assure this high quality.
2. To assist in the development of a well-integrated personality, enjoying life with no reliance upon false superiorities or inferiorities but with a stability rooted in a capacity for accurate self-appraisal.

3. To clarify thinking about personal and public health matters, to remove the superstitions, the false beliefs, the ignorance; and to substitute the accuracy of science, where available, for the darkness of falsehood and misbelief.

4. To participate in the development of a security against the threats and destructive forces of the world through the acquisition of scientific knowledge, the formation of scientific attitudes, and the practice of scientific behavior.

5. To enrich the life of the community and commonwealth through the collective action of individuals well taught in the advantages of health measures to be taken for the common good.

6. To establish the ability in students to see cause and effect, to recognize consequences, and thus to preserve life and the fullness of it.[5]

An examination of the key words of the objectives shows that they are action orientated - behavior, enjoying life, thinking, participate, rich, establish. They imply healthful living rather than the study about health. Learning about health is not enough. It is important, of course, but the child needs opportunities to practice and build his own health patterns and make his own decisions regarding what is good and what is bad health practices.

In a camp setting, health is an integral part of every activity. Habits and attitudes toward healthful living are under a twenty-four hour surveillance of the teacher and her assistants. In such an environment the teacher can see that the health habits and attitudes developed are desirable ones.

The outdoor education program provides meaningful and direct experience in many areas of the health curriculum. These experiences can easily be related to classroom teaching. They may also extend beyond what is taught in the classroom and require instruction as the experiences are taking place.

In the classroom students learn the necessity for body cleanliness. In the lower grades teachings begin with brush-

[5]Delbert Oberteuffer, School Health Education, (Rev. Ed.) New York: Harper and Brothers, 1954. p. 54.

ing teeth, washing hands, cleaning finger nails, bathing, and general body cleanliness.

When youngsters are in camp they not only learn first-hand from leaders who supervise these experiences but they learn from each other. Social relationships within the group work well towards accomplishing the teaching and learning of good health practices in regard to body care. Experiences also relate to teachings that take place in the classroom regarding all other aspects of body care such as medical exams, immunizations, preventive medicines, first-aid, clothing, food and rest. Learning also occurs regarding safeguarding each other from contagious disease, colds and natural hazards. Following are examples of some areas in the health curriculum which receives a great deal of emphasis at camp.

SANITATION

The teachings of sanitation become more meaningful in a camp setting. If every camper does not give attention to and work for general camp cleanliness and proper disposal of waste the entire camp family is adversely affected.

Many campers have experienced uncomfortable situations and sleepless nights when they have become careless with food disposal and food storage around their shelters. They have learned that poor sanitary practices invite mosquitoes and other insects, rodents, animals and frequently putrid odors. Campers sometimes experience stomach disorders because of obvious poor sanitary practices in dishwashing and general camp cleanliness. The good teacher or leader can prevent all these undesirable experiences by providing adequate instruction in the classroom and a re-emphasis while the experiences are taking place.

The problem of disposal of human waste is a real one in camp. Real camping experiences take the youngsters to areas where provisions must be made by the students for waste disposals of all kinds. Learning experience in cleanliness and sanitation is real and meaningful. The success of the experience is determined on how well good health practices are taught.

Students are given an opportunity to study general camp and community sanitation problems. How is the waste disposed of and treated in a camp? In the community? Where does it all go? What happens to the garbage and trash in a camp? In the community? Who is responsible?

Who protects the public from poor sanitation in restaurants? Grocery stores? Other food sources? Do we have any protection from insects and rodents? These are some of the interests of students when they are provided with direct experiences with sanitation problems of their own.

FOOD - (PLANNING, PREPARATION, SERVICE)

The outdoor education program provides experience for students in all phases of the food and water health instruction. First hand experience and observation where food is grown, how it is grown, what makes it grow bigger and better, how it is cultivated and cared for, how it is harvested, how it is packed, inspected or treated for consumer use, and what are the many problems involving getting the food to the table. Many schools have quite extensive garden and food production programs. They receive experiences in planting, cultivating, processing, shipping and marketing the food. Many concomitant learnings occur as the result of these programs in areas of conservation, chemistry, zoology, botany, economics, sociology, arithmetic, and other subjects.

Another important phase of the food program involves the study of dietetics. Learning occurs from the simple explanations in early grades to more complicated scientific learning in high school and college.

In a typical outdoor education experience, a large number of the meals are prepared by the students in their small group living units. Lecturing on a well balanced diet in the classroom usually means that "mother should hear what the teacher is telling me, " or "we should invite the cooks in from the cafeteria who prepare our noon lunch. "

When classroom instruction involves meal planning for a real experience in selecting, buying, and cooking meals, it suddenly has a significant meaning for the student. In school camping, teachers will make the nutrition unit which is studied on the various grade levels in the classroom real and meaningful--something to put into practice here and now. Scientifically planned meals prepared in a hygienic manner are essential to the health and happiness of the children.

When many meals are cooked by the small camp units, the campers become more cognizant of the real meaning of food in relation to their bodies. They often view food in terms of its contribution to vitamin and mineral, protein, carbohydrates and other content. They also are made aware of the effect of food on bones, organs, skin, elimination, muscle, glands, teeth and other parts and functions of the body.

Other important experiences which students have regarding food include the proper storage, preparation and cooking, seasoning, serving, and conservation.

Water is always a problem in most outdoor education experiences. In the short duration experiences, water is usually carried in containers from the school building. Some learning experiences are involved in even these simple problems of transporting and storing water. In the more advanced program in outdoor education, it becomes necessary sometimes to locate water, learn of its source, its condition in terms of sanitation, its treatment, storage, use, and conservation for camp living. Children in camp learn to know that they can make water pure by boiling it and that spring water is more likely to be pure than surface water. Not only do students learn about water in terms of the individual health needs; they also learn many other important things regarding water and its importance to our economy and our existence.

One of the valuable contributions outdoor education makes to the interpretations of health curriculum in school is the opportunities for observation, investigation and in many cases the use of the many plants found in the woods which provide food, medicine, dyes, decorations, poison, and other products that are only seen or used in bottled or canned form.

An experienced camper who has the knowledge and skills for outdoor living could in many instances live in the woods on the food nature has provided through plants and wildlife.

FIRST AID

The teachers and students are often the responsible individuals for first aid when they leave the classroom. Away from the immediate health services of the school doctor or nurse, children and teachers are on their own. It is important that they anticipate the dangers and the possible happenings and prepare the first-aid kit to meet them.

The first-aid kit becomes an important and meaningful item in preparation for an experience away from the school.

The outdoor education program provides a variety of learning and doing experiences wherein safety instruction and first-aid knowledge and skill becomes necessary and important. Almost every kind of first-aid practice proposed in the various text books will have application to a school camp program and in most cases to an outdoor education program of shorter duration.

When students are made to feel and understand that many of the things concerning first-aid being discussed in the classroom will affect their living in a few days at camp, it becomes more important and meaningful. Teaching safety, first-aid and health in preparation for a real experience about to take place will be learned better by the students. The institutional phase of this program and the learning process becomes more emphatic and meaningful as the students enjoy the various experiences associated with the teachings. The teachings have real meaning when they are applied to the experiences taking place.

Many situations which children are confronted with in a school camp require a knowledge of first-aid if they are to live safely and comfortably in the woods. Among the many problems encountered at camp which require first-aid are: sunburns, insect bites, bee stings, snake bites, poison ivy, poison oak, cuts and abrasions, sun stroke, allergies and many others.

PEST AND WEED CONTROL

The best way to learn and understand how to protect oneself against all pests, insects, and poisonous plants is to have real experiences with them. It is necessary to take some knowledge concerning these health hazards to the woods, but students will learn the true meaning of protection when they come face to face with the problems.

Most of the above mentioned hazards have been eliminated in the city or the home. Elimination has its problems and undesirable qualities in a natural setting. The learning becomes one of skill and knowledge in protection against and living with these hazards. Concomitant learnings have taught the plan and balance of nature in regard to pests, (including animals) insects, rodents, snakes, and weeds. Disrupting this balance may be more hazardous to health in the long run than the benefits derived from immediate elimination of the problem.

In some instances in immediate living areas it becomes necessary to eliminate these hazards and to do so is good health practice.

A study of the habits, breeding places, life cycle, and kinds of annoying pests, insects and weeds become important from the stand-point of health knowledge. It is also important to know how they may be eliminated, controlled or protected in terms of the most desirable health practices. It is important to know how to protect or treat oneself when this becomes necessary.

CLIMATE AND WEATHER

Living in a day and age where most students ride to and from school and to and from almost every place they are going, the climate and weather does not provide the challenge or the need for care by individuals that once was a necessity. Day by day living has been quite easy because of so many modern conveniences that shield men from weather and climate.

The outdoor education program provides a new learning experience in the study of weather and climate as it relates to health. Many diseases, physical discomforts, and illnesses are related to the care and protection of the body from climate and weather conditions.

Some of the more common hazards associated with outdoor living include sun burn, windburn, dampness, rain, lightning, tornadoes, snow, sleet, hail, ice, humidity, dust, pollen, other air impurities, gases, heat, and cold.

In an outdoor education program, students are encouraged to challenge nature when it appears feasible, safe, and educationally beneficial to do so. The best way to study climate and weather is to become involved with it and learn first-hand what must be done to protect oneself in the way of clothing, shelter, and living outdoors. It is not necessary to call off the days educational experience in the out-of-doors if students have the knowledge and skills to cope with the weather. From a health standpoint the participant soon learns how to adjust through self preservation where weather and climate do not become a major deterrent to living and learning outdoors.

NATURAL HAZARDS

Nature has provided an unlimited number of areas of scenic and aesthetic beauty. Many of these areas can only be enjoyed and studied by hiking to and through them. Some of these areas are challenging but dangerous to students because of the steep cliffs and mountains, treacherous paths, rugged rocks and boulders, swift flowing streams, heavily wooded areas, heavy thickets, vines and weeds, and other phenomena of nature which is interesting. Areas of this kind need to be surveyed and studied by teachers before extensive use is made of them for educational purposes. Students may also enjoy learning experiences in safety and precaution as they enjoy trips and hikes to these areas. Students are made aware of such things as proper hiking techniques including clothing and gear; observations for falling rock, tree limbs, and land slides; selecting secure resting places; danger of avoiding hazards such as quicksand, whirlpools, large game habitats, power stations and other man-made hazards; and proper conduct and knowledge concerning all water activities. Knowledge and skill necessary for the safe enjoyment and the resultant educational benefits derived from these experiences is essential for teacher and students.

Another important phase of the health and safety program consists of an inspection and understanding of the camp area and surrounding areas to be used for programs.

Children as well as staff should be involved in the elimination of poison ivy and poison oak, in seeing that dogs or camp pets are immuned against rabies, in seeing that shelters are water proof, in locating sites suitable for wind storms and tornadoes, and in filling eroded ditches or marking off other hazards to talking at night.

This type of program combines a rich experience for the learners in both mental and physical health.

SUMMARY

Modern existence has been both a blessing and a burden to the health of man. While modern science has helped him to conquer many dreaded diseases, it has also put him under greater stress and strain. The incessant change in man's habit patterns, the rigid and scheduled urban life, the relentless pressures of the modern competitive society, the strain due to uncertainty of financial or economic status, the worry over war and world conditions and many other characteristics of modern life, together with a relatively sedentary existence, tend to adversely affect the health of man.

Man has not always led a sedentary life. For century upon century his existence required hard work involving the use of his body in the open. He ate heavy foods and fed a hungry body that needed lots of energy. Modern life has taken away the necessary toil but man has not yet learned to make physical and mental healthful adjustment to this life. He gets too little recreation, too little exercise, and too many calories.

The public schools are beginning to assume their rightful responsibility in teaching health to all children. The better schools are combining health experience with instruction. By providing health service and a healthful environment, children are better able to understand health and through practice it becomes a part of their life.

The informality of the outdoor classroom is more conducive to a healthy democratic climate. Dictator tactics often employed in the formal classroom are hard on the teacher as well as on the pupils. The teacher who can share responsibilities with her pupils will be a better, a happier, and a healthier teacher. Outdoor education encourages informality, shared experiences, and an atmosphere of fun in learning.

Outdoor education is an ideal setting for teaching health habits and attitudes. Living twenty-four hours a day with a group of classmates, health becomes something real, something that must be dealt with, something that must have attention and not something to study or prepare for later in life.

In addition, the teacher is with her pupils not six hours a day as in the classroom but night and day. The health instruction which may or may not be put to practice at home can be properly supervised by the teacher and properly practiced by the children.

Questions and Projects

1. In what ways does health education present greater administrative problems than most other phases of the school program?

2. Make a list of the health problems of one-hundred years ago and a list of the health problems confronting the people of today. What factors account for the difference?

3. Write the National Safety Council for latest state and national statistics on accidents and safety.

4. What factors give rise to the increasing problems related to mental health in this country?

5. What advantages does the teacher have in teaching health in a camp setting over teaching health in a classroom?

6. What part do students have in maintaining a healthful school environment? A healthful camp environment?

7. List the advantages and disadvantages of both direct and incidental teaching of health.

8. What is the relation of health education and physical education in the schools? In a camp setting?

9. How is health related to the other objectives of education?

10. Of what value is it to have a world-wide approach to health as exemplified by the World Health Organization?

11. Select one of the following topics for further study:

> Exercise and Health
> Sleep, Rest and Relaxation
> Control of Communicable Disease
> Health Knowledge and Health Attitudes
> Health Instruction in a School Camp.

12. The nature of the modern school is such that an imaginative teacher has to set up contrived experiences to teach some aspects of health and safety. List the real situations in healthful living that children may experience in a school camp.

Selected References

Anderson, C. L., *School Health Practice.* St. Louis: The C. V. Mosby Company, 1960.

Basowitz, Harold, et al., *Anxiety and Stress.* New York: McGraw-Hill Book Company, 1955.

Brownell, Clifford Lee, *Principles of Health Education Applied.* New York: McGraw-Hill Book Company, 1949.

Eaton, Joseph W., *Culture and Mental Disorders*. Glencoe, Illinois: Free Press, 1955.

Grout, Ruth E., *Health Training In Schools*. (third ed.) Philadelphia: W. B. Saunders, 1959.

Oberteuffer, Delbert, *School Health Education*. (third ed.) New York: Harper and Brothers, 1960.

Willgoose, Carl E., *Health Education In The Elementary School*. Philadelphia: W. B. Saunders Company, 1959.

World Health Organization, Division of Public Information, *A Strategy For World Health*. Geneva, 1956.

Chapter 10

LEISURE TIME EDUCATION

"Universal leisure is the soil from which must inevitably come a universal culture." [1]

—*Raymond B. Fosdick*

The introduction of an abundance of leisure time into the American social structure is opening up a large number of challenging and perplexing opportunities for all American citizens.

NEW LEISURE

Modern leisure has a much different connotation than it had a few decades ago. For many years the Aristotelian concept of leisure was widely accepted by educators and philosophers. Leisure was considered as the reward for work or as "time off" which work had earned. It was regarded as necessary time for creative advancement by individuals in all cultural and scientific endeavors. Time off from work was a goal for each individual to attain. Leisure was something that man longed for and sought after to do the many things he had always dreamed of doing.

Part of this Aristotelian concept is still important to modern leisure; however, it still does not encompass all the ramifications of "free time" associated with modern society.

The contributions of science, philosophy, medicine, law, education, business, and agriculture have all made

[1]Raymond B. Fosdick, The Old Savage In The New Civilization. New York: Doubleday Doran and Company, 1934. p. 110.

leisure for the masses a reality. Progress in these fields have also contributed concomitant problems for the masses in adjusting to the new leisure. Leisure means more than "time off from work." Soule states that:

> Leisure is not to be equated with idleness, especially not with the enforced idleness of one who is deprived of work which he would prefer to free time, either because he likes his job and the community of interests with which it provides him, or because he needs products and services which he cannot buy because his income without work is insufficient. Unemployment is not leisure. Neither is retirement leisure, insofar as it is not freely chosen by the retired. The concept of leisure implies the absence of compulsion to work arising from want of material goods and services. It implies free choice in the use of one's time whether for work or for play. A member of the traditional "leisure class" may indeed work hard at some self-chosen occupation. Many of the greatest intellectual and artistic achievements have been stimulated, not by commercial demand, but by the interest and dedication of men who could choose how to spend their lives because they did not have to make a living.[2]

The new leisure is exploding many early American traditional beliefs; it is creating a new way of life; it is causing new behavior patterns and new social habits; it is changing the emphasis on the efforts of labor and the emphasis on the production of goods; it is believed to be the underlying cause of many social problems; it is helping to provide a richer and fuller life for the masses; and it is frequently regarded in varying ways as a blessing, reward, utopia, or a stigma and curse.

Unfortunately, there has been little constructive effort applied toward study or planning for the new leisure.

The new leisure has been studied more toward its contribution to our economy than to its contribution to our culture and individual growth. Business leaders have viewed the new leisure as an opportunity to sell more goods and to produce different kinds of goods to use during leisure time.

---

[2]Wilma Donahue, (editor) Free Time--Challenge To Later Maturity. Ann Arbor: The University of Michigan, 1958. p. 65.

America has taken the Chamber of Commerce approach to leisure rather than the educational-cultural approach. Henry Ford the great inventor and industrialist admirably expresses this point of view when he said people with more leisure must have more clothes, greater variety of food, more transportation facilities and more services. He always contended that increased leisure led to increased consumption which, in turn, led to greater production. Fosdick further expands on this traditional viewpoint of leisure:

> . . .America is not thinking primarily of leisure in relation to culture; it is thinking of leisure in relation to the development of new needs. Not leisure to live, but leisure to buy! . . .

> . . .Our attention seems to be focused on producing things rather than people, with output set up as a god. We are absorbed in the mechanical processes by which things are created. We are interested in pushing these processes into all the interstices of our lives. We have not only mechanized our industry but we have mechanized our leisure. Our free hours have taken on the color of our working hours. Just as the machine has stereotyped our tasks, so it is stereotyping our play. Just as self-expression and spontaneity in industrial life have been crushed out for thousands of workers by the processes of mass production so self-expression and spontaneity in leisure hours are being undermined by mechanical devices. Leisure today takes mainly a receptive instead of an expressive form. The mechanical piano, the phonograph, the radio, the movie, create an atmosphere of passivity. Many of us do not to any great extent participate as individuals in our own leisure; seldom do we contribute any element of originality or preference. The same forces that have gone into the big business of providing our necessities have gone into the big business of providing our amusements. "Our souls sit on the bleachers and watch a game played no longer by us but for us." Leisure means freedom, but if a man's freedom consists in efficiently amusing himself according to standard formulas, or subjecting himself to the passive reception of standard relaxations, then he is not really free. He is as much the victim of the machine process as he is when, for eight hours a day of high-speed production, he monotonously turns a series of screws, as the moving belt goes by him in a vast repetitive rhythm.

> In such an atmosphere of strain and escape, of pressure
> and reaction, culture cannot easily find a home. Cul-
> ture is the product of real leisure, or unhurried hours,
> of quiet absorption in things for their own sake. It
> cannot be approached by short-cut paths; it cannot be
> won by efficiency methods; it cannot be spread by ro-
> tary presses or radios. The application to the spiri-
> tual life of the philosophy of mass production must
> inevitably create a society bleak and shallow.[3]

We must soon recognize the fact that the social and
cultural progress of this country will rise and fall depending upon how our citizens use their leisure.

Accomplishments in technology and the rewards of
automation have deprived workers of the many constructive
opportunities and experiences that work once provided.
MacIver states that:

> Back in the days when unremitting toil was the lot of
> all but the very few and leisure still a hopeless
> yearning, hard and painful as life was, it still felt
> real. People were in rapport with the small bit of
> reality allotted to them, the sense of the earth, the
> tang of the changing seasons, the consciousness of the
> eternal on-going of birth and death. Now, when so
> many have leisure, they become detached from themselves,
> not merely from the earth. From all the widened hori-
> zons of our greater world a thousand voices call us to
> come near, to understand, and to enjoy, but our ears
> are not trained to hear them. The leisure is ours but
> not the skill to use it. So leisure becomes a void,
> and from the ensuing restlessness men take refuge in
> delusive excitations or fictitious visions returning
> to their own earth and no more.[4]

A few decades ago, man could expect to receive most
of the necessary rewards from work to sustain his needs for
creativity, mental and physical health, family solidarity,
and inner-satisfactions. Today's worker must depend on
his leisure time to substitute for these much needed experiences.

[3]Raymond B. Fosdick, The Old Savage In The New Civilization. New York:
Doubleday Doran and Company, 1935. p. 111-113.

[4]Erick Larrabee, and Rolf Meyersohn, Mass Leisure. Glencoe, Illinois: The Free
Press, 1958. p. 122.

Wrenn and Harley summarized this need when they
made the following observation:

> Very many people, and especially young people, are now
> employed in factories where they engage in routine,
> monotonous tasks often requiring little physical exer-
> tion or skill and almost no mental effort. Much the
> same is true of many office workers and store clerks,
> whose numbers have also increased greatly in recent
> years. In their leisure time these people wish to
> escape from their work, but their work has not taken
> enough from them to leave them satisfied simply with
> relaxation. Neither has it given them the social,
> cultural, or creative experiences without which most
> people feel their lives to be incomplete. It is during
> their leisure that people like these must now look for
> satisfactions that in other days they would have found
> in their work or else would have had no time for.
> Their leisure problem is not how to rebuild what work
> tears down but how to obtain what work does not af-
> ford.[5]

It would be well if leisure automatically produced culture; or if leisure was viewed universally as a rich and de-
serving reward for the masses. With wise planning and
proper education these accomplishments might be assumed.

Many people now have their leisure and appear to be
unhappy about it. Linden states that:

> Since we already know that to many individuals enforced
> leisure is neither sought after nor desired, we are
> confronted with the interesting philosophical paradox
> that the reward, leisure, is often unrewarding. Un-
> doubtedly this is owing to a variety of sociological
> and individual psychological factors that seem to be
> characteristic of our stepped-up and intensely busi-
> ness-like American pattern of living. I am convinced
> that not just the aging, but everyone in our society
> needs to learn how to be leisurely. Not only because
> psychiatry is my specialty and interest but also be-
> cause of the opportunity I have to see the social

[5]C. G. Wrenn and D. L. Harley, Time On Their Hands. Washington, D.C.:
American Council on Education, (Prepared for the American Youth Commission),
1941. p. 56.

casualties of our way of life do I conclude that the uses of leisure constitute a mental health problem.[6]

Many individuals are faced with the reality that they must retire before they are ready. To these workers, leisure is not always looked upon as a blessing or reward. Several studies have recently been made concerning the attitudes of the retired worker toward his new leisure.[7] Friedman's comment on some of these studies indicated that retired workers were not happy with their new found leisure.

> Indeed some observers' comments on the earlier studies have implied that retirement is an unwanted blessing and that work, and not leisure, is the most desirable condition for man.[8]

It is not leisure itself that causes an individual to be unhappy, dissatisfied, delinquent, or mentally ill. The fault lies in the fact that we have made little preparation and have provided little education for intelligent and creative use of leisure. Misspent leisure has been associated with juvenile delinquency, crime, gambling, drug addiction, and almost all of the social ills found in today's society.

All Americans need is to give to leisure time the same zestful approach that she gives to business and industry. There needs to be recognition of its cultural importance; there needs to be extensive education regarding its significance and use; and there needs to be adequate facilities, equipment, and leadership for its enjoyment. With these supporting developments new leisure can be a reward and a blessing; without them it will become a curse.

Joseph Devereux made a strong point of this when he states:

> This much is certain: The employment of leisure is a social problem which we shall have to face much more seriously in the decades ahead. Americans have become

[6]Wilma Donahue, et al. (Editors), _Free Time--Challenge To Later Maturity_. Ann Arbor: The University of Michigan Press. 1958. p. 77.
[7]Ibid., p. 121.
[8]Ibid., p. 122.

experts at consuming goods. Now they must learn to consume leisure. They have instinctively sought meaning and inner reward from within their work. Now they must seek equivalent satisfaction outside their work.[9]

Some factors have held back an intelligent acceptance and an intelligent use of leisure time. One of the more significant deterrents to the development of proper attitudes toward leisure is the traditional belief concerning leisure and the traditional thoughts concerning business success.

AMERICAN TRADITIONAL BELIEFS ON LEISURE

Our American forefathers left no doubt in the minds of men as to their beliefs regarding work and leisure. The business of opening and settling a new continent was wrought with trials and tribulations that demanded full cooperation from every individual. The hard struggles and cooperative effort needed to conquer the wilderness and to provide a subsistence for the families left little time or concern for leisure. The pioneers regarded work with a religious fervor. It meant subsistence, social prestige, and economic progress. Leisure and recreation were often regarded as a waste of time and did not represent efforts toward the higher goals of life. In many instances idleness and leisure were regarded as a sin against God. It was also regarded as a crime against society punishable by imprisonment. Some of the earliest laws concerning leisure and recreation were passed in the early 1600's. These laws were primarily aimed at prohibiting all forms of amusement and misuse of time. Laws of this nature were to be found in Virginia, Massachusetts, and other New England areas.

The Puritan influence against the "pleasures of life" gave religious support to the early curse that was placed on leisure.

One of the frequently quoted articles outlining the early Puritanical beliefs regarding leisure appeared in the *Methodist Discipline* of 1792 and refers to the policy of Cokerbury College toward leisure:

[9] C. Joseph Devereux, "The Emerging American Scene," The School Review Chicago: University of Chicago Press, 1958.

We prohibit play in the strongest terms . . . . The
students shall rise at five o'clock . . . summer and
winter . . . . Their recreation shall be gardening,
walking, riding, and bathing without doors, and the
carpenter's, joiner's, and cabinetmaker's bench within
doors . . . . A person skilled in gardening shall be
appointed to overlook the students . . . in this recreaation . . . . A master shall always be present at the
time of bathing. Only one shall bathe at a time and
no one shall remain in the water above a minute. No
student shall be allowed to bathe in the river . . . .
The students shall be indulged in nothing that the
world calls play. Let this rule be observed with the
strictest nicety; for those who play when they are
young will play when they are old.[10]

These early concepts never won complete support
even among the early settlers because there were many individuals and groups who felt that recreation and leisure was
necessary to life; however, these early concepts regarding
leisure have made a lasting impression upon American philosophy regarding leisure.

The strong influence and indoctrination of thinking regarding the righteousness of labor and the contempt for leisure was successfully passed on from generation to generation. The biblical strength of these concepts unfortunately
did not change and did not keep pace with the rapid changes
that were taking place in American society. Leisure time
was a reality; but it was difficult to believe or accept as
fact.

It has been only during the last few decades that there
has been a noticeable change in the American philosophy regarding leisure time.

In the early 1900's, when leisure became a recognized
reward for many individuals it was regarded as a "critical
social problem." This was partially due to the fact that it
was the beginning of a new social force in American democracy; but it was also due to the fact that there was still a
strong current of feeling against leisure that was inherent
in the minds and teachings of many people.

[10]Youth Leaders Digest I (December 1938). p. 195.

Today, the concept of leisure and recreation is gradually losing its stigma, including its classification of being a "critical social problem." Leisure is something that is real and the reward of all Americans; it is now being viewed as an opportunity, a challenge, and a cultural and healthful necessity.

American traditions are having quite a detrimental influence on leisure time opportunities. One of our greatest assets concerned with economic and financial progress becomes the greatest stigma concerning wise use of leisure. The emphasis on standardization, mechanization, and the purchase of goods.

America is trying to apply the same techniques to leisure in capturing the dollar as she applies to man's work and business.

It has been pointed out earlier that most cultural progress occurs during leisure time and most materialistic advances occur during work. America is attempting to harness her leisure time inheritance primarily for materialistic gains. Raymond B. Fosdick outlined some of our American concepts regarding leisure when he stated:

> . . . In the mechanization of industry and in the consequent growth of free time, America is well in advance of other nations. Yet when it comes to comparisons on a cultural basis, only a one-hundred per cent patriot, blind to realities, would venture to give us a very prominent position. Indeed, there are few signs in America of a fresh, vital, indigenous culture. We are educating for efficiency and not for the good life. We are educating for civilization and not for living. Culture is frankly not our objective; we do not use our leisure as a means of obtaining it. . .[11]

Modern technology and invention together with medical and social advancement has brought to America a revolutionary way of life. She is fast approaching the development of an economy that will provide security and plenty for all.

[11]Raymond B. Fosdick, The Old Savage In The New Civilization. New York: Doubleday Doran and Company, 1934. p. 111-113.

Americans have developed so many machines to do their work and to do their figuring, and in some cases to do their thinking, that these blessings may be a curse if man frees himself only to degenerate and not create.

Education appears to be the one best approach toward making leisure time a rich American reward.

LEISURE TIME AND YOUTH

Some of the social and welfare legislation and practices that are having quite a bearing on leisure time responsibilities for youth involve child labor, school legislation, negligence and liability, social security, workman's compensation, and special statutory laws.

Several facets of our legislative program have almost eliminated youth from employment in places where they once enjoyed the experience, responsibility, creativity, and financial rewards of work. Well meaning welfare workers, labor leaders, management, educators, and legislators have annually amended and revised laws concerning child labor, tort, negligence and liability, school attendance and military obligation to the degree that it has almost created forced leisure for youth.

The age at which a child may be gainfully employed is continually rising: Approximately 50 years ago one in every five youngsters from age 10-15 was gainfully employed. Today this figure would probably be insignificant since most states prohibit employment until the age of 16. [12] Not only is the age limit becoming higher before youth may be employed but additional restrictions are introduced which prohibit the number of hours per week they may work; the time of day they may be employed; the kind of work they may do; and the places where they may be employed. In a recent case in Kentucky it was decided by the courts that the operation of a power lawn mower fell within the limitation of

[12]William H. Freeberg, *Law and Liability of Municipal Charitable and Private Corporations For Conducting Recreation Camps*. Doctoral Thesis, Indiana University, 1949. p. 57-61.

kinds of machinery a child could operate. The operation of this machine was only possible when the youth reached the age of twenty-one. Industry shuns youth when it involves considerations for employment. Most states have laws which make an individual, company, or corporation liable for the negligent acts of its employees. In most cases where minors are employed (in many cases hard to determine) the employer may be regarded as negligent *per se* for hiring one not mature enough to handle the responsibilities of the job expected of one who could be employed and would be considered a prudent individual. Many other legislative considerations such as workman's compensation, social security, and other statutory laws must be considered by employers before they will employ youth.

The male students who graduate from high school are still perplexed and do not understand all that is necessary in order to make intelligent decisions regarding their military obligations. Most high school graduates have accepted with pride and dignity their obligations to serve their country and train themselves to defend the principles for which it stands. The number of services available to youth and the vast number of ways he may serve and be trained are quite confusing.

In many instances the periods of indecision, waiting, and final acceptance to military duty involves misspent time by youth. This time of military indecision might also be added to the many causes of extended leisure with which youth are confronted.

It might be recognized that most of the legislation now being passed in behalf of youth is done primarily for their benefit and primarily for their well being. However, too much of this legislation being passed is inconsistent with the present day needs of youth. Some of these laws might be considered as being more beneficial to labor and management; other laws can be regarded as over-protection for youth; many laws are inconsistent with educational purposes (camp work experiences, etc.); and still other laws restrict youth in education, work and play.

School laws are usually not broad enough in scope to allow for leisure time activities for youth. School codes frequently limit the numer of hours, days, and in some cases weeks that school may be in session. There are restrictions on leadership assignment and teachers used for leisure time programs. The "lighted school house" and the week-end recreational programs now being advocated for leisure time education and activities are in some states not legally possible. Most school codes have certainly not encouraged leisure time assignments and the use of teachers, facilities, and money.

Legislation thus far has been a one-sided affair concerning itself primarily with limitations and restrictions for youth. There has been very little thinking, planning, effort or education to provide youth with compensatory programs of work and creativity. Legislation appears to be against them rather than for them. America has endowed youth with nothing but leisure; but has failed them in not providing education and opportunities for its use. Youth has had no voice in the dictatorial legislative plans that have been made for them. America needs the same dedicated support and responsibility to pass legislative programs that will compensate for the enforced leisure imposed upon her youth. At this time, plans for creative programs for youth to develop interests, attitudes, appreciations, knowledge, and skills regarding leisure time activities have not kept pace with the vigorous efforts of interested groups who have legislated leisure time. The abundance of leisure time enjoyed by youth, coupled with lack of parental interest and guidance, and lack of challenge and interest in the schools have caused quite a challenge to American democracy. It has been estimated that "20% of all the boys in the nation will have had their day in court--as juvenile offenders-- before their 18th birthday."[13]

The nation becomes alarmed when it has an unemployment figure of six per cent. All of the facets of the economy are exploited to correct this situation.

Why cannot American's get excited about the problem of youth? One of the best solutions to the leisure problem for youth is through proper education, purposeful work ex-

[13]American Recreation Journal, "Americans Are Looking For New and Better Ways To Use Their Growing Leisure Time, " August/September, 1960. p. 16.

perience, recreation, and religious training. America is short changing youth in each category for the benefit of materialistic, economic, and social expediency.

She must re-evaluate the purposes and principles of democracy in terms of its future existence. The future of America lies in the success of her educational programs for youth in terms of their preparation for vocations, professions, citizenship in a democracy and their leisure; at present America has been ignoring or sidestepping this problem. She must realistically face this problem today, now, or the course of our future will be uncertain!

LEISURE TIME EDUCATION AND THE SCHOOLS

There needs to be a concentrated effort on the part of educators, economists, sociologists, poets, and philosophers in the study of leisure and its impact on modern day society.

Will the new leisure be characterized by boredom, idleness, apathy, promiscuity, immorality, physical degeneration, mental stagnation, waste, juvenile delinquency and senility? Are some of these social ills now the result of our new leisure or are there other factors or combinations of factors involved?

America needs to give the same dedicated time and attention to the study of this new approach to living as she has to the study of materialistic and economic influences in our society.

She has barometers, statistical analysis, computations, indices, standards, and check and balance procedures to guide and direct the economic conditions in our modern society.

There would be greater social progress in America if she focused as much attention to other social problems as she has to those concerned with materials and finances.

America cannot afford to let scientific progress and economic insurance outstrip her abilities to solve social changes and social problems.

Leisure time presents one of the greatest social changes that confronts all Americans.

Little planning has occurred which would indicate that we are ready to assume responsibilities for mass leisure.

There has developed within recent years an increased amount of pressure on the schools to spend more time in teaching mathematics, physics, chemistry, and natural science courses. Public pressure is demanding this emphasis because of their concern for the loss of prestige in the scientific race to explore outer space. There is also a feeling that America has not nearly enough scientists and engineers to meet the challenge of the new age in science. Many schools and colleges have accepted this appeal with rigorous action and have revamped their curricula to include more courses and more time allotments in these various areas.

The methods used for teaching these courses, to a large extent, have reverted to the emphasis on drill and memorization. Parents would like to have the teacher, "make their children learn." This method of teaching is best reserved for the classroom. Outdoor education to accomplish the same purpose might receive critical evaluations.

Mass education for all students in these specialized areas, together with the disciplined methods of instruction, may be one factor which is causing the increased number of student "drop-outs" at the high school level. The wisdom of this rush for mass education and all out emphasis in these scientific areas at the expense and sacrifice of other subject matter teachings will be debated for many years.

The tremendous scientific advances made in recent decades has brought with it many valuable contributions to living but it has also introduced many new social and welfare problems that thus far are not too well solved. The same amount of time and emphasis is needed in education to help individuals solve these social problems. Scientific progress is of no avail if we cannot keep pace in social maturation. Our loss in prestige to other countries might

realistically come faster through social decay than by any
lack of genius in the scientific realm.

The leisure time reward is one phenomena that scientific progress has given to America. Are the schools educating for leisure time? Is America in danger of graduating
a mass of "leisure time illiterates or morons"? What
should the balance in our educational program be?

A large majority of students now attending elementary
school might very likely be confronted with a thirty-two hour
work week and a fifty hour leisure time week.

In speaking about the leisure time of our present day
worker, Marion Harper, Jr. states:

> . . . Along with a forty-hour work week, his fixed time
> segments include a fifty-six hour sleep week, a ten
> hour transportation week, and let's say arbitrarily a
> six hour grooming week, along with a ten-and-a-half-
> hour dining week. (Assuming thirty minute meals and
> omitting discretionary time spent around the table.)
> This means a leisure week of forty-five-and-one-half
> hours, or five-and-one-half hours longer than the aver-
> age work week.[14]

Educational leaders have frequently stated that one of
the functions of all schools should be to teach "worthy use
of leisure time." Most schools have only given lip service
to this belief and it is difficult to find many schools who can
say they are actually educating for leisure. Many individuals point to the athletic programs as an indication that
they are doing creditable things toward leisure education.
The athletic program and physical education program provide only one facet of the recreational needs of individuals.
This is particularly true when participants reach middle
age or older. At this point in life, the vigorous, highly
competitive sports for which many athletics prepare are
no longer feasible for recreation purposes. Most individual and dual sports may be enjoyed for a lifetime. Even in
this area of physical recreation the schools are not teaching
most of the students. Wrenn states:

[14]Recreation Magazine, January, 1961. p. 14.

The opportunity for athletic participation that school offers the average young person has been comparatively small. If a boy has a natural aptitude for some sport, he can develop it through the school team. But such a lad has relatively little need of organized physical recreation. On the other hand, the youngster who would benefit most from practice in games and sports is not likely to add to the school's prestige in this field, and he has consequently been neglected. There has been some improvement in recent years, but we are still far from the point where schools will accept the responsibility of seeing that all their students have an equal opportunity to take part in the more physically beneficial forms of recreation.

Out-of-school youth have even less chance of filling any substantial portion of their leisure with sports and outdoor activities. For the most part, such pastimes require facilities they do not have, and there is no agency or combination of agencies that has yet been able to make them generally available.[15]

The development of skills and knowledge concerning physical recreation activities is a vital necessity for the growth and physical fitness of youth. Education for leisure in this area has been badly neglected. There are examples of excellent physical education programs in a few scattered schools throughout the United States. These programs are exceptions rather than the rule.

Schools for the most part have done little planning and have shown little concern in education for leisure concerning physical recreation activities.

At the President's Conference on Fitness of American Youth held in 1956, Vice-President, Richard M. Nixon pinpointed some weakness in the present Leisure Time educational pursuits. Some facts revealed that:

1. Fewer than 50% of our high school students are exposed to physical education programs.
2. More than 90% of our elementary schools have no gymnasia.
3. Only 1,200 of America's 17,000 communities have full-time recreation leadership.

[15]C. Gilbert Wrenn, and D. L. Harley, Time On Their Hands. Washington, D.C.: American Council on Education, 1941. p. 6.

4. About 40% of the men in our Armed Forces during World War II were unable to swim 50 feet.
5. Almost 90% of the nation's elementary schools have less than the recommended five acres of land necessary for essential play areas.

The country as a whole has been negligent in planning for our future leisure time needs. The American Institute of Park Executives in their report on "The Crisis in Open Land" reveals how sub-divisions, highways, airports, and other commercial and public interests are robbing cities of precious park and recreation land. There is also a study which points out in further detail how negligent we are as a country about our concern for developing land, facilities, and leadership for leisure time use. Marion Clawson's, "Statistics On Outdoor Recreation,"[16] points out the need for immediate action to develop new areas and protect what areas we have for leisure time use.

This lack of interest on the part of educators towards physical education and towards physical recreation activities has been the cause of great concern by many national leaders. In a recent article for the Sports Illustrated Magazine, President John F. Kennedy pointed out that:

> As a result of the alarming Kraus-Weber findings President Eisenhower created a Council on Youth Fitness at the Cabinet level and appointed a Citizens Advisory Committee on the Fitness of American Youth, composed of prominent citizens interested in fitness. Over the past five years the physical fitness of American youth has been discussed in forums, by committees and in leading publications. A 10-point program for physical fitness has been publicized and promoted. Our schools have been urged to give increased attention to the physical well-being of their students. Yet there has been no noticeable improvement. Physical fitness tests conducted last year in Britain and Japan showed that the youth of those countries were considerably more fit than our own children. And the annual physical fitness tests for freshmen at Yale University show a consistent decline in the prowess of young Americans; 51% of the class of 1951 passed these tests, 43% of the class of

[16] Resources for the Future, Inc., Washington, D.C., April 1958.

1956 passed, and only 38%, a little more than a third,
of the class of 1960 succeeded in passing the not
overly rigorous examination.[17]

Many areas of the school program, where leisure time
education might occur, are limited to the better or more for-
tunate students. In the areas of art, crafts, music, debate,
theater work, and other active and cultural subject-matter
fields, those students who show some proficiency and ability are encouraged to continue. Those who desire to learn
these activities, only reasonably well for their own enjoyment, are discouraged. Many students are discouraged because of economic limitations. The teachers who are responsible for teaching these subject-matter areas are in
most instances artists. They strive for perfection, genius,
dedication, and artistic production. These objectives are
far above the average person's need to enjoy these subjects
for recreational purpose. Time and staff are not available
for leisure time education. Musical instruments are expensive; leadership is expensive; materials and equipment
are expensive; educational values are measured in terms
of today's dollar. The products turning out in terms of leisure time education and preparation will be our most expensive human error.

Statistics are not available on what the schools and
communities are providing in the way of leadership, facilities and equipment for leisure time pursuits in the Fine
Arts and cultural areas. It is reasonable to believe that
the statistics would be as bad or even worse than those
concerned with physical recreation.

Dr. Jay B. Nash[18] conducted a twenty year survey
with approximately a thousand people to determine many
interesting things concerning their leisure time use. Most
of the participants who took part in the survey had reached
adulthood.

This survey substantiates previous discussions and

[17] John F. Kennedy, "The Soft American," Sports Illustrated Magazine, December 28, 1960.
[18] Jay B. Nash, Philosophy of Recreation. St. Louis: C. V. Mosby, 1953. p. 15.

gives a clearer picture of the school's disregard for leisure time education.

The study revealed that 70 per cent of the hobbies individuals participate in were learned before the age of twelve. These life interests in these hobbies reveals that 70 per cent started in the home and only 10 per cent started in the schools.

This study also revealed that in only 6 per cent of the cases the classroom teacher was given credit for teaching the hobby.

Most of the teaching and learning occurred in the home.

This becomes even more significant in today's society since our homes are becoming more mobile and disintegrated. Statistics reveal that in the near future more than 75 per cent of married women will be gainfully employed. There is also noticeable increase in the number of "moonlight workers," where the father works at two jobs.

Two questions immediately must be answered. Whose responsibility is it to educate for leisure?; and who will assume this responsibility?

The schools can do much more than they are presently doing. It would appear that if schools do not assume more responsibility for leisure education many *more* youth will be neglected.

The many school clubs, intra-mural programs, special interest activities, and other organized student groups have always been an important function of the schools. These programs have been considered as of secondary importance in the school curricula. They have usually been designated as programs not important enough to be conducted during school time. They are out-of-class or after school functions; extra-curricula activities; optional school activities; and more recently have been kindly called co-curricular activities.

The number and amount of such programs and the leadership provided to conduct these programs varies according to the size of school; the economic status of the

school district; and the policies governing each school.
Some schools have no co-curricular activities, but many
schools have outstanding programs. Credit is given to
students for their participation in co-curricular activities
in several cities and teachers are also given supervisory
credit on teaching loads.

The co-curricular functions of the school is one place
where leisure time education could be emphasized a great
deal. This can be accomplished through better planning,
more leadership, better facilities, and an adequate budget.

Some credit must be given to our schools for teaching
students "wise use of leisure. " Inherent in each subject
matter field are opportunities for teaching knowledge and
stimulating creative expressions that carry over into leisure
time use. The lessons are not specifically directed for leisure time use but because of the nature of the instruction it
does contribute indirectly and in some cases to a great extent to worthy use of leisure. Hobbies, special interests,
and many "out-of-school activities" are outgrowths of the
lessons learned in the classroom.

Too few schools provide the necessary leadership to
direct the interest and motivation of students that has been
generated in the instructional program. Many students receive inspirations and feel an urge for creative activity as
the result of classroom teachings. These motivations soon
fade away because of lack of opportunity for expression or
outlets that schools are not able to provide.

It is quite evident that our educational system needs
some careful study in terms of its contribution to leisure
time education. Will we be able to combat public pressure,
American traditional beliefs, restrictive school law, inadequate budgets, and apathy towards this problem before it is
too late ?

A great deal may be accomplished through the outdoor
education program toward the wise and constructive use of
leisure time. This program by no means solves all the
answers but it does contribute a great deal to leisure time
education.

OUTDOOR EDUCATION AND LEISURE TIME

The outdoor education program provides inherent opportunities for developing a creative spirit within each student. There are many experiences which provide opportunities for self-expression and self-motivation. The teacher's role becomes one of developing the educational process by continually providing experience where the creative spirit will be kept alive. Students who develop this creative spirit and maintain it for a lifetime have reached a major goal in preparing themselves for leisure. In some instances, the creative spirit becomes almost as important to a person's leisure as learning skills and knowledge concerning a variety of recreational activities.

The emphasis in education and in outdoor education might well be on developing the creative process rather than the creative product; this is particularly true as it concerns leisure time.

One of the most popular leisure time activities today is to become a member of a club or organization. Within each club or organization there are many committees and each individual is certain to be appointed to one or more responsibilities. This form of group activity is one of the more constructive forms of leisure and it makes a desirable contribution both to social progress and to the individual.

Some attempts are made and some success is accomplished in preparing students for these activities in the classroom.

The outdoor education program, and especially the school camp, provides a natural class organization for developing attitude and skills necessary for the enjoyment of group activities. Camping teaches the art of living and it also teaches the art of living together.

The small unit or tent group might represent a small committee. The total camp group might represent the total membership of the club. In a camp experience the students receive excellent guidance and consul from teachers in practicing good behavior patterns, in democratically arriving at

decisions, in accepting responsibilities, in enjoying the
activities and in helping others to have a rewarding and
enjoyable experience.

Some research is now being conducted to determine
the value of small group living in camp. Larrabee and
Meyersohn state:

> The wilderness camping group is of necessity a small
> group, and currently there has been considerable inter-
> est in the general study of small groups. There are at
> least three relations for such study. First, the small
> group is seen as a social microcosm so that presumably
> much can be learned about the larger society from its
> analysis. Second, large social structures are thought
> to be tied together in part by the functioning of small
> groups. Third, one's conception of self is formed,
> maintained, and altered in the matrix of close intimate
> relations.

> An abiding question in small group research asks how an
> organization arises--how the activities of members be-
> come geared into one another so that a so-called "sys-
> tem" is established. Establishing a set of complemen-
> tary activities--a division of labor--among the members
> of a camping group is undoubtedly an operation on which
> the success of the venture stands or falls. Mutual
> recriminations among the campers we observed seemed
> invariably to stem from some unsatisfactory apportion-
> ment or carrying out of camping tasks.[19]

Leisure should imply a certain amount of time for
relaxation, meditation, inspiration and the development of
aesthetic appreciation and skills. An examination of the
leisure time habits of the American people will show a
noticeable lack of these qualities in their use of leisure
time. Most Americans regard leisure as a time to do the
many things they have always wanted to do. This leisure
reward arrives in the form of a vacation or week-end and
there is usually a scramble and an all out effort to satisfy
this urge of freedom or urge of escape. More time, effort,
planning, perspiration, argument, frustration, and hustle
goes into a leisure time experience than is normally put

[19] Erick Larrabee and Rolf Meyersohn, _Mass Leisure_. Glencoe, Illinois: The Free
Press, 1958. p. 300.

into an individual's work. Relaxation and meditation are not usually associated with leisure in America. Culture should emanate as a result of leisure time. Education for cultural developments during leisure has not been emphasized or specifically planned for students in our educational system.

It is extremely difficult for teachers, if not impossible, to guide and direct students into an understanding of what is meant by relaxation and meditation while teaching in a typical classroom situation. It would be almost impossible to provide an experience which would have real meaning within the four walls of the schools. Yet, this learning experience is often cited as an important goal in education. Donahue states that:

> The goal of education should be not so much to teach as to offer the opportunity to experience growth of the total personality, including, of course, exercise of the mind and the aesthetic skills. These are counsels of perfection, of course, but they ought not to be generalities meaningless in the daily routine and operation of our schools, as in many cases they are. If we can but produce a generation healthy and vigorous in both body and mind, capable of appreciating individual differences, and bent on seeking the best use of their limited time, when they are free of the job as well as when they are on it, we shall be practicing a preventive medicine which will make life much easier for the doctors, medical and social.[20]

Another of the inherent leisure time educational objectives that outdoor education provides for the student is the development and maintenance of physical fitness. Outdoor education implies participation rather than spectatoritis; it implies action rather than idleness; it implies creativity rather than formal discipline; it implies natural outlets rather than man-made activities; it implies individual reward rather than mass accomplishments; it implies self discipline rather than regimented bells, whistles and militaristic commands; and it involves physical exercise asso-

[20]Wilma Donahue, et al., Free Time--Challenge To Later Maturity. Ann Arbor: University of Michigan Press, 1958. p. 76.

ciated with the motivations of a challenging outdoor program rather than artificial exercises planned to develop big muscles--and usually for no purpose. All of these contributions that outdoor education offers to the aims of education in this particular area may be considered as valuable contributions to physical fitness. Outdoor education's contribution encompasses the broader concept of physical fitness science. It fulfills the recommended development of physical, social, and mental health of the student.

In the outdoor education program, physical fitness is developed simultaneously with the students search for knowledge. The student must hike, explore, lift, pull, swim, paddle, and perform many physical chores to accomplish the education goals of outdoor education. The mind and body must function as a unit to acquire knowledge.

President John F. Kennedy states that:

> For physical fitness is not only one of the most important keys to a healthy body; it is the basis of dynamic and creative intellectual activity. The relationship between the soundness of the body and the activities of the mind is subtle and complex. Much is not yet understood. But we do know what the Greeks knew: that intelligence and skill can only function at the peak of their capacity when the body is healthy and strong; that hardy spirits and tough minds usually inhabit sound bodies.[21]

The development of physical fitness is often considered as a natural outgrowth of a student's participation in a well planned outdoor education program. School camping fulfills these objectives most successfully because this experience is usually of longer duration.

Strenuous physical activity becomes an inherent part of the program as students explore, discover and search for knowledge. Many of the recreation activities which are planned for students who participate in outdoor education programs will provide physical, mental, emotional, and social experiences so necessary to total fitness. All stu-

[21]John F. Kennedy, "The Soft American", Sports Illustrated. December 26, 1960.

dents enjoy and benefit from an outdoor education experience. Athletic ability or physical powers, artistic or musical ability, are not criteria for participation.

OUTDOOR RECREATION IN AMERICA

In chapter one there was a brief discussion of the outdoor recreation picture in terms of the number of Americans at play. A brief review here may serve to show how from 40 to 50 billions of dollars are spent in recreational pursuits.

American's spend close to $11,000,000,000 for pleasure traveling, $1,000,000,000 on movies, another 2 to $4,000,000,000 on gardening and do-it-yourself projects, $30,000,000 for art supplies, over $100,000,000 worth of backyard grills and about $35,000,000 to $50,000,000 for building model airplanes, ships and other models.

Despite the apparent surge of wholesome recreational activities, America is far from solving the leisure problem. A nation educated to work does not accept an invitation to play without a struggle. Leisure time education is lagging far behind the needs and demands of society. Just as education had to struggle for acceptance in the days of Horace Mann, recreation and leisure time education is battling through societies adjustment to the golden age of leisure.

In spite of warnings and pleadings of outstanding scholars of sociology, colleges and universities are slow to add courses in recreation and leisure-time skills. While it is acceptable to offer courses in touch football, basketball and track and field, educators frown on leadership training and participation in basketweaving, fishing, and other valuable carry-over activities.

One of the notable exceptions to a lack of interest in outdoor recreation on the university level is the general acceptance of the outdoor education project which is sponsored by the American Association of Health, Physical Education and Recreation. The project, under the leadership of Julian Smith, Michigan State University is concerned with recreation as well as education.

382

Workshops sponsored by state departments and universities are concerned with activities, both educational and recreational, such as safety, hunting, shooting, gun handling, fishing, casting, camping, boating, fire prevention, conservation, law observation and health practices.

RECREATION SKILLS IN CAMP

The school camp provides a wonderful laboratory for teaching children carry-over skills which may lead to hobbies and leisure-time pursuits the rest of their lives. The authors are not interested in drawing a fine line between which of these are educational and which are recreational. They are confident that regardless of how they may be classified they are worthwhile and should be a part of the education of every boy and girl in America.

Some of the leisure time skills which are taught in a good school camp include:

Games and stunts	Fishing
Hunts--treasure, scavenger, etc.	Wood crafts
	Whittling
Singing and Storytelling	Arts and crafts
Dramatics	Camp Hobbies
Folk and Square Dancing	Discovering native materials
Ceremonials	Working with native materials
Vespers	Participating in cookouts
Camp Fire Programs	Hiking
Swimming and boating	Swimming
Skating, skiing, sledding	Dramatic presentations
Archery	Quiet game activities
Photography	
Fly tying and bait casting	

SUMMARY

Today, according to sociologist David Reisman in his book *Lonely Crowd*, the average American citizen has more than 3,000 hours of leisure a year. This golden age of leisure has been the dream of man through long centuries of hard and back-breaking work.

Now that he has abundant leisure time, he is at a loss to use it. Spending almost $50,000,000,000 for fun and play, he still is living a life of boredom.

Although his society is moving from a world of work to one in which machines have made possible a world of leisure, the public schools are still preparing graduates for the former society.

Unless the schools begin, and begin immediately, to assume the responsibility of preparing the youth for the new age, America is in for trouble.

Past civilizations have left their records for all to study. Many sociologists have grasped the full meaning of their lesson but seem to be powerless to get the attention of their contemporaries. It is past time that educators give more attention to one of the major problems of modern society--educating youth for leisure time.

Questions and Projects

1. Discuss the implication of "education for the worthy use of leisure time." What must be considered in what is meant by education for leisure?

2. How would you enrich the elementary school curriculum to prepare pupils for the age of leisure? High school? College?

3. A class member may write to Dr. Julian Smith, College of Education, Michigan State University, to determine the scope and purpose of the A.A.H.P.E.R. Outdoor Education Project.

4. From the standpoint of recreation, what are the chief social problems?

5. What are some of the major social, political, and economic forces that have conditioned the growth and development of recreation in America?

384

6. Is the leisure time activities of the American people contributing to American culture?

7. Do you regard recreation as a function of the school? Why or why not?

8. What factors are contributing to the recent emergence of recreation as an integral phase of the total school program?

9. How did the early settlers in Colonial America compensate for a lack of organized recreation?

10. Discuss this statement - "A nation's culture is determined more by its recreation than by its education."

Selected References

Department of Supervision and Curriculum Development, *Toward A New Curriculum*. Washington, D.C.: National Education Association, 1944.

Donahue, Wilma, et al., (Editors) *Free Time, Challenge To Later Maturity*. Ann Arbor: University of Michigan Press, 1958.

Fosdick, Raymond B., *The Old Savage In The New Civilization*. New York: Doubleday Doran and Company, 1934.

Hutchinson, John L., *Principles of Recreation*. New York: The Ronald Press Company, 1951.

Larrabee, Eric and Meyersohn, Rolf, *Mass Leisure*, Glencoe, Illinois: The Free Press, 1958.

Meyer, Harold D. and Brightbill, Charles K., *Community Recreation*. Englewood Cliffs, N. J.: Prentice-Hall, Inc., 1956.

Nash, Jay B., *Philosophy of Recreation and Leisure*. St. Louis, Mo.: The C. V. Mosby Company, 1953.

Neumeyer, Martin H. and Neumeyer, Ester S., *Leisure and Recreation*. New York: The Ronald Press Company, 1958.

Wrenn, C. Gilbert and Harley, D. L., *Time On Their Hands*. Washington, D.C.: American Council On Education, 1941.

Chapter 11

SCOPE OF OUTDOOR EDUCATION IN THE UNITED STATES

The time is opportune to initiate forward-looking programs of educational activities outside the walls of school buildings through which boys and girls may find a new vision of America— clearer, truer, more satisfying—in the freedom and reality of God's out-of-doors.

—*S. D. Shankland*

Surveys and reports indicate that there is an active and growing interest in outdoor education in America. There are increasing numbers of local, state, and national workshops and conferences on school camping, conservation, nature study and other areas of outdoor education. The number of school camps, school gardens, school forests, and other types of outdoor activities show a steady increase throughout the United States. Agency and church sponsored camps are mushrooming even more rapidly. Governmental agencies such as the Forestry Service, National Park Service, and Fish and Wildlife Service are providing more and more camping facilities for families and groups but are still far behind the public demand. Further evidence of public interest in, and recognition of, the possibilities of education and recreation in the out-of-doors is reflected in recent legislation in Michigan, New York, Wisconsin, California and Montana, and several other states.

In order to get a picture of the scope and status of outdoor education in the United States today, a discussion of the current practices in schools, universities, churches, and other agencies and institutions will be helpful. A number of outdoor education programs in successful operation in various sections of the United States will be examined.

OUTDOOR EDUCATION IN THE SCHOOLS

Teachers have been taking their classes out of the classroom almost as long as there have been formal schools. Most of these field trips or excursions have been educationally focused upon one subject matter field. The use of the out-of-doors and observations of society in action cannot be considered as being universally accepted by all teachers in our modern school programs. For many school districts, it is against local policy to leave the school; and in other school districts, there is little encouragement given to this type of education. Teachers are not willing to provide this experience, and public opinion, in many places, does not accept this type of program. There are many public schools throughout the United States who have recognized the values of outdoor education as a means to better education. Some of the more popular means of accomplishing the outdoor educational experiences include field trips and excursions, park school plans, school gardens, school farms, school forests, school day camps, school resident camps, and the educational mobile unit.

FIELD TRIPS AND EXCURSIONS

The school journey, field trips, and excursions have received the approval of most educators as a valuable media of instruction. They are used in practically all areas of the curricula and by schools in every state of the union. The school journeys are used primarily to provide first hand observation of things of interest that help students understand, interpret, and formulate ideas concerning materials they are studying in the classroom.

Trips and excursions are administered and planned in numerous ways. Some are for a few hours and others for as long as a week or more. The school field trip has become so universally accepted that recent statistics are not available on how extensively they are used through the nation.

A survey of educational indices and popular journals in the various fields of study indicate that practically every subject matter area has found valuable uses for the field trip. They have been used extensively in all parts of the United States. One example of the growth in popularity of field trips can be found in studies of the number of refer- ences found concerning field trips. According to one study there were 450 references to field trips in 1938 and 700 in 1947.[1] The number of magazine articles and conference reports at educational meetings indicate an ever increasing number of schools using field trips, school journeys, and excursions for educational purposes.

Quite a number of the larger cities are publishing catalogues of school journeys for the benefit of their teach- ers. Los Angeles Public Schools publish a catalogue in which more than 150 field trips are listed, and the Milwau- kee, Chicago, and New York schools offer similar services to school administrators and teachers.

A promising educational trend is developing toward the integrated use of community resources. School field trips are used as part of extensive resource studies. The Committee on Southern Regional Studies and Education with headquarters at the University of North Carolina has given significant impetus to this approach to resource materials. State Departments of Public Instruction, Schools of Educa- tion in colleges and universities, and Curriculum Depart- ments of local school systems are currently assisting in the development of resource units for various grade levels and subject areas. Michigan State College, for example, has a program under way for resource unit preparation in Agri- cultural Education.

Some school boards have encouraged the use of field trips by official proclamation. In Madison, Wisconsin, the school board proclaimed:

> Field trips and excursions outside the classrooms and school buildings and grounds under the supervision of members of the school staff are considered by the Board of Education as an extension of the classroom and an integral part of the educational program.[2]

[1] Gertrude Forrester, Methods of Vocational Guidance. Boston: D. C. Heath and Company, 1951. p. 40

[2] Charles F. Schuller, The School Administrator and His Audio-Visual Program. Washington, D.C.: National Education Association, 1954. p. 10.

388

In a recent report on field trips conducted in the New York City public schools, a total of 552 trips were taken by 25,359 students in 33 of the 35 high schools from June, 1954, to June, 1955.[3]

One of the most ambitious field trip programs concern a public high school in New York City. This particular school system hopes to make a field trip possible for all 200 academic classes in the school system.

During the school year 1955-56, Metropolitan Vocational High School began a program of field trips with the ambitious goal of providing a trip for each of its 200 academic classes. One hundred and twenty-five classes took a field trip. The goal was not quite realized due to the newness of the project and the delay in evaluating the trips. The following year the field trip program was continued with the expectation of providing the opportunity of a field trip for every academic class in the school.

In Lincoln School in Manchester, Ohio, the kindergarten youngsters take field trips to study nature and then use their experiences in the play activities of the classroom.

In New Britain, Connecticut, the laboratory schools of Central Connecticut State College each year plan field trips of short duration to the city parks and other outdoor localities from the kindergarten through the high school. In addition, upper grades take trips to the Springfield (Massachusetts) zoo, to the old whaling seaport, to Yale University and the Peabody Museum, and occasionally to New York City by railroad train where they visit the United Nations, Chinatown, the Stock Market and numerous other interesting areas.

The field trip when properly planned and conducted is now considered an important part of most American public school systems.

[3]William Hamm, "The School and Community," High Points. April, 1955. pp. 5-33.

PARK-SCHOOL PLAN

The Park-School program is designed primarily to supplement the school classroom in instruction related to nature and the out-of-doors. With the park-school development in recent years, several programs in outdoor education are significant.

School and park departments are cooperatively developing areas with a wide variety of plant and animal life. They are providing formal areas for planting and wildlife, and also are allowing large tracts of land to remain in their natural state.

Practical experience and demonstrations are made possible through projects of erosion control on park land adjacent to schools. Projects for providing food and cover for wildlife are common experiences for school children. Some school-park programs grow horticulture stock for landscaping, wildlife purposes, and erosion control.

School forests, arboretums, gardens, farms, and nature trails are all important developments in this media of instruction called the Park-School Plan.

Museums and zoos serve as complementary and contributing experiences for children in their study of outdoor education. Live animal libraries, living plants and insects, rock and mineral samples, soil samples, and conservation demonstration projects are an integral part of these programs.

Children experience, plan, and conduct projects in conjunction with these museums; learning experiences occur in nutrition, fertilization, care and upkeep of living plants and animals; observation of living phenomena, and group cooperation is practiced in planning and sharing responsibilities. Programs of this type are becoming widespread in the elementary schools and may be observed in many states throughout the country. Other developments in the Park-School Plan include amphitheaters, picnic areas, and other recreation areas.

In the Park-School Plan the park departments usually purchase and maintain the land around the schools and make it available to schools as an outdoor education laboratory. The park and school personnel work harmoniously to adapt the area to its most successful educational use.

The American Institute of Park Executives as early as 1939 went on record in support of outdoor education when they appointed a committee on Nature Study. In 1950, Robert Mann, Chairman of the General Session on Outdoor Education said, "We have a vital function in this movement which, like a snowball, is gaining size and momentum all over the continent."

THE SCHOOL GARDEN

There is nothing fundamentally new in the school gardening programs. Many school systems throughout the United States have used gardening as a teaching device since the turn of the century. The school garden has been popular in European countries much longer and more extensively than in the United States.

During World War II gardening in the United States was probably at its most productive peak due to the emphasis on the Victory Garden Campaign. Gardens flourished across the entire nation for obvious economic reasons and were sponsored by home, school, and community groups. Many schools and clubs have continued a program of gardening activities since World War II because of the sheer joy of working together in a worthwhile cooperative venture and because of the many obvious educational and recreational values.

Educators throughout the country, while promoting the Victory Garden for economic and patriotic reasons, found that well-planned and properly supervised activities in gardening enrich and vitalize the school curriculum.

Many examples of good gardening practice may be found in the United States ranging from the one-teacher rural school gardens to several acres used in large city systems such as Los Angeles, New York, Cleveland, and Minneapolis.

Minneapolis has an excellent school gardening program which is run by the schools in cooperation with the local Parent-Teachers Association. In the spring and summer of 1956, there were 2,223 school gardens in fifty-two elementary school districts.

In the schools of our newest state, Hawaii, gardening has long been recognized as a very important means of motivating students in almost the whole range of school subjects. Here the school gardening programs are developed with the Office of Agricultural Education and Elementary Education in the Department of Public Instruction. These departments believe that in a perfectly natural way, gardening contributes to the other fields of teaching and learning, and tends to integrate the learning process to make it effective. Its value as a subject, or as an end in itself, becomes apparent when considering the importance of gardening, avocationally and culturally, in Hawaii today. The school gardening program in Hawaii includes such units as:

1. Planning the garden
2. Preparing the soil for planting
3. Fertilizing
4. Planting
5. Irrigating
6. Thinning, spacing, transplanting
7. Weeding, cultivating
8. Controlling insects and related pests in the garden
9. Controlling plant diseases
10. Harvesting, cleaning, grading, marketing.

The general objectives as determined for the state of Hawaii are as follows:

1. To provide an environment and a succession of worthwhile experiences which will help the pupil to progressively improve his behavior, and to assist him in acquiring the necessary skills and knowledge.

2. To encourage the pupils in making careful observation, exploration, and experimentation in the activities pertaining to gardening.

3. To encourage the pupil to become intimate with

the plants he cultivates and the interrelation that exists among the various forms of life in the garden.

4. To encourage the pupil to learn more about the nature of plant growth, requirements for good plant growth, and the cultural practices that bring about good plant growth.

5. To utilize the activity and work experiences in gardening as a "hitching post" to other fields of teaching and learning thereby establishing a more life-like situation.

Other examples of school gardens may be found in New Britain, Connecticut; Overland Park, Kansas; Claiborne County, Tennessee; San Mateo, California; Whittier, California; Chester, South Carolina; Indianapolis, Indiana; Montgomery County, Maryland; Knoxville, Tennessee; Rock Island, Illinois; Fulton County, Georgia; and many other schools throughout the country.

SCHOOL FARMS

The school farm is fast becoming an integral part of many school programs. The school farm is used as a laboratory and also as a means for providing work experience. Most of the farms are fully equipped with a diversified sample of farm animals, grains, pastures, orchards, farm equipment, and other necessary facilities and equipment for the modern farm. Children get valuable experience working with the animals, planting and harvesting crops, and doing the many farm chores necessary for good farm practices.

The school farm of Battle Creek, Michigan, is a good example of a farm used as a laboratory of learning for children of all grade levels. Several other good school farm plans exist in the United States but too many are used exclusively for the use of agriculture classes. Some schools that do not own their own school farm have worked out cooperative plans with community spirited farmers who make arrangements for children to visit their farms at specified times through the year.

SCHOOL FORESTS

Many public schools throughout the United States have

taken advantage of legislation which was enacted several decades ago permitting the establishment of county, township, village, city, and district forests. In many schools the Agriculture Department took the initiative in securing land and developing lands for reforestation and conservation study. The use of the school forests in the educational program has unlimited possibilities. It can be used for selection, purchase, planning, work experiences, research, and development of many other programs characteristic of forest land.

Many schools provide experiences for children in tree planting on or near their own school grounds. Other school districts which are closely associated with reforestation projects or state and national forests, become actively engaged in forest conservation projects through the cooperation of the various governmental forestry service offices. In many cases public lands are entrusted to schools for reforestation and conservation practice.

Among the leaders in programs of school forestry are Michigan, Wisconsin, and New York who now have over 300 school forests in their states. Other states such as Florida, and Ohio are rapidly increasing their school forest programs.

Schools in 41 counties in the state of Ohio now utilize 66 school forests. The total amount of land in this state devoted to school forests is 2,023 acres, which makes the average school forest in this state larger than 32 acres in size.

In the state of Florida, school forests are under the Vocational Agriculture departments of the high schools. Fifty-five secondary schools in this state operate school forests. One high school in Five Oak, Florida, operates two forests--one of 80 acres and one of 10 acres. The average acreage per school forest in Florida is more than 74 acres, with one school in Deland, Florida, operating a forest of 640 acres. The total number of acres devoted to school forests in Florida is 4,109.

In Texas the one school program most note-worthy of name is in Tyler, although many other schools in this state are in the planning stage of beginning school forest programs. The Texas Forest Service conducts many forestry workshops in conjunction with schools.

Four communities in Oklahoma, Walliant, Tahlequah, Brushy Ridge, and Beachton carry on school forest programs. All programs are carried on in conjunction with the local F. F. A. chapter. The state of Oklahoma also has an annual Youth Forestry Camp at Beavers Bend State Park that lasts for a period of one week. This camp has as its objectives:

1. To teach each boy the general fundamentals of good forestry as they apply to the multiple use of timberland.

2. To offer each boy an opportunity to enjoy six days of constructive recreation along with his work.

3. To develop each boy as a junior leader and to encourage him to pass to others in his community the knowleege he gained and activities he experienced while in camp.

Many other schools own and operate their own school forest. Nevada County, Arkansas, for example, provides a school forest for every school. Merrill, Wisconsin, purchased a tract of cut-over land for developing a school forest movement by passing legislation in 1931 providing for county, township, city, village, or school forests. This act has resulted in over 600 school forests amounting to some 65,000 acres of state land. Other states are beginning to follow the excellent example set by Wisconsin and many scattered school systems in over one-half the states are today working in school forest programs.

In some areas special interests are closely tied in to conservation education experiences. Maine is a great deer hunting state, and in some schools in Maine considerable emphasis is placed on gun and hunting safety, and compass and map work. Many hunters each year are shot mistakenly and often accidentally, and many hunters usually get lost in the woods. Conservation education has real meaning as youngsters learn not only safety but a great deal about the total conservation problem.

SCHOOL DAY CAMPS

The day camp in schools is a recent educational innovation. The day camp can best be described as an all day camp in which only the noon meal is involved and the children return to their homes in the evening. The day camp is often thought of as a program that is a fore-runner to the resident school camp. However, in many school systems it has become very highly acceptable as an educational media and will remain as an important phase of the school program.

The day camp must be within easy transportation distance from the school or the living quarters of those using the camp. Day camps usually operate from morning until late afternoon, however, some continue until late evening and involve the preparation of the evening meal.

The day camp can be operated most economically because of the elimination of sleeping quarters and the simplicity of the eating arrangements. Children can bring a sack lunch from home, may cook their own meal, or combine both methods.

The site for the day camp may be found in a nearby park, at a farm, a national forest, or other places secluded enough to offer privacy and natural surroundings for study.

One of the most noted day camp programs being conducted by schools is found in the Cook County Forest Preserve in Chicago, Illinois. Here public school districts annually provide a day camp experience for 2000 students. There is also a day camp program for Chicago teachers which provides teacher training experiences for over 200 Chicago teachers.

THE EDUCATIONAL MOBILE UNIT

Some schools have introduced a travel camping program as part of their outdoor educational program. These trips are taken on school time, weekends, holidays, and during the summer vacation periods. Some of the noted programs are those in Atlanta, Georgia, and the Roslyn Public Schools in New York. Students and teacher plan trips to observe places of historical interest and to observe and investigate interesting things in the natural science field. These trips are combined with adventurous travel, cooking, caring for themselves, and many social experiences of a recreational nature, and also in group living.

A unique program in travel camping is conducted by National Camp, Matamoras, Pennsylvania. Dr. L. B. Sharp, the director, has devised a travel camp trailer with room for materials of interest for programming, equipment, and provisions for preparing food for twelve campers and two counselors. The trailer is equipped with the basic essentials necessary for complete and comfortable living on the road. Experience in campcraft, group planning, adventure on the road, and educational experience through first hand visitations is made possible in an exciting and pleasurable way.

SCHOOL CAMPING

School camping programs, although found in over thirty-five states in the United States, are given their greatest emphasis in California, Michigan, Texas, Wisconsin, Indiana, and Illinois.

Outstanding examples of school camps operating today are found in the school districts of San Diego, California; Tyler, Texas; New Castle, Indiana; Battle Creek, Michigan; Austin, Texas; Los Angeles County, California; Frederick County, Maryland; Long Beach, California; Racine, Wisconsin; Milwaukee, Wisconsin; Roslyn, New York; Greensboro, North Carolina, Highline, Washington; Clairborne County, Tennessee; Carbondale, Illinois; Marion, Illinois; DuQuoin, Illinois; Cleveland Heights, Ohio; Manitowoc, Wisconsin; and close to three hundred more school districts.

There is every indication that this number is increasing and will more than double in the next ten years as the present experiences are evaluated and the possibilities made known to educators.

SPECIAL EMPHASIS PROGRAMS

In many schools, teachers of specialized subject matter areas conduct a variety of outdoor education programs to supplement their classroom teaching. These special project-field trip combinations are generally found in the fields of Biology, Forestry, General Science, and Physical Education. Some of the specialized projects include such things as aquatics, craft schools, hunting and gun safety workshop sessions, study of the propagation of fish in the school tank and in the Conservation Department hatcheries, special one-week workshops with emphasis on a specialized subject matter area such as Biology.

In many schools throughout the country there are clubs and organizations whose primary interest may be in a specialized area in the natural science field or in an area that closely relates to the outdoor education program. There are outing clubs, biology clubs, astronomy clubs, hunting and fishing clubs, camp craft clubs, hosteling clubs, bird watching clubs and many others. Through many of these clubs and organizations some very interesting hobbies, discoveries and research concerning the out-of-doors have been produced.

COOK COUNTY FOREST PRESERVE DISTRICT

The Conservation Department of the Cook County Forest Preserve District has an outstanding program in outdoor education for both public schools and adults which was started in 1945. The Forest Preserve's Conservation Department has improved both the quantity and quality of natural science and outdoor education in the public schools. They have done this chiefly through public relations and leadership education. As a result of their work more and more schools are hiring competent naturalist-teachers. The chief methods of promoting outdoor education is through the publication of a weekly nature bulletin (since 1945), lectures and movies on outdoor education to school assemblies, teacher education courses in cooperation with Chicago Teachers College, demonstration lessons, field trips, pilot studies in the out of doors and day camping.

It is estimated that during the past year the department's personnel reached close to 250,000 children and adults. There are no means of estimating the countless numbers reached through the weekly radio and television programs, and the newspaper articles which originate from the department.

OUTDOOR EDUCATION
IN COLLEGES AND UNIVERSITIES

In a recent study conducted by William E. O'Brien of the Recreation and Outdoor Education Department, Southern Illinois University, he discovered that there were approximately 275 colleges and universities teaching some kind of camp leadership course. These courses are being offered by departments of Education, departments of Recreation and departments of Physical Education. Some universities have special departments in Outdoor Education such as is found at Northern Illinois University, and some departments have a dual title with Outdoor Education being emphasized such as the Department of Recreation and Outdoor Education at Southern Illinois University.

In another survey made by Noel P. McGregor at Kansas University, he determined that only nine colleges and universities own and operate their own camping programs. This number has been increased considerably in the past decade.

There are many other opportunities existing through college and university areas in regard to implementing academic study through outdoor education by all university departments.

In addition to the campus many colleges and universities have extensive farms, forests, abandoned strip mine areas, formal gardens, arboretums, museums, many varieties of laboratories, small lakes and streams, and a variety of other resources usually not seen by most of the students that could be made available for all classes in any college or university. Some of the more significant kinds of programs to be found involving leadership training and teacher training in outdoor education programs at the college and university level include the following:

1. Lecture courses on camp leadership and camp administration where instruction is confined to lectures and follows the normal procedure for most college class work.

2. A combined lecture and field experience with the major emphasis being in the lecture courses.

3. A combined lecture and field experience in camp leadership where university students are required to participate in a camp leadership experience for one week duration or more with school children who are taken to camp through a local school board.

4. A camp counseling experience may be a part of the practice teaching requirement or made an optional part of the total practice teaching program. In some instances no credit is given for this experience, and in some universities credit is allowed toward the practice teaching requirement. At Clear Lake Camp there were approximately 300 practice teachers who selected a one week camp counseling experience without credit in connection with practice teaching from Michigan State and Western Michigan University.

5. Some colleges and universities require a school camp experience of one week's duration or more for all the teachers in the educational training program. Northern Illinois University requires all elementary education majors to have school camp experiences in their sophomore, junior, and senior years.

6. At least thirty-two colleges and universities require field experience as part of the camp leadership and outdoor education leadership training program. The amount of time varies considerably from one to twelve weeks. The kind of program also varies from a formal lecture period with one week field experience to an integrated instructional program of a twelve week field experience where the instructor is the camp director and the counselor meetings held weekly are considered a formalized lecture period.

7. In some colleges and universities the programs consist of integrated offerings from a number of university departments which cut across many areas of instruction. At Southern Illinois University there are a number of camps located at Little Grassy Lake. Campers consist of mentally retarded, both educable and trainable, all types of orthopedically handicapped, campers with speech and hearing defects, normal children, and children with social and emo-

tional problems. The camping program is considered a laboratory to be used by any University department which feels that they can enrich their program by giving students direct experiences in the out-of-doors and direct experiences in counseling the campers. At the present time fourteen different departments are offering twenty-four courses for credit in conjunction with this program. There are approximately 300 campers for a ten week period and approximately 250 University students participating in various parts of the program.

8. Many colleges and universities have special interest camps. Some of the more noted specialized camps of this kind include:

The Geology Camp

Here the major emphasis is on field mapping which includes problems in stratigraphy, structure, paleontology, physiography, and economic geology. It also includes study of the principal minerals and rocks of the earth's crust, emphasizing origin and identification, and the physical processes active in producing the surface features of the earth.

The Field Biology Camp

The Field Biology Camp is more commonly conducted on a day camp basis, but in some instances there are special camps for the study of field biology. Most of these camps consist of a study of representative plant groups, classification and evolution of the plant kingdom. They include also a study of the basic relationships of plants to the life of man--the history, geography, crop ecology, production, consumption, and uses of plants and plant products of economic importance.

Forestry Camp

Several colleges and universities now have established forest camps. They deal primarily with the importance and use of forests, their management and conservation, methods and principles of measuring contents of trees, stands of timber and rough wood products, and the application of yield tables and growth studies. There is also consideration given to the recreational use of forest lands.

Music Camp

The National Music Camp of Interlochen, Michigan, is a good example of using the relaxed climate of a camp setting for promoting a special interest. Sponsored by the University of Michigan, the music camp is nationally known. In addition to instruction and experience in performance in art, music, dance, and drama, children spend their leisure hours in outdoor recreation such as swimming, canoeing, sailing, nature lore, sports, and overnight camping.

ORGANIZED CAMPING IN THE UNITED STATES

Organized camping has become an integral part of programs of many organizations in the United States. Practically every youth serving agency has included the organized camp as part of their total program. In many cases it is the basis of the program, or the most important part. It has often been stated that if "outing" is taken out of "scouting" the purpose of the Scout programs, both Boy Scouts and Girl Scouts, is lost. Some of the various kinds of organized programs now flourishing in the United States are the church camps, the youth serving agency camps, governmental agency sponsored camps including both municipal and state, public school camps, parochial school camps, camping by colleges and universities, handicapped agency camps, and private camps.

It is estimated that each summer between five and six million boys and girls attend the various camps which are sponsored by various agencies. There are from 12,000 to 20,000 organized camps in the United States today.

The organized camping movement began in the late 1800's and within a very short period of time almost every type of agency accepted camping as part of its program.

CHURCH CAMPING

The first church camps in America were established for the purposes of recreation and Christian and religious education. Most church camps established up until the 1940's were the "camp-meetings" and the "church-institutes." Church camping as a vital part of the program of Christian and religious education is relatively new.

The purposes of church camping in modern day society have not changed a great deal except that almost every denomination of churches in America now considers camping a very important part of their religious training program. Ensign states that:

> Church camping may be thought of as living together happily in the out-of-doors in a Christian community being built by followers of Christ. Or it may be thought of as a twenty-four hour-a-day opportunity to put into practice the Christian principles we often only talk about. The camp setting provides campers with countless opportunities to deepen their understanding of God and his purposes.

> Church camping is part of the total program of the Church for the Christian education of its people--both children and adults. It can be one of the most meaningful experiences in this total program because by its twenty-four hour-a-day nature it is more intense and all-encompassing. It can be the vehicle for developing a deepening awareness of creation, for discovering the more satisfying ways of living in group situations, and for bringing an individual to a closer understanding of his relationship to God, to others, and to the natural world about him.[4]

The church was slow to recognize the inherent values in teaching Christianity through camping. Their early attempts were the interdenominational camps at Camp Winnepesaukee in New Hampshire, Camp Kanestake in Pennsylvania, and many other interdenominational camps in various parts of the country.

---

[4]John and Ruth Ensign, Stewards In God's World. Richard, Virginia: John Knox Press, 1953. p. 20.

It has only been in the last quarter of a century that churches of all denominations have used camping for inspiration and development of religious ideals in compliance with their particular faith.

An example of the remarkable growth of church camping is illustrated by Sheeder: "Nine Protestant denominations which had a total enrollment of 1,000 junior high campers in 1930 reported 165,000 in this age bracket in 1950."[5]

The same trend is cited by Catholic educators. The Belleville Diocese purchased a large tract of land in Southern Illinois and are now in the process of readying it for camping for Catholic youth. The Catholic Church has organized a national camping organization with headquarters in Washington, D.C.

The Jewish faith is also using camping to further their religious teachings. They have many camps which are used for religious teaching combined with outdoor recreation. In some New England states the services of the Jewish Rabbi are provided free to camps of other denominations or interdenominational camps to teach the folklore and meaning of the Jewish religion, thus promoting understanding.

Camp Ben Frankel, a three week camp designed primarily for religious instruction is held each summer at the Giant City State Park near Makanda, Illinois. In addition to religious instruction the children of Camp Ben Frankel participate in horseback riding, archery, fishing, sports, campcraft, and many other recreational activities through the cooperation of the Recreation and Outdoor Education Department of Southern Illinois University. Some of the trends in church camping include:

1. The summer school vacation, until rather recently, was also considered "vacation" time for the church. Now the summer is filled with educational experiences. The church-sponsored summer program of Christian Education now includes leadership schools, conferences of many kinds,

[5]Franklin I. Sheeder, "Church Camping," International Journal of Religious Education March, 1959. p. 13.

workshops, seminars, consultations, retreats, institutes, resident camping, day camping, trip camping, go-and-see tours, trailer-travel camping, caravans, assemblies and service projects.

2. The development of guidance material for new phases of camping--camping with families, day camping, camping with senior highs, church-sponsored camp trips.

3. The steady increase in numbers of persons participating year-by-year means more campers, more leaders, more camps, more materials, more preparation, more guidance, more professional staff--in short, a greater demand upon our resources of budget and personnel.

4. The rapid increase in the number of properties owned by our churches for the purposes of Christian Education. The denominations represented in the National Council are investing between fifty and seventy-five million dollars in these properties.

5. More careful recruitment and training of camp counselors.

6. The development of a "camping" pattern as different from the "conference" pattern.

YOUTH AGENCY CAMPS

Most youth agencies began in the late 1880's to include camping as part of their over-all program. The first camp of the Young Men's Christian Association was organized in 1885 by Sumner F. Dudley. The first Y.M.C.A. Camp consisting of six to eight boys was conducted at Pine Point . on Orange Lake near Newburgh, New York. The second summer the number grew to twenty-three boys and by 1891 the campers increased to eighty-three.

From the seed sown by Dudley in 1885 has grown a world-wide Y.M.C.A. camping movement reaching many thousands of boys in camps located in all parts of the world.

The Fresh Air Camps, developing as a part of social service, had their beginning in New York City. The first Fresh Air Camp for underprivileged children was established in 1872 on Staten Island and was sponsored by the Children's Aid Society of New York.

Life's Fresh Air Fund and the *Tribune* Fresh Air Fund were organized to raise monies for camping for the underprivileged. In 1925 Dr. L. B. Sharp was appointed Executive Director of the Activities of *Life's* Fresh Air Fund, and directed the organization of the camps. Dr. Sharp changed the name from *Life's* Fresh Air Farm to *Life's* Camp, changed many policies and placed the program of camp activities upon an educational basis.

The first Boy Scout Camp with professional leadership was established in 1910. During this year there were over twenty councils established near New York, Philadelphia, Boston, Columbus, and other larger cities. Today there are over 600 Boy Scout camps with a daily capacity of 60,000 boys.

Girl Scout camping was first organized in 1912 at Savannah, Georgia, by Juliette Low. Mrs. Low's purpose was to provide simple living under camp conditions for as many girls as possible. The Girl Scouts hold a nation-wide training program annually to provide leaders for their small unit camping program.

The Camp Fire Girls began in the home of Mrs. Luther Gulick and then moved to a private camp on Lake Sebago, Maine. Mrs. Gulick worked up a manual of camping and outdoor activities and on March 17, 1912, made it public. This date is considered the birthday of the Camp Fire Girls.

The Young Women's Christian Association's first summer camp was officially opened at Asbury Park, New Jersey, sixty-six years ago by President Grant. In recent years the Y.W.C.A. has organized a Girl Reserve which provides outing experiences for girls of high school age.

There are now several hundred national and state youth serving agencies who provide camping experiences for boys and girls.

PRIVATE CAMPS

Private camps began in the early 1890's concurrently with all other types of camps. Most of these camps were organized for profit and emphasized recreational activities, outdoor living, and nature studies.

Today the Association of Private Camps estimate that there are over 7,000 private camps located in every state of the Union.

CAMPS FOR HANDICAPPED

Another phase of outdoor education which is making tremendous growth both in terms of numbers served and quality of program is camping for the handicapped.

Probably the pioneer in camping for the handicapped is the National Association for Crippled Children and Adults. Many state associations have been operating camps for several years and the association holds an annual workshop or conference for camping personnel each year. Outstanding camps operated by the state societies of the National Association of Crippled Children and Adults are found in Minnesota, Wisconsin, Connecticut, Pennsylvania, Indiana, Ohio, and many others. At this writing the Kentucky Society is in the process of building a new camp.

The National Association for Retarded children added camping to their program at their national conference in Philadelphia in 1958. This occurred because many local associations were operating camps and requested that they be given a chance to discuss their mutual problems.

An outstanding example of camping for the mentally retarded is conducted at the Egyptian Camp for the Mentally Retarded at Southern Illinois University. Mentally retarded campers are referred to the camp by the Egyptian Association for the Mentally Retarded. The program is conducted by the Recreation and Outdoor Education Department for a two-fold purpose--providing leadership experience for teachers and others who plan to work with the handicapped and to provide a unique opportunity for the mentally retarded to live and learn in the out-of-doors.

The United Cerebral Palsy Association has recently moved into camping as a means of enriching the lives of the handicapped--both children and adults. The theme of the Association's national institute in Pittsburgh in 1959 was "The Development of Guidelines and Standards on the Creative Use of Leisure Time for the Cerebral Palsied."

Many camp leaders from all parts of the country related experiences at this institute held to discuss and improve programs for handicapped children and adults.

Other camps which are either in existence or are being prepared care for people with such handicaps as diabetes, the blind, the hard-of-hearing, the cardiac, the muscular dystrophy, and other crippling diseases.

CAMPINGS MANY PURPOSES

An examination of the various kinds of organized camps in existence today reveals amost every kind of camp imaginable. It would appear that camping might be the answer to all mental, physical, moral, and social ills. Some of the areas of specialization found in various camps include those of recreation, health development, religion, military training, remedial school work, school camping, social adjustment, psychological adjustment, rehabilitation, handicapped camps, and camping for the aged. Interwoven throughout all camps, no matter what their specialty, can be found the list of objectives consisting of development of health, character, education citizenship, conservation, and recreation.

Historically, educators should have been aware of the tremendous educational potential that has existed in supervised experience possible in living and learning in the organized camp. Camping has always been used as one of the most forceful media of education and indoctrination for the youth of the world. Down through the ages, most of the notorious, despotic leaders latched on to the camping idea as a means of indoctrinating youth to the many isms and potential ideologies. By controlling youth in this manner, despotic leaders built up a sense of fear, loyalty, pride, and admiration for their political ideals. These programs usually killed the initiative of youth, and they were not permitted to do any thinking of their own except as it contributed to the ideals specifically advocated by the military or political wish of a dictator, king, or chieftain.

In early Sparta, youngsters were taken from their parents at the age of six and indoctrinated into the military ideals of the Spartan leaders. They were taught to steal,

408

cheat, plunder, and know only one leader--their emperor. By the same token, they were probably the most physically fit group of young people ever to exist.

Since this time every leader has realized that in order to perpetuate their political viewpoint, no matter what it may be, they must first capture the youth of a nation, indoctrinate them, and control their thinking, keeping them healthy and physically fit to do the duties and work proposed by the national leader.

Programs of this kind were used successfully by Caesar, Hitler, Mussolini, Stalin, Franco and by many of the Greek leaders.

During the depression, school administrators had their eyes opened to an extensive camping program that had all of the desirable qualities of a supplementary approach to education. The Civilian Conservation Corps was a necessary relief program. The work and the results of this national camping venture with its many valued programs will long be remembered by the American public.

The aims of the Civilian Conservation Corps included:

1. To develop in each man his powers of self-expression, self-entertainment, and self-culture.
2. To develop pride and satisfaction in cooperative endeavor.
3. To develop as far as possible practicable and understanding of the prevailing social and economic conditions to the end that each many may cooperate intelligently in improving these conditions.
4. To preserve and strengthen good habits of bodily health and of mental development.
5. By organizing such vocational training as is feasible, but particularly by vocational counseling and adjustment activities, to assist each man better to meet his employment problems when he leaves camp.
6. To develop an appreciation of nature and country life.[6]

[6]James L. Mursell, Principles of Democratic Education. New York: W. W. Norton and Company, Inc., 1955. pp. 200-201.

World War II terminated the CCC, but in its nine
years some great steps had been taken. The team of boys
planted nearly three billion trees and built over 150,000
miles of trails and fire lanes. They strung 85,000 miles
of new telephone lines and put up 4,000 fire towers, 45,000
bridges, and thousands of buildings. Humphrey points out
further benefits:

> They built several million check dams against soil ero-
> sion, and did improvement cuttings and thinnings on
> about four million acres of forests. They saved mil-
> lions of acres by prompt fighting of small fires before
> they got out of control and protected the trees from
> attacks by insects and diseases. They also helped re-
> place sage brush with forage grasses on nearly forty
> million acres of brushy range lands.[7]

The CCC was essentially a relief organization and
designed primarily to serve young people who were in difficulties because of the economic situation of the time. The
development of these federal camps indicated that there
was a serious weakness in the school systems at this time.
The most serious weaknesses were other than finances.
Mursell states:

> When the depression hit American youth, all the public
> high school had to offer was, in the main, an academic
> curriculum with some rather ineffective vocational
> trimmings that were regarded as infra dig.---The un-
> mistakable lesson to be drawn is that the program of
> the comprehensive school must be made more realistic,
> more genuinely serviceable, less shackled by meaning-
> less traditions, more sharply focused on balanced gen-
> eral education for successful living, special education
> for occupations, work experience, active employment,
> guidance and placement, cooperation with public employ-
> ment agencies, financial aid to help some students meet
> the hidden cost of schooling--all within the framework
> of the comprehensive school. . . .

> No doubt the CCC camps were well on the road to becoming
> an established supplementary educational program to our
> present day public schools. This program no doubt could

[7]Hubert H. Humphrey, "A Plan to Save Trees, Land, and Boys," Harper's Magazine.
January, 1959. p. 54.

have become one of the most significant federal education programs of the century. In many respects this
would have had a very disastrous effect upon the concept of the old American tradition of local control of
education.[8]

Although these educational institutions were abolished
primarily as a result of World War II, there is still strong
support nationally to reinstate the CCC camps. There are
several Bills before the present 85th Congress that are being studied very carefully. One Bill, H. E. 1893, introduced by Congressman Dent is a Bill to authorize establishment of a youth camp recreation program to assist those
organizations which have for their purpose the providing of
healthful outdoor and camp training for indigent children.

The revival of the talk concerning the need for these
supplementary programs should be carefully studied and
analyzed by our school people today because the benefits
from school camping as an educational media have very
definitely proven highly successful. The schools can ill
afford to have Federal competition with a camping program
that would surely have immediate acceptance and gain in
popularity and be doing the things that schools have neglected
to do.

NATIONAL OUTDOOR EDUCATION ORGANIZATIONS

Teachers and youth leaders interested in gaining
background information on resources or in developing programs can secure a wealth of documentary materials,
audio-visual aids, teaching handbooks, bulletins, guides,
pamphlets, charts, maps, resource speakers, and other
valuable help from the many national governmental and
private agencies and organizations.

The federal government through its many departments
has issued many useful and inexpensive bulletins which may
be purchased from the Superintendent of Documents,

[8]James L. Mursell, Principles of Democratic Education. New York: W. W. Norton
and Company, Inc., 1955. p. 202.

Washington, D. C.   Among the governmental agencies concerned with various phases of outdoor education are:

Bureau of Biological Survey, Department of Agriculture, Washington, D.C.

Conserves wildlife; acquires and maintains bird refuges and game preserves; administers wildlife conservation laws; cooperates in development of improved methods of propagation of fur and other animals.

Bureau of Fisheries, Department of Commerce, Washington, D.C.

Develops methods of regulating the fish industry and supply in the interest of conservation; administers Alaska fisheries and fur-seal industries, and care of the Pribilof Island natives; administers laws for the protection of Florida coast sponges; and enforces the law regulating the interstate shipment of large and small-mouth black bass.

Bureau of Reclamation, Department of Interior, Washington, D.C.

Directs investigation of irrigation projects, has supervision over construction of Boulder Dam and the development of the Colorado River Basin; also over the Grand Coulee Dam and Columbia River Basin.

Extension Service, Department of Agriculture, Washington, D.C.

Sponsors 4-H Clubs whose work includes a conservation education program.

Federal Power Commission, Washington, D.C.

Organized to administer the Federal Water Power Act which provides for the improvement of navigation thru the development of water power on streams subject to federal jurisdiction or on public lands by private and governmental agencies acting under licenses issued by the Commission, licenses so issued to be subject to conditions prescribed to promote navigation and to conserve water-power resources for the public good. It is authorized to conduct general investigations of power resources.

Forest Service, Department of Agriculture, Washington, D.C.

Has general administration of national forests; conducts forest research; promotes improved forestry

practices; regulates grazing in national forests;
manages watersheds protected by national forests;
supervises forestry emergency activities of the
Civilian Conservation Corps; cooperates in development of state forests.

Geological Survey, Department of Interior, Washington,
D.C.
Classifies public lands and examines geologic structure, mineral resources, and mineral products of the
national domain; conducts investigations on quantity,
distribution, mineral quality, availability, and
utilization of water supplies in the United States,
and studies production of hydroelectric power for
public use; examines and classifies public lands as
to their mineral resources and their value for power
development; supervises oil, gas, and mining operations on public lands included in prospecting permits
and leases under mineral leasing laws.

National Forest Reservation Commission, War Department,
Washington, D.C.
Purchases such forested, cut-over, or denuded lands
within the watersheds of navigable streams as in its
judgment may be necessary to the regulation of stream
flow and the production of timber.

National Park Service, Department of the Interior,
Washington, D.C.
Directs protective work toward preserving national
parks for all generations and utilizing them to the
best advantage for the benefit and enjoyment of the
visitor; furnishes public educational service in
national sciences, history, and archeology, in connection with areas under its care; participates in
the Emergency Conservation Work program and supervises work camps engaged in recreational development
on state, county, and municipal areas; cooperates
with regional and state planning boards and conservation agencies.

Soil Conservation Service, Department of Agriculture,
Washington, D.C.
Promotes use of soil conservation practices in agriculture; conducts research and demonstration projects
in soil conservation; directs erosion-control activities of soil conservation district offices. The
S.C.S. has local offices in each county.

In addition to the governmental agencies there are many private clubs and organizations promoting nature, hiking, outings, conservation and other recreational or educational experiences in the out-of-doors. Many of these groups have organized into sectional, state, and national organizations in order to better achieve their objectives and gain the mutual benefit which comes from united effort on a larger scale.

Some national organizations promote outdoor education as one phase of their program as a supplement, or as a technique, in achieving their set objectives. Among these groups are the Girl Scouts of America, the Boy Scouts of America, the Campfire Girls, the Young Men's Christian Association, the Four-H Club, and the Boys Club of America. Each of these organizations have contributed much to the cause of conservation, nature lore, campcraft, and other phases of outdoor education.

Other professional organizations which are interested in outdoor education as a part of their total program are the National Recreation Association, the American Association of Health, Physical Education and Recreation, the National Parks Association, and the American Institute of Park Executives.

The National Recreation Association has its headquarters at 8 West Eighth Street, New York 11, New York. Although it is a service organization for the entire field of recreation, it has many good publications on camping in general and especially on day camping as it applies to recreation.

The American Association for Health, Physical Education, and Recreation as its title implies covers a wide area of interests. It is a division of the National Education Association with headquarters at 1201 Sixteenth St., N. W., Washington 6, D. C. The Association publishes a monthly journal and other helpful materials on health, physical education, and recreation.

The Outdoor Education Project under the direction of Julian W. Smith is sponsored by the American Association of Health, Physical Education, and Recreation. The purpose this project is to awaken interest in outdoor education, provide leadership at the various workshops, and point up the possibilities for programs in the various states. The project has been held in thirty-three states.

The American Institute of Park Executives with headquarters at Oglebay Park, Wheeling, West Virginia, publishes a monthly journal, *Parks and Recreation*. The Institute has given great emphasis to outdoor education through its park-school plan.

The Student Conservation Program of the National Parks Association offers opportunities for high school and college youth to make significant contributions to the conservation of natural resources and at the same time acquire experiences which may lead to an interesting vocation. The Association with headquarters at 1300 New Hampshire Avenue, Washington 6, D. C. publishes the *National Parks Magazine*.

Among the national organizations which foster and promote interest in nature, conservation, and outdoor life as their primary objectives are: The American Camping Association, The Outdoor Education Association, The National Audubon Society, The American Forestry Association, the Intercollegiate Outing Club Association, The Association of Private Camps, The Soil Conservation Society of America, The American Youth Hostels, National Wildlife Federation, and The Wilderness Society.

THE AMERICAN CAMPING ASSOCIATION

The American Camping Association is dedicated to furthering the interests and welfare of children and adults through camping education and recreation. As an outgrowth of a conference of camp directors in 1903, the present organization was formed in 1924 as the Camp Directors Association. The name, American Camping Association, was adopted in 1935.

The current membership of the Association is well over 8,000 people. It includes camp directors, counselors, board members, and other persons interested in camping. Membership is open to people of all races and creeds.

Private, organizational, church, public, institutional, and specific purpose camps are represented in the American Camping Association membership.

are: The objectives of the American Camping Association are:

1. To further the welfare of children and adults through camping.
2. To extend the recreational and educational benefits of out-of-doors living.
3. To provide for exchange of experiences and successful practices, and for development of materials, standards and other aids for the progress of camping.
4. To serve as the voice of camp leaders in national and local affairs.
5. To interpret camping to related groups and to the public.
6. To stimulate high professional standards of camp leadership.
7. To give emphasis in camping to citizenship training in keeping with the principles and traditions of American democracy.

The Association is organized for democratic government, as much of the work of the Association is carried out through National Committees in the areas of standards, leadership, membership, program, publications, public relations, research and other important facets of camping. The Association operates a national office at Bradford Woods, Martinsville, Indiana, employing an Executive Director, Assistant Executive Director, and office staff.

The American Camping Association serves practically everyone interested in camping from camp directors to the campers and their parents. The Association gives assistance to parents seeking the right camp for their children, offers consultant services for camp directors and owners, develops and conducts leadership courses, holds local and national workshops and conventions, provides a counselor placement service, encourages and conducts studies and research on topics dealing with camping, and improves the general camping practices through formulation and adaptation of a set of recommended camp standards.

THE OUTDOOR EDUCATION ASSOCIATION, INC.

The Outdoor Education Association, with headquarters at 800 South Illinois Avenue, Carbondale, Illinois is devoted exclusively to the promotion of outdoor education. It is a national, non-profit, tax exempt, educational organization supported by voluntary contributions and memberships. Its purpose is to extend the benefits of outdoor education-- through schools, colleges, and public and private agencies --to youth and adults throughout the country.

The Association publishes a newsletter, various educational pamphlets and brochures and a monograph, *Extending Education* semi-annually.

The objectives of the Outdoor Education Association in "preparing today's camper for tomorrow's world" are:

1. Promotion of living and learning in the out-of-doors as an integral part of education and organization programs.
2. Dissemination of information through materials, publications, and films.
3. Training of leaders at National Camp in summer sessions, short institutes, pilot and demonstration projects and workshops.
4. Research and study of problems and new frontiers in the operation of children's camps and related projects.
5. Field service and consultant assistance--to communities, agencies, and institutions--on program surveys, plans for camp layout, leadership training programs, and study groups.

The Association's concept of outdoor education was pioneered by its present director, Dr. L. B. Sharp, over a quarter of a century ago. This concept of utilizing the open country to extend the child's knowledge and individual development has gained wide acceptance through the years largely through the efforts of Dr. Sharp.

The Outdoor Education Association conducts workshops

for advanced leadership training in outdoor education and camping at National Camp located in the Pocono Mountains at Matamoras, Pennsylvania. The camp, overlooking the beautiful Delaware Valley, comprises a large tract of woodland and meadows adjacent to thousands of acres of state forest offering an abundance of wildlife and geographical phenomena.

National Camp for advanced leadership preparation was founded in 1940 in response to a growing need for qualified leadership in outdoor education, including school camping in all parts of the country. Hundreds of youth leaders, teachers, college faculty members, administrators, and camp personnel have attended its regular summer sessions and special institutes. As greater numbers of schools and organizations turn to the out-of-doors for a more realistic approach to the present day needs of American youth, there is an increasing demand for qualified leadership.

National Camp is devoted to advanced study and practice. Participants are helped to develop specific plans for their own schools, colleges, organizations, or communities. The regular session is a practice field course in administration and leadership of outdoor education with special emphasis on the development of year-around programs. Students learn through field trips, group conferences, general sessions, research, and participation in all phases of camp living. Construction of shelters and equipment, hiking, overnight camping, menu planning and food marketing, accounting, nature and conservation activities, trips, and explorations are among the practical experiences offered. Faculty members are nationally known leaders in education and camping. A similar program with modifications is followed in short institutes and workshops and special sessions for church camps and other institutions.

Among the institutes and workshops offered by the Outdoor Education Association at National Camp are:

> School camping groups
> Trailer Travel camping workshop
> Small group, decentralized camping skills
> Trailer travel leadership course
> American Youth Hostel course

Counselor leadership course
Outdoor education and school camping workshop
Church camp leadership
Pole Bridge Camp for boys and girls, and
Special leadership camp for older youth

THE AMERICAN NATURE ASSOCIATION

The American Nature Association, with headquarters at 1214 16th Street, N. W., Washington 6, D. C., was founded in 1922 to stimulate public interest in every phase of nature and the outdoors and to further the practical conservation of the great renewable natural resources of America.

The Association conducts a conservation department, carries on campaigns for road beautification, elimination of unsightly billboards, discourages cruelty in hunting, and provides illustrated lectures and motion pictures on conservation and wildlife. There are over 75,000 members who are concerned with such problems as education, soil, water, pollution, public lands administration, forests, National parks, wilderness, wildlife, fisheries, and rural roadside environment.

The voice of the Association and its official publication, *Nature Magazine*, is published ten times a year. A non-commercial publication, published at a deficit that is made up from membership dues and endowment income, the magazine goes to some 15,000 schools and libraries, in addition to the membership of the Association. In addition to the *Nature Magazine* the Association publishes *Birds of the State, Bird and Animal Book, Nature Almanac,* and many education reprints and special bulletins.

THE IZAAK WALTON LEAGUE OF AMERICA

The Izaak Walton League of America has over five hundred chapters in thirty-three states not including the major junior chapters for boys up to eighteen years of age. The League is set up in community chapters with a tradition of *responsible* and *united* action assured by its unique and democratic structure. There are over five hundred men's chapters, over seventy women's chapters, a growing nucleus of high school chapters, and many state divisions all chartered by the national organization which is chartered by the state of Illinois and recognized by the Federal government as a non-profit, non-sectarian, and non-political scientific and educational organization.

Delegates to state divisions and to the national conventions are selected by vote of members in each chapter, giving each member a voice in establishing local, state, and national policies that all members support whole-heartedly.

The League's tradition of conservation action began in 1922 when a group of fifty-four outdoorsmen met in Chicago to stop the widespread and arrogant abuse of America's rich heritage of fish, wildlife, and scenic resources.

The purpose of the League is to develop opportunities for the enjoyment of the out-of-doors through encouragement of protection, restoration, and conservation of woods, water and wild life. The Izaak Walton League engages in activities which promote sound conservation practices. They are active in supporting legislation for control of stream pollution, for acquiring public forest lands, and for development of wildlife and wilderness areas. Individual chapters sponsor junior chapters and aid them in activities concerned with the enjoyment and perpetration of the out-of-doors resources.

Teachers and youth leaders may get further information on how to organize a chapter in a local community by writing to the Izaak Walton League of America, 1326 Waukegan Road, Glenview, Illinois.

Further insight into the purposes of the League are shown in the pledge which the members make upon joining:

I believe in the aims and purpose of the Izaak Walton League of America, and pledge my aid and support in the protection and restoration of America's soil, woods, waters, and wildlife; to help increase opportunities for outdoor recreation and safeguard public health; to hunt and fish in accordance with the law and to respect the property rights of others; and to further the League's efforts to foster the wise use of all natural resources.

The League publishes the *Outdoor America* magazine monthly, and in addition is a good source for booklets, films, maps, and charts.

The underlying philosophy of the League is summarized in its *Handbook of Instruction for Chapter Officers:*

1. The Izaak Walton League is devoted to the wise use of our America's natural resources in a measure compatible with the continued and future welfare of all Americans.

2. The League consistently works toward eliminating pollution of public waters on the premise that water which has been given to all peoples shall be maintained in usable condition for everyone.

3. The League opposes the granting of special privileges in connection with our Federal lands, including National Parks, wildlife refuges or any areas for the purpose of commercializing and despoiling any areas which should be retained for public benefit.

4. The League has long pioneered the encouragement of teaching conservation in the schools, so that growing generations will be better informed in the safe-guarding of their rich heritage of resources, --its soil, woods, waters, and wildlife.

5. The League, which consists of chapters for both men and women, is not a hunting or fishing organization. Many of the League members neither hunt nor fish. Its membership is drawn from all walks of life. The common bond between all members is the desire to stop the senseless waste of America's outdoor heritage.

6. The League has no political, commercial or sectarian attachments . . . It has no axe to grind . . . Will not be "bought" or "bargained with." It jealously guards its reputation for integrity of purpose and its constant vigilance against any attempted misuse or abuse of America's soil, woods, waters and wildlife.

7. In a nutshell . . . The League maintains that, "Conservation is as non-partisan as patriotism."

THE NATIONAL AUDUBON SOCIETY

The headquarters for the National Audubon Society is 1130 Fifth Avenue, New York 28, New York. Their membership numers 6, 500 adults and over 200, 000 children, the latter enrolled in over 4, 000 Junior Audubon Clubs.

The purpose of the National Audubon Society is to arouse public appreciation of the beauty and economic value of wildlife and to stimulate action to preserve and protect it; to preserve an adequate breeding stock of all native wild life; to preserve environmental conditions of ample food, water, and cover; to fix guardianship responsibility on federal, state, or competent private agencies to safeguard all species threatened with extinction.

The Audubon Society encourages the establishment of sanctuaries, the enactment of legislation to eliminate pollution of inland and marine waters, the limitation to emergencies in the use of poison as a method of wild life control, and the regulation of hunting and commercial use; promotes the establishment of permanent primitive areas, combats public works such as draining projects when seriously destructive to wild life and its habitat yet not of clearly demonstrated public benefit, combats wasteful lumbering, opposes overgrazing on public lands; opposes widespread killing of predatory wild life, urges the elimination of the practices of paying bounties, and discourages vermin campaigns; advocates legislation establishing the teaching of nature appreciation and the biological basis of wild life conservation as part of the regular school curriculum, trains teachers and other youth leaders to develop genuine lasting interest in wild life and its conservation, prepares and distributes conservation material and natural science facts among children, and maintains research fellowships at universities as a means of basing conservation policies on biological facts. In 1936 the National Audubon Society inaugurated the Aubudon Nature Camp where teachers, principals, superintendents, camp counselors and youth group leaders from all over the United States and Canada have enrolled each year.

The *Audubon Magazine,* published bi-monthly and *News on the Wing,* published quarterly, are the publications

of the Audubon Society. In addition the Society publishes
many helpful outdoor teaching guides for teachers and youth
leaders.

THE AMERICAN FORESTRY ASSOCIATION

The American Forestry Association, with headquarters at 919 17th Street, Washington, D.C., has a membership of over 14,000.

The purpose of the Association is to promote the protection, preservation, and wise use of the forest resources
of the United States, together with the complementary resources of soil, water, wild life, and outdoor recreational
facilities to the end that these resources may contribute in
a larger and more permanent way to the social and industrial welfare of the people.

The American Forestry Association initiates campaigns to bring about further state and federal laws designed
to protect the public interests in the use and preservation of
natural resources; conducts special campaigns to protect
trees and forests against devastation by forest fires, tree
insects, and tree diseases; conducts group vocation trips
to the national parks during summer months in order to
give laymen an insight into the resources of these public
reservations; provides the public with information on forest,
wildlife, conservation and other conservation fields; also
provides books and sporting and travel equipment at special
discount. Activities for youth include the promotion of special forestry contests among boys and girls in different
states, cooperation with outdoor clubs and groups in the
planting of trees, and sponsoring of special educational
projects in schools to awaken the younger generation to
the needs of protecting forests from fire.

The Association publishes *American Forests* monthly
and *Conservation* bi-monthly. In addition they publish special booklets, pamphlets and a few books dealing with forestry.

THE INTERCOLLEGIATE OUTING CLUB ASSOCIATION

In 1932, delegates from eight New England college
outing clubs met on Mt. Moosilauke to exchange ideas and

suggestions for the mutual betterment of their outing club programs. At this time they decided to set up a College Week plan whereby a week before classes open in the fall, the outing clubs would get together for a week of camping, mountain climbing, and other outdoor activities. The College Week met with great success and is practiced by many college outing clubs today.

The Intercollegiate Outing Club Association has met every year since 1932 for the purpose of exchanging ideas, promotions of outing projects, and aiding new club members in organizational and program problems.

In recent years the Association has increased its membership considerably. Among the many college outing clubs belonging to the Intercollegiate Outing Club Association are: Dartmouth, Syracuse, University of New Hampshire, Rensselaer, Massachusetts Institute of Technology, Amherst, McGill, Vassar, Cornell, Princeton, Wisconsin, Purdue, Swarthmore, Harvard, and Yale.

ASSOCIATION OF PRIVATE CAMPS

The headquarters for the Association of Private Camps is 55 West 42nd Street, New York 18, New York. A full time Executive Secretary and a staff administers the activities of the Association and is available for information and counsel on camp problems at all times.

The Association is composed of men and women who are actively engaged in the direction of privately conducted children's camps. It is incorporated, non-sectarian, and non-profit. It was established in 1940.

The primary aims of the Association of Private Camps are the advancement of camping as a vital and progressive force in the education and recreation for the children of the nation. Through mutual cooperation it seeks to elevate the standards and advance progress in children's camps. It helps to maintain a high degree of professional ethics and develops wholesome relationships among the many men and women who devote themselves professionally to children's camping.

The stated purposes of the Association are:

To provide a media for the exchange of ideas on camp philosophy, program methodology, and problems related to management and operation for the benefit of the members of the Association and the public it serves, and

To promote among private children's camps the highest possible ethical and professional standards.

Some of the many services which the Association of Private Camps offers its members are: counselor placement bureau; research and study groups; camp referral service; printed camp forms including counselor application blanks, employment contracts, medical certificates, and other administrative forms; insurance help through a cooperative project of the insurance committee and several large insurance companies; legislative advice and opinions concerning State and Federal legislative matters; public relations; buyers guides, and setting camp standards in administration, leadership, program, facilities, health, safety, and sanitation.

Since 1947 the Association has conducted a convention each year with increasing success. This annual function has attracted thousands of persons interested in camping for children and has served to stimulate interest and broaden the scope of benefits available to children. Experts in various fields and specialists of national reputation have graced the list of speakers at the national conventions. In addition hundreds of suppliers have come together at this convention to display their products for inspection of the camp leaders.

The proceedings of the annual camp conventions of the Association of Private Camps are duplicated each year and mailed to each member of the group. Much help in the way of professional advice and practical information pertaining to the operation of a private camp is included in these yearly proceedings.

SOIL CONSERVATION SOCIETY OF AMERICA

The Soil Conservation Society of America, has its headquarters at 838 Fifth Avenue, Des Moines 14, Iowa.

The Soil Conservation Society of America is dedicated to the advancement of the science and art of good land use. Here the teacher, technician, researcher, and administrator from all fields relating to land use, join with business, industrial, farm and organizational leaders to find common meeting grounds. Through membership of professional and practical conservationists, the Society has become a strong and world wide "voice" in soil and water conservation. Members have many opportunities to share information, experiences and fellowship through chapter, state, regional and Society meetings. Through membership the individual lends his influence in an organized approach to advance the cause in which he is vitally interested.

The Society publishes the widely read *JOURNAL OF SOIL AND WATER CONSERVATION,* now in its 14th volume. Here in readable and pictorial form, technical information is contributed by members and other leaders. The JOURNAL is secured through membership in the organization. In addition the Society publishes many conservational materials and special publication such as *Journal of Soil and Water Conservation, Our Watershed Resource, Land Utilization in the United States, The Wonder of Water, The Story of Land,* and *Down the River.*

Governed by a council of five officers and eight members elected by the total membership, much of the Society's work is carried forward by the one hundred local chapters. National committees have produced many benefits to members, including the first soil and water conservation glossary, a series of popular booklets, studies relating to watershed development, wetland management, effects of urbanization and other problems involving land use.

More than 10,000 conservation leaders, many with specialized backgrounds of experience, training and affiliations, have joined the Society to better serve the objective of advancing the science and art of good land use.

Members are located in all states, territories, Provinces of Canada, and in seventy-two other countries. Dues are $5.00 a calendar year. Individuals having professional training and experience in some phase of the soil and water conservation movement or related fields are eligible for professional membership. Interested leaders and individuals join as members. Libraries, institutions, schools or firms become subscribers.

Individuals desiring to give greater support may become sustaining members for $25.00 or more. Business firms, organizations, institutions, and industries may obtain sustaining membership for $100.00 or more.

Chapters located throughout the United States, Puerto Rico, Canada, and in South America increase the benefits of membership. The national or international aspect of The Soil Conservation Society of America gives a broader and more varied and interesting aspect to the problems of conservation in the Americas. Members of local chapters who are primarily concerned with local problems are able to see how their problems relate to the problems of the nation and of the world.

THE AMERICAN YOUTH HOSTELS, INC.

The American Youth Hostel, Inc. is a member of the International Youth Hostel. The headquarters of the Hostel is located at 14 West 8th Street, New York 11, New York.

The purpose of the American Youth Hostels is to help all, especially young people, to a greater understanding of the world and its people, primarily through out-of-doors educational and recreational travel. Youth hostels provide simple accommodations in scenic and cultural areas. The AYH is a non-profit, non-sectarian, non-political corporation organized exclusively for charitable and educational purposes, and open to all regardless of race, creed, or religion. It is tax exempt by ruling of the U.S. Treasury Department, and contributions to AYH are deductible.

The AYH National Leadership Training Course, held each year during the month of June, is required of leaders of group hosteling trips sponsored by AYH National Headquarters, and is open as well to youth leaders who plan to include hosteling in their own educational or recreational programs. The course provides discussion and practical experience in the application of leadership skills to hosteling in their own situations, combined with an intensive study of modern leadership techniques.

For further information apply to the Travel Director, American Youth Hostels, 14 West 8th Street, New York 11, New York for Bulletin 1.

NATIONAL WILDLIFE FEDERATION

The national Wildlife Federation with headquarters at 1412 16th Street, N. W. , Washington, D. C. , is a national federation of state level organizations expressing an interest in the conservation of wildlife and other natural resources and representing a cross section of conservation interest within the state.

Membership in any state is limited to one organization which must be representative of that state's conservation interests, and must adhere roughly to the principles and objectives of the National Wildlife Federation and be operated along commonly-accepted business principles. There is nothing to prevent several state-wide organizations from banding together or council being accepted as the NWF affiliate in that state.

The National Wildlife Federation is financed through the sale, by direct mail, of the celebrated Wildlife Stamps and related materials. These, issued annually and depicting a variety of flora and fauna, are responsible for virtually the entire annual income of the Federation. The remainder of the income is from contributions, donations, and the sale of materials utilizing stamp subjects or Federation art work.

The Federation sponsors a program of educational grants and fellowships to individuals and organizations for conservation education projects and research. Many of these are given to students who are carrying on research in educational phases of conservation work. Local and state organizations have received support from the Federation for research studies.

The Federation offers a variety of organizational aids for its affiliates and other conservation groups at state and local levels. Each year the Federation distributes nearly a million leaflets and educational items to these organizations, as well as to schools and the general public through

428

its Education Servicing office and the annual Wildlife Week program. Most of these materials are furnished without charge. Listings of the Federation's free and low-cost conservation publications are available upon request.

The Federation also publishes and distributes a semimonthly newsletter, the CONSERVATION NEWS. This contains latest information on activities in the resource management and conservation fields throughout America and is made available to interested persons without charge. The CONSERVATION REPORT, a weekly analysis of conservation legislation before the U. S. Congress, is another Federation publication that is offered to the public as a free educational service.

THE WILDERNESS SOCIETY

The Wilderness Society is a national conservation organization incorporated in the District of Columbia to secure the preservation of wilderness . . . to carry on an educational program concerning the values of wilderness and how it may best be used and preserved in the public interest . . . to make and encourage scientific studies concerning wilderness . . . and to mobilize cooperation in resisting the invasion of wilderness . . . . In the National Wilderness Preservation System there are 82 wilderness, wild, primitive, and roadless areas within the national forests, 48 primeval national parks and monuments, 20 national wildlife refuges and ranges, 15 roadless and wild areas on Indian reservations. There also are state parks and preserves where wilderness is protected. The Wilderness Society's most particular, immediate purpose is to defend these areas . . . . Its long-time, broad purpose is to increase the knowledge and appreciation of wilderness, wherever found.

The by-laws of the Wilderness Society say: "This Society shall be composed of individuals who feel that the entire nation and they themselves are losing something of value when a highway is built in a wilderness, when a primeval forest is logged, when airplanes bring the noise of urban life into a wilderness and destroy the charm of remoteness, or when mechanical civilization encroaches in any way on the last remnants of wilderness left for themselves and their posterity. " . . . . They believe that wilderness is a valuable natural resource that belongs to the people and that its preservation--for educational, scientific, and recreational use--is part of a balanced conservation program essential in the survival of our civilized culture . . . .

The Society publishes *The Living Wilderness,* issued quarterly, illustrated with photographs, paintings, drawing, and maps, and including articles, narratives, poems, reviews, and news . . . . It makes personal investigations of wilderness areas and problem . . . . It brings wilderness needs to the attention of those concerned with public-land policies . . . . It mobilizes support for wilderness preservation and tells members, other organizations, and the public about proposals that threaten this preservation . . . . It represents wilderness interests at public hearings . . . . It attends conservation conventions and other meetings to discuss current needs and opportunities in wilderness preservation . . . . It joins with other organizations in co-operation for the conservation of all natural resources . . . . It encourages members to work for the preservation of natural areas in their home localities . . . . It maintains an office in the nation's capital.

SUMMARY

A study of the scope of outdoor education in America reveals many types of outdoor education programs in every state of the Union. Some type of outdoor education program is used by practically every youth serving agency. The most prevalent types include: journeys and field trips, day camps, gardens, sanctuaries, park plans, forests, farms, overnight and extended resident camps, hosteling, and club activities involved with some special outdoor interest.

Private camps are serving the youth of America well but many children cannot afford the cost of this excellent service. Welfare agencies provide camping experience for the underprivileged. Children of middle income families, unless they belong to the Y. M. C. A., Y. W. C. A., the Boy or Girl Scouts, or other youth serving agency, are denied a camping experience. It is up to the public schools to provide for these children.

Many excellent organizations concerned with outdoor education are reaching young people in their homes. The National Audubon Society and the Izaak Walton League of America are good examples. Other organizations such as the American Camping Association, the Outdoor Education Association, and the American Association of Private Camps are doing a wonderful job in promoting leadership and setting high standards in camping and outdoor education.

Organizations such as the American Forestry Association, the Soil Conservation Society of America, the National Wildlife Federation, and the Wilderness Society are primarily interested in supporting and educating for good conservation practices.

Questions and Projects

1. What are the types of outdoor education conducted by schools, churches, and agencies?

2. Write the American Institute of Park Executives to ascertain the scope and purpose of the park-school plan.

3. What advantages will the educational mobile unit, designed by Dr. L. B. Sharp, offer to schools and other agencies or institutions? What might be some disadvantages?

4. List as many valuable educational activities as you can think of that are afforded by a school garden.

5. Are there any groups or organizations in your community which are promoting outdoor education? If so, visit them and determine their purpose and services offered.

6. A committee may be appointed to write for further information as to the function and services offered by the associations listed in this chapter. Reports of findings should be made to class.

7. Write the national headquarters of your church to determine what is being done by your denomination in Christian education through use of church camps.

8. The state of Maryland has a unique program whereby the State Departments of Conservation helps schools to operate a school sanctuary. Write for more information on this unusual promotion of wildlife by the state through the public schools.

9. As a member of a team, make a survey of your community and list the educational possibilities in the community for field trips and other types of outdoor education.

10. Make a study of outdoor education in your state.

11. Develop a teaching outline which may be used by a sixth grade teacher for a school garden, a school forest, or a school farm.

12. Interview the Girl Scout leader, Boy Scout leader, Y.M.C.A. leader and other agency leaders in your community to determine the extent that their group is using outdoor education.

Selected References

Bathurst, Effie G. and Hill, Wilhelmina, *Conservation Experiences For Children.* (Bulletin no. 16) Washington, D. C.: U. S. Department of Health Education and Welfare, 1957.

Clarke, James Mitchell, *Public School Camping.* Stanford California: Stanford University Press, 1951.

Department of Public Instruction, *Guide To School Camping For Wisconsin.* (mimeographed bulletin) Madison, Wisconsin: Department of Public Instruction, 1956.

432

Department of Public Instruction, *School Experiences In Camp*. (Bulletin no. 420) Lansing, Michigan: Department of Public Instruction, 1948.

Department of Supervision and Curriculum Development, *Toward A New Curriculum*. Washington, D. C.: National Education Association, 1944.

Macmillan, Dorothy Lou, *School Camping and Outdoor Education*. Dubuque, Iowa: Wm. C. Brown Company, 1956.

National Recreation Association, Recreation Magazine, *Camping and Outdoor Education*. March, 1961.

Smith, Julian W., *Outdoor Education For American Youth*. Washington, D. C.: American Association For Health, Physical Education, and Recreation, 1957.

Western New York School Study Council, *Education Beyond Four Walls*. (mimeographed bulletin) Buffalo: University of Buffalo, 1959.

Chapter 12

A LOOK TO THE FUTURE

To the educators of the future a major mystery of the development of their profession in the first half of the twentieth century will surely be the slowness with which camping was adopted as a functional part of the school system.

—American Youth Commission

Man has conquered many worlds and pushed out on many frontiers since Hannibal sat on the east side of the Alps and cried because there were no new worlds to conquer.

Not only has man expanded Hannibal's world to seven continents and thousands of islands but he is now ready to establish beach heads on the moon and on other planets.

Man has made great strides in other fields, too. He has made incredible progress in unveiling the secrets of nature. He has made the earth yield more abundantly than ever before in human history. He has made unbelievable strides in technology and automation. He has pushed back the threats of disease with wonder drugs and vaccines and has prolonged man's life span to an unbelievable age. Scientists felt, that through the conquest of disease, man would not only be healthier and live longer, but would live happier.

From the beginning of the new century man's mind has been filled with wild dreams and extravagant hopes. Sociologist believed that it would be possible to abolish poverty and eliminate crime. Industrialists claimed that the machine age would give man so much free time that universal education and culture would reach incredible heights. Religious leaders, thinking that improvements in transportation and communication would bring closer world-wide relationships with all mankind, dreamed of the brotherhood of man being near at hand.

- 433 -

And now man has unlocked the door to the atom, resulting in an inexhuastible source of power to build, to heal, and to open new avenues for a healthier and happier life.

In view of the astonishing progress man has made through science and technology and in view of the wonderful promises which scientists say the future holds for mankind, it would seem that the modern age would be one of peace and hope.

Yet the very opposite prevails. The world is full of turmoil. Man lives in fear of his neighbor and wars threaten to destroy the world. Insecurity and tension mounts as man struggles from one generation to the next. We find ourselves spending most of our monies building implements of destruction and living a life full of fear, apprehension, and insecurity.

WHY HAS MANKIND FAILED?

Let us turn to the schools. While man's educational system cannot be entirely blamed for the "nature of man", we are doing very little to help his plight. It appears that educators have been more interested in administrative techniques than they have in the function and goals of education. They have been more interested in imparting knowledge than they have in developing wisdom. Critical thinking or the wisdom to use knowledge does not receive as high a mark as the ability to repeat facts, either written or oral.

Another reason for the disharmony and conflicts in world affairs is the fact that the dollar has replaced the Golden Rule as the goal of man. Here again the schools do very little but accept societies goal. The National Education Association periodically publishes the increased earning power which an education promises to the young men and women. Fathers and mothers send children to college "so they won't have to work as hard as I did." A successful man in America is associated with the wealthy man. Cultural achievements are subordinate to materialistic advancements.

Unless the public schools can start helping society solve the pressing problems of the changing times, there is little hope for the future. It is now time for educators to think in terms of what the schools can do to help students, not only to adjust, but to work constructively to improve society.

Education for tomorrow demands that we re-examine the entire school curricula and start at once to make constructive changes which are compatible with the new goals in education. This may involve an extended school year, more teachers, more budget, more mobility of classes, and a score of other changes. It is imperative that changes be made. Education for American youth can no longer come from the tombs.

As science and technology advances, so must the educational insights and methods change. All that was good in the 1920's will not necessarily work in the 1960's. New methods and new patterns will emerge. Teaching machines will appear. Educational television will be used. There will be a closer student-teacher relationship. Teachers will find methods which will avoid pedagogical verbalism and theorizing and will employ methods that develop creativity, inventiveness and critical thinking.

In the past year a group of business firms alarmed at the poor caliber of graduates from schools of business placed a full page advertisement in several leading magazines pleading for colleges to give them good strong liberal arts graduates who could spell, write, speak, meet people, and be at ease with life. If we can get such men, they went on to say, we will teach them the necessary business skills.

Other professions are beginning to feel the same way. The schools are not keeping abreast with society's present day needs.

The great social and economic development of the American people and the complete severence of a great segment of humanity from nature and the soil which sustains them would seem to demand an outdoor experience for all youth.

Outdoor education has been fully justified both educationally and economically as an important contribution to the total education program. There is every reason to believe that this phase of education will continue to grow at a rapid rate. The use of the outdoor education techniques in California and Michigan should only serve as a forerunner for future development throughout the United States. Many other states are accepting its philosophy. It can only expand.

Outdoor education, and particularly a school camp, provides a setting unequalled for teaching and for student learning.

How can we live together?

How can we care for our bodies?

How can we save our resources?

How shall we play?

Before the schools can answer these questions, they will have to help the teachers and students with the answers.

THE SCHOOLS NEW FUNCTIONS

. . . Teachers are not pedagogues. They cannot discharge their obligations by saying to pupils: "There is your Virgil; in the corner are the birches; learn your Virgil." Society will not let them rest content with such a procedure, even if they are inclined to do so. Nor are they so inclined. Moved by the ancient command to search out all things under the sun and by the spirit of science to seek new knowledge endlessly, teachers are pioneers, not mere camp followers. Their task is not limited to preserving and passing on a heritage of knowledge and treasured experience; they must take account of advancing knowledge, add to it when they can, sift and create as well as accumulate.

...Unless they do this they fall under the dead hand; knowledge will advance without them, in spite of them; and society, finding death, not life, in the schools, will withdraw support. Or perhaps society itself, deriving no nourishment from education and ceasing to

grow, will ossify, if not disintegrate. Hence, educators cannot abide by the record alone. It unfolds
in their keeping. They too are stirred by the quest-
ing spirit, spurred by the examples of the great thinkers and doers whose record they keep, stimulated by
the currents of thought in society itself. So moved,
they are literally compelled to enlarge their own
powers, to enrich their own minds, and ever anew to
chart their own obligation. . . .[1]

It has not always taken an Industrial Revolution to
cause Americans to make adjustments and improvements
in our educational systems. The Industrial Revolution did
cause schools to keep abreast to the best of their abilities
in providing education so students might prepare themselves
for the many social and economic changes. Our public
schools have fulfilled the educational needs associated with
the Industrial Revolution. We now appear to be in another
kind of revolution which is more fantastic and rewarding
than the Industrial Revolution. The new revolution consists
of one in which there will be phenomenal progress in social
and welfare advancements; outer space discovery and use;
technology and automation with machines that will work,
think, and play for man; and the shrinking of the earth's
surface so all countries may unite in friendship, economic
security, scientific advancement, and social compatibility.

Education has made many changes over the past few
centuries. Some changes have been slow, others have been
fast. When war and other social problems arose, our educational systems were quick to make the necessary adjustments. We have advanced in education from providing
schools for the few to providing schools for the masses;
from a 3 months school to a 9 and 10 month school; from
a one room school house to magnificent buildings with
modern classrooms and laboratories; from low standards
of teaching to excellent standards of teaching.

America will meet the new challenge facing education

---

[1]Educational Policies Commission, Policies For Education In American Democracy.
Washington, D.C.: National Education Association of the United States, 1946.
pp. 58-60.

today. It will be met forcibly and quickly by educational
and other professional leaders. From their leadership will
come many educational improvements.

Improvements in outdoor education programs will include the following:

1. Educators and national leaders will be much more
cognizant of the value of outdoor education. Education will
become more attached to the students' experiences. Teachers will provide new and direct experiences, for students,
which are associated with the subject matter being taught.
They will approach outdoor education with freedom of conscious and with the support from both administrators and
parents.

2. Educational institutions who are concerned with
teacher training cannot for long remain "aloof" to the need
for outdoor education teachings. In the next decade most
universities and colleges will require teachers to have
some experiences in methods of teaching out-of-doors.
Teacher training programs like those in Illinois, Michigan,
New York, California and Indiana, will improve and tend to
serve as a guide for outdoor education teaching methods.

3. School laws, now quite restrictive and dictatorial,
will be amended and broadened to permit many desirable
educational programs which are having difficulty finding
their way into our schools. Legislation will be advanced
and proposed by professional educators who are primarily
interested in the student. There will be less legislation
proposed by outside groups and individuals whose primary
interest involves the American dollar.

4. School boards and school administrators will take
the leadership in acquiring and preserving open space. For
one hundred years or more schools have sold and given land
away. This is particularly true in those states that bene-
fited from the Northwest Ordinance of 1787, where each
16th section of land was set aside for schools. Leadership
must come from many sources to preserve and conserve
natural areas for park, recreation and outdoor education
purposes. The need is greatest in metropolitan areas, but
it is still necessary for rural areas. The professional

educator will join hands with others to acquire large tracts of land for school use. It would be well if more than one acre per student were the goal.

5. There will be greater team work and cooperative effort between park departments, schools, and city recreation departments. In school and out-of-school programs will be provided which will fill the educational void in the teaching of conservation and leisure time activities.

NEW YOUTH PROGRAM

Today in America, there is a great need for a sound educational program for teen age youth who have dropped out or who have recently graduated from high school. We can no longer ignore our idle youth.

One program that is essential at this time is an Educational-Vocational-Recreation camp.

Various camp ideas have been proposed for youth of this age, including a suggestion that the old Civilian Conservation Corp Camp idea be restored.

To restore the old C. C. C. Camp idea under auspices and direction of the military authorities would be a grave error. Programs of this nature will serve democracy best if they are maintained under the auspices and direction of our educational systems.

Many of the functions of the C. C. C. Camps could still be maintained but the total program would have to be supplemented by other kinds of programs with new educational objectives.

The activity phase of the program would consist of work experience and teachings in conservation, recreation, vocational training, and special subject matter areas.

The program would include guidance, counseling, testing, health, and placement services.

Inherent in the program would be emphasis on and experiences in democracy and democratic group living.

Professional leadership would be provided through the public schools or universities and would consist of leaders trained to teach and work with teen-age youth.

Programs for both boys and girls are essential.

The program would involve cooperative planning and effort among all governmental units located within a given area. All levels of government, federal, state, county, special district, and local would be involved in the education program.

It is hard to understand why legislators freely appropriate money to build penal and correction institutions, but are adverse to spending money to help children avoid such institutions. Juvenile delinquency is on the increase and will get worse before it improves. Penal institutions will not contribute to solving the problem. They will increase and expand as America fails to provide for her youth.

Public sentiment will soon change and answers will be sought through education rather than correction. This day cannot be postponed too long.

INDEX

Adler, Mortimer J., 51

Agassiz, Louis, 111

Age of Indiscretion, The, 66

Alcuin, 158

Algonquin Camp, 190

America, 262

America The Beautiful, 263

American Council on Education, 332

American Forestry Association, 414, 422

American Institute of Park Executives, 373, 413, 414

American Nature Association, 418

American Youth Hostels, Inc., 414, 426

Anaragoras, 147

Aristeides, 153

Aristotle, 57, 151-152

Art, 246

Arunta Tribe, 138

Association of Private Camps, 406, 414, 423

Atlanta (Georgia), 209

Audubon Magazine, 421

Audubon Nature Camp, 421

Automation, 5-8, 22, 23, 38, 286

Bacon, Francis, 172

Bagley, William C., 51

Balch, Ernest, 188-189, 203

Battle Creek (Michigan), 212

Basedow, Johann Bernard, 169

Battle Hymn of the Republic, 263

Bode, Boyd, 52

Boys' Club Camps of America, 201, 413

Boy Scouts of America, 413, 202

Brameld, Theodore, 53, 74

Brumm, R. P., 195

Brunsmade, Mary Gunn, 196

Bryant, William Cullen, 264

Bureau of Biological Survey, 411

Bureau of Fisheries, 411

Bureau of Reclamation, 411

Butts, R. Freeman, 136

Camp
    criteria, 230
    program, 230, 282
    purpose, 229

Camp Directors Association, 191-192

Camp Fire Girls, 405, 413

Camping, 185, 407-408

Camping at the Mid-Century, 203

Camping Magazine, 223

Charlemagne, 157-158

Child Labor Laws, 286

China, 144

Church Camps, 192, 402

Chocourua, Camp, 188

Citizenship, 48, 76

Civilian Conservation Corps, 408

Clear Creek Camp, 198

Clear Lake Camp, 213, 399

Climate, 351

Cole, Luella, 156

Cole, Percival, 114

Comenius, 3, 101, 114, 165-168

Communication Arts, 247

Competition, 77

Confucius, 145

Conant, James B., 60

Conservation
    concepts, 315-318
    democracy, and, 307-309
    education, and, 312-315
    legislation, 310
    outdoor education, and, 320-324
    principles, 318-320
    school responsibility, and, 309

Consumer Education, 78

Cook County Forest Preserve, 397

Cooperation, 107-109, 221, 223

Correlation, 110-112
Cousins, Norman, 329
Creativity, 82, 121-126
Curricula, 245-248
Curriculum and Outdoor Education,
    240-243
Communication, 9-13,
Counts, George S., 252
Culture, 2

Dark Ages, 155
Day Camp, 394-395
Declaration of Human Rights, 271-273
Declaration of Independence, 262
DeMerritte, Edwin, 190
Democracy, 69, 221, 251, 307-308
    belief in God, and, 260-261
    criteria for, 301-302
    education, and, 65, 273-275, 281
    experience, and, 258-260, 299-301
    in camp, 295-299
    meaning, 252-255
Democritus, 150
Dewey, John, 52, 72, 73, 98, 174-175
Displaced Persons Act, 14
Dudley, Sumner F., 200-201, 404
Durant, Will, 231

Ecclesiasticism, 168
Edison, Thomas, 7-8, 285
Education
    as growth, 72
    as life, 72
    as reconstruction of experience, 73
    as social progress, 73
    democracy, and, 273-275, 281
    function, 74
    goal, 80
    health, and, 331
    leisure, and, 369-376
    society, and, 42-45
Educational Policies Commission, 46, 49
Egyptians, 140
Egyptian Association for the Mentally
    Retarded, 406
Eisenhower, Dwight D., 85, 127, 267,
    328

Emerson, Ralph Waldo, 71, 264, 265
Emile, 169
Erasmus, 161-162
Essentialism, 50-51
Ethridge, Mark, 294
Excursions, 386
Exercise, 330
Extending Education Through School
    Camping, 199
Extension Service, 411

Family, 21-22
Federal Power Commission, 411
Field Biology Camp, 400
Field Trips, 386
First Aid, 350
Fitness, 126-129
Food, 348-349
Fontaine, Albert L., 190
Ford, Henry, 8
Forest Service, 411
Forestry Camp, 400
Fosdick, Raymond B., 365
Four-H Club, 413
Franklin, Benjamin, 285
Frederick County (Md.), 227
Fresh Air Camps, 201, 404, 405
Froebel, Friedrich, 172
Frontier, effects of, 22
Frost, Robert, 265
Fulbright Act, 37

Galileo, 163
Geological Survey, 412
Geology Camp, 400
Girl Scouts of America, 202, 405, 413
Good Will Camps, 192-193
Greece, 147-155
Greenbrier, Camp, 191
Gregg, A. S., 191
Gunn, Frederick William, 196, 197, 203

Harvard, Camp, 189-190
Health, 75
    classroom teacher, and, 337-339
    definition, 328
    education, and, 331

environment, and, 339-341
instruction, 344-347
legislation, and, 334-336
objectives, 345
outdoor education, and, 336-337
service, 341-344
Henckley, George W., 192-193
Henderson, C. Harford, 191
Henry, Patrick, 26, 265
Herbart, Johann Friedrich, 171-172
Hullehen, Walter, 191
Human Relations, 47, 77, 220, 269, 276, 278
Human Resources, 28
Hutchins, Robert M., 51

Idealism, 50
Idlewild, Camp, 191
Immigration, 14
India, 143
Indianola, 191
Industrialization, 2, 6, 7, 19, 24, 437
Informality, 116-120
Integration, 110-112
Intercollegiate Outing Club Association, 414, 422
International Geophysical Year, 99
Investigation, 104-106
Irvington Health Camp, 198
Izaak Walton League, 418-419

Jackson, Andrew, 266
Jefferson, Thomas, 266, 280
Jordan, David Starr, 104

Keewaydin Camps, 191
Kellogg Foundation, 198
Kennedy, John F., 267, 373, 380
Kilmer, Joyce, 101-102, 264
Kilpatrick, William, 52

Latin School, 166
Laws of nature, 81
Leadership, 243
Leisure, 357, 33-34
culture, and, 361
definition, 358

education, and, 369-376
mass leisure, 29
outdoor education, and, 377-379
science, and, 5
traditional viewpoint, 359-360, 363-364
wise use, 78
Leisure Class, 30
Lincoln, Abraham, 266
Living Wilderness, 429
Longfellow, Henry W., 264, 285
Los Angeles, 224
Low, Juliette, 405
Lowell, James Russell, 266, 285
Luther, Martin, 164

MacLeish, Archibald, 2
McBride, Robert, 203
Marist Brothers, 193
Martineau, Harriet, 22
Masters, Edgar Lee, 129
Mathematics, 246
Meditation, 81-82, 113, 115
Middle Ages, 155-160
Minority Groups, 255-256
Monilaw, William, 191
Montaigne, 168
Moral Issues, 4
Moral Values, 79
Music, 246
Music Camp, 401

Napoleon, 11
Nash, Jay B., 374
National Association for Crippled Children and Adults, 406
National Association for the Retarded, 406
National Audubon Society, 414, 421
National Camp, 417
National Forest Reservation Commission, 412
National Parks Association, 413, 414
National Park Service, 412
National Recreation Association, 413
National Wildlife Federation, 414, 427
Nature Magazine, 418
Naturalism, 169-170
Natural Resources, 25-26
Natural Science, 247

Nature Science Camp, 190
Nichols, William Ford, 189
Nixon, Richard M., 371
Northern Illinois University, 84
North Mountain School of Physical
    Culture, 187
Northwest Ordinance, 82, 438

Observation, 96-104
Otis, James, 265
Outdoor America, 420
Outdoor Education, 436, 438, 56,
    225-226, 206, 210, 303
        concepts, 234
        conservation, and 320-324
        leisure, and, 377-379
        need for, 226-227
        objectives, 217
        principles, 228
        program areas, 228, 212
        scope, 217
Outdoor Education Association, 414, 416
Outdoor Education Project, 413

Participation, 121-122
Park-School Plan, 389
Perennialism, 50, 51-52
Pestalozzi, Johann, 92, 170-171
Petrarch, 161
Pettit, Henry S., 191
Physical Education, 247-248
Physical Fitness, 75, 380
Pickard, Jerome P., 15-16
Pinchot, Gifford, 27
Plato, 150
Pope, Alexander, 80
Population, 14-15, 17-18, 38
Pragmatism, 50
Prehistoric Man, 139
Presidential Oath, 265
Presidents Conference on Fitness, 372
Private Camps, 187
Progressivism, 50, 52-54
Psychological Digest, 267
Pygmalion, 23
Pythagoras, 149

Quintilian, 155

Reconstructionism, 50, 53
Reflection, 81-82
Reformation, 163
Renaissance, 160-163
Renssalaer Polytechnic Institute, 174
Ritter, Carl, 92
Rome, 153-155
Roosevelt, Camp, 198
Roosevelt, Franklin D., 24, 267, 271, 293
Rothrock Joseph, 187
Rousseau, Jean Jacques, 169

Safety, 75
Saint Ann's Camp, 193-194
Salute to the Flag, 262
Sanctation, 347-348
Sarachens, 158
School Camping, 195, 219
School Farms, 392
School Forests, 392, 394
School Garden, 390, 391-392
School of the Mothers' Knee, 166
Science, 3-4, 36-37, 81
Self Expression, 82
Self Government, 279
Self Realization, 46
Semetic Nations, 146
Sen, Mme Sun Yat, 292
Sharp, L. B., 199, 207-208, 234, 396, 416,
    405
Smith, John, 265
Smith, Julian, 413
Social Contract, 169
Social Science, 247
Society, 2, 75
Socrates, 3, 150-151
Southern Illinois University, 399
Soil Conservation Service, 27, 412
Soil Conservation Society of America, 414,
    424
Spencer, Herbert, 173
Spiritual Values, 79
Spragne, John, 191
Suburbanization, 15, 39

Star Spangled Banner, 263
Status Quo, 3
Stuart, Jesse, 264
Student Conservation Program, 414

Talbot, Winthrop, 190
Taylor, J. Madison, 197
Technology, 2, 37
Thales, 149
Thamus, 142
Thoreau, Henry David, 32
Tools of Learning, 76
Traditionalism, 50
Transportation, 9, 35, 38
    airplane, 11
    automobile, 10
    railroads, 9-10
    waterway, 10
Truman, Harry, 294
Twentieth Century Fund, 29

UNESCO, 37-38
United States Geological Survey, 28
University and Travel, 166
United Cerebral Palsy Association, 406

Urban Land Institute, 15
Urbanization, 15-16, 39

Vergerius, 45
Vernacular School, 166

Watt, James, 6-7
Weather, 351-352
Webster, Daniel, 266
Wells, H. G., 42, 275
Western New York State, 214
What Knowledge Is Most Worth, 173
White, Paul Dudley, 330
Whitehead, Alfred North, 64, 110
Whitman, Walt, 263
Whittier, John Greenleaf, 264
Wholeness, sense of, 80
Wilderness Society, 414, 428
Wilson, Edward S., 191
Wilson, Woodrow, 266
William of Ockham, 164
Work, 284-286
Work Experience, 287-289

Young Men's Christian Association Camps,
    200, 404, 405, 413